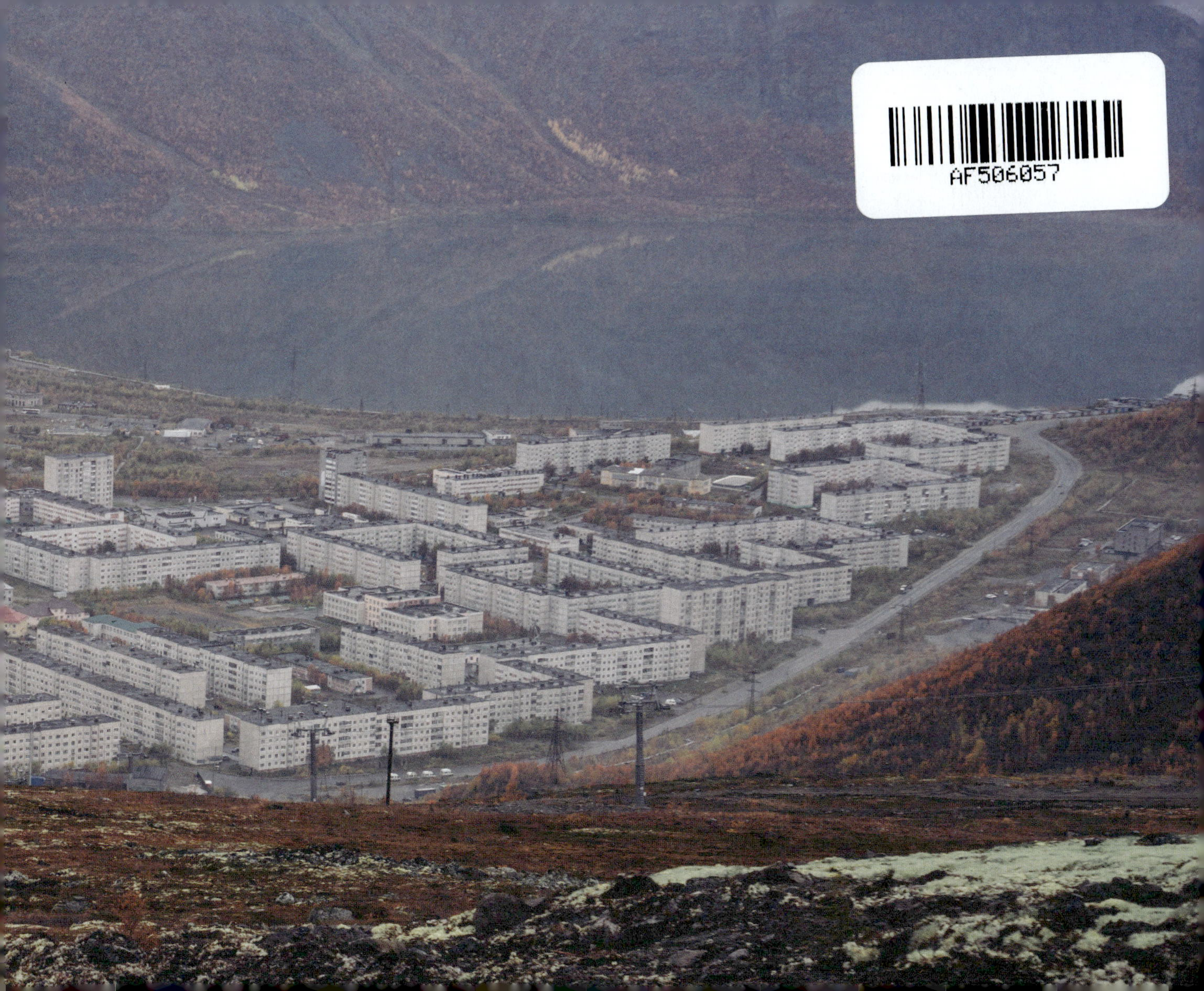
AF506057

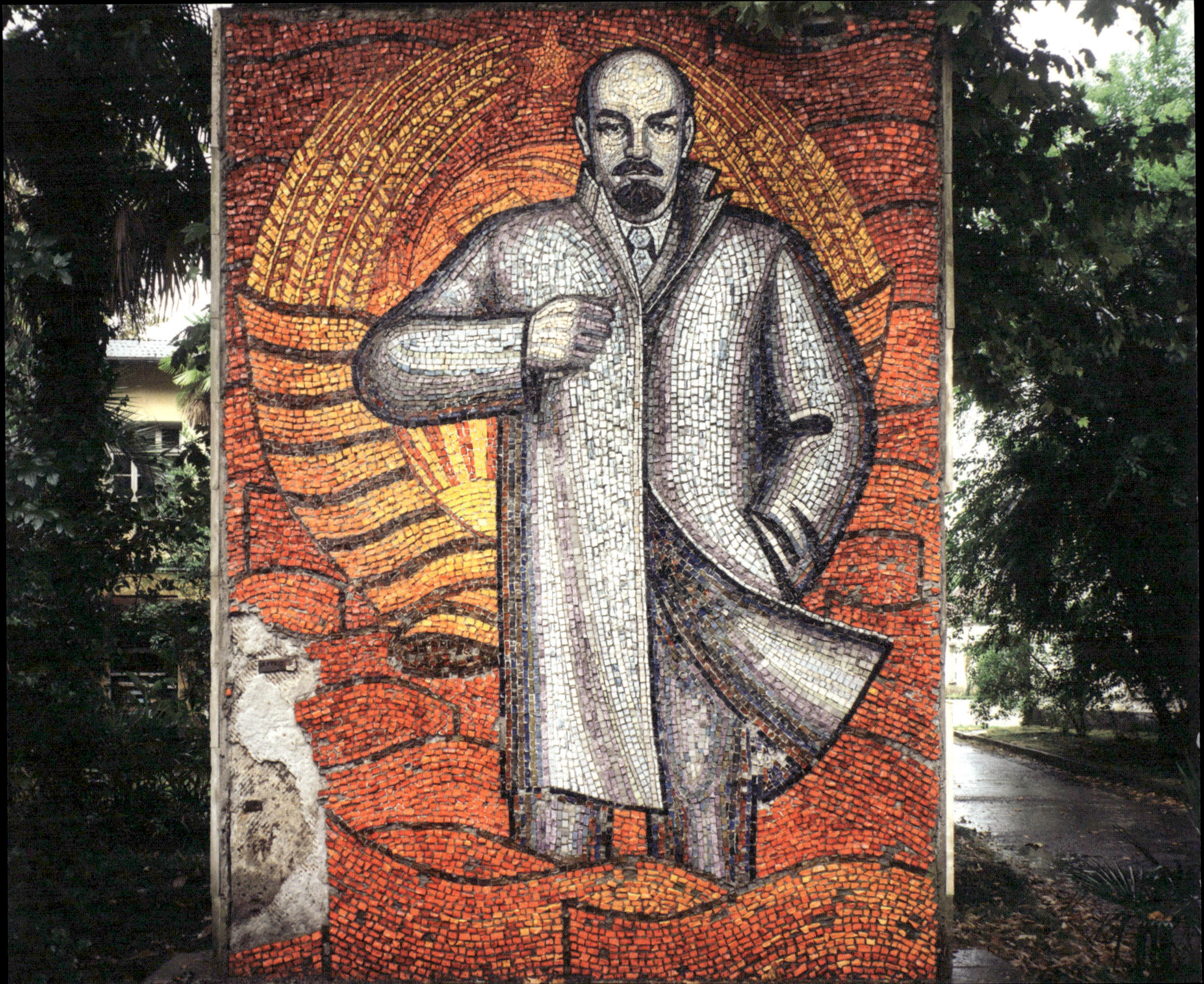

СОВЕТСКИЕ СЕЗОНЫ

SOVIET SEASONS

ARSENIY KOTOV

FUEL

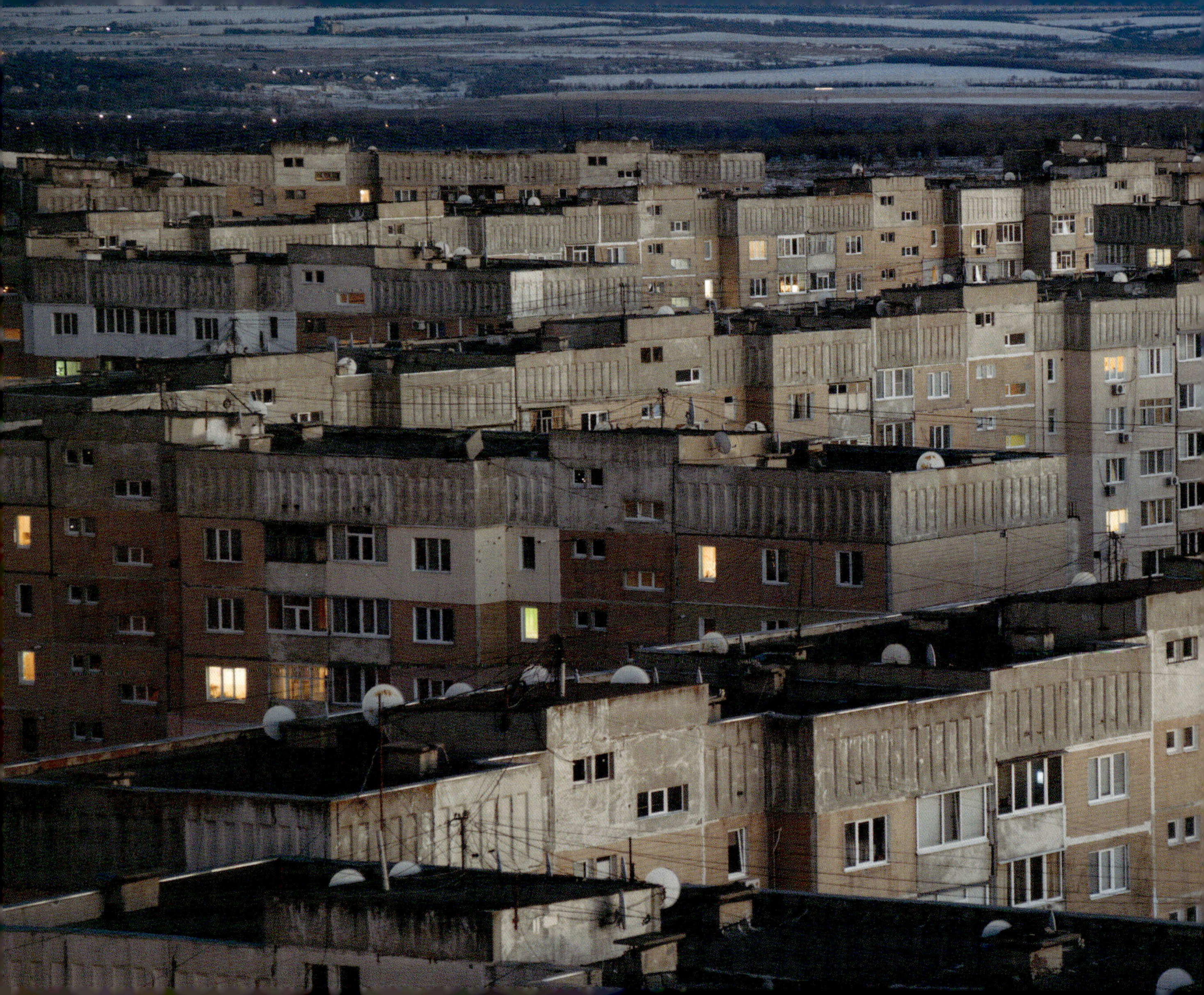

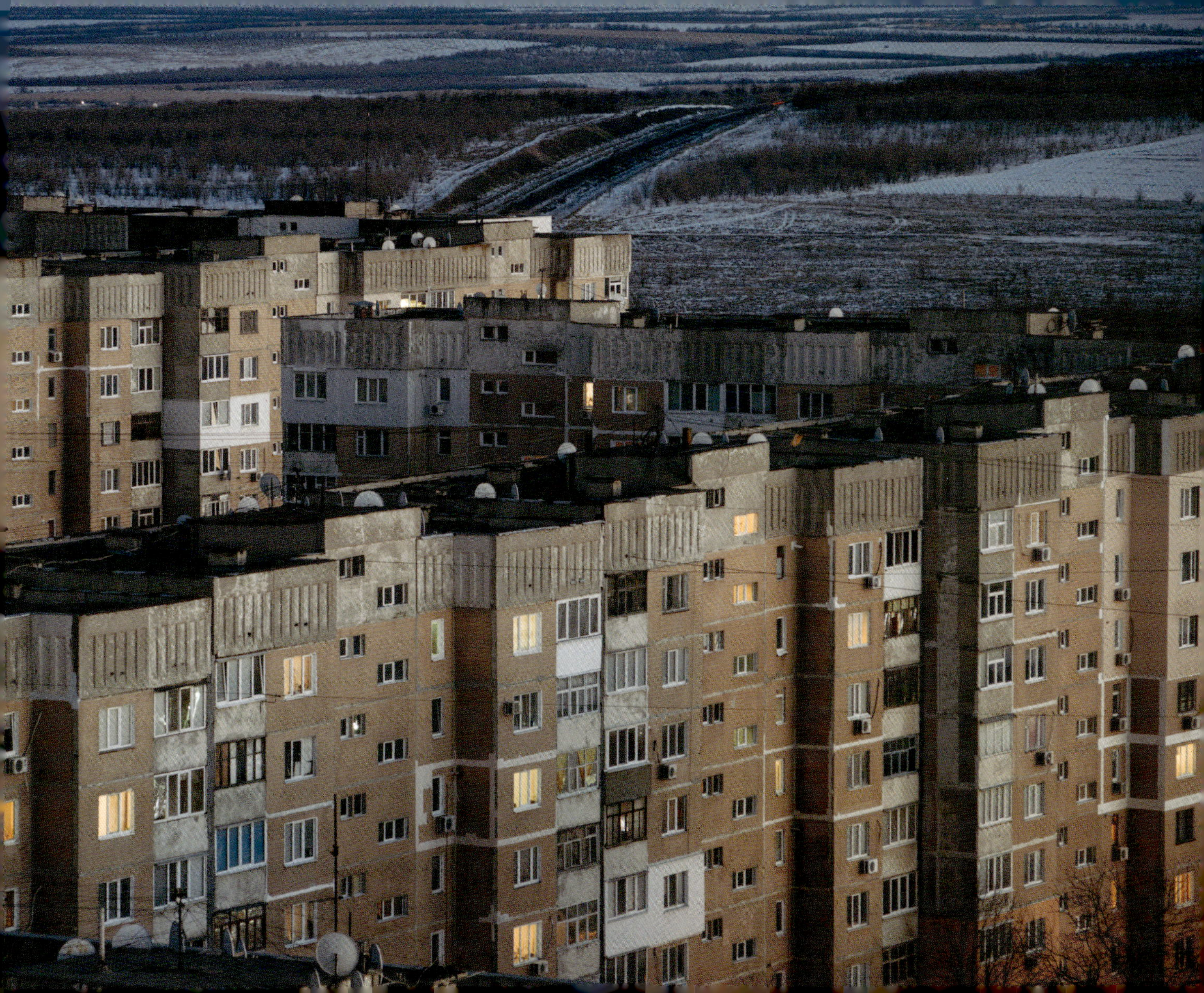

INTRODUCTION

After finishing my first book *Soviet Cities* (which documented prominent Soviet modernist architecture in the major cities of the former Soviet Union), the focus of my travels shifted to more remote, infrequently visited locations. This book is a collection of photographs I took in areas as diverse as Siberia, Central Russia, Ukraine and the Caucasus.

During winter 2019, I travelled extensively throughout Siberia, a vast region that occupies most of Russia but contains only about 11 per cent of the country's population. I visited many of the region's major cities, and the distance between them – never less than 700 kilometres – gives a sense of the scale of the area. Later that winter I gratefully accepted a job as a construction worker in Norilsk. I had long dreamed of reaching this city, but as flights are prohibitively expensive, I had kept postponing the trip. Despite my career in the building industry not working out, I spent about six weeks there, photographing the surreal and beautiful landscapes, sometimes with snowdrifts reaching as high as the third floor of the buildings.

The European part of Russia is my homeland and I have visited almost all its large cities. During the lockdown of spring 2020, despite travel restrictions, I was able to hike along the Volga from Samara to Ulyanovsk, stopping at towns and villages along the way. I then stayed for a month in Moscow, visiting nearby cities including Vladimir, Obninsk and Kaluga.

Every summer for the past seven years, I have travelled to different parts of the Caucasus, including all the regions of the Russian Caucasus and all the republics of Transcaucasia. In this land of glaciers and ancient settlements, I have been impressed by the juxtaposition of mountain landscapes with the panelled apartment buildings so familiar to those of us living in post-Soviet towns and cities. The lifestyles and beliefs of local inhabitants vary greatly from one region to the next – for instance, Georgia resembles a European country while neighbouring Chechnya has become like an Islamic state within Russia. In small villages and remote towns, traditional ways of life endure, with people surviving through subsistence farming and herding.

Following the Euromaidan of 2014 and subsequent conflicts, travelling to Ukraine has become difficult for Russians. For this reason, I tried to see as many places as possible in one trip, visiting Kiev and several large industrial cities in eastern Ukraine including Kharkiv, Dnipropetrovsk and Krivoy Rog. Finally, I journeyed on to Pripyat and Chernobyl, where in autumn I witnessed this extraordinary site being reclaimed by nature.

previous page
South Quarter
LUHANSK, UKRAINE
(UNRECOGNISED LUHANSK PEOPLE'S REPUBLIC)

Blue portal
Suzdalka District
YAROSLAVL, RUSSIA

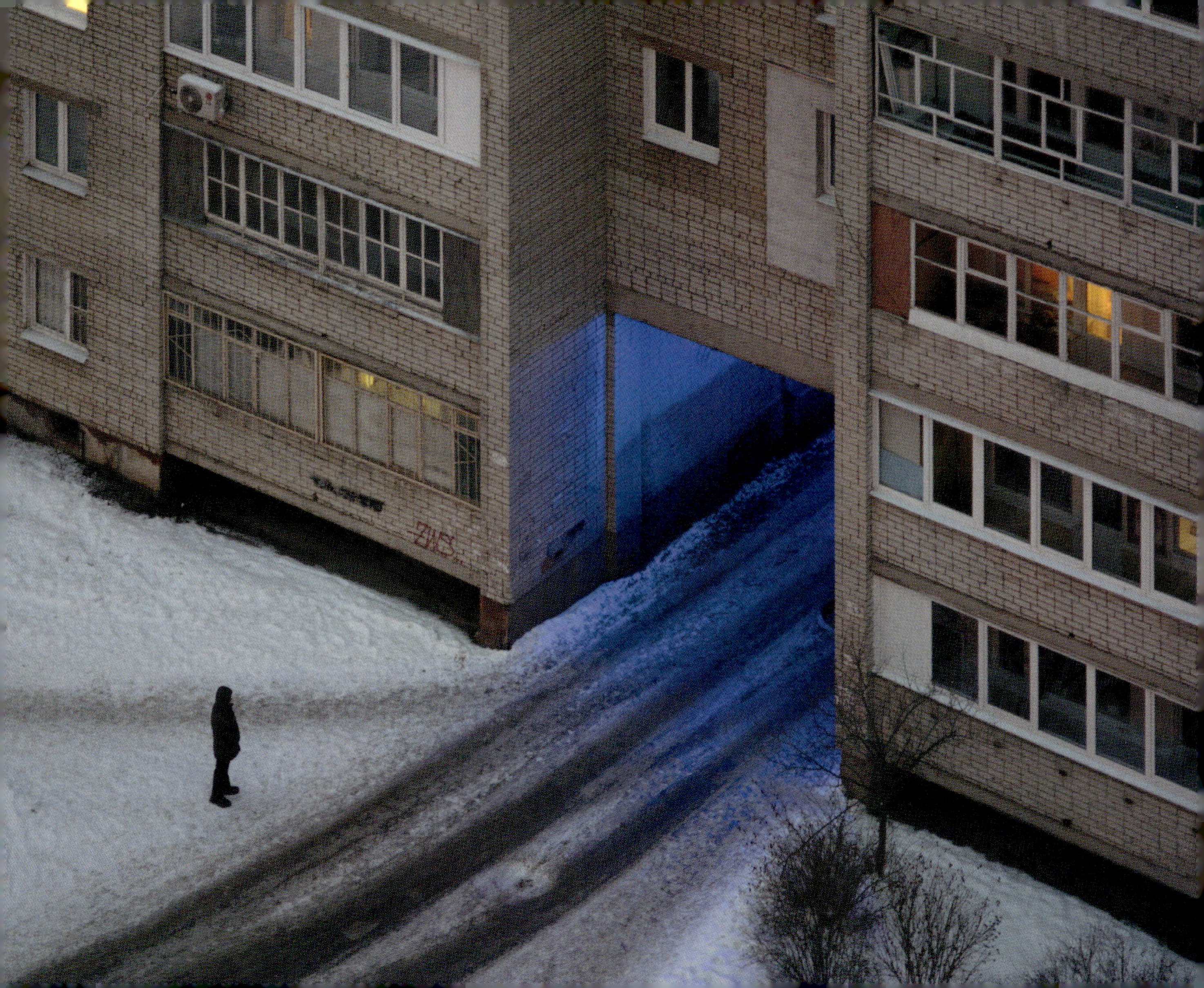

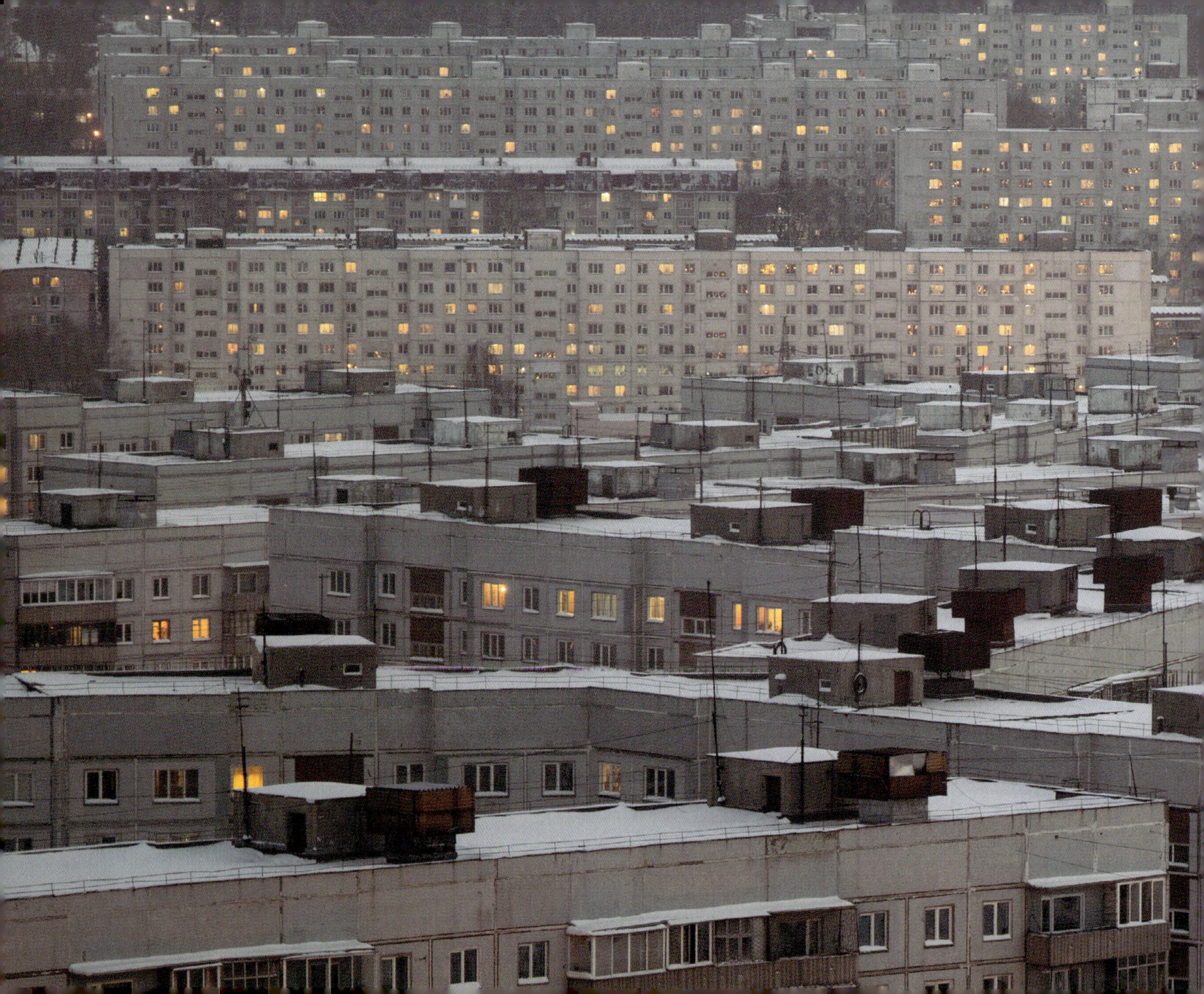

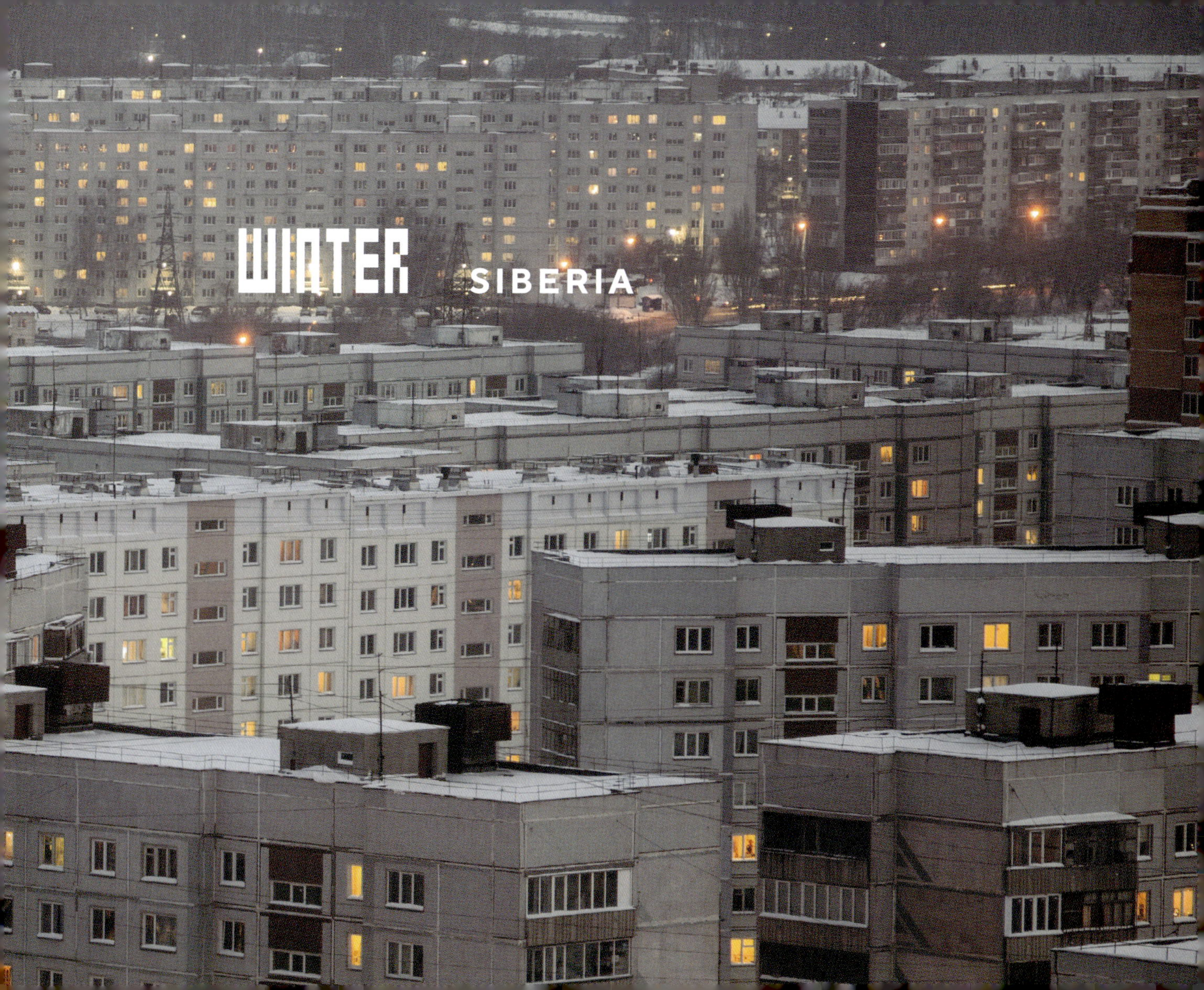

WINTER
SIBERIA

SIBERIA

Siberia is vast, stretching all the way from the ridges that flank the Pacific Ocean in the east to the Ural Mountains in the west. To the north it meets the Arctic Ocean; to the south it borders Mongolia. It is almost half the size of our country, an area equal to all of Europe or all of the United States.

Siberia is so huge that it spans several distinct natural environments. On the Arctic coast of the far north lies a harsh treeless tundra, a realm of mosses, lichens and stunted shrubs. The lowlands stretch to the edge of the ocean and penetrate inland along the river valleys. Here the glacial fossil ice can be 15 metres thick or more, frozen ground from which tusks and sometimes even entire carcasses of extinct mammoths have been unearthed.

The natural riches of Siberia are enormous. There is coal from the Kuznetsk and Yakutia; iron ore from the Angara river basin and Khakassia; base metals from the Transbaikal, the Far North and Altai. Gold, diamonds, graphite, the raw components for aluminium, as well as phosphate and other elements for chemical fertilisers and more recently oil have also been discovered. How much more wealth lies untapped in the interior of this immense land?

While Siberia is home to people of many nationalities, most of the population is Russian, arriving in these vast expanses of challenging terrain at the end of the 16th century. Before the Russians came Cossacks, usually hunters and fur trappers.

The Russians crossed this huge, rugged and uncharted landscape to reach the Pacific Ocean in just over 50 years. They built fortresses and created strongholds, securing a new territory. Then the servicemen and peasants arrived. Prospectors, farmers and builders cultivated a land that had previously known only snares and spears. Through continual hard work, the Russian people gradually developed the sparsely populated province, ploughing fields, establishing villages and towns and building the world's longest railway.

But it is only through the Soviet regime that Siberia has been transformed into a new country. As it begins to rise to prominence, we must redraw the economic map almost entirely. The East is growing at a faster rate than any other region as its immense resources are comprehensively brought into production. The path of our country towards Communism increasingly requires more natural materials, and nowhere are these more abundant than in Siberia. Nothing compares with the transformation of the land during Soviet times – and above all with the transformation of the Soviet East: Siberia. 'Staggering. Imagination with grandiosity,' wrote Alexei Maximovich Gorky. 'Fabulous pictures of Siberia's future are unfolding.' And we are already very close to the realisation of these fabulous pictures!

My Russia, N.N. Mikhailov, 1964

previous page
5th and 6th Microdistricts
NOVOSIBIRSK, RUSSIA
Built between the 1970s and 1990s

Abandoned office for the construction of the Nadezhda (Hope) Factory
NORILSK, RUSSIA

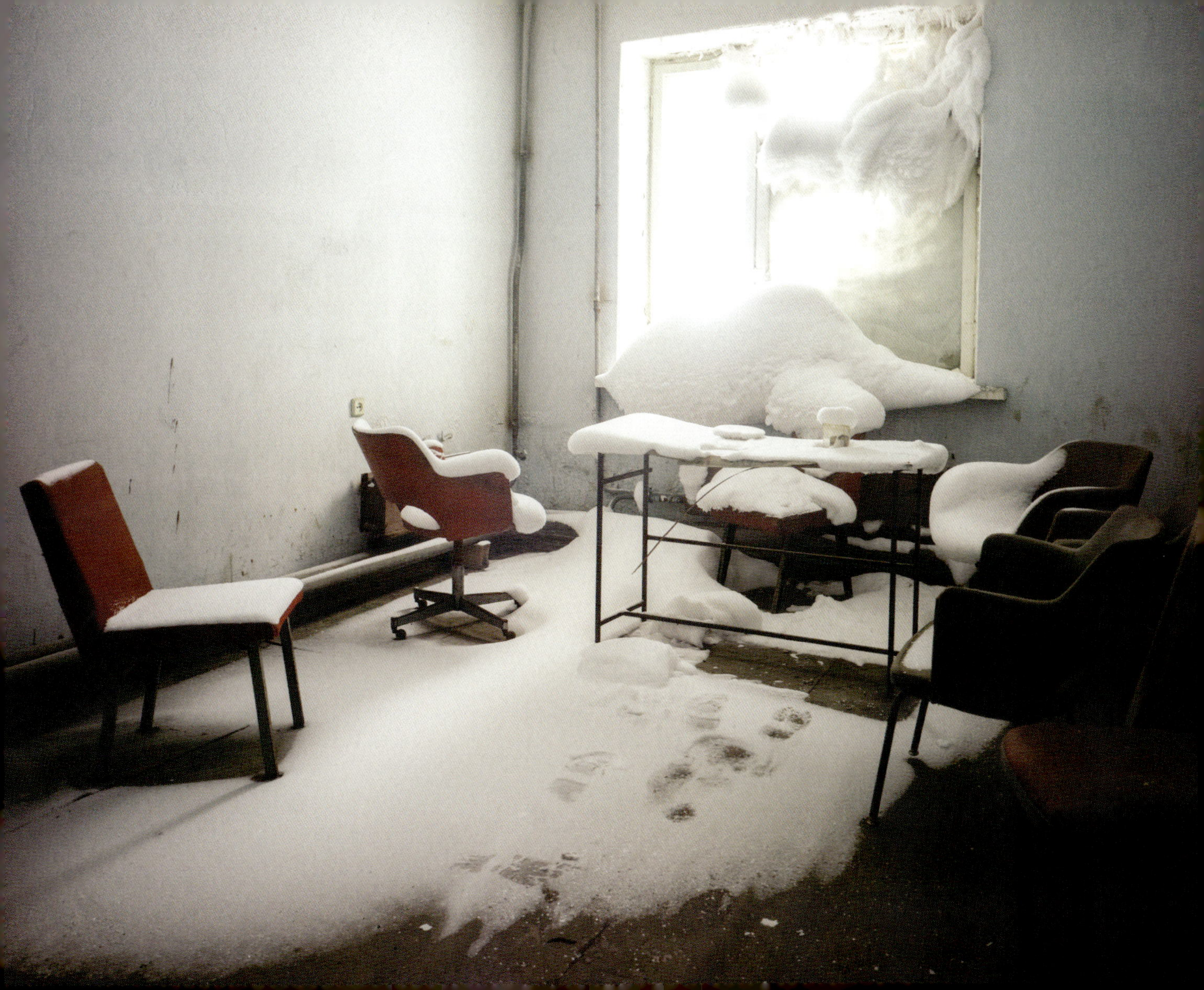

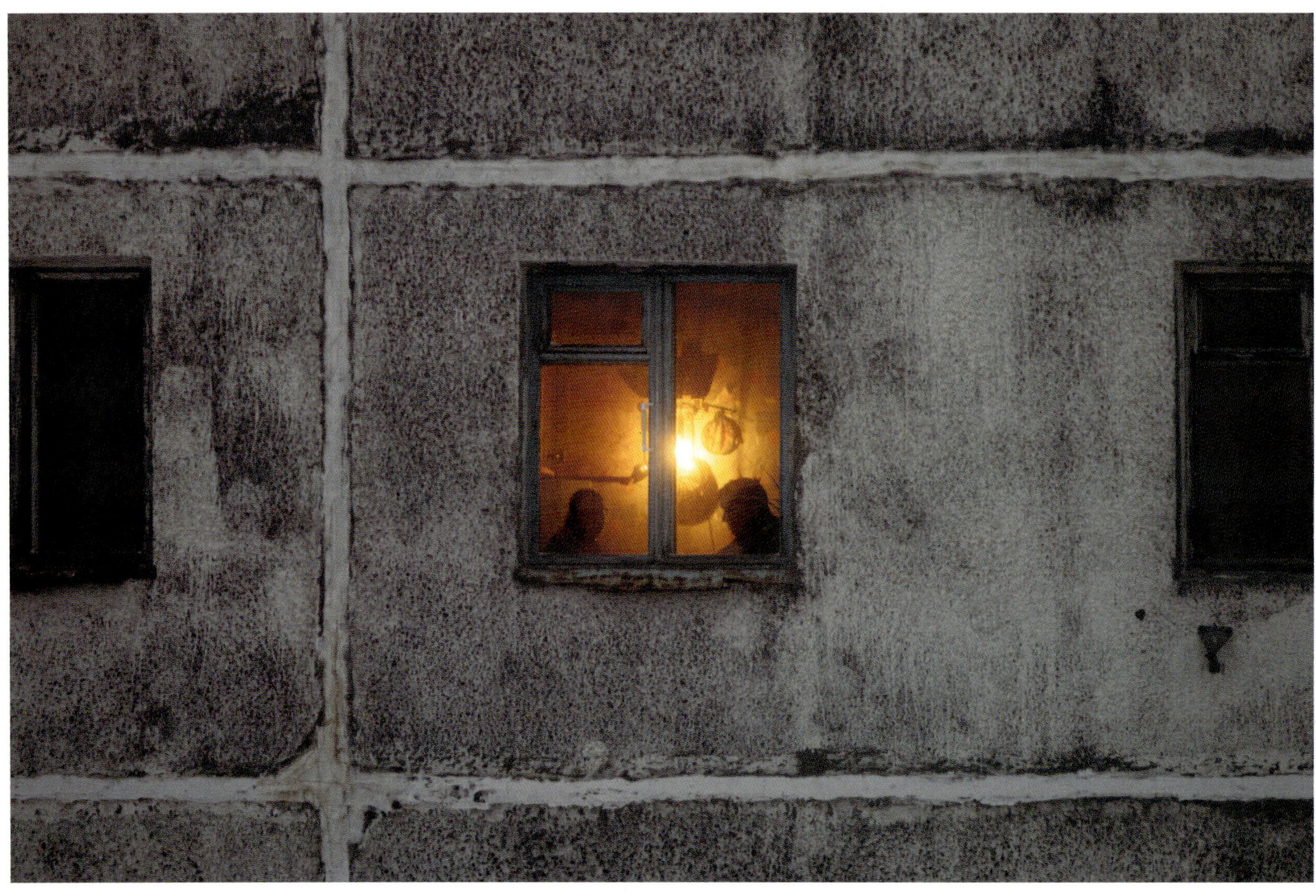

Housing block, Kayerkan District
NORILSK, RUSSIA
Built in the 1980s

Kayerkan is a district in Norilsk with a population of around 23,000. In severe weather, residents of the area who work in the city centre cannot return to their homes, so schools, kindergartens, the theatre, museum and other public buildings are equipped for them to stay overnight.

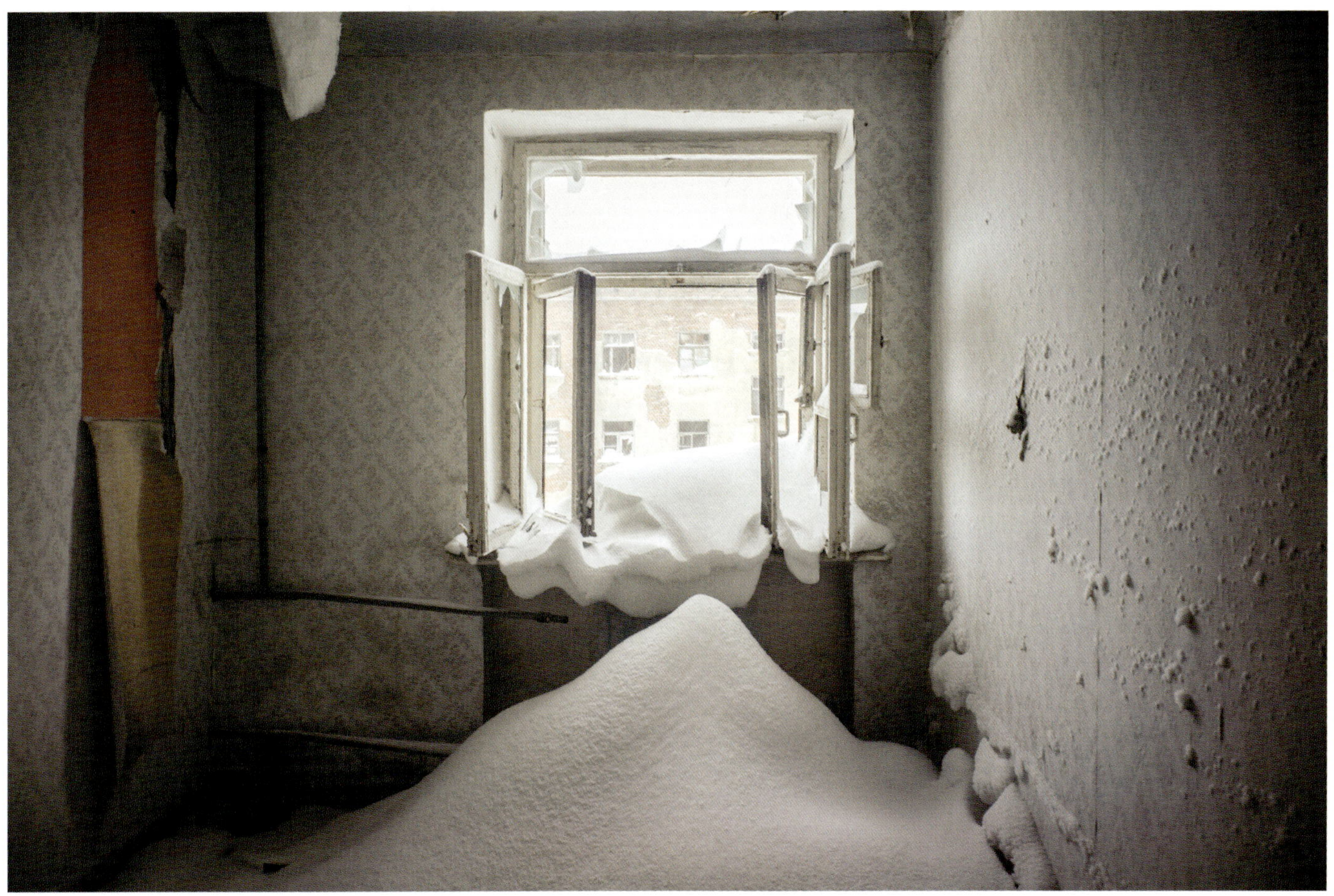

Snow drift inside an abandoned house
NORILSK, RUSSIA
Built in the 1950s

The early buildings of Norilsk were built on strip foundations set on a rock base, but even under this sections of ice can be found. When the ice melts, cracks form in the foundations and the buildings become unfit for habitation. Their residents are then resettled elsewhere.

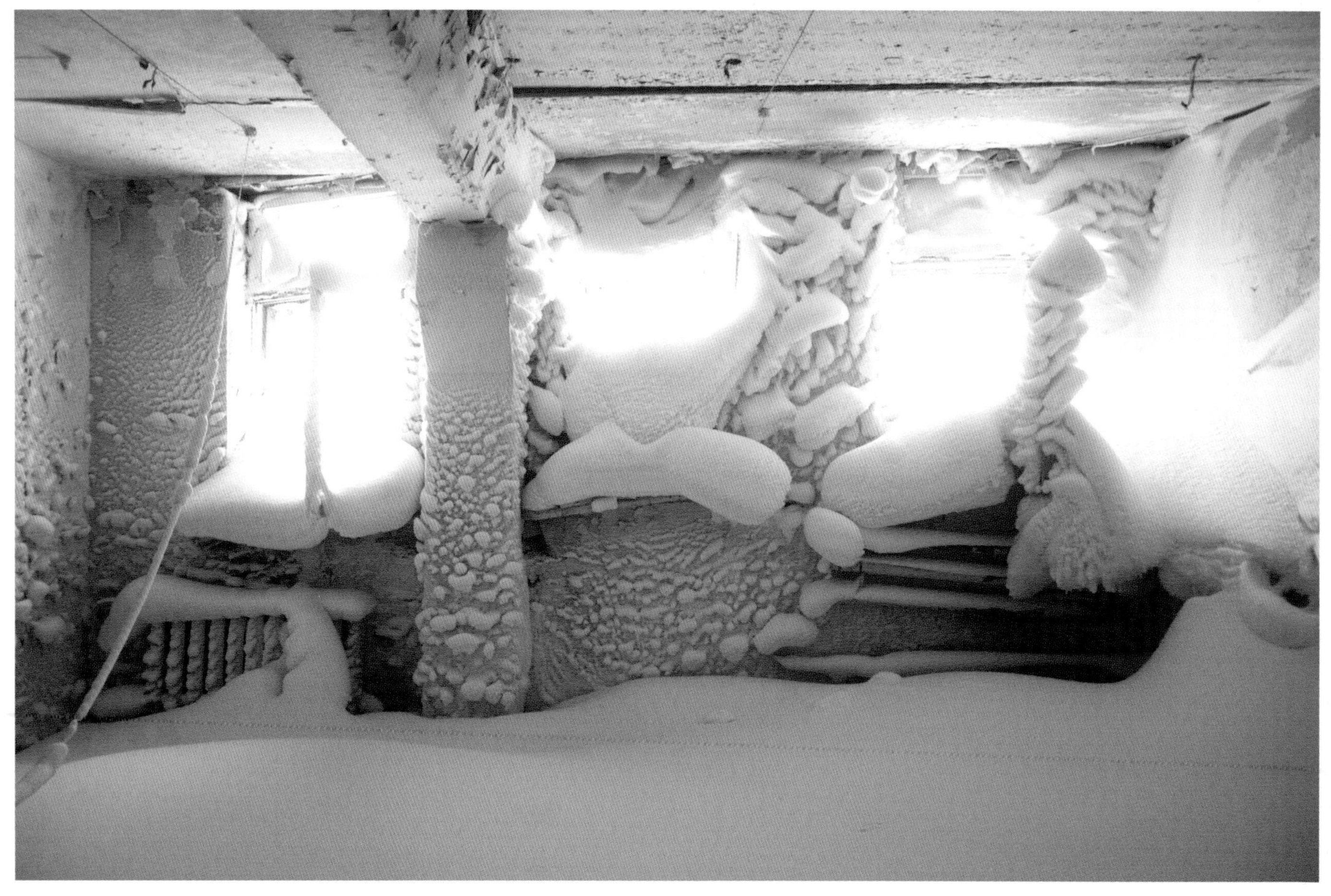

Interior of an abandoned workshop building
NORILSK, RUSSIA
Built in the 1970s, abandoned in the 1990s

Main hall, office for the construction of the Nadezhda (Hope) Factory
NORILSK, RUSSIA
Built in the 1970s, abandoned in the 2010s

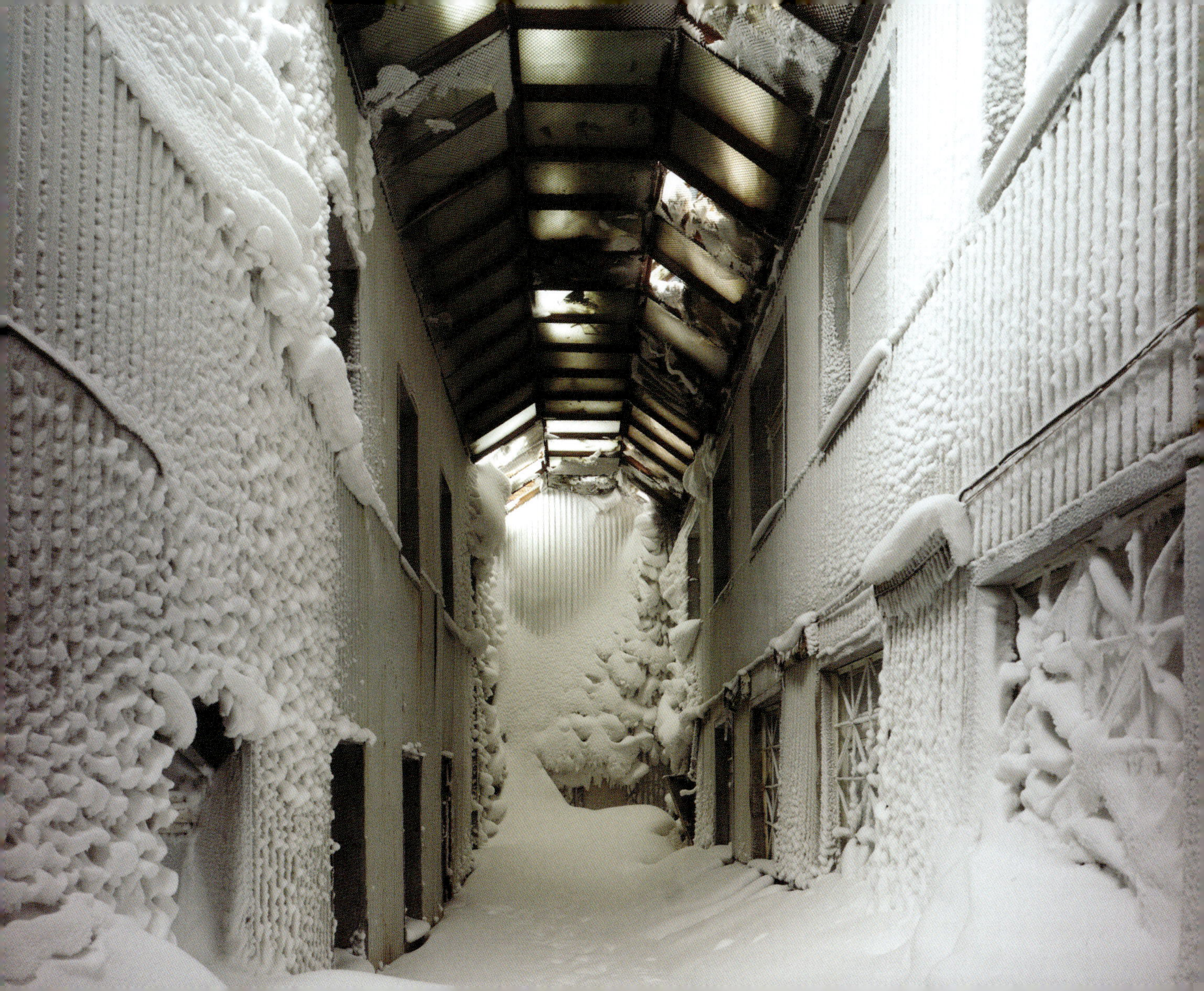

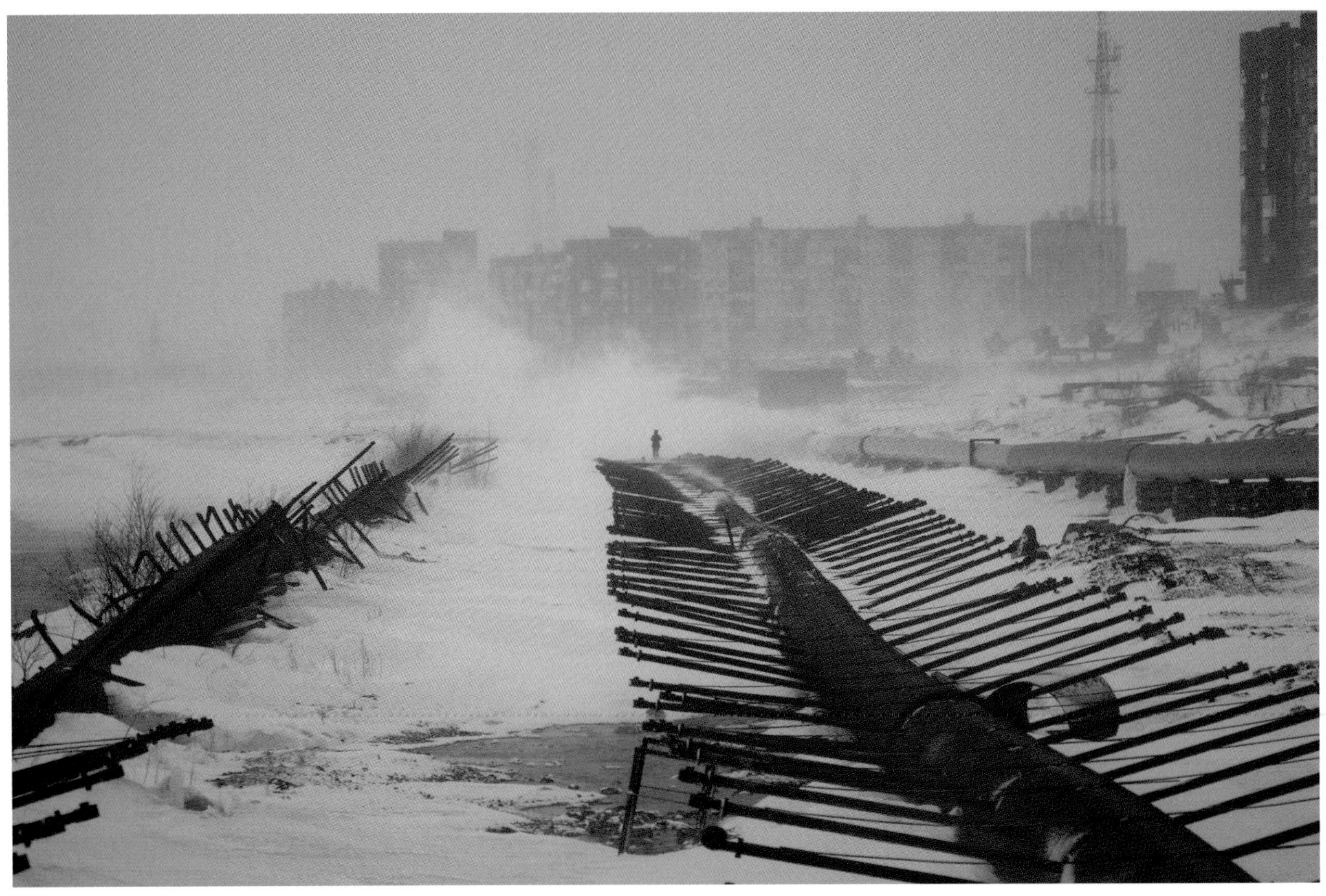

Cooling systems for turbine condensers
Combined Heat and Power Plant No.1
NORILSK, RUSSIA

Commissioned in 1942, Norilsk Combined Heat and Power Plant No.1 was the first power plant within the region's energy sector. It provides electricity to the industrial district and is the only source of energy for heating for the city of Norilsk.

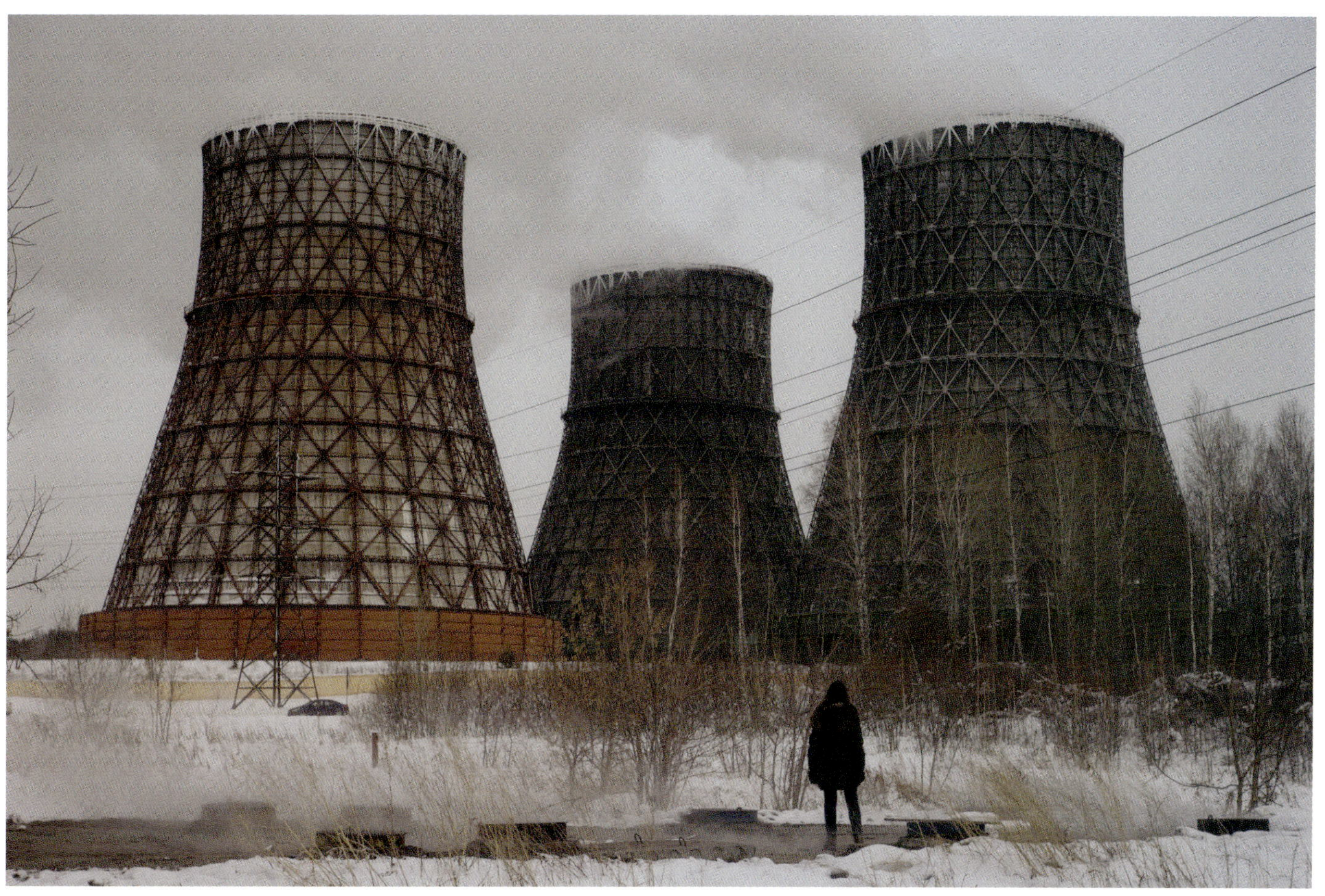

Cooling towers
Combined Heat and Power Plant No.5
NOVOSIBIRSK, RUSSIA

In 1971, the USSR Council of Ministers decided to build Combined Heat and Power Plant No.5 in Novosibirsk. At that time, the facility had one of the largest outputs of any thermal power plant in the country, with a capacity of 1.2 GW.

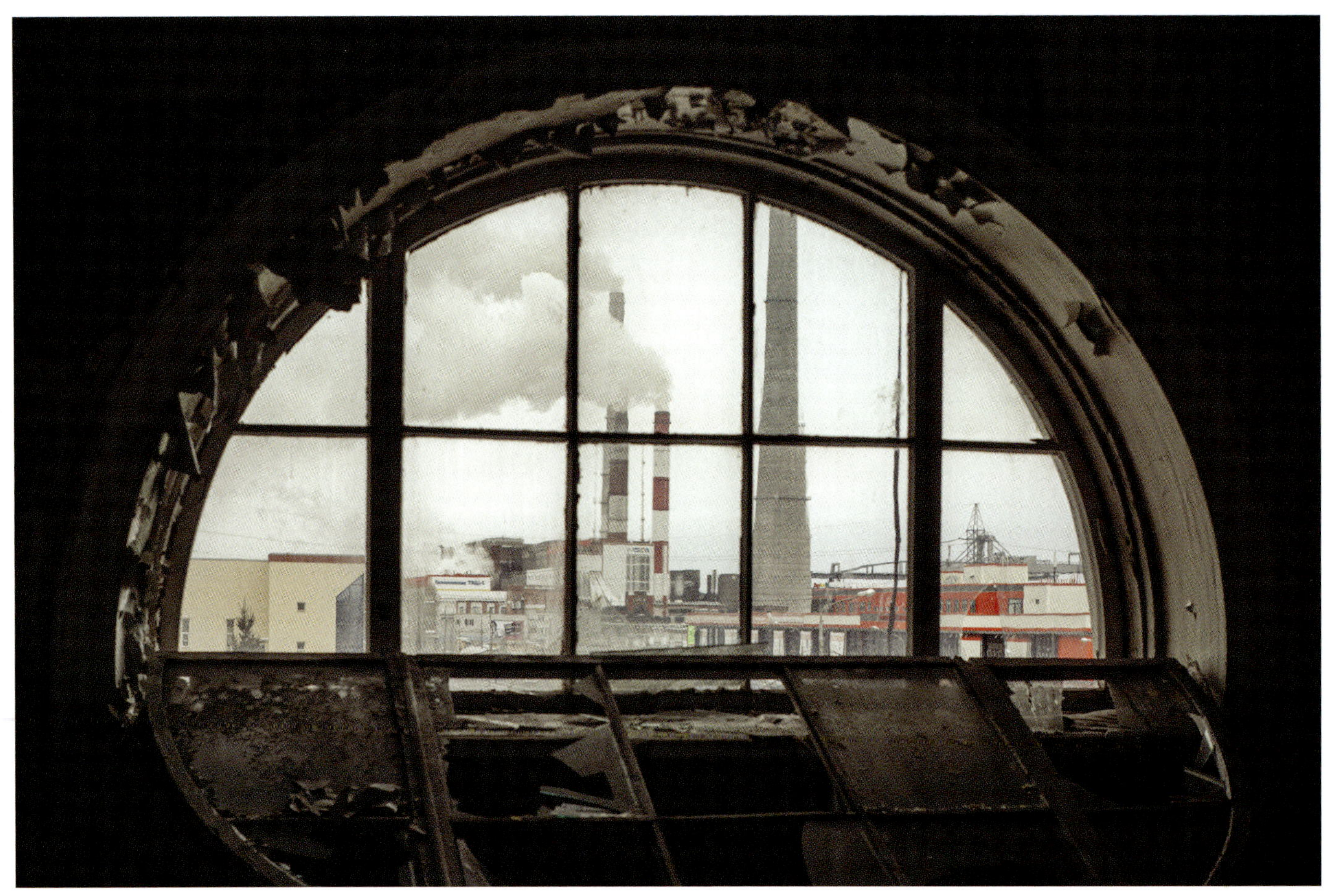

View of power plant chimneys from the abandoned
Palace of Culture, built for workers at the plant
KRASNOYARSK, RUSSIA
Commissioned in 1943

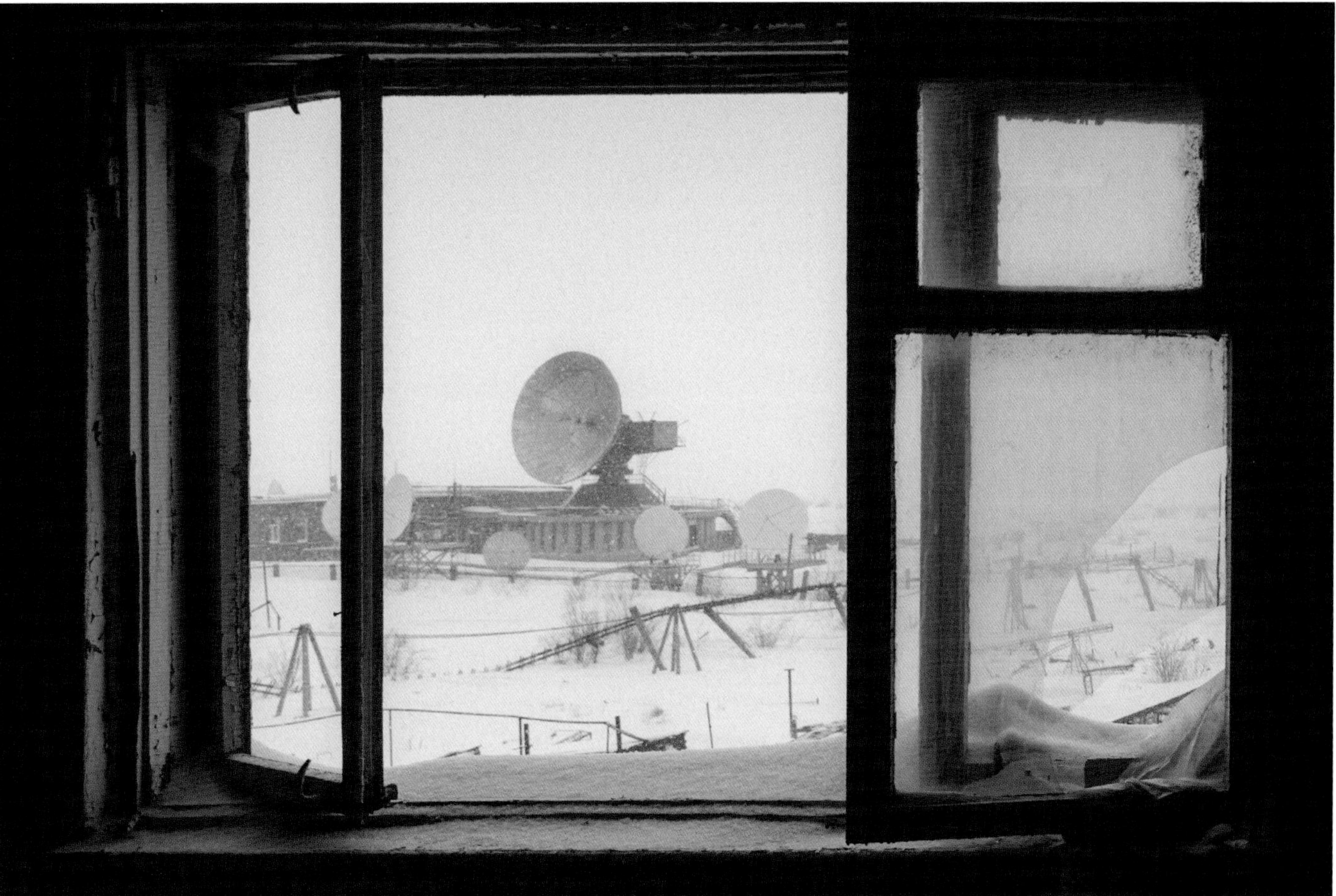

Orbita Receiving Station
NORILSK, RUSSIA
Built in 1967

This was the first Orbita space communications receiving station to be built in Krasnoyarsk oblast. It allowed the people of Norilsk to watch television programmes transmitted by Molniya 1 satellites from Moscow across the USSR.

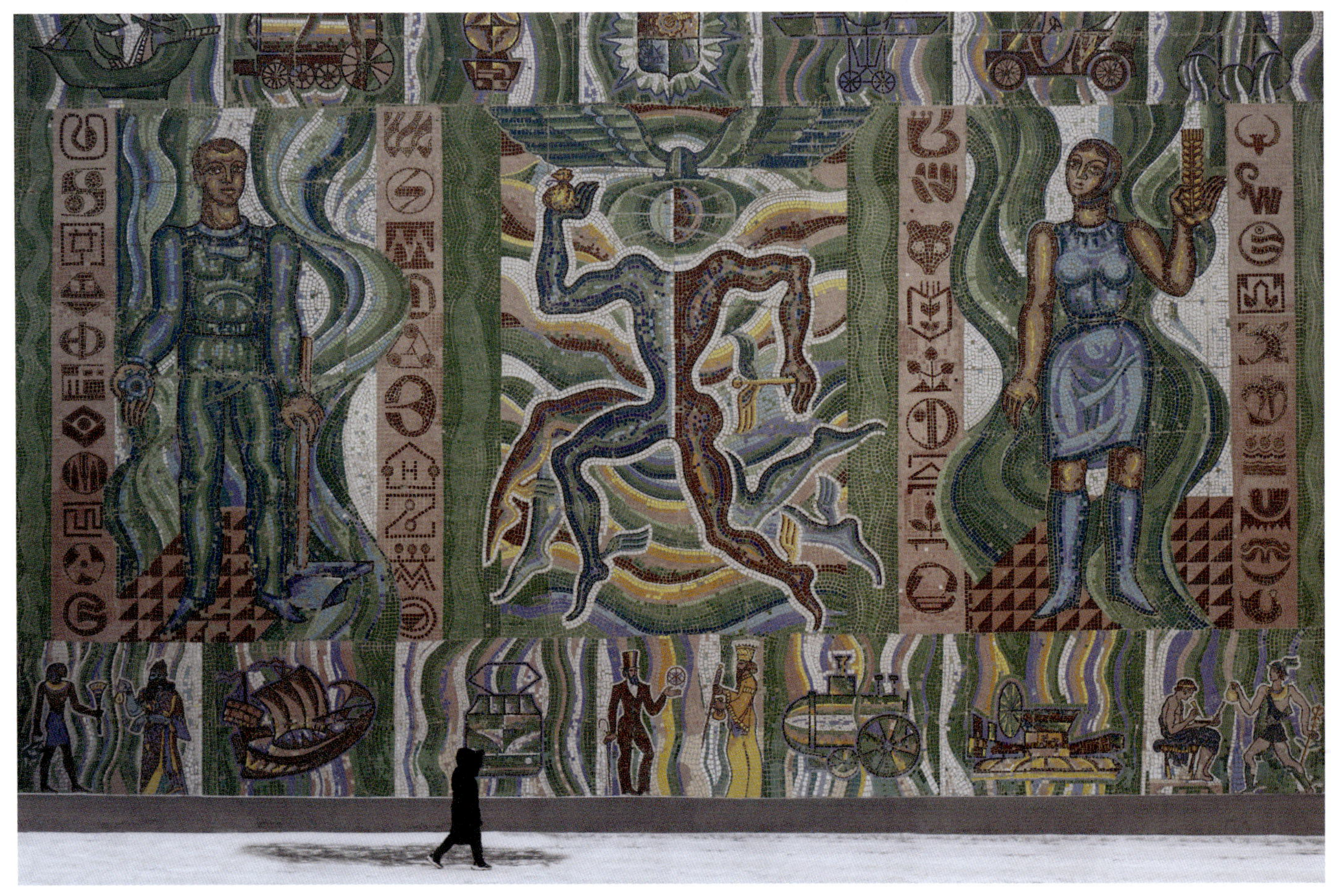

Central Department Store mosaic
KURGAN, RUSSIA
Created in the 1970s
Designer: Y. Kozminykh

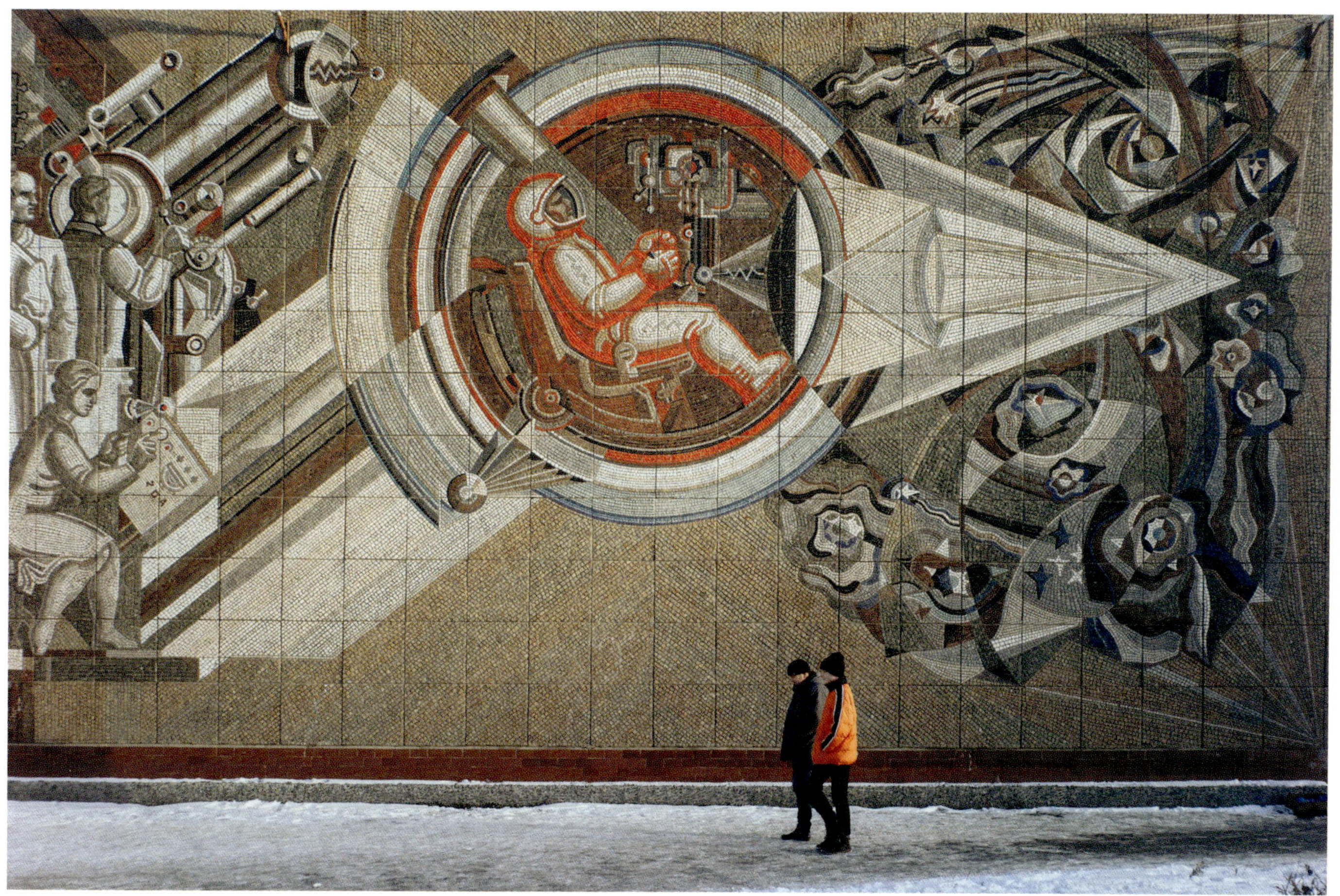

'Conquering Space' panelled mural
Technical College
CHELYABINSK, RUSSIA
Created in 1976

This mosaic was made by the artist V.G. Mishin. It pays tribute to the extensive preparatory work of scientists, engineers and designers in the process of space exploration. The figures depicted here are inspired by Tsiolkovsky, Korolev and, of course, Gagarin himself.

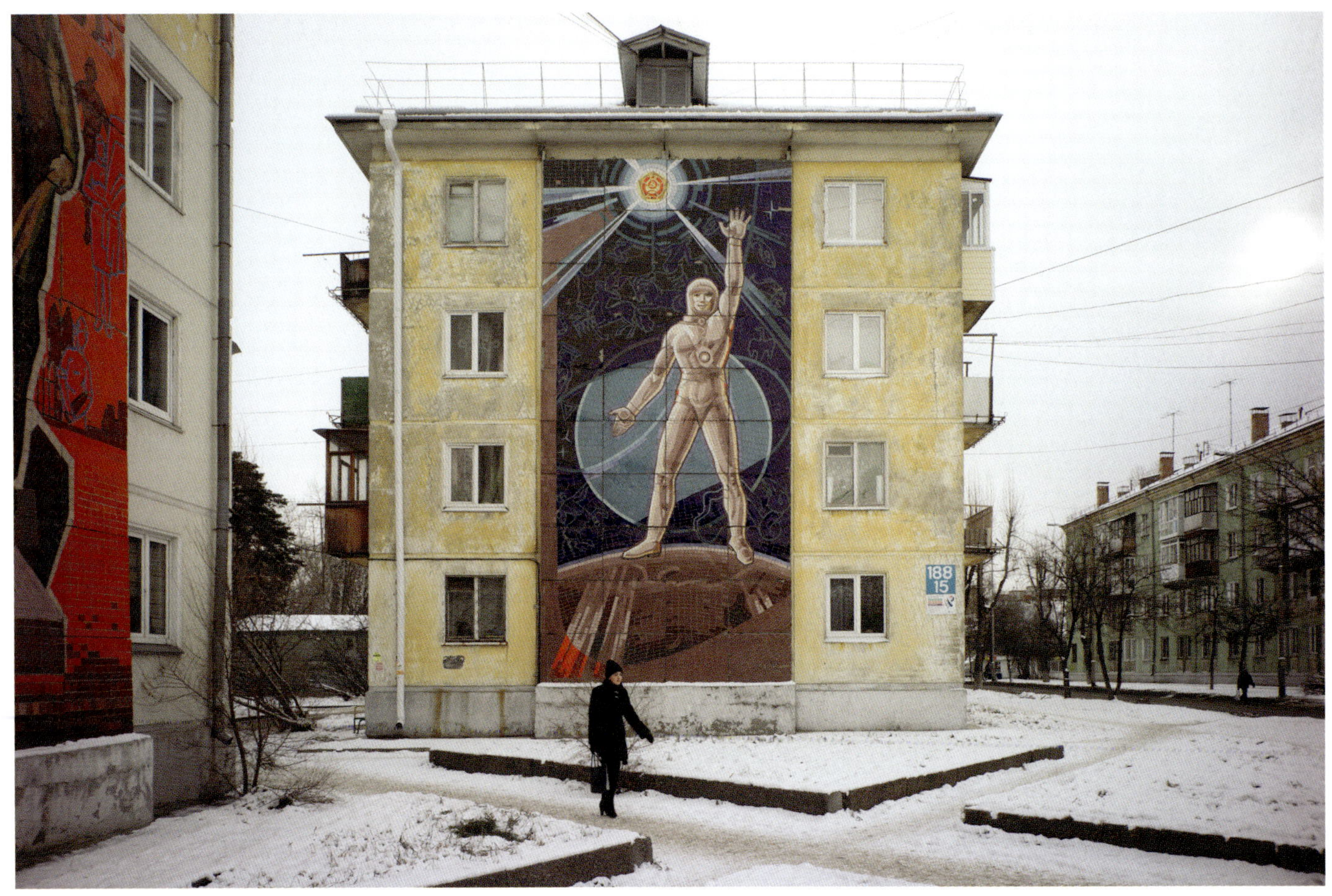

Soviet mosaics
ANGARSK, RUSSIA
Created between 1969 and 1975

These seventeen mosaic murals are devoted to important Soviet
historical events and themes such as the Decembrist Uprising, the
October Revolution, the Great Patriotic War and space exploration.
They depict famous people from various eras – Pushkin, Lenin,

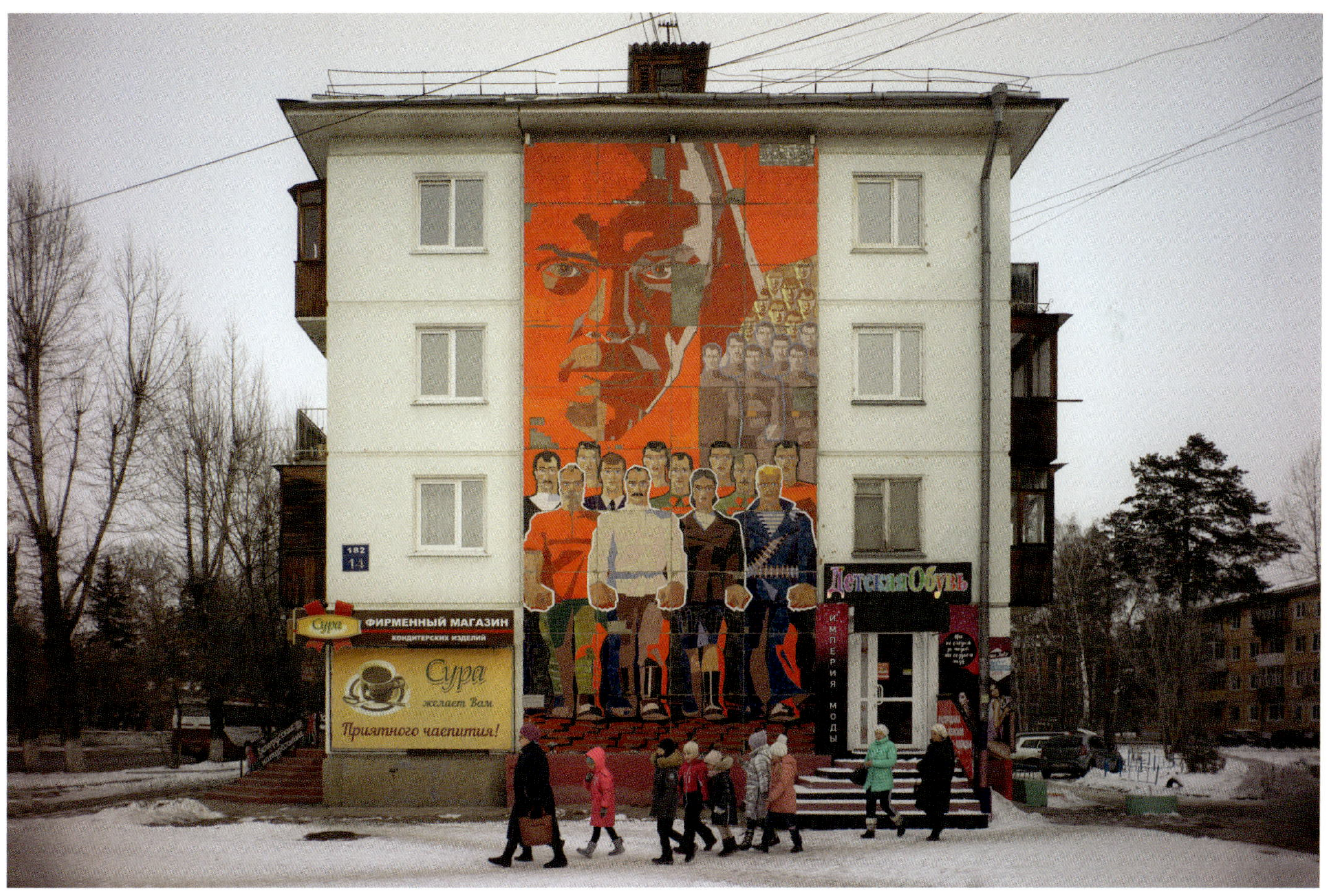

Tsiolkovsky and Korolev – and are united by a common aspiration: the desire to build a better future for the Soviet people. They were designed by a team of artists (N. Gorokhov, K. Voevodin and others) as works of art for the general population rather than for a select elite.

The murals were intended as a message to future generations of citzens from people who lived in an era of visionary creators and dreamers. Today the Angarsk mosaics are widely recognised as a unique monument to the age of Socialist Realism.

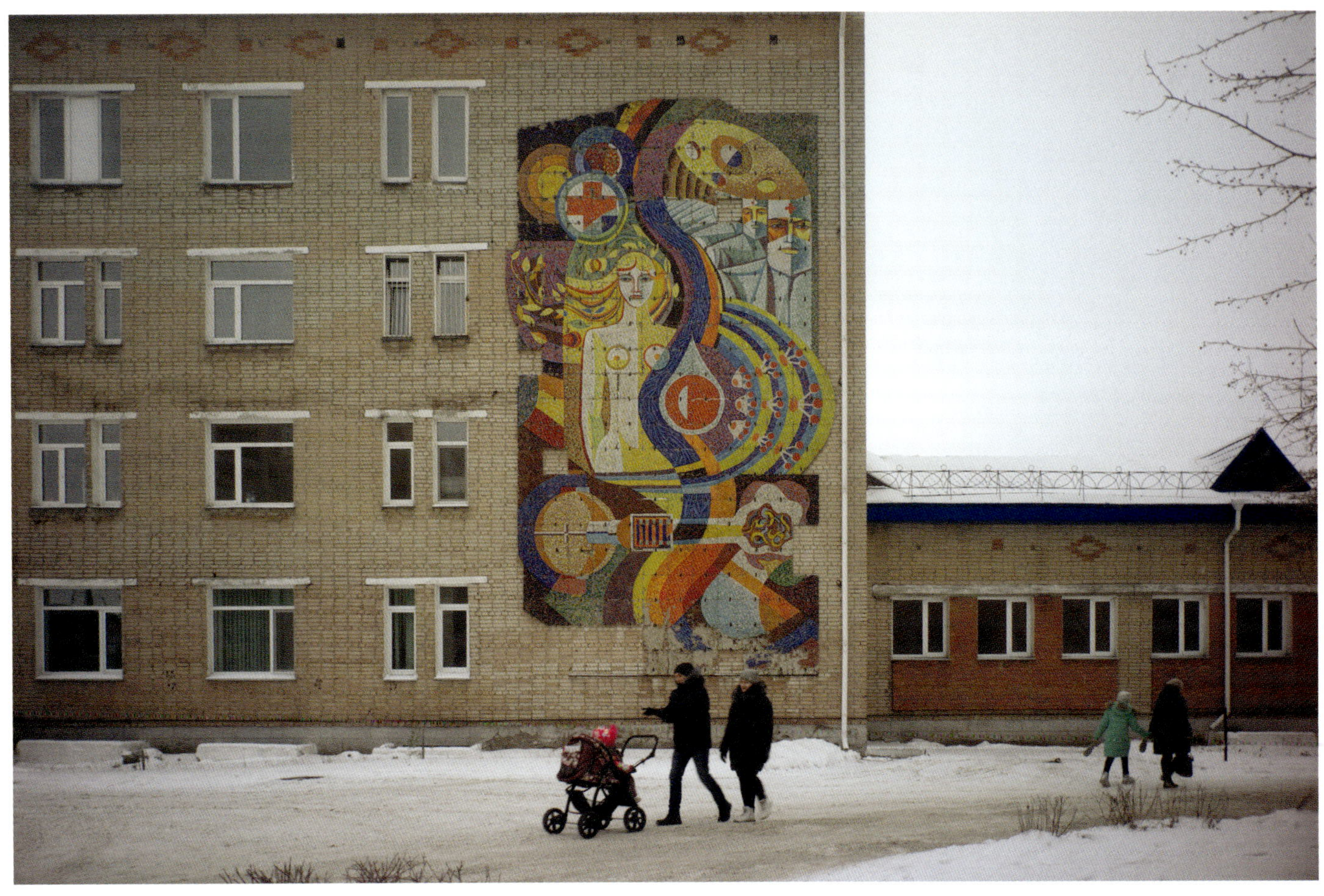

Mosaic on the Old Railway Hospital
PETROPAVLOVSK, KAZAKHSTAN

This city in northern Kazakhstan has a population of 219,000. In 1752, a fort was constructed on the Ishim river to strengthen the southern border of the Russian Empire. In 1918 it became a centre for the White movement, fighting the Reds, but Soviet power was restored in 1919.

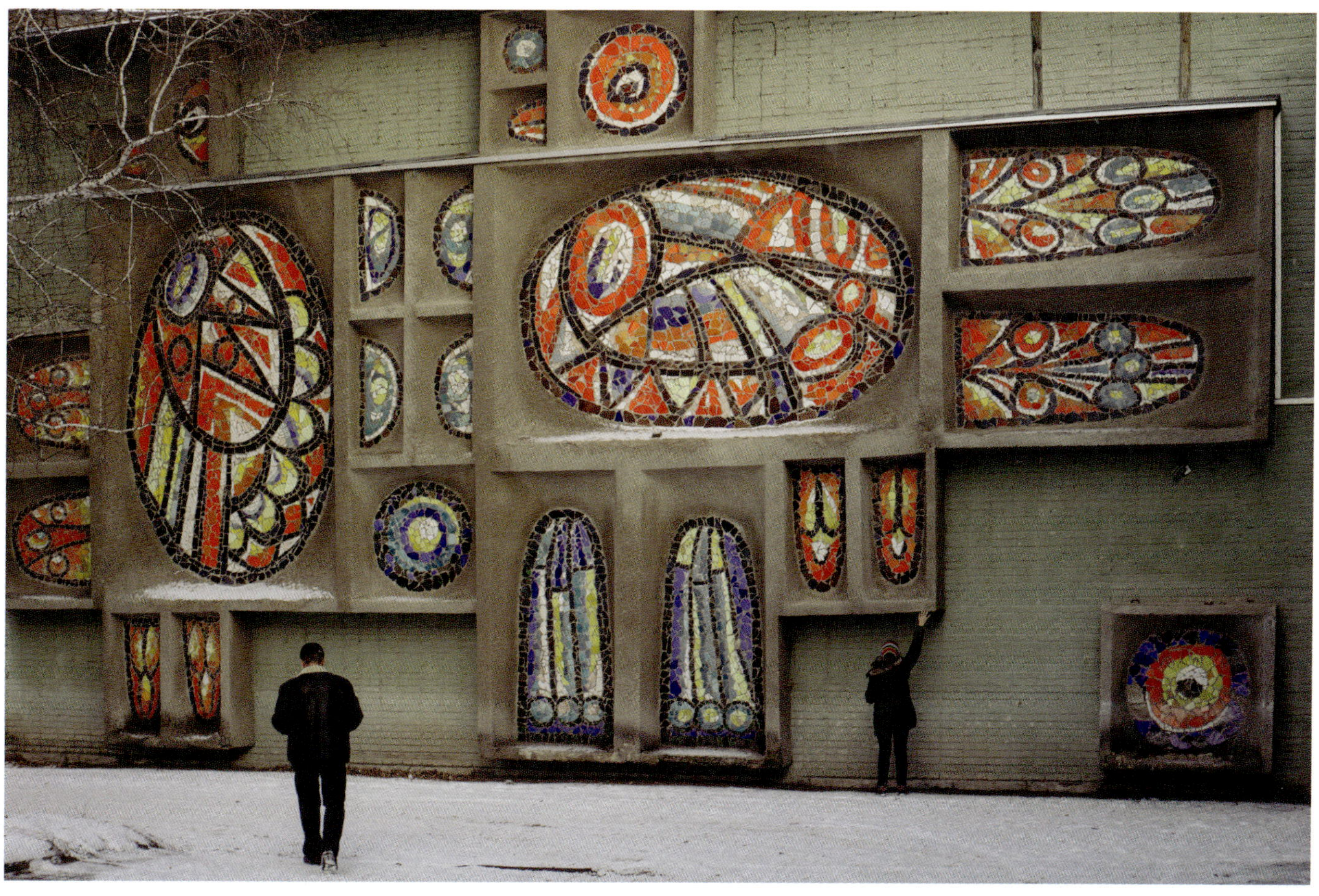

Bas-relief mosaic with birds
ZHELEZNOGORSK, RUSSIA

Zheleznogorsk (previously Krasnoyarsk-26) is a restricted city with a population of 83,000. It was built in 1950 to accommodate workers at Kombinat No.815, an underground plant that played a significant role in the production of weapons-grade plutonium.

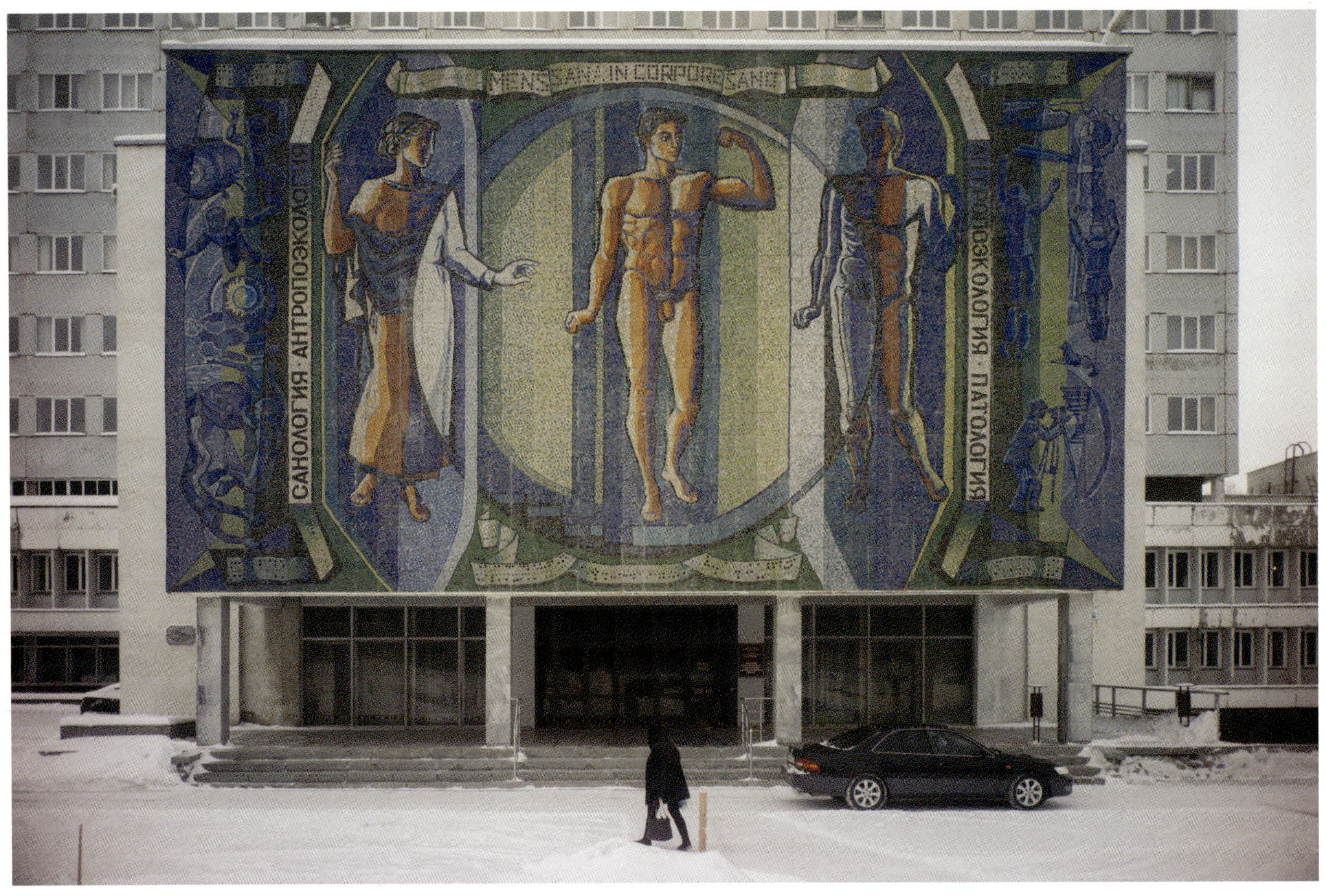

'Man and the Science of Medicine' panelled mosaic
NOVOSIBIRSK, RUSSIA
Created between 1979 and 1989
Designer: V. Kiryanov

The huge mosaic is situated above the entrance of the Institute of Clinical and Experimental Medicine, a department of the Siberian branch of the Academy of Sciences. It took creator Vasily Kiryanov nearly ten years to complete.

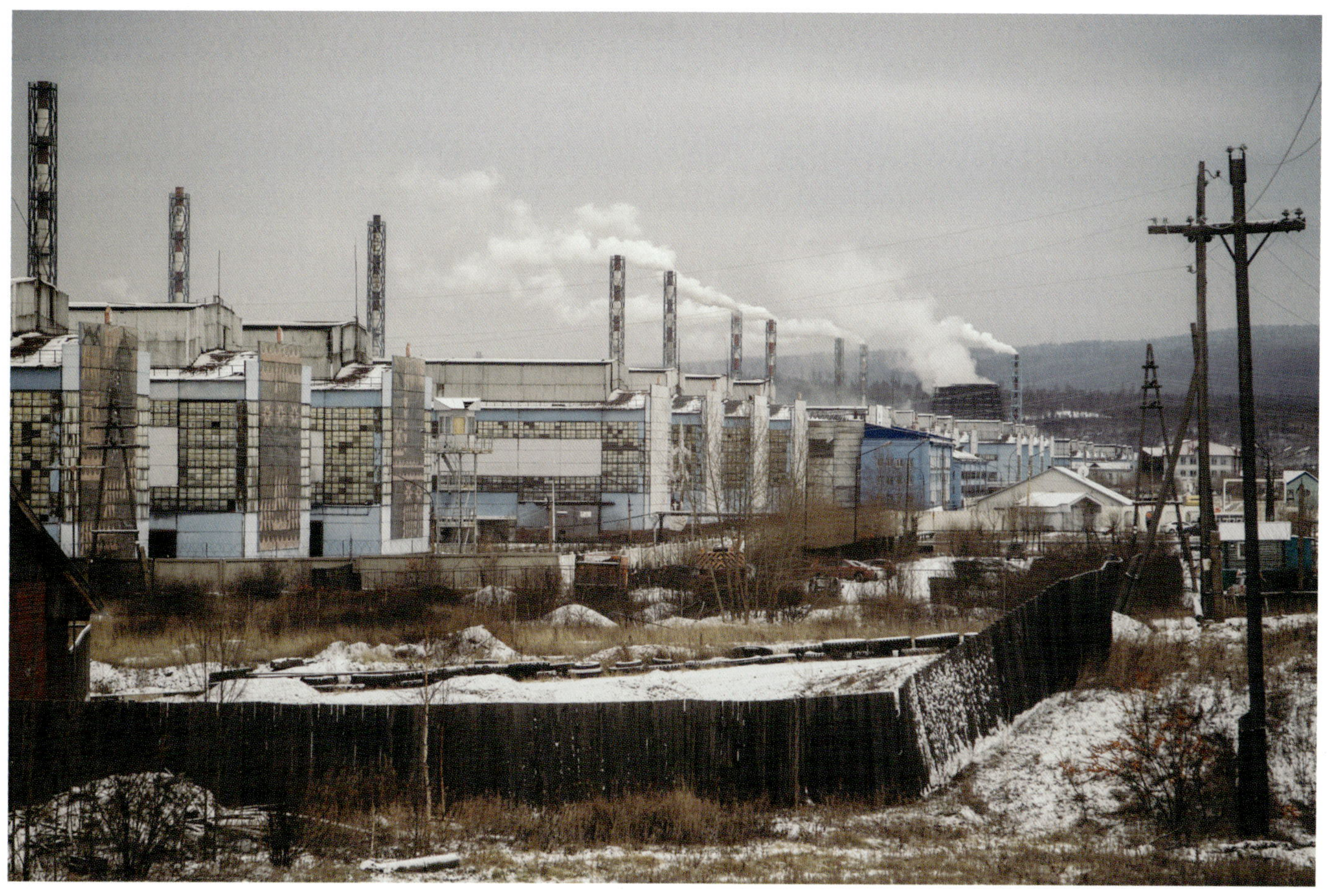

Bratsk Aluminium Smelter
BRATSK, RUSSIA
Founded in 1966

The Bratsk Aluminium Smelter is the largest in the country and one of the largest in the world. This site produces 30 per cent of the total Russian aluminium output and accounts for 4 per cent of total global production.

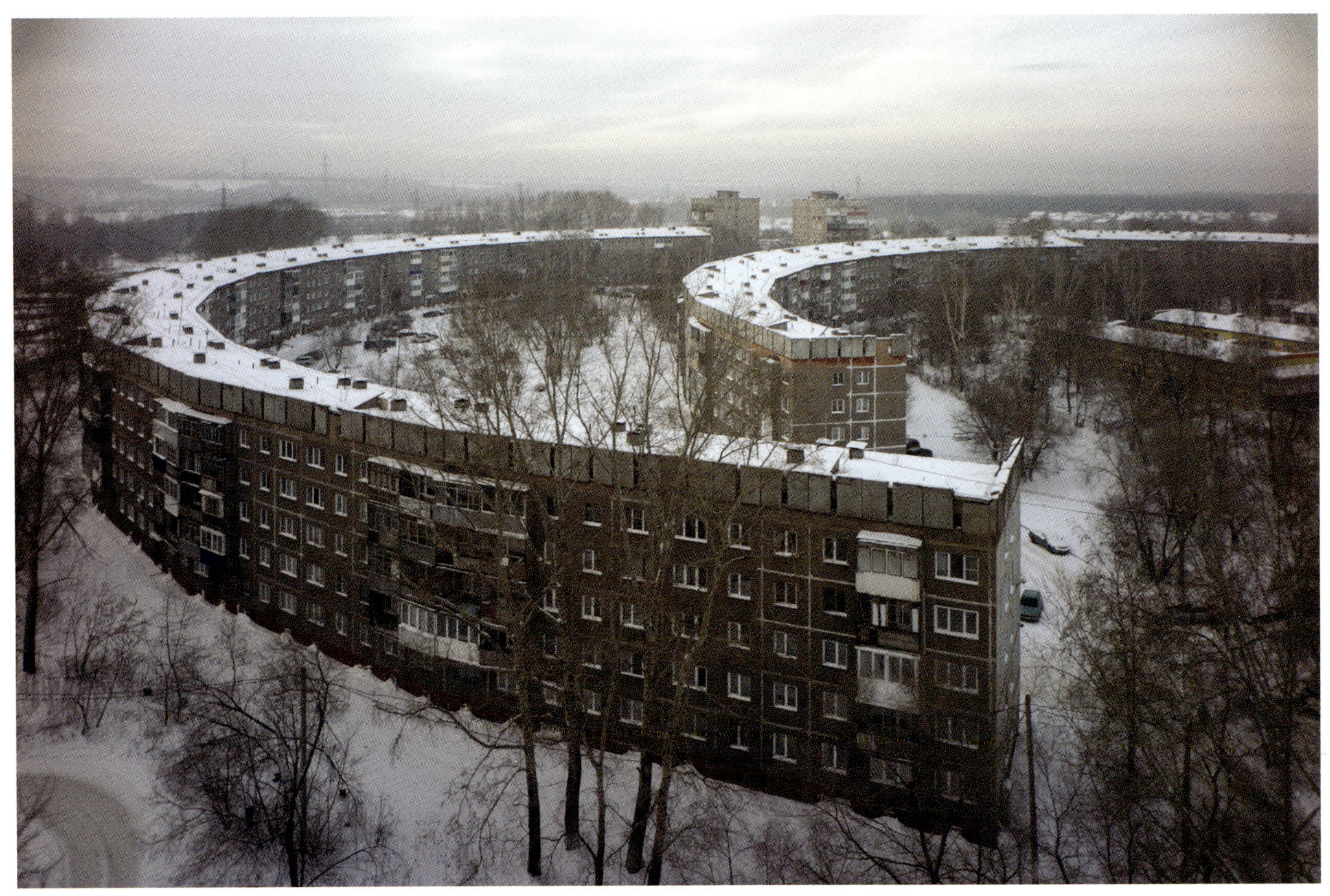

'Rocker' buildings
Zavodskoy District
NOVOKUZNETSK, RUSSIA
Built in 1973

Named after their unusual arc-shape, these two 'Rocker' apartment buildings were constructed for employees of the Novokuznetsk Metallurgical Plant. The idiosyncratic dwellings have become a local landmark.

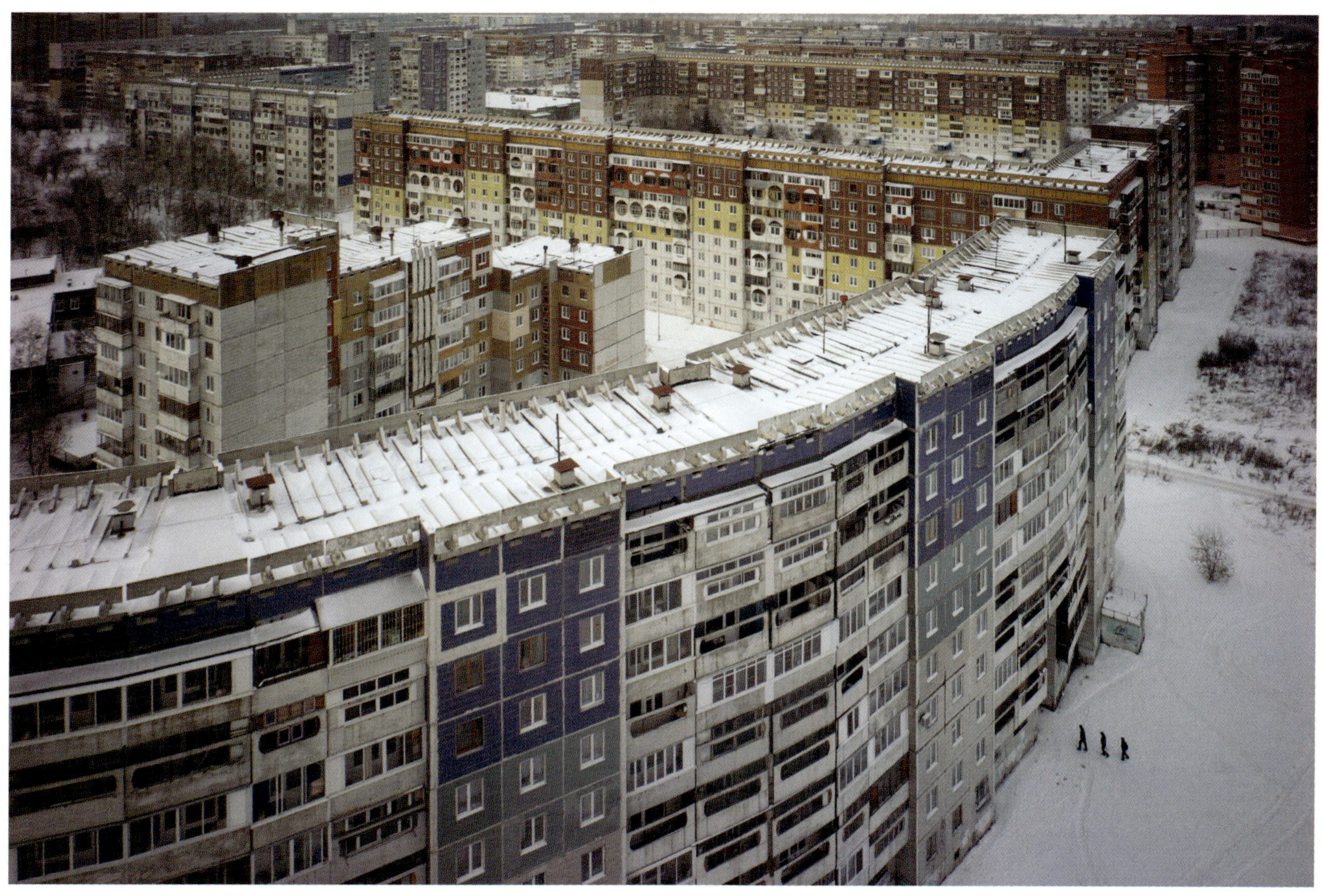

Shalgotaryan Microdistrict
KEMEROVO, RUSSIA

Following a governmental decree of 1979, this neighbourhood was built in conjunction with workers from Hungary as a symbol of Kuzbass-Hungarian friendship. The district was named after the Hungarian city of Salgotarjan, which is twinned with Kemerovo.

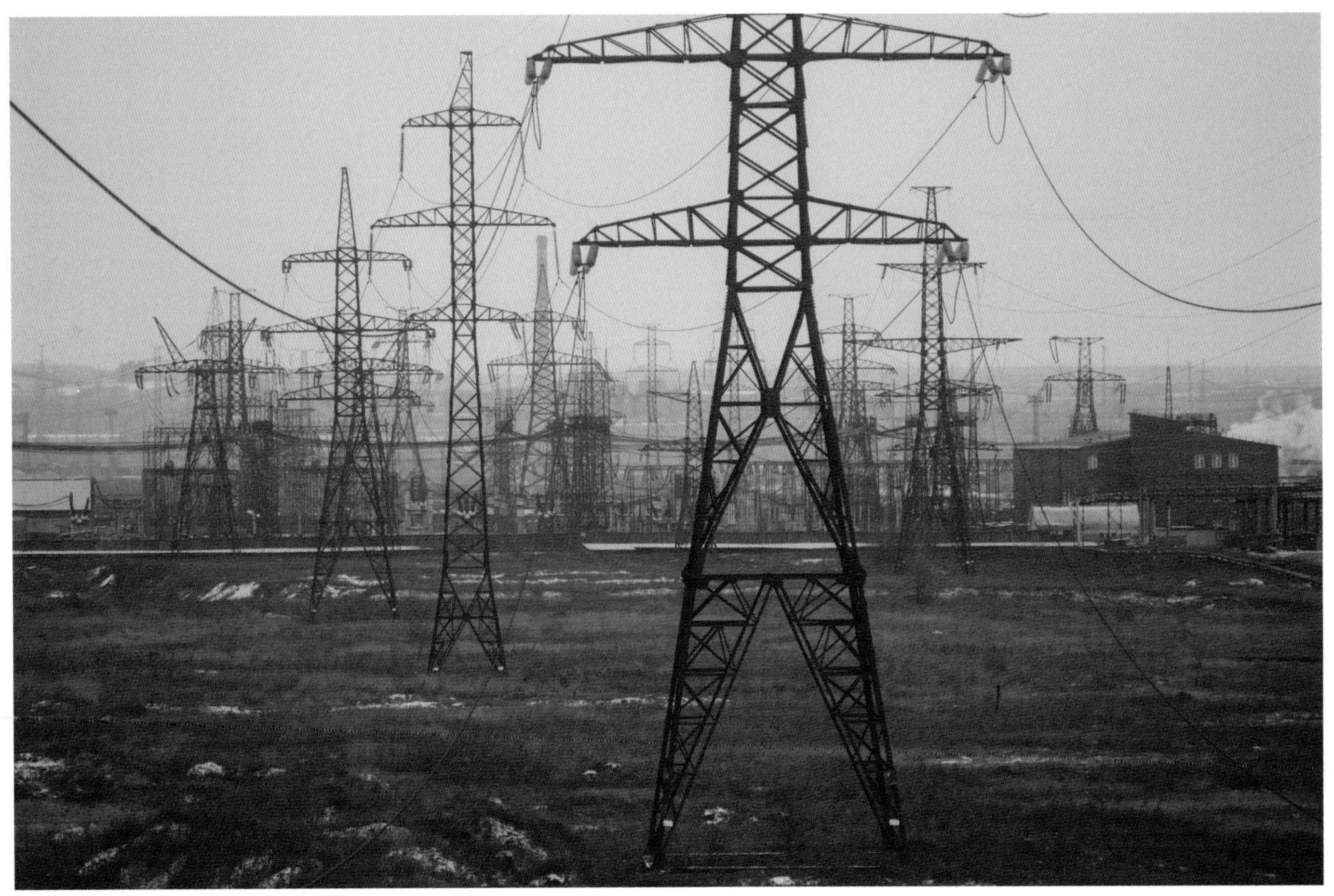

Aluminium Factory power lines
KRASNOYARSK, RUSSIA

This vast smelter is powered by the Krasnoyarsk Hydropower Plant and consumes around 70 per cent of its output. The production complex includes 25 electrolysis cells, three foundry units and an anode mass-production facility.

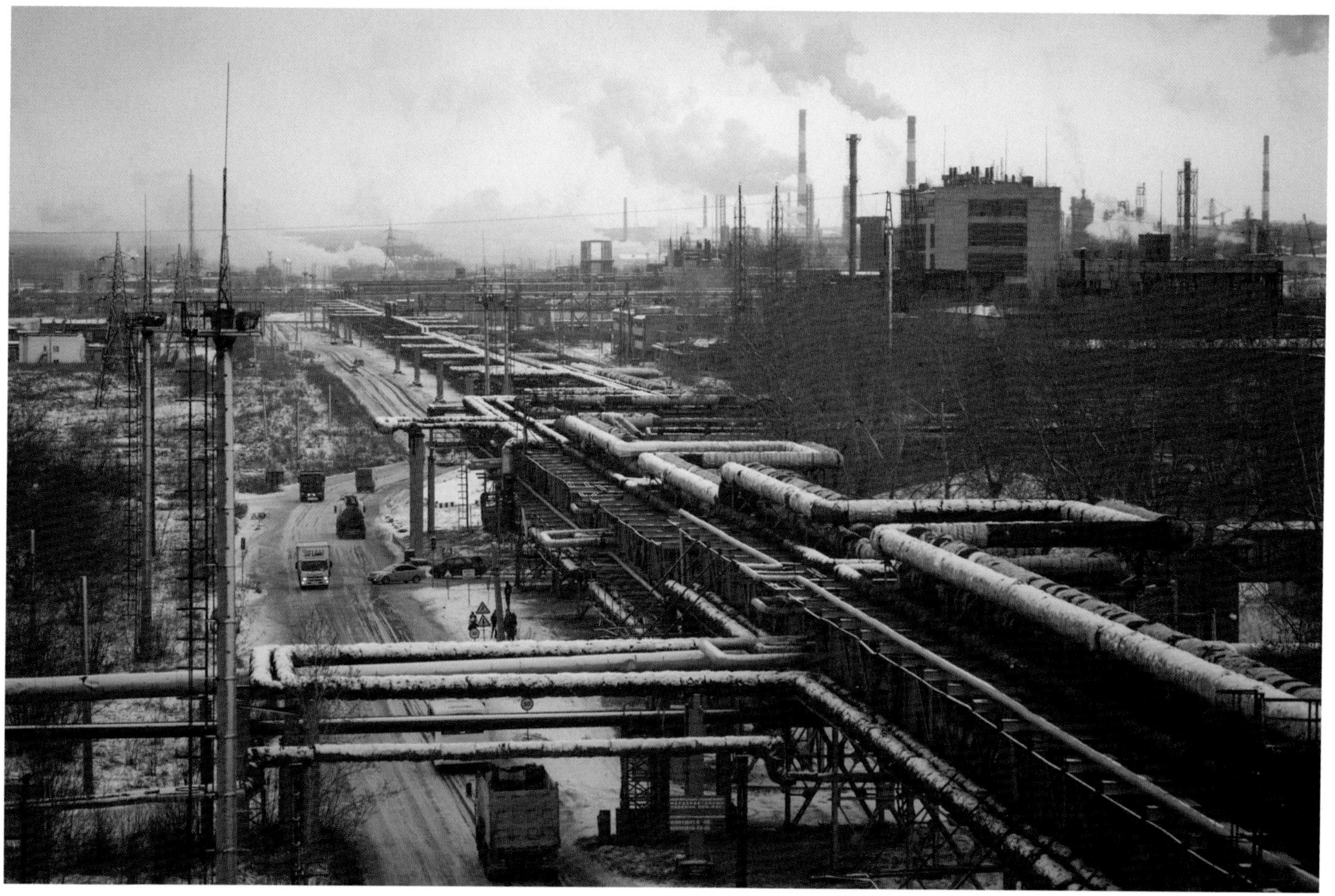

Petrochemical Plant pipeline
ANGARSK, RUSSIA

The government decree on the establishment of the Artificial Liquid Fuel Combine was issued in 1945. Over time, the combine grew into Eastern Siberia's largest enterprise for the refining and manufacture of oil products, eventually giving rise to the city of Angarsk.

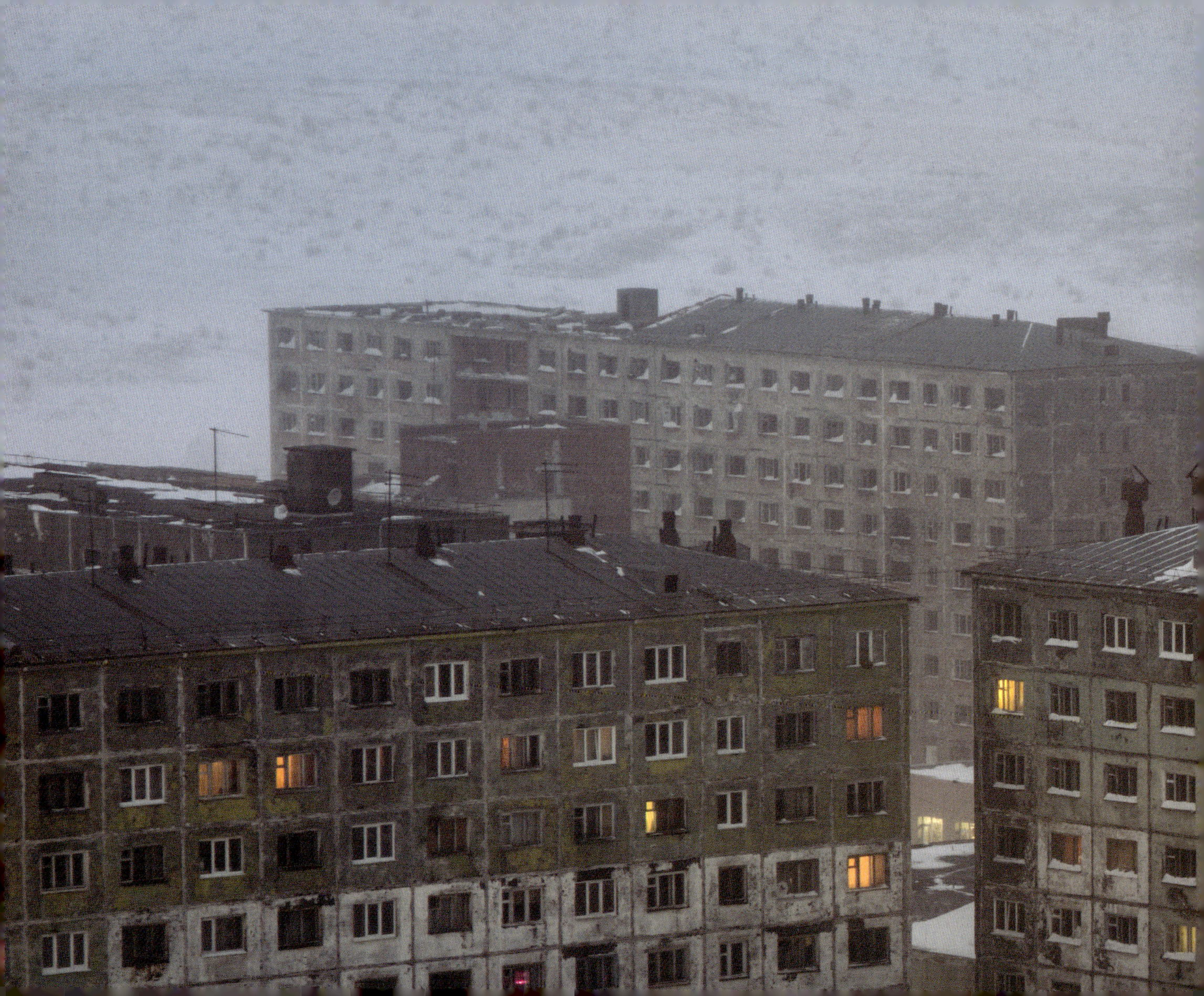

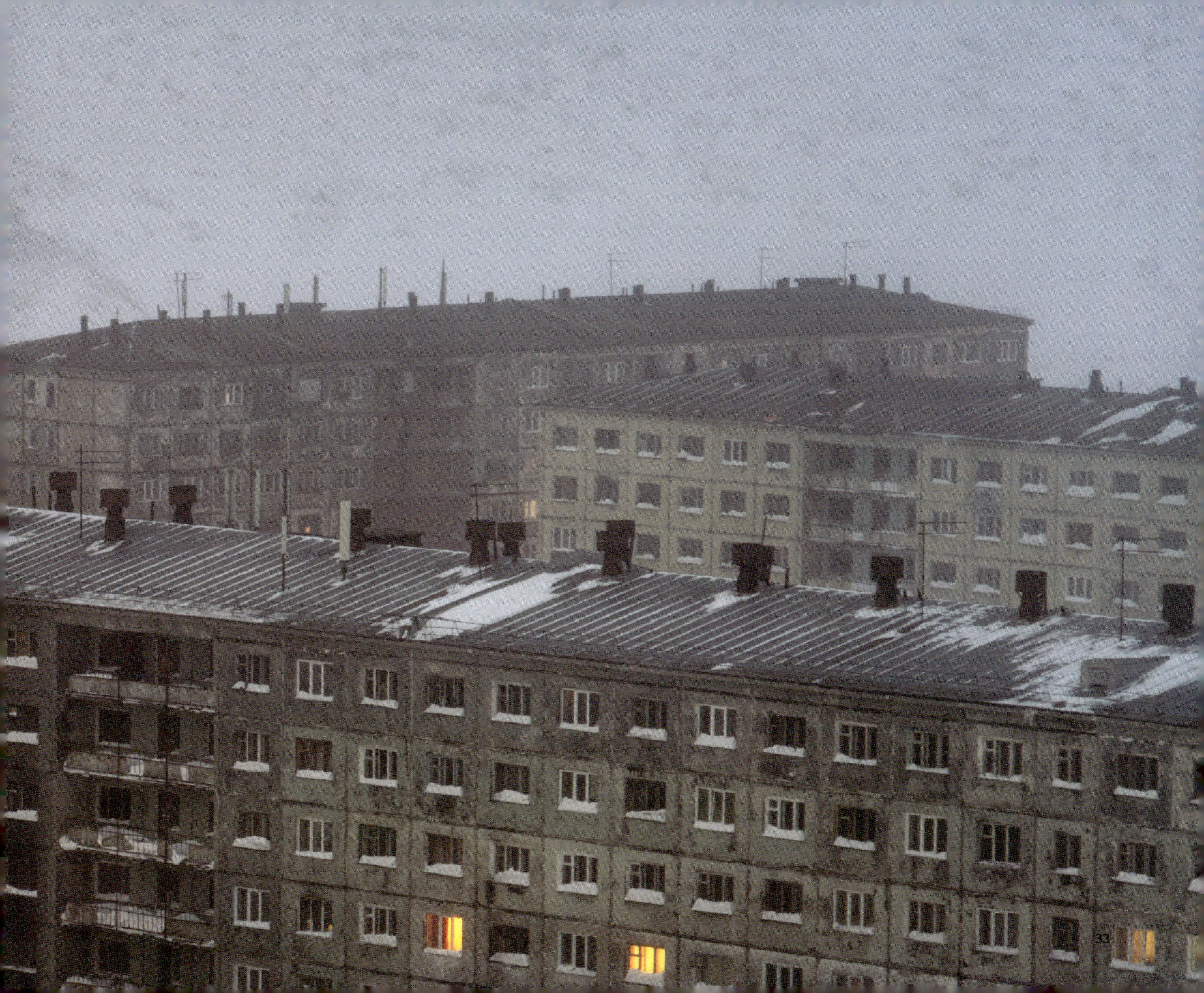

NORILSK

Usually, when people say 'terra incognita', they are referring to distant, unexplored lands. But in Norilsk, this 'unknown land' lay under our feet. It was difficult to walk on and impossible to drive over – swamps in summer, snowdrifts as tall as a man in spring... Yet it was to be built upon.

For half the year, the surface could not be broken even with a crowbar – it was hardened by cold, ringing as steel. Bonfires were lit; the ground was thawed. Workers removed a layer of earth and the bonfires were lit again. Eventually they reached rock. The rock served as a foundation, on top of which a workshop could be built. If you dig the ground you quickly find ice like cement. Ice as a mineral is well known to the geologists of Norilsk, where its veins penetrate even the density of the bedrock.

The minerals mined by the Norilsk Combine have developed within the bowels of the Taimyr Peninsula. In this midnight land, nature's resources lay hidden until man discovered them – riches greater than our sunniest regions could dream of. The Norilsk ore district alone includes deposits of copper-nickel, iron ore, coal, natural gas, lead, zinc and mercury...

The city of Norilsk came into being through the Norilsk Mining and Metallurgical Plant, and the factories, mines and shafts draw their lifeblood from the abundance of the Taimyr region.

The three resources on which Norilsk is built are nickel, cobalt and copper – these are the glory and pride of the entire city. Norilsk has discovered and extracted the valuable ores of the Polar terrain. It has become the northernmost mining and metallurgical centre in the country, and one of the largest in the world.

From its very first steps, Norilsk set world records in the area of constructing a city on permafrost. Such an array of issues on such a scale were not to be found anywhere else: the study of the thermal conditions of the soil, the determination of its load capacity, the observation of the permafrost in developed areas, water supply, sewerage, foundations, the secrets of building bridges and dams...

The experience of the first decade of construction allowed the team of designers headed by Mikhail Kim to establish the basic 'Methods for the Formation of Structures on Permafrost'. In 1966, this work gained the team the highest state award – the Lenin Prize. One of their most striking discoveries was the efficacy of piling to enable deep foundations in Norilsk, where 250,000 piles were drilled into boreholes within the frozen permafrost soil. It is on these that the residential areas of Norilsk stand.

Norilsk – Cities of the Krasnoyarsk Region, Anatoly Lvov, 1985

previous page
Semi-abandoned outskirts of the Kayerkan District
NORILSK, RUSSIA

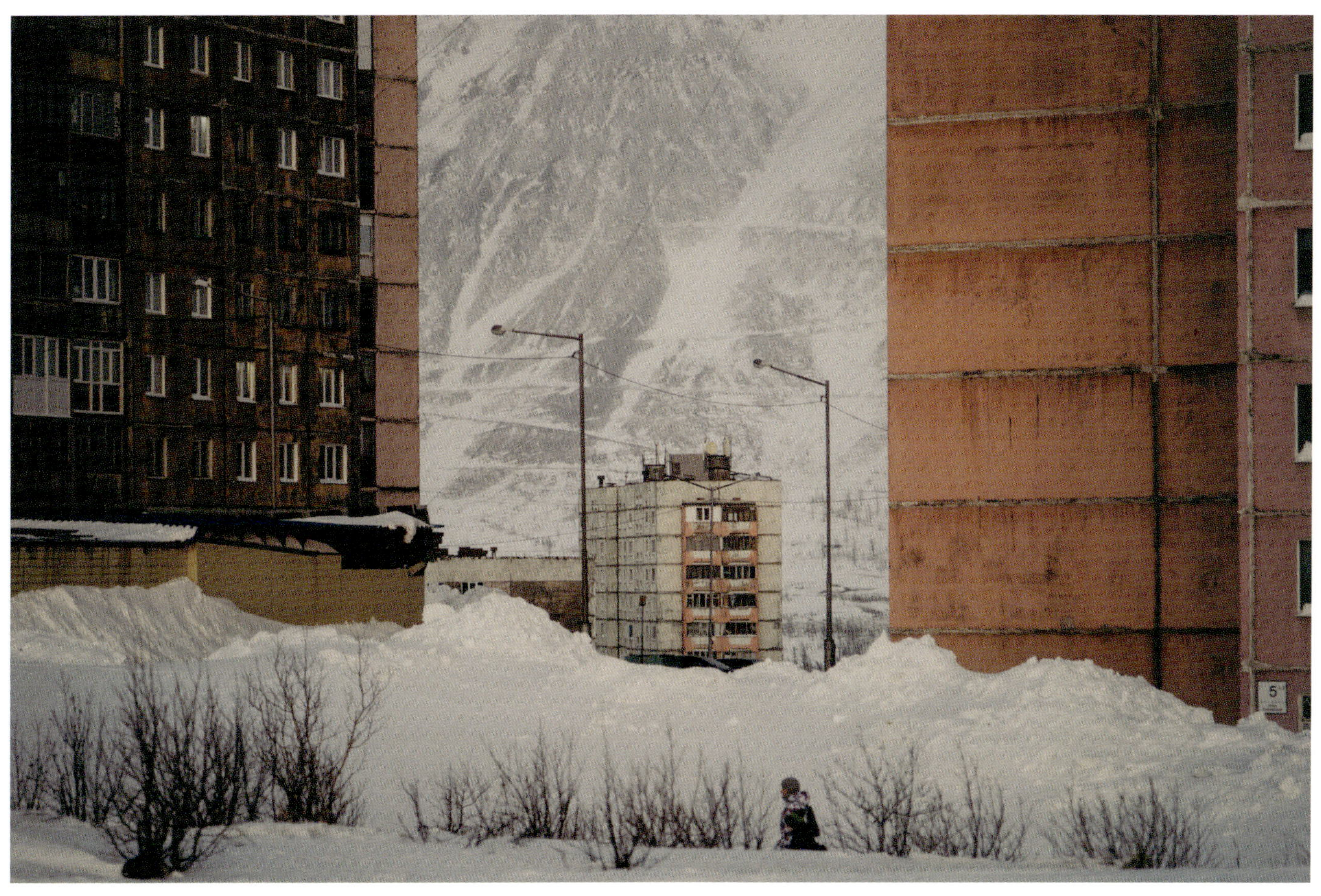

5th Microdistrict, Talnah
NORILSK, RUSSIA

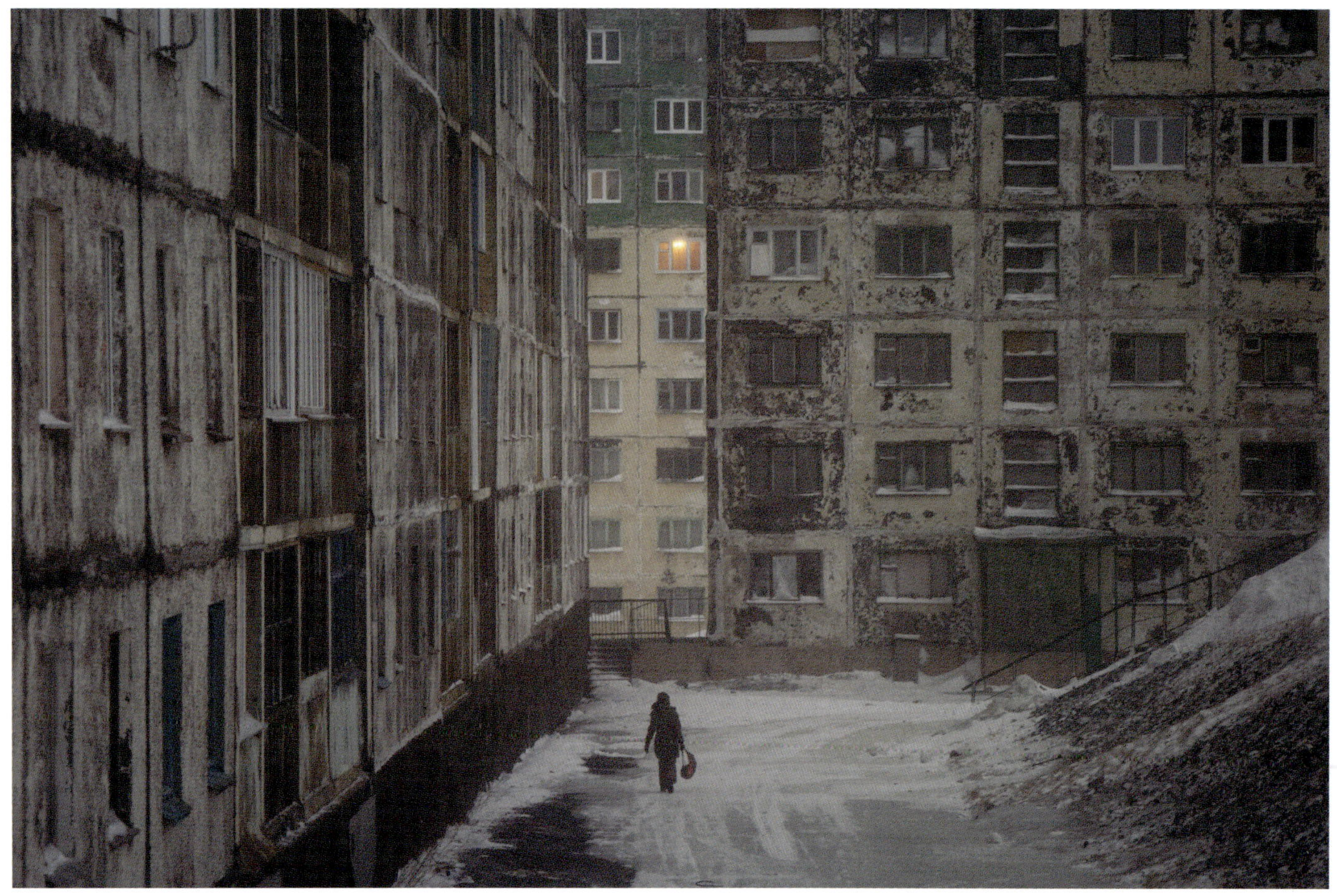

Kayerkan District
NORILSK, RUSSIA

The Kayerkan settlement was developed as local coal deposits began to be exploited. The area grew further as residents were employed to build and operate the Nadezhda Metallurgical Plant, the largest enterprise in the Norilsk region.

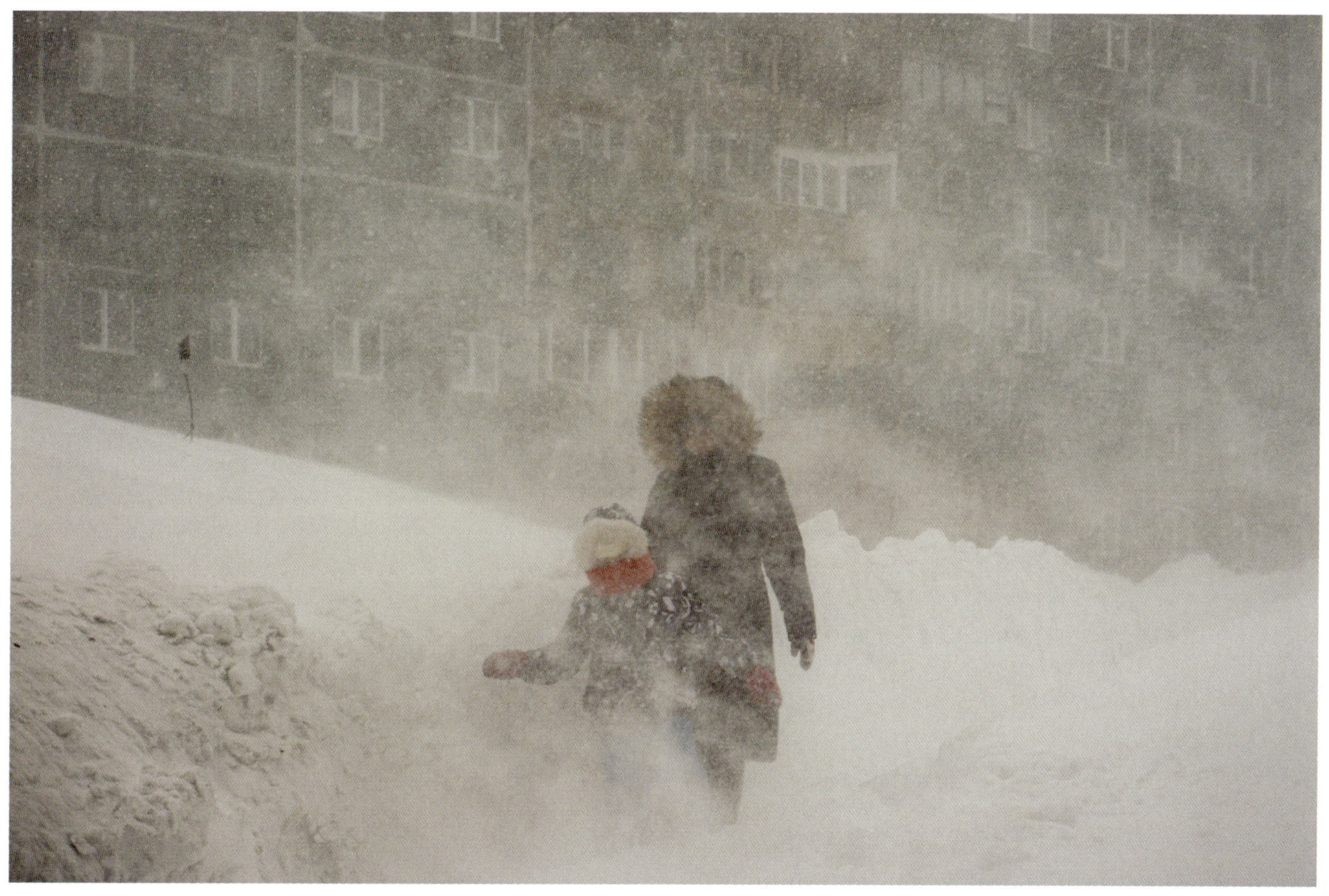

Walking to school in a blizzard
Talnah District
NORILSK, RUSSIA

The exploitation of the Kharaelakh deposits and the construction of a workers' camp began here in 1963 following the geological expedition of G. Maslov, who discovered a rich deposit of copper-nickel polymetallic ores.

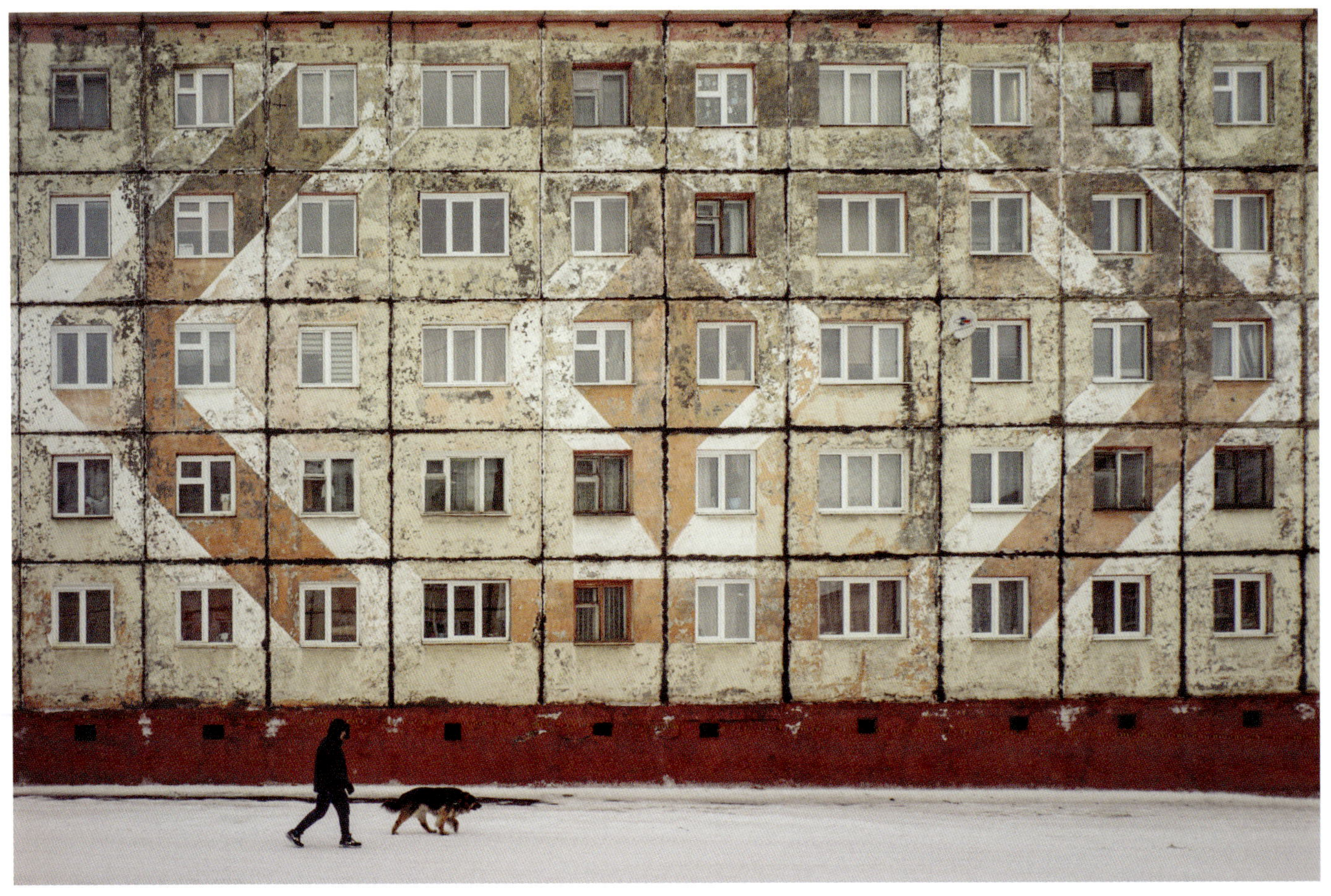

Painted building in the Central District
NORILSK, RUSSIA
Built in the 1970s

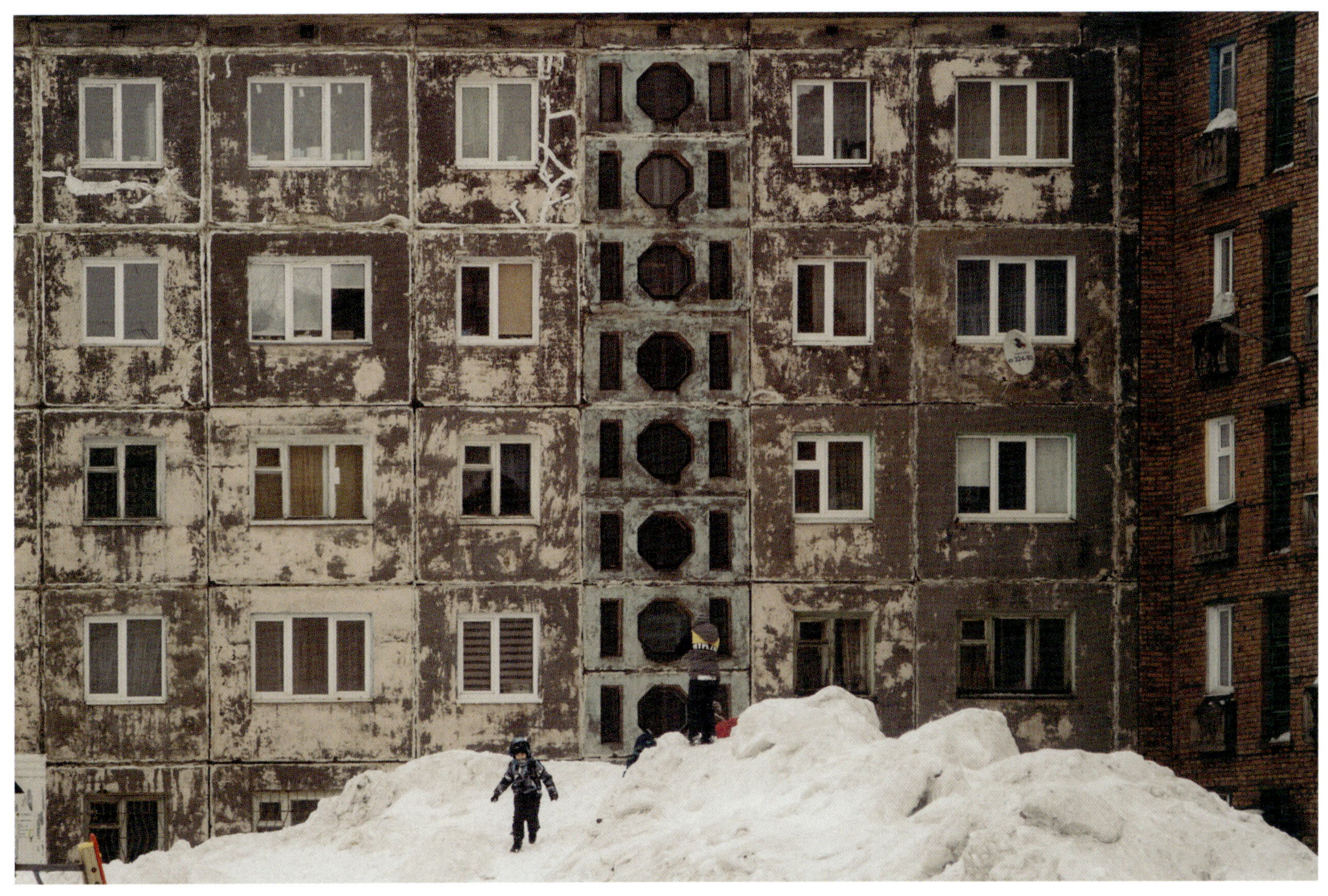

Snow drifts in the Central District
NORILSK, RUSSIA
Built in the 1970s

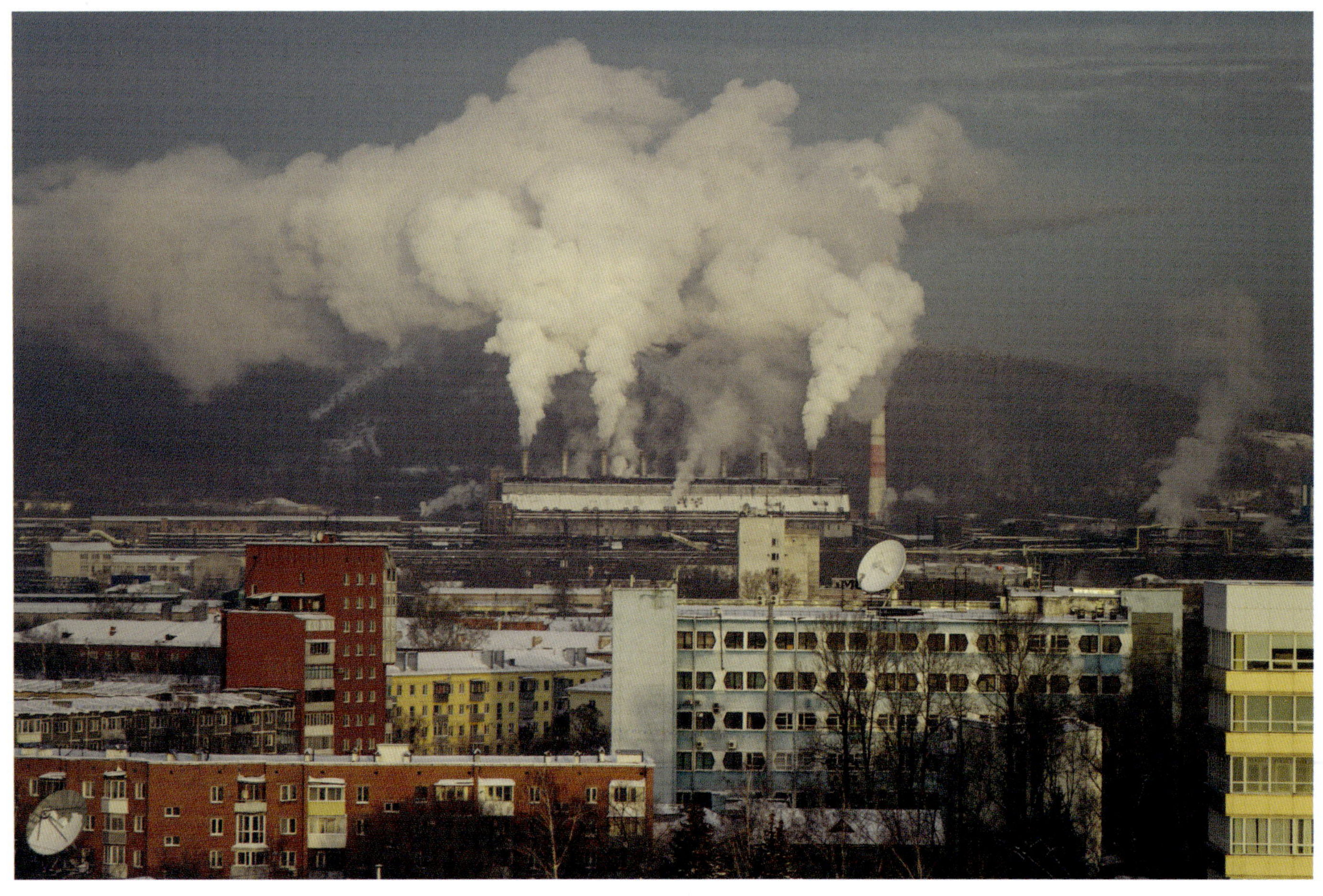

Metallurgical Plant
NOVOKUZNETSK, RUSSIA

In the winter of 1929, a second, substantial coal and metallurgical centre was established here. Thousands of Komsomol members helped with its construction. Fires burned continuously to thaw the frozen ground so that foundations could be laid for 41 furnaces.

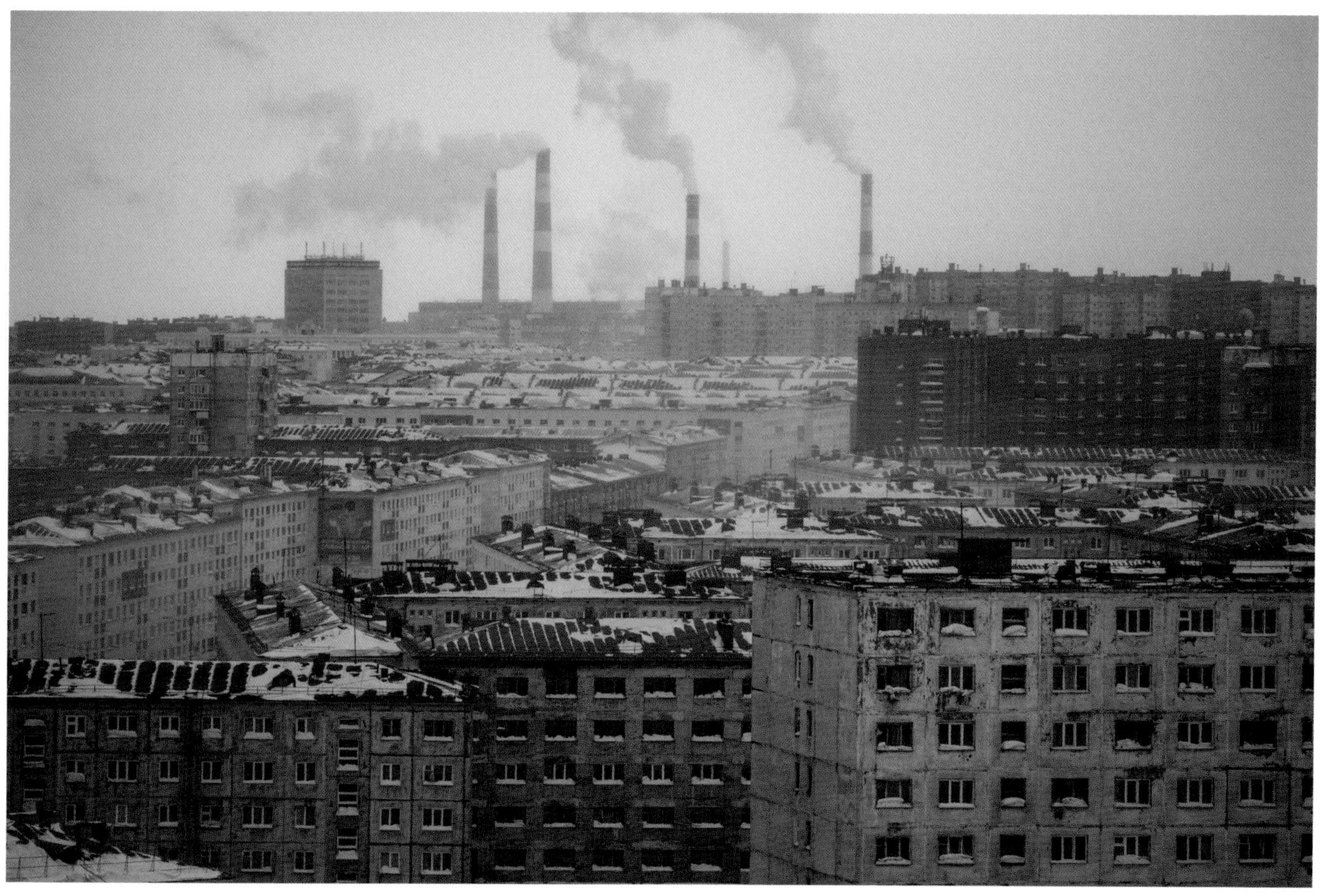

Chimneys of Combined Heat and Power Plant No.1
NORILSK, RUSSIA
Built in 1942

Combined Heat and Power Plant No.1 is a source of electric power for the city and its factories. It is the only source of heat energy for the main industrial site, the city of Norilsk and the neighbouring Oganer housing community.

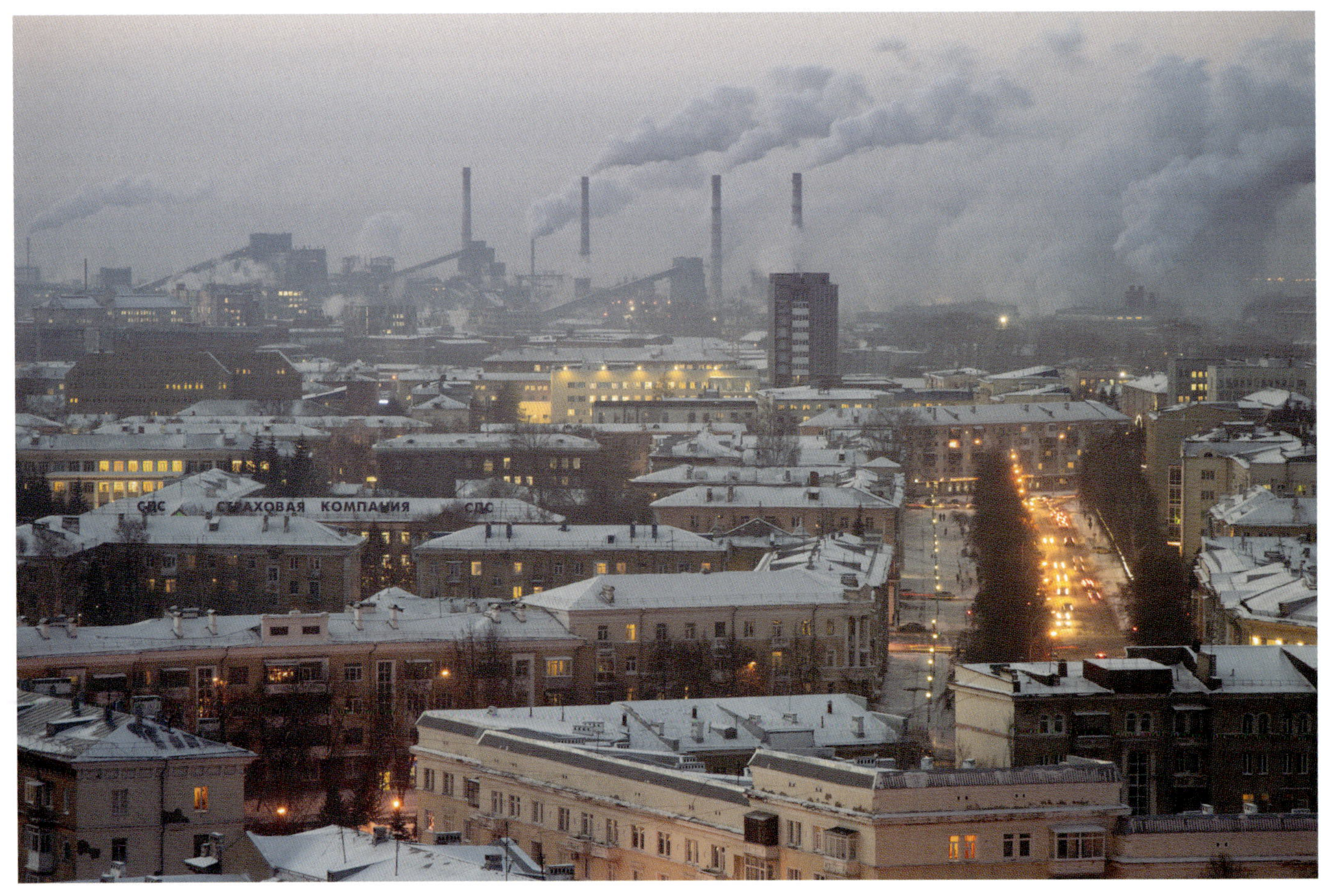

Coke Plant
KEMEROVO, RUSSIA

Construction of the Kemerovo Coke Plant began in 1915. During World War I, two ignition batteries were built, burning between 30 and 60 tonnes of coke a day. On 2 March 1924, a date which became the plant's birthday, a coke battery of 50 furnaces was commissioned.

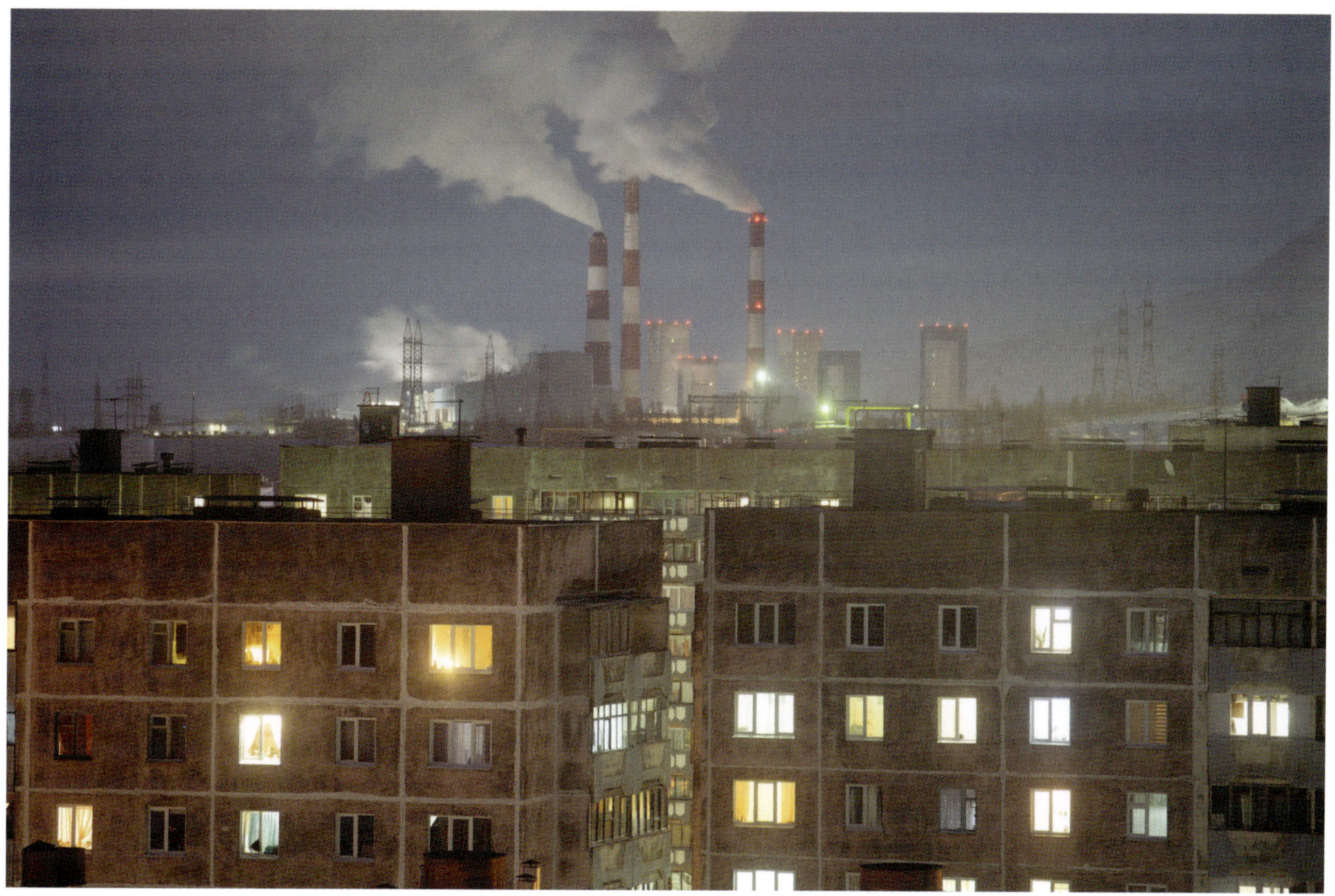

Combined Heat and Power Plant No.2 and copper mines,
viewed from residential buildings of the Talnah District
NORILSK, RUSSIA

In 1965, not far from Talnakh, one of the largest copper reserves in
Russia was found: the Oktyabrskoye deposit. This discovery led to
the formation of the biggest underground mine in the Soviet Union,
reaching depths of up to 1,100 metres.

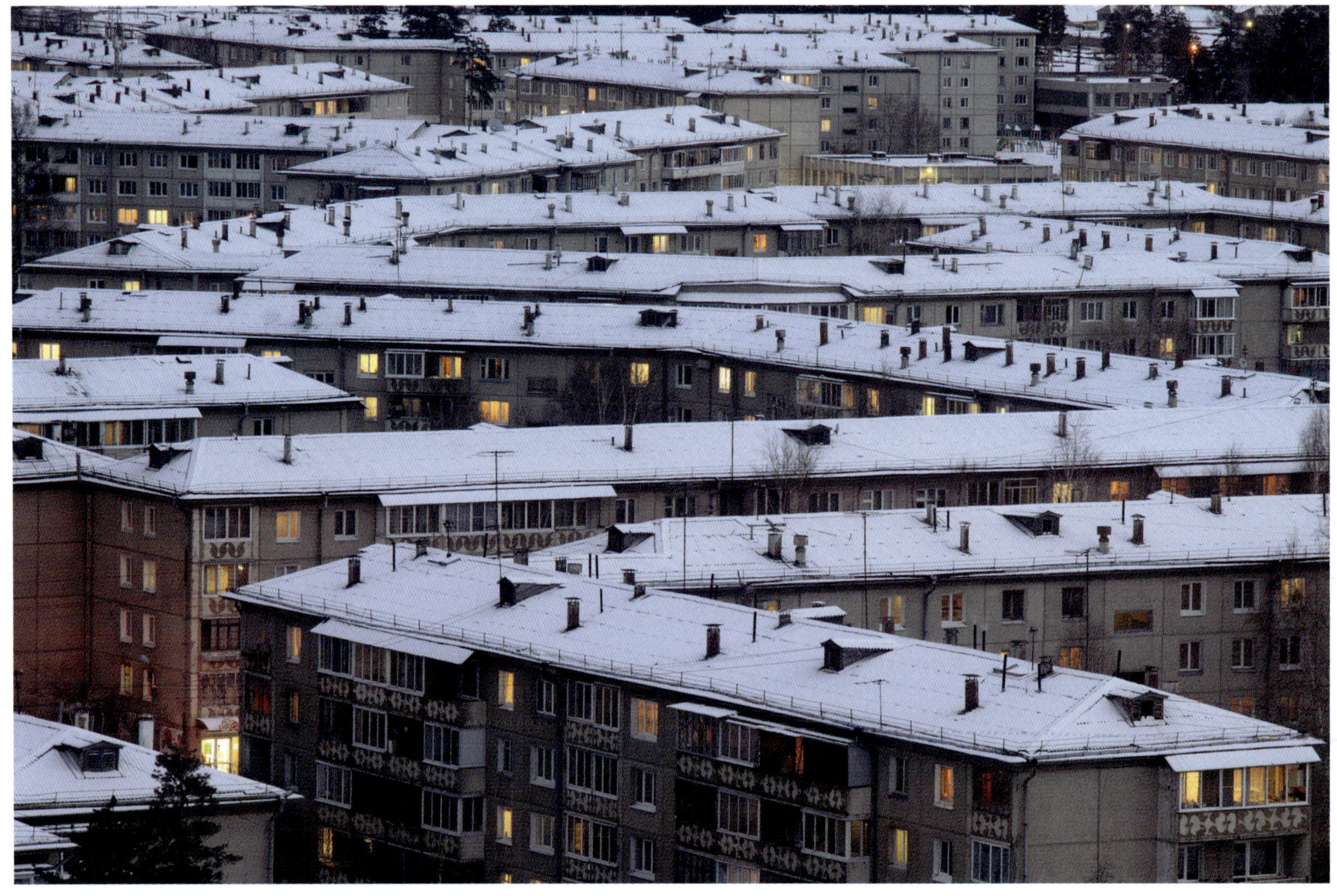

I-335 Series panel housing blocks, 17th Microdistrict
ANGARSK, RUSSIA
Built in the 1960s

Angarsk is a petrochemical city in Eastern Siberia with a population of 224,630. It was established in 1945, when an artificial liquid fuel plant was sited near the Angara river. The equipment used in the factory formed part of German war reparations.

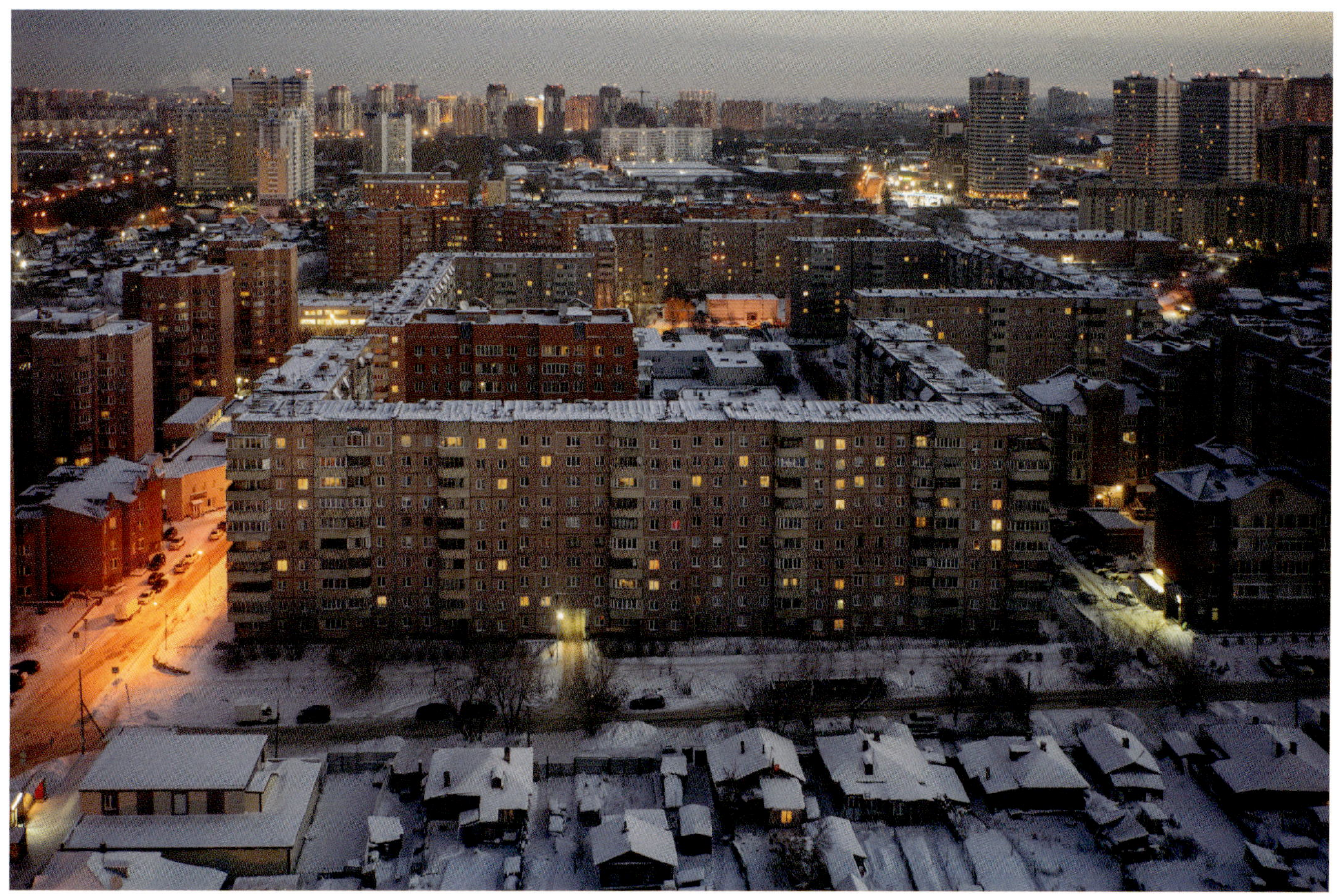

Shevchenko housing estate
NOVOSIBIRSK, RUSSIA
Built in the 1980s

Shevchenko housing estate was developed in the 1980s as an elite neighbourhood, accommodating mid-level officials. As well as improved versions of typical panel apartment blocks, brick high-rises incorporated duplex apartments, exceptional for Soviet-era Novosibirsk.

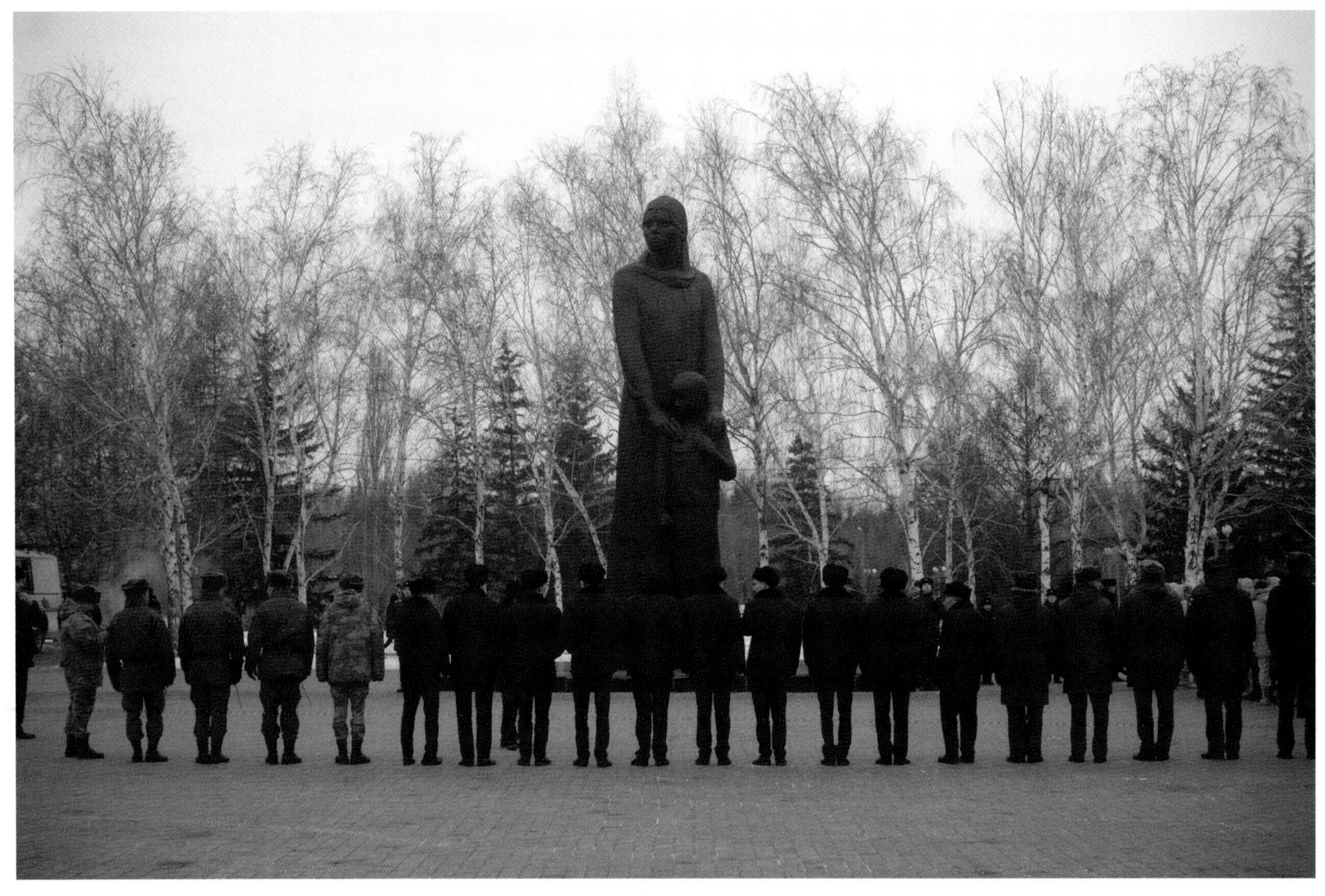

'Siberian Mother with Her Son'
OMSK, RUSSIA
Erected in 1959
Designer: V.N. Antoninov

This 9-metre tall monument represents those who suffered to forge victory and then helped to restore the country after the Great Patriotic War (World War II). The birch trees planted behind it are intended to represent the Motherland.

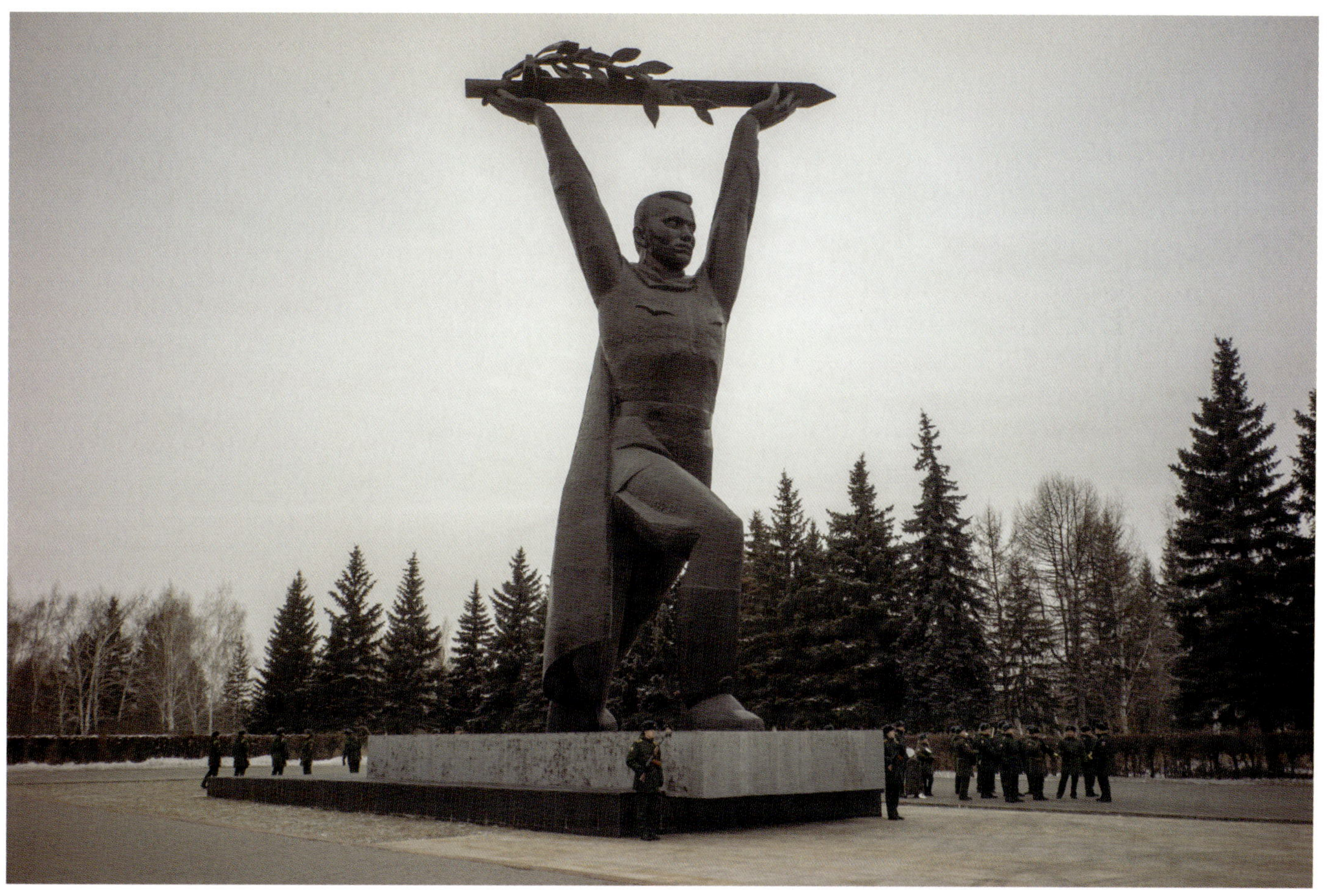

Victorious Soldier Monument
OMSK, RUSSIA
Erected in 1975
Designers: D.B. Ryabichev, N. Kovalchuk

This 14-metre tall sculpture depicting a cloaked soldier symbolises victory in World War II. He holds aloft a sword on top of which rests a laurel branch. The memorial was unveiled on 9 May 1975, the 30th anniversary of Victory Day.

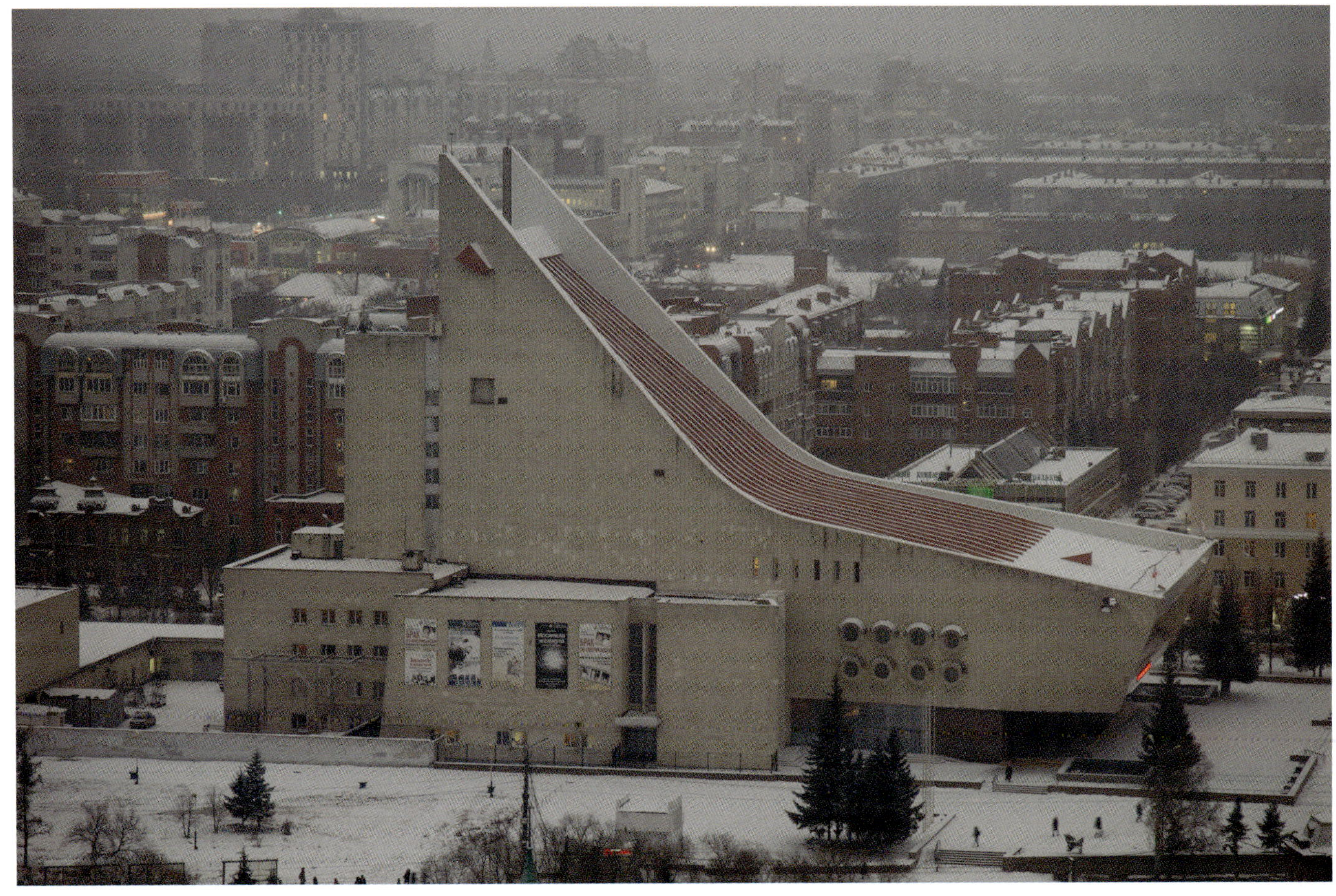

State Musical Theatre
OMSK, RUSSIA
Built in 1981
Architects: D. Lurie, N. Stuzhin, N. Belousova

Situated in the historical centre of Omsk, the modern form of this building divided opinion. Developed in 1969 at the Mezentsev Scientific Research Institute for Theatre and Sport Facilities, the 1,200 seat theatre building is known as the 'springboard'.

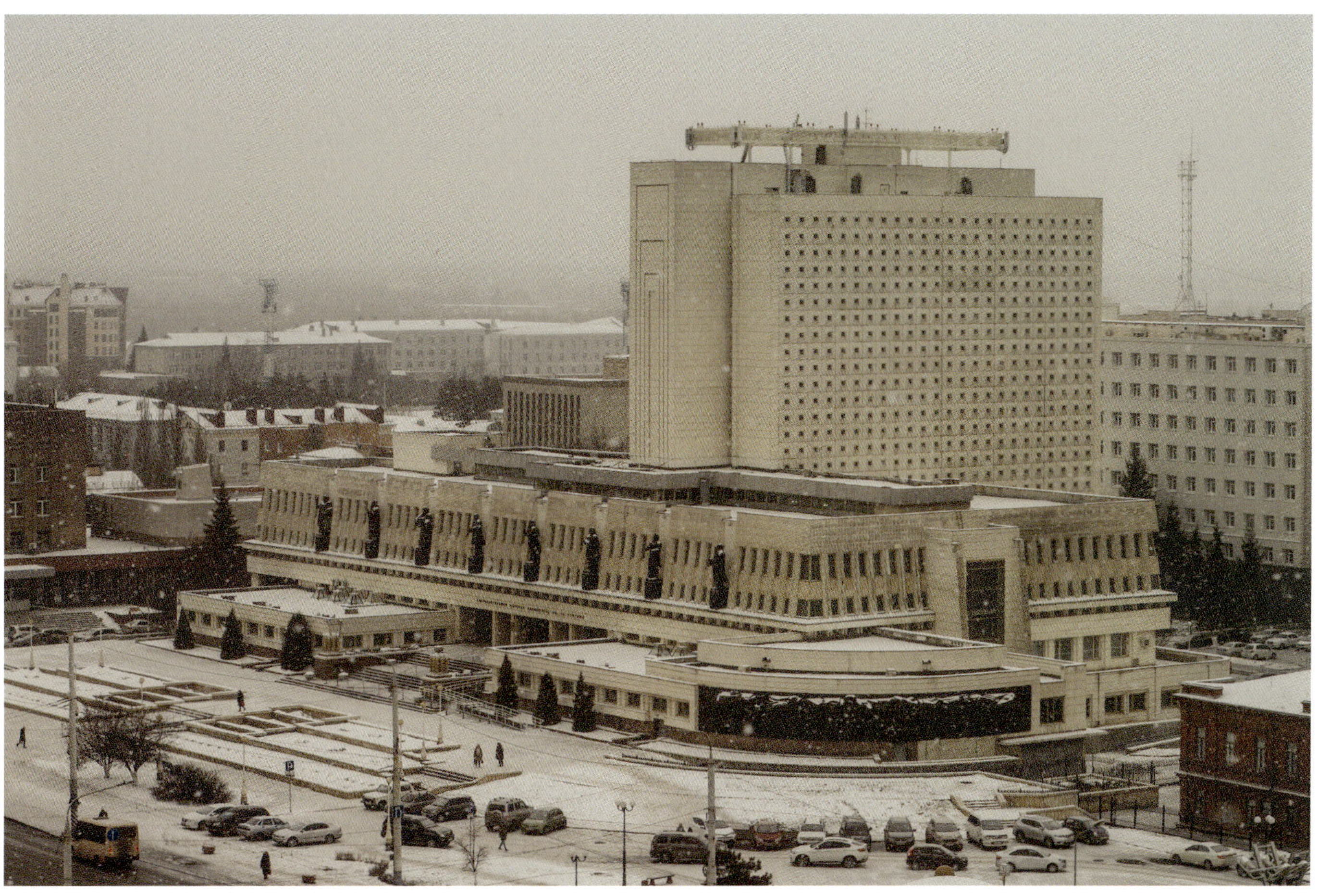

A.S. Pushkin Library
OMSK, RUSSIA
Built between 1986 and 1995
Architect: V. Trokhimchuk

Eight figurative sculptures, each 3.5 metres high, are set in niches along the main façade of the building. Constructed from hammered copper, they depict prominent historical Russian personalities who are the embodiment of the Homeland.

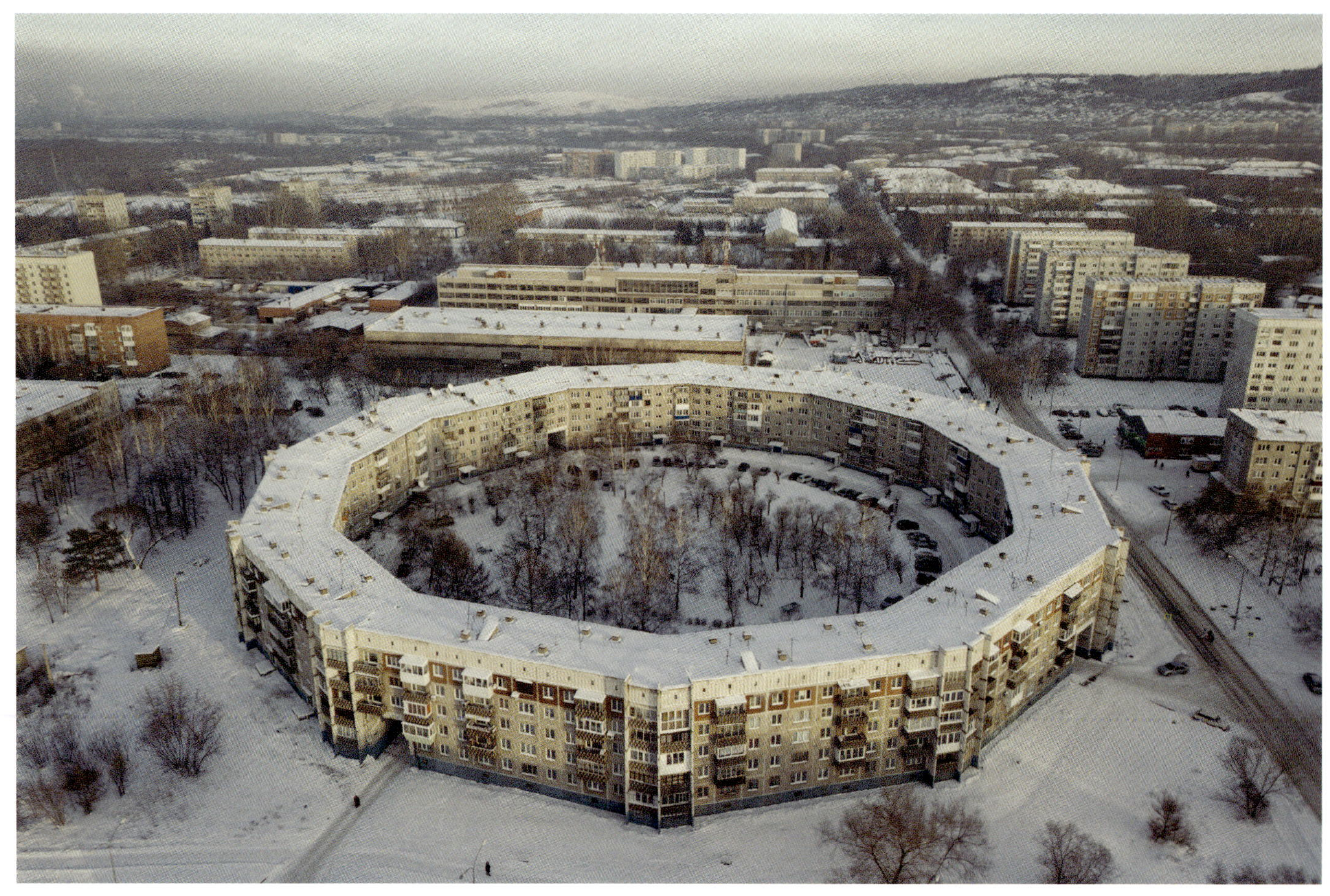

Shaybale Building
NOVOKUZNETSK, RUSSIA
Built in 1974

This residential apartment building is situated in Novokuznetsk, an industrial city on the banks of the Tom river. The sides of the Shaybale are constructed from typical 5-storey panel sections from the 1-464 A-17 series of prefabricated building materials.

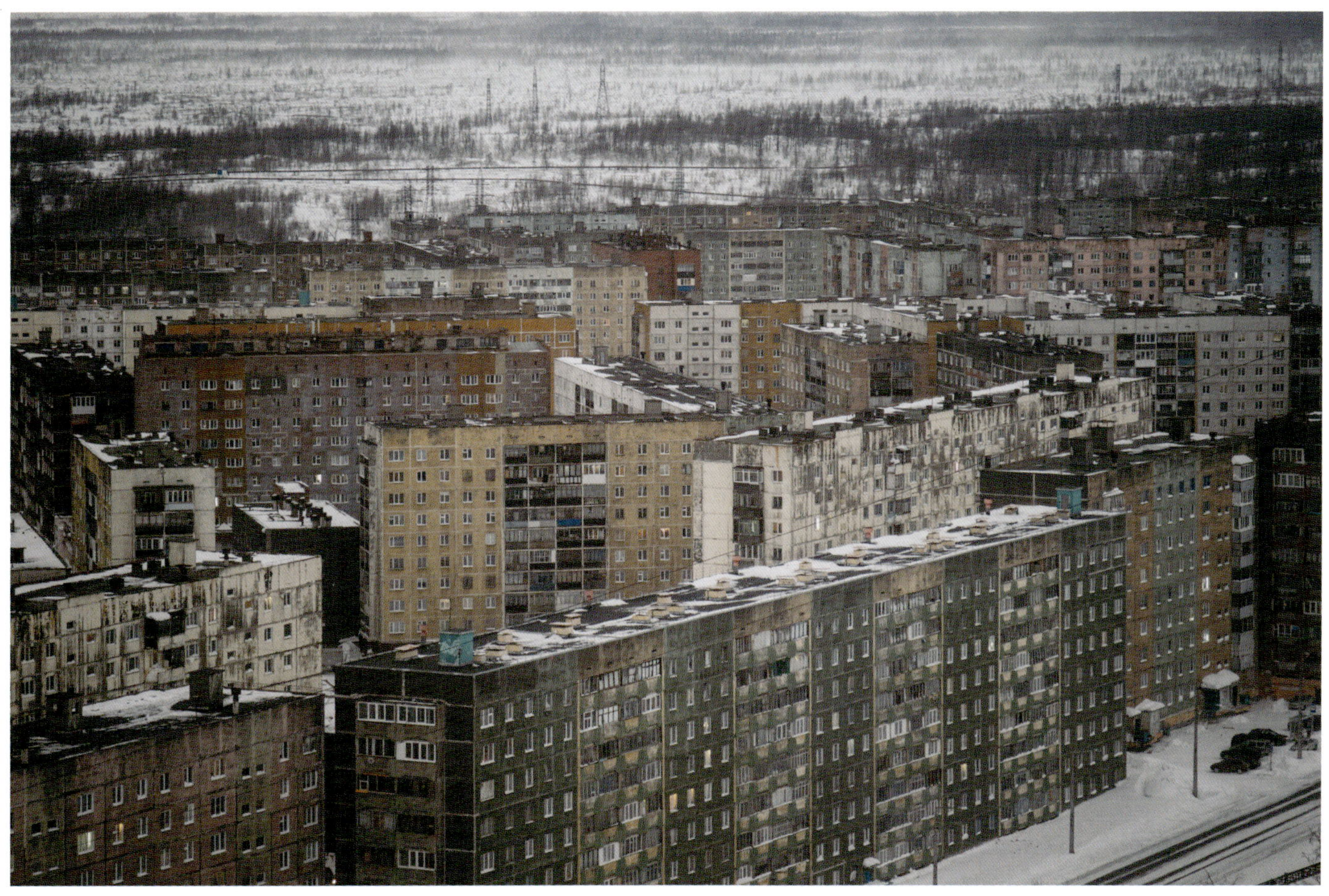

4th Microdistrict, Talnakh
NORILSK, RUSSIA
Built in the early 1980s

In 1982, the settlements of Kaerkan and Talnakh were remodelled into towns. Talnakh town consisted of 5 schools, 12 kindergartens, 18 shops, a library, community centre and pool. In 2005, it was stripped of town status and merged into the city of Norilsk.

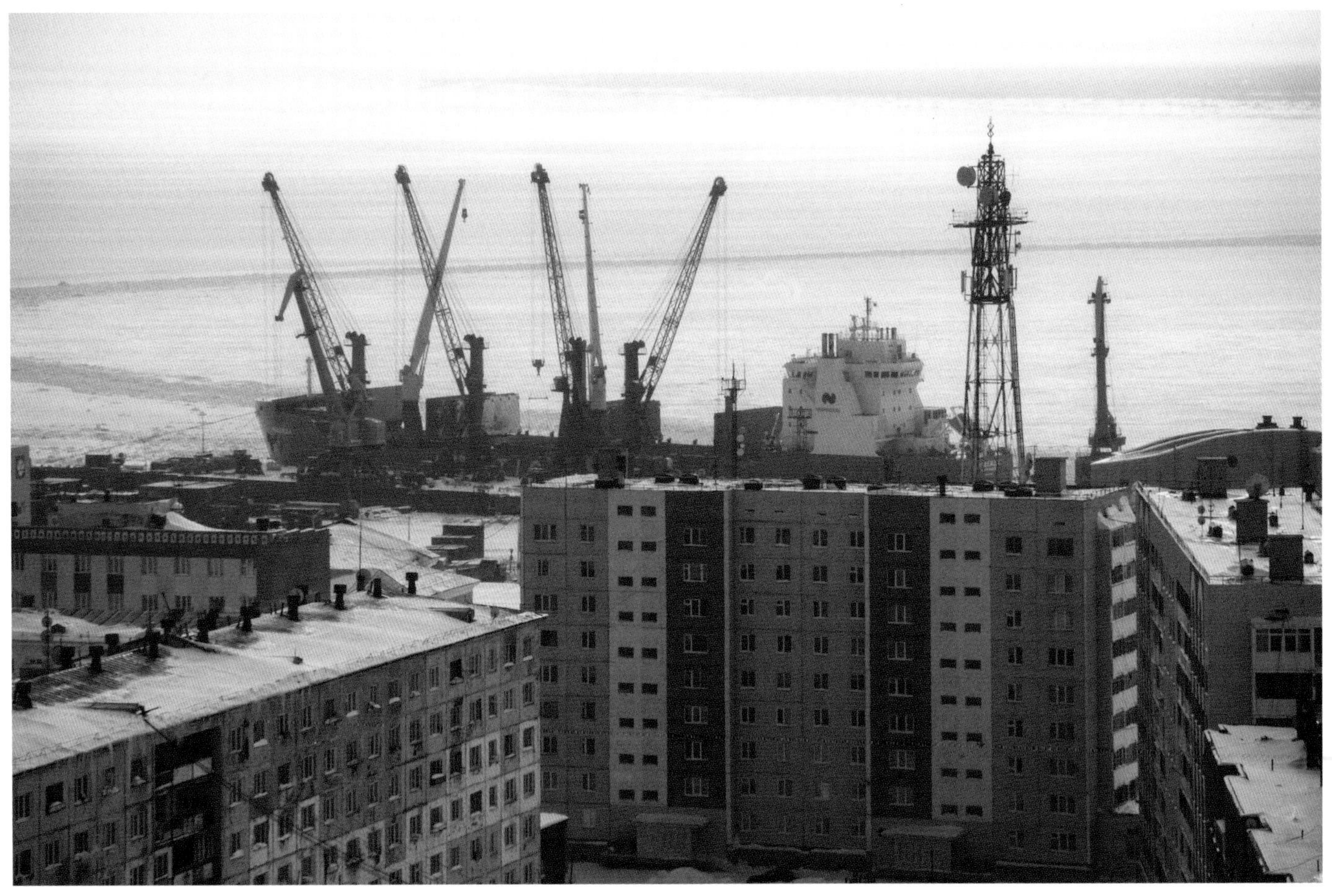

Seaport Piers
DUDINKA, RUSSIA

Dudinka is the largest seaport in Siberia. It is connected by sea to the ports of Arkhangelsk and Murmansk throughout the year, and by the Yenisei river to Krasnoyarsk and Dikson Island during the summer navigation season, when the river is not frozen.

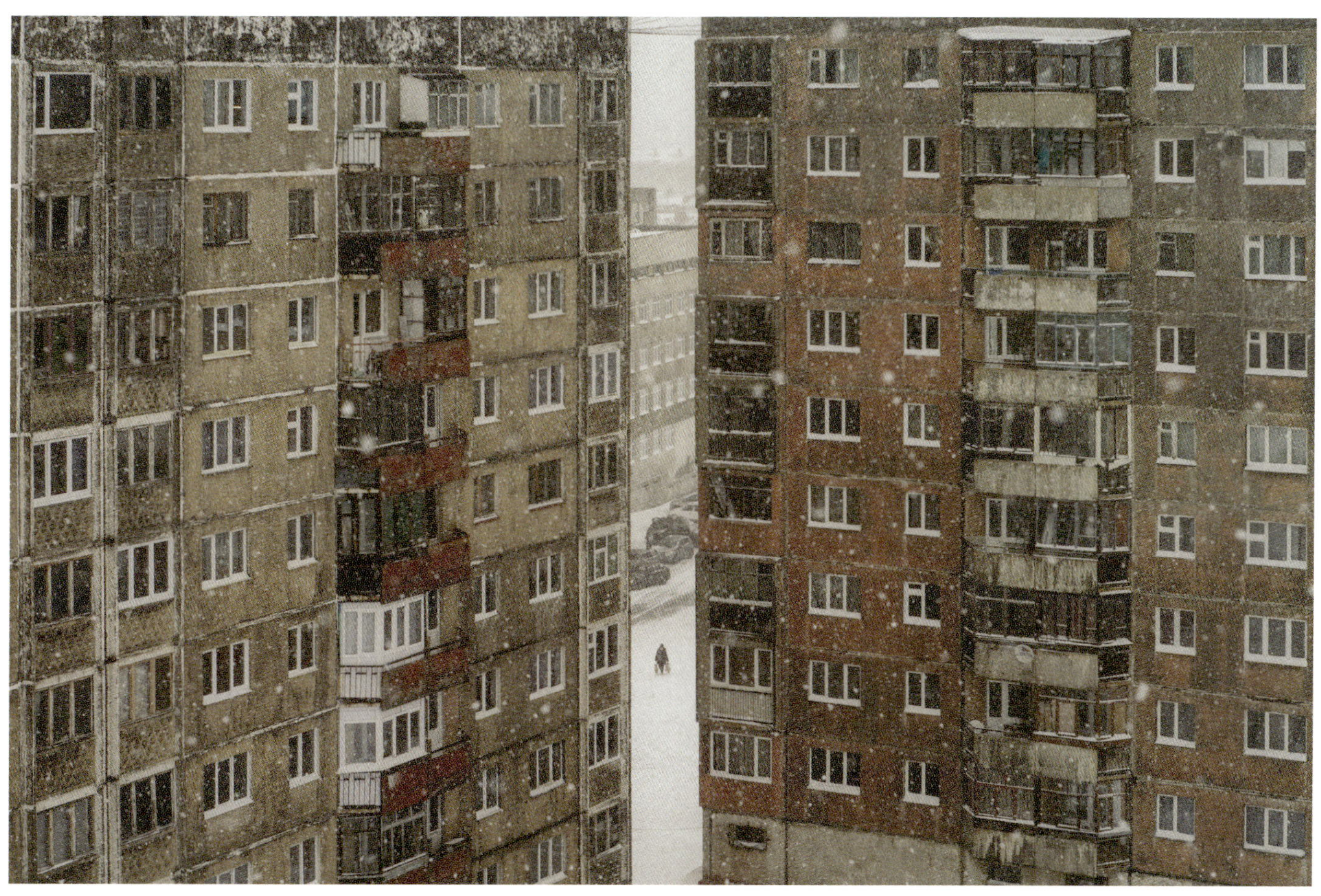

10th Microdistrict
NORILSK, RUSSIA
Built in the 1980s

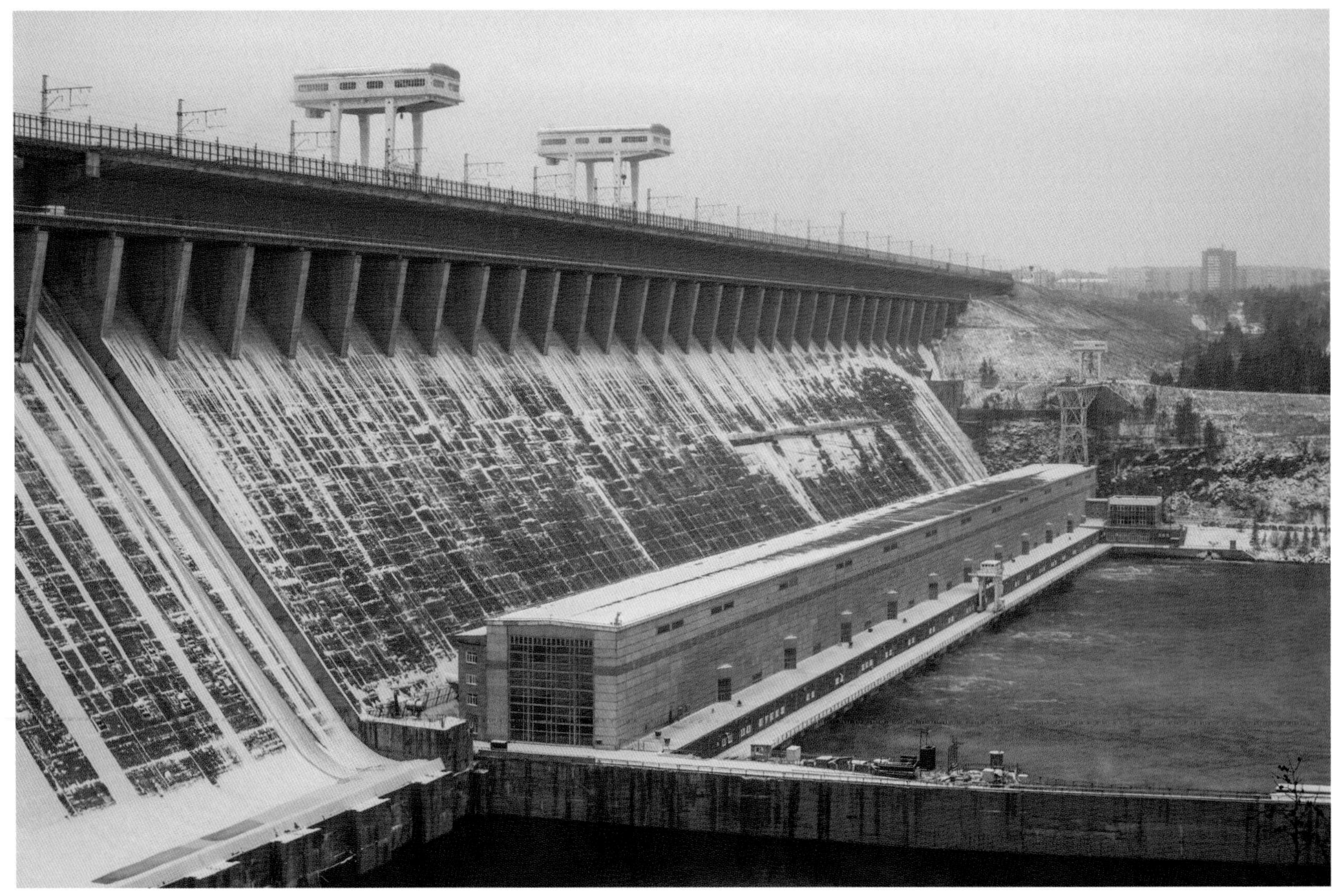

Bratsk Hydroelectric Power Plant
BRATSK, RUSSIA
Built in 1966

The decision to build the Bratsk Hydroelectric Power Plant was made in 1954, at a time when the country lacked the resources to simultaneously develop its space, nuclear and aviation industries, areas that had gained importance during the Cold War. The hydropower

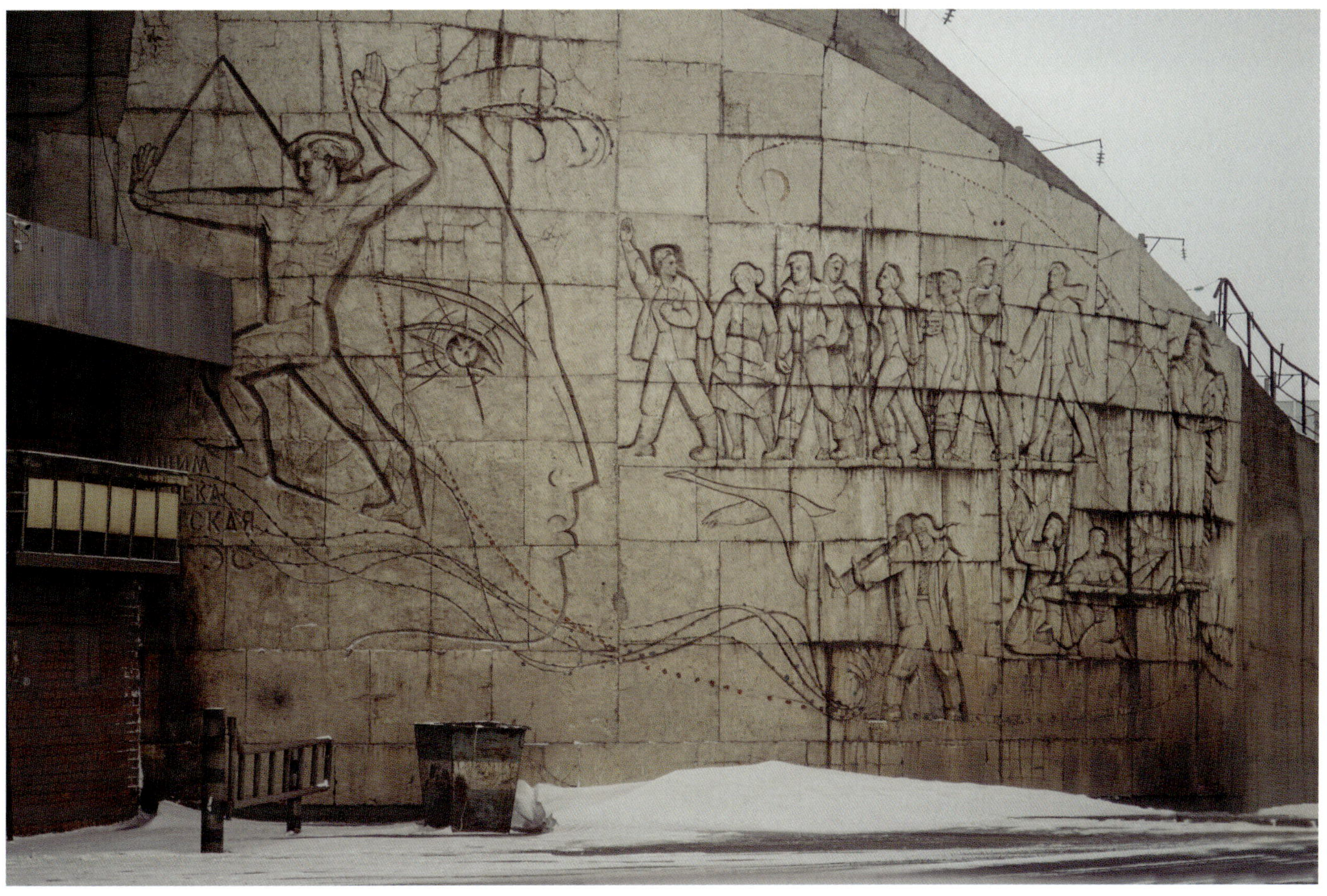

industry convinced the government that utilising the Angara and Yenisei rivers would help eliminate power shortages in Siberia, which until then had been reliant on coal. In addition, Bratsk was to be the location for the country's largest aluminium plant, which required huge amounts of power but would provide vital materials for the space and aviation programmes. Declared a Komsomol priority construction project, it received great public attention. The completed plant became a symbol of industrial development in Siberia.

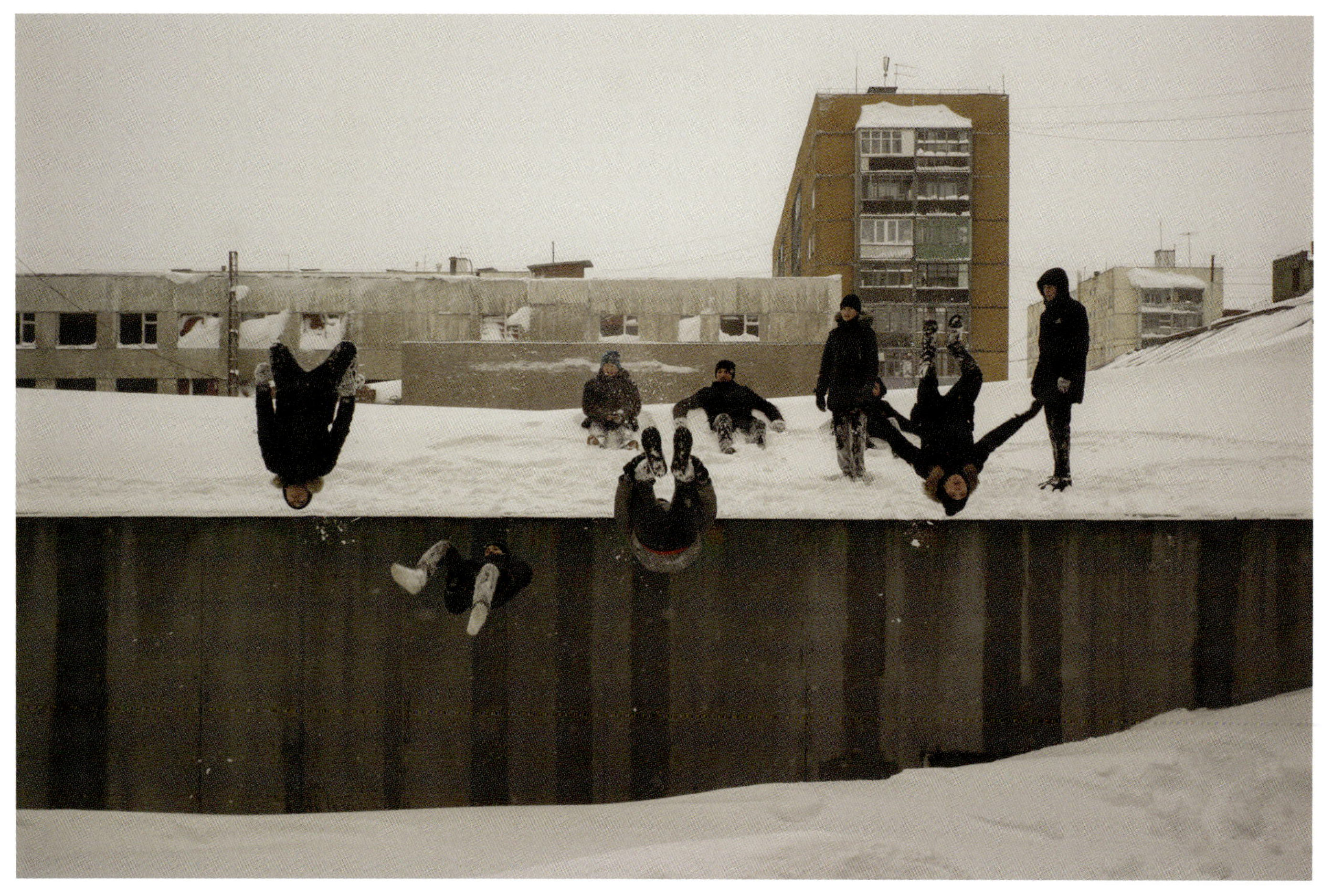

Playing in the snow, Talnakh
NORILSK, RUSSIA

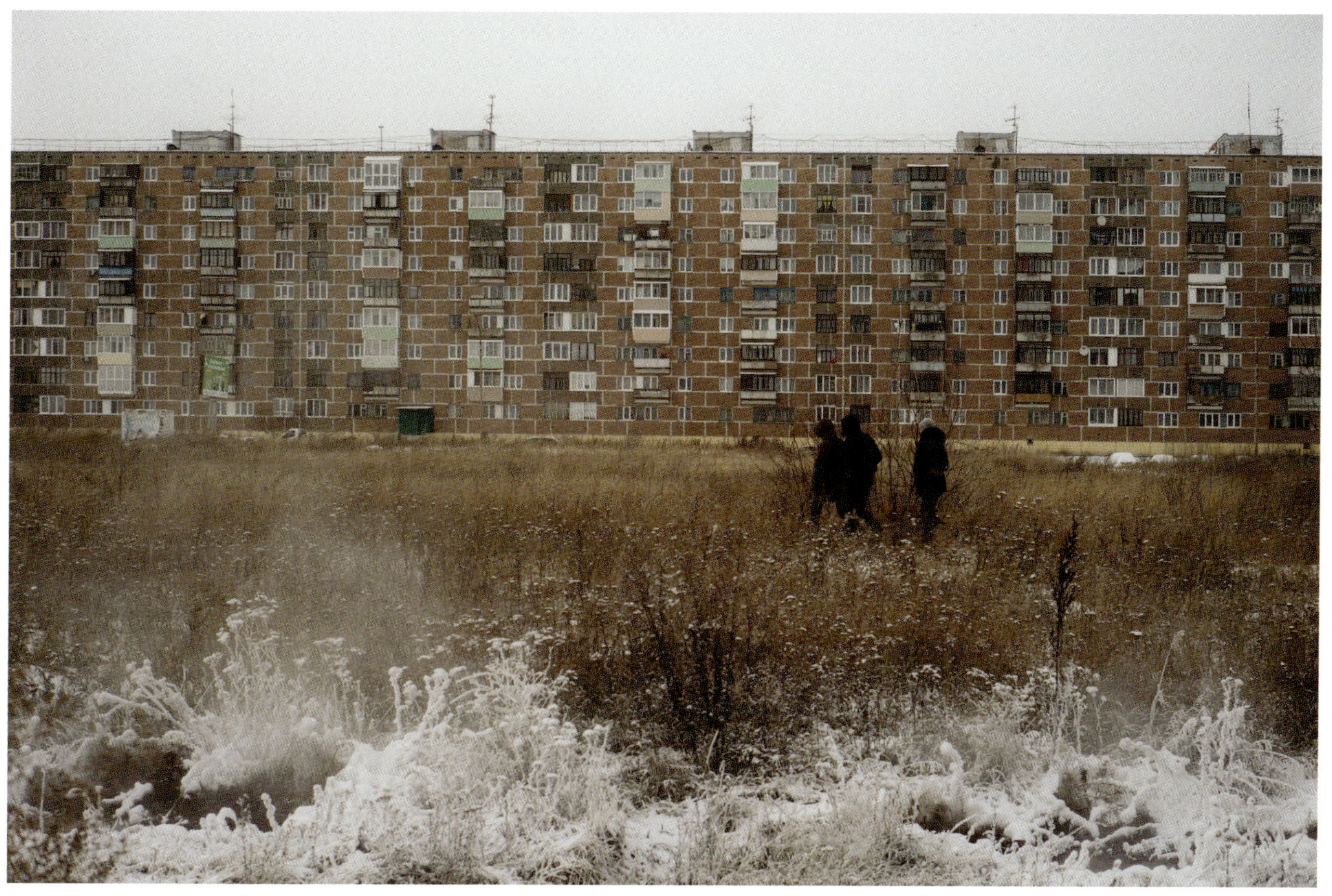

14th Microdistrict
BRATSK, RUSSIA

Founded as a fortress in 1631, the city of Bratsk was developed in 1955, alongside the construction of the hydroelectric power station. Today Bratsk serves as an important industrial base, supporting the development of Eastern Siberia and the Far East.

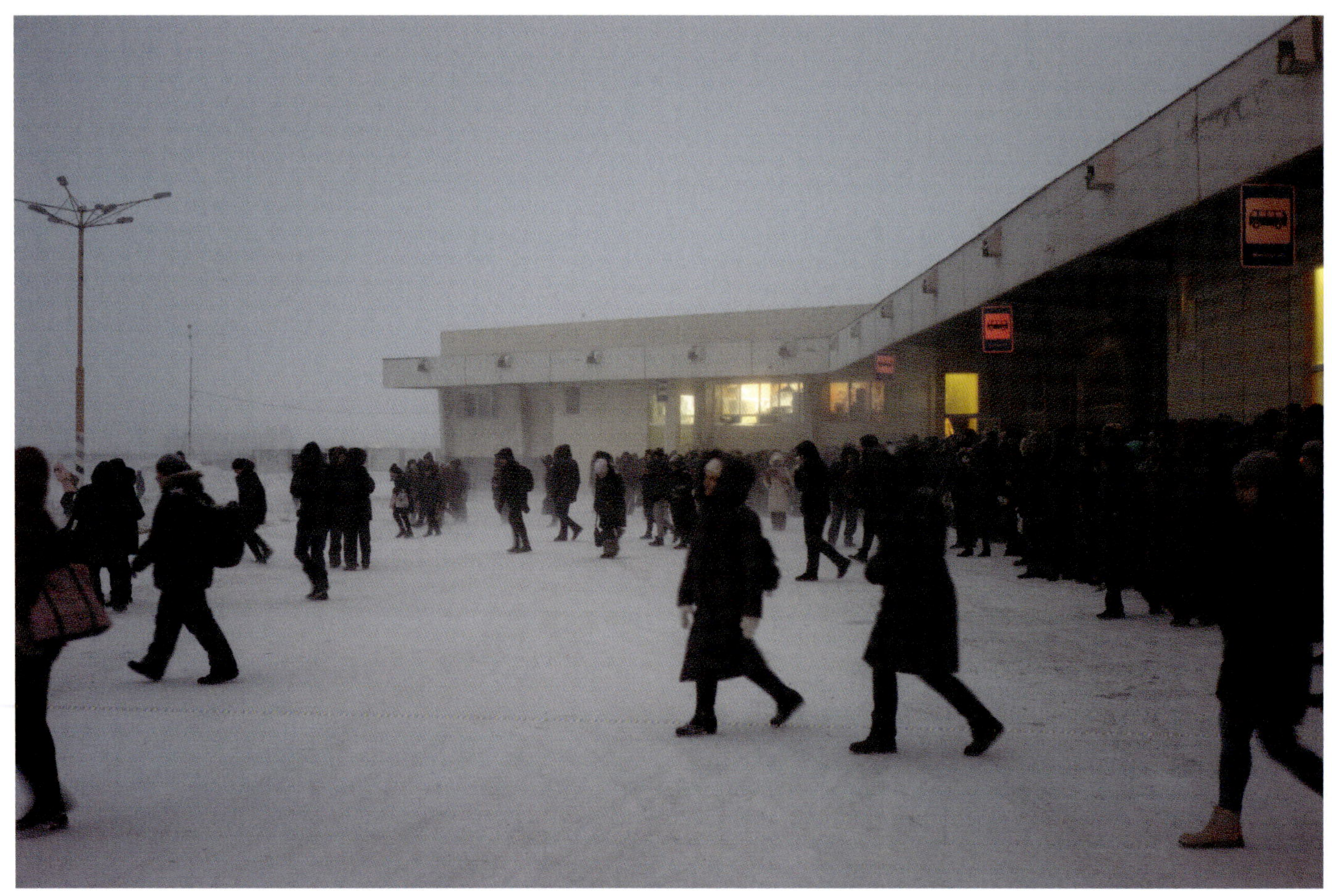

Norilsk Bus Station
NORILSK, RUSSIA

In bad weather, the road to the neighbouring district becomes difficult to negotiate. In order to transport people safely from one district to the other, a column of buses assembles twice a day, led by a snow-clearing vehicle.

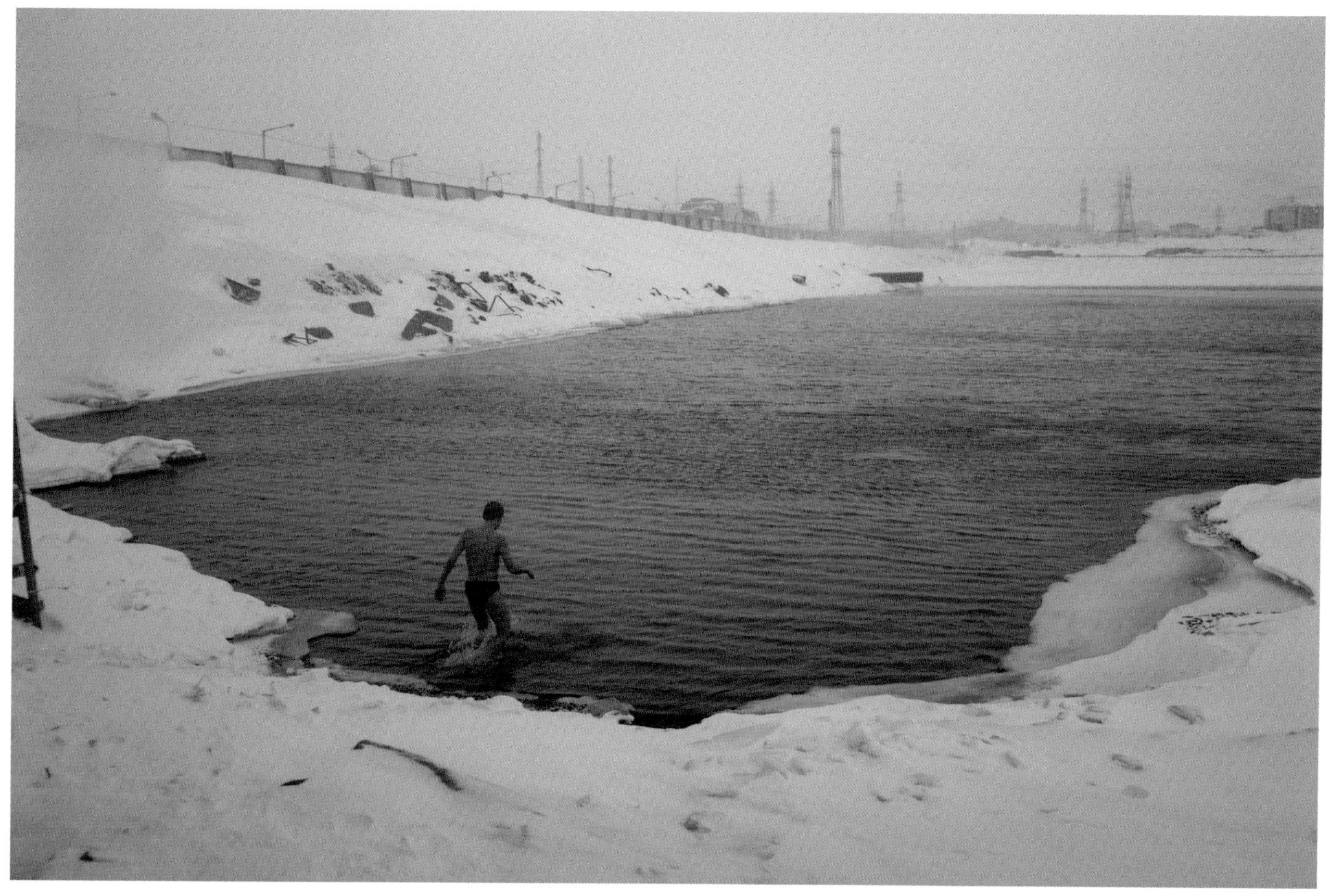

Winter bathing in Lake Dolgoye
NORILSK, RUSSIA

Hot water generated from Norilsk Combined Heat and Power Plant No.1 is discharged into Lake Dolgoye to prevent the water from freezing. This makes it a popular spot for winter swimmers, despite the water temperature being close to zero.

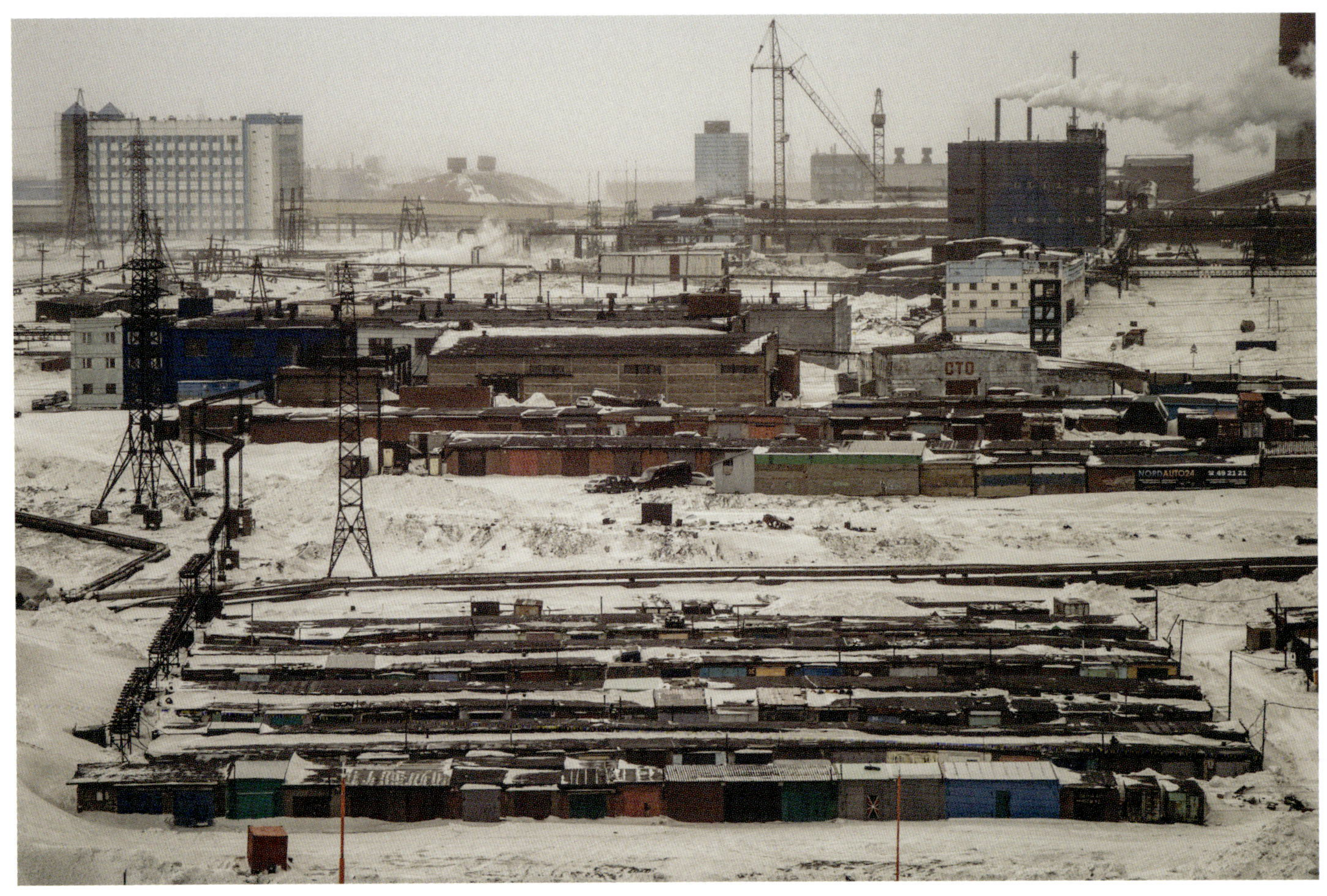

Garages near the Nickel Plant
NORILSK, RUSSIA

In the early 1970s, the mass production of relatively cheap cars made them accessible to regular citizens, regardless of party or social status. To solve the issue of storage, hundreds of square kilometres of iron and brick garages were built, cluttering the landscape. Usually located

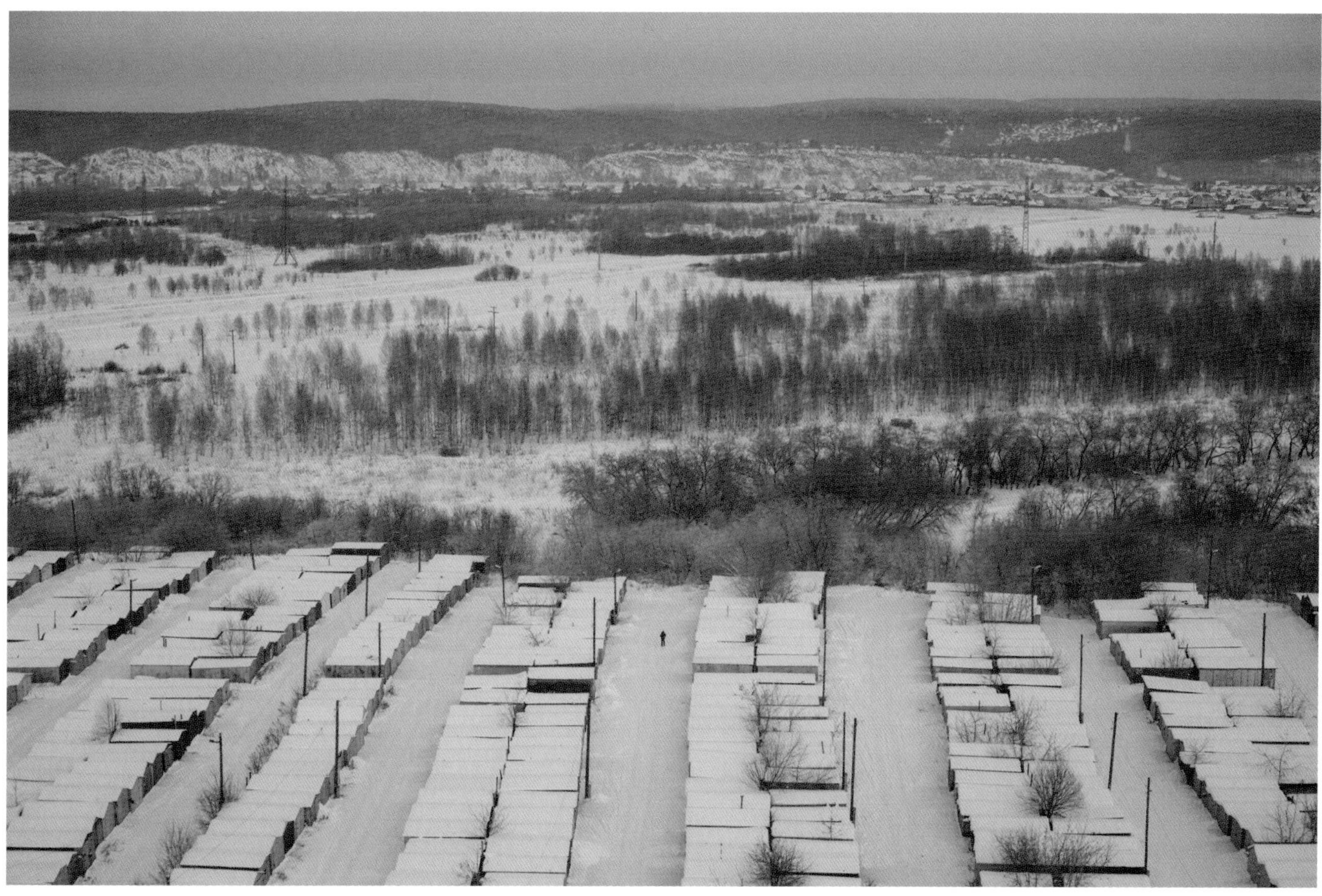

Komsomolsky garage cooperative
KEMEROVOV, RUSSIA

in suburbs, these buildings became second homes by default. Unlike apartments, they were not given away by the state: housing was vital, but garages a luxury. Ownership was mostly through cooperatives, the membership of which required money and connections.

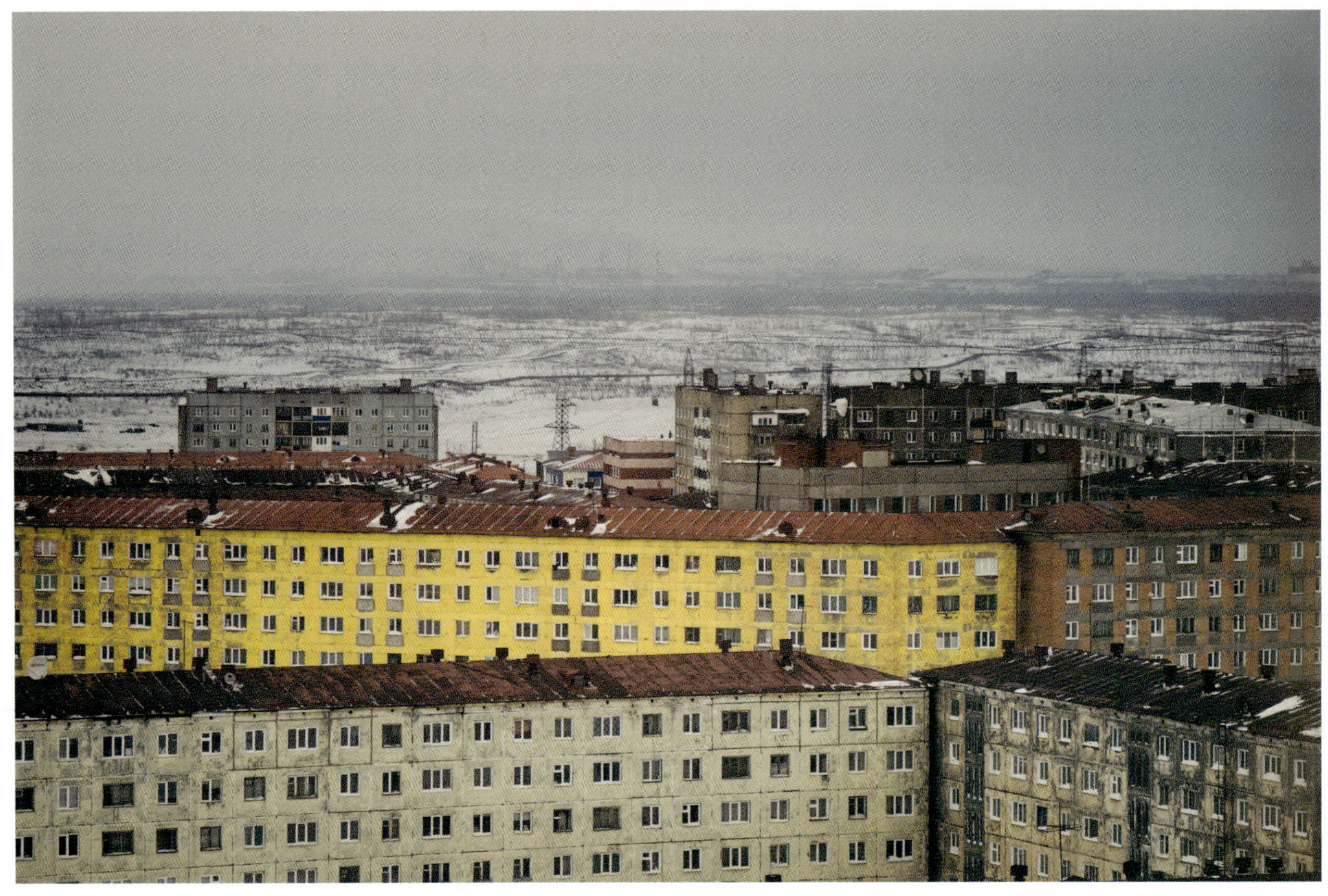

Landscapes of the Central District
NORILSK, RUSSIA

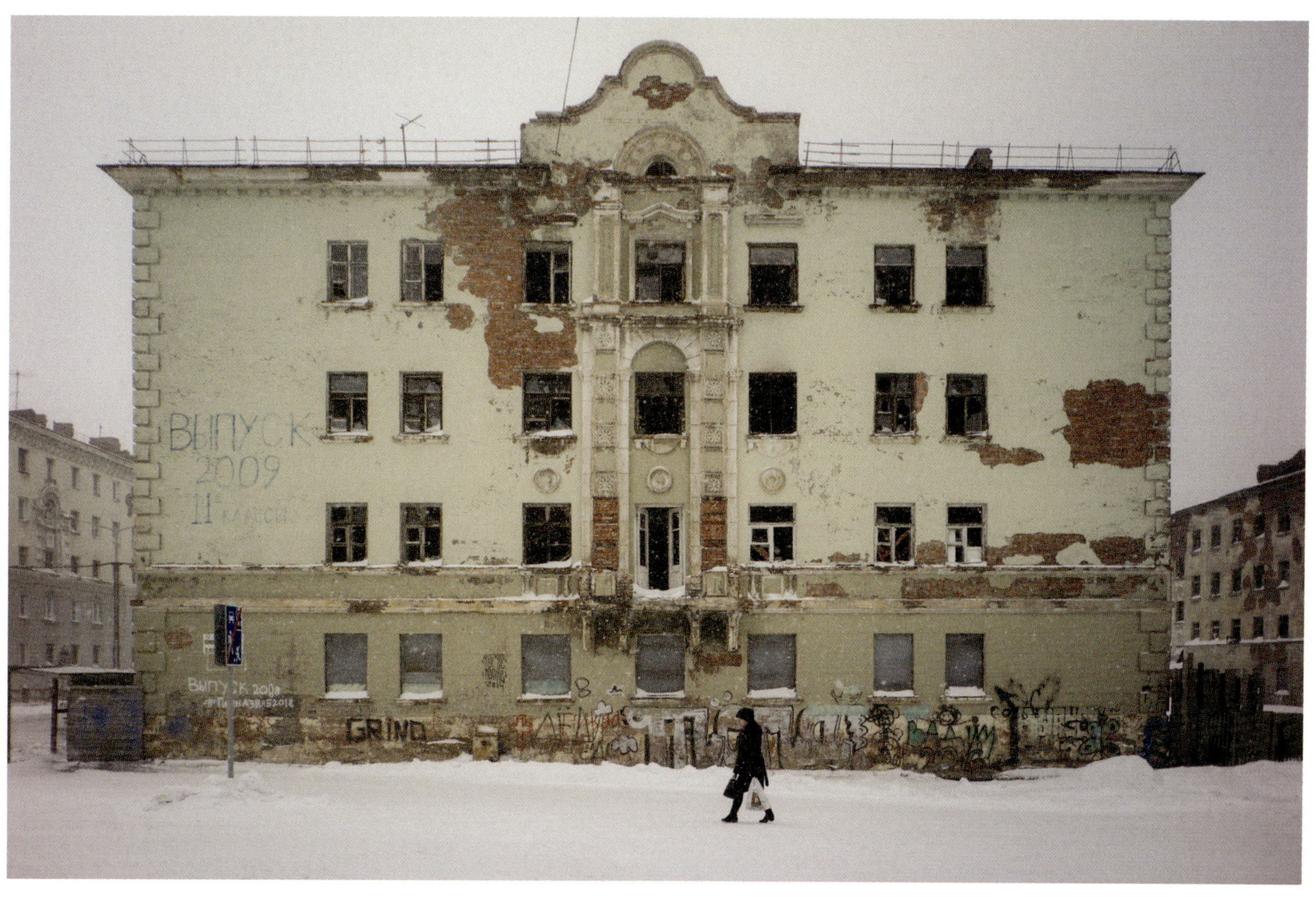

Abandoned buildings in the 21st Quarter
NORILSK, RUSSIA
Built in 1950s

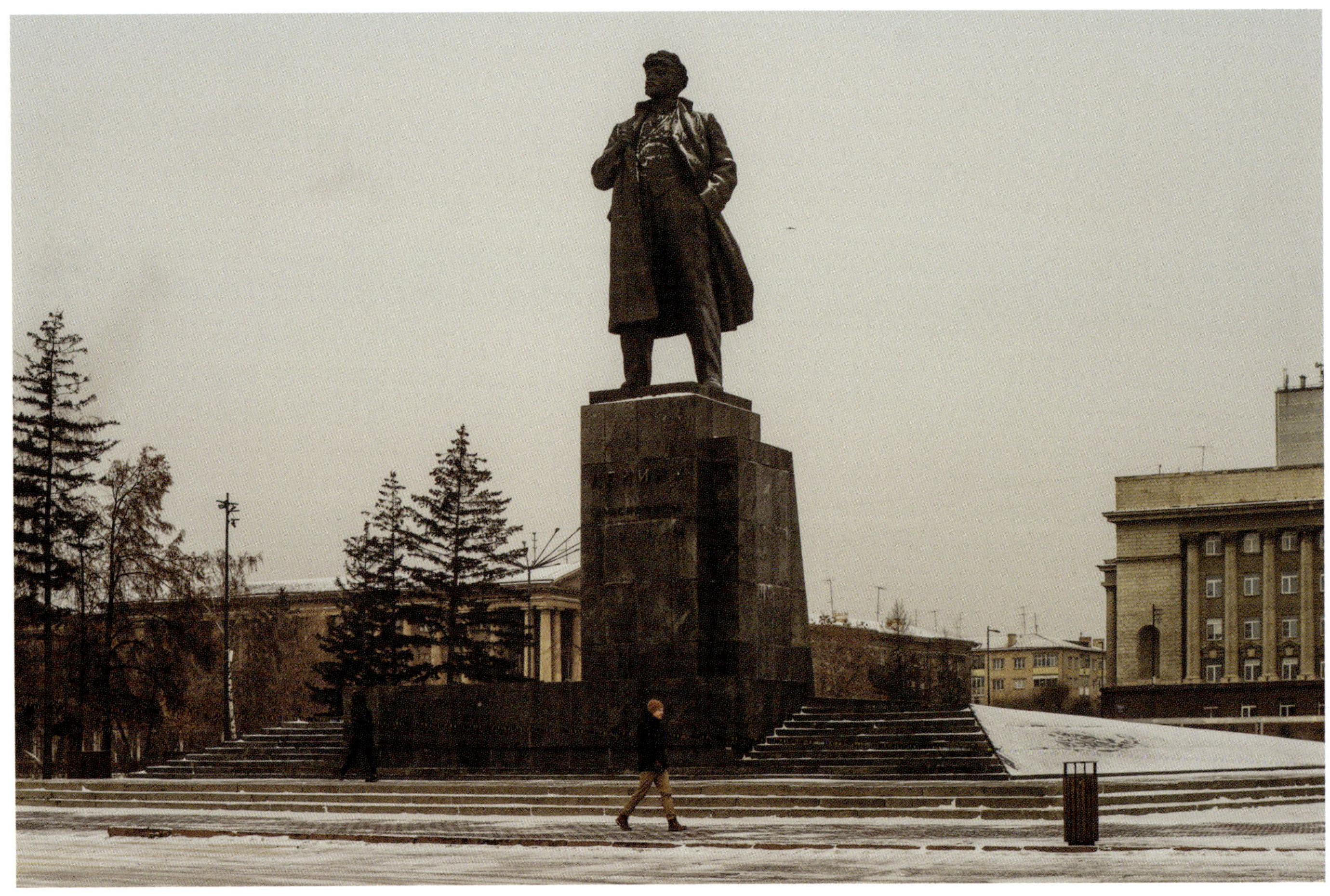

Lenin Monument in Central Square
KRASNOYARSK, RUSSIA
Erected in 1970
Designers: V. Pinchuk, Yu. Ishkhanov and S. Speransky

This monument was unveiled on the 100th anniversary of Lenin's birth. The designers intended to convey 'the energy and pathos of the leader of Revolutionary battles, consonant with the power of the Yenisei river and the distant horizon line'.

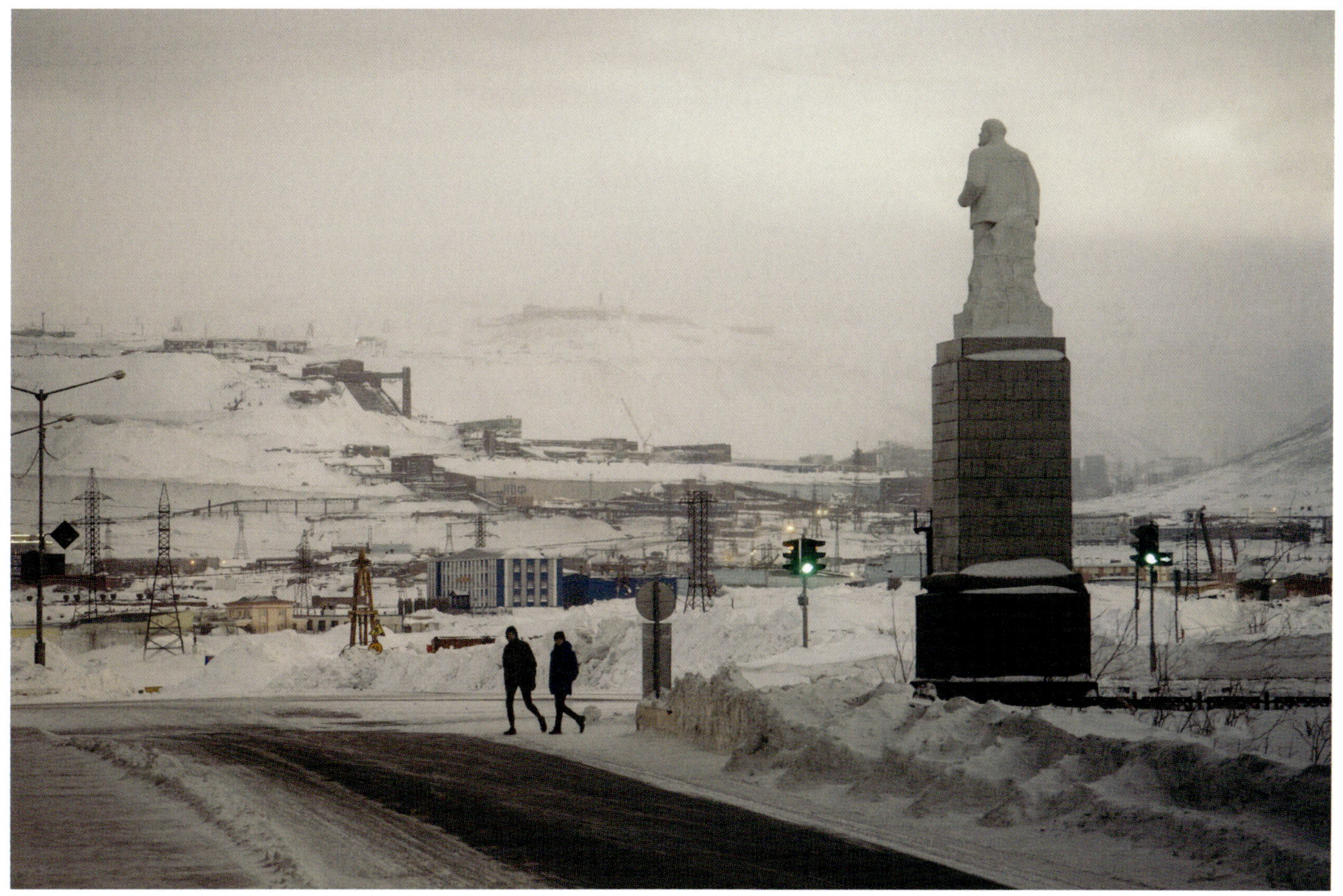

Lenin Monument
NORILSK, RUSSIA
Erected in 1953

This sculpture of Lenin was made at the Murmansk art workshops and delivered to Norilsk in 1953. The statue is constructed from reinforced concrete and is a copy of the sculptor Sergei Merkulov's original work.

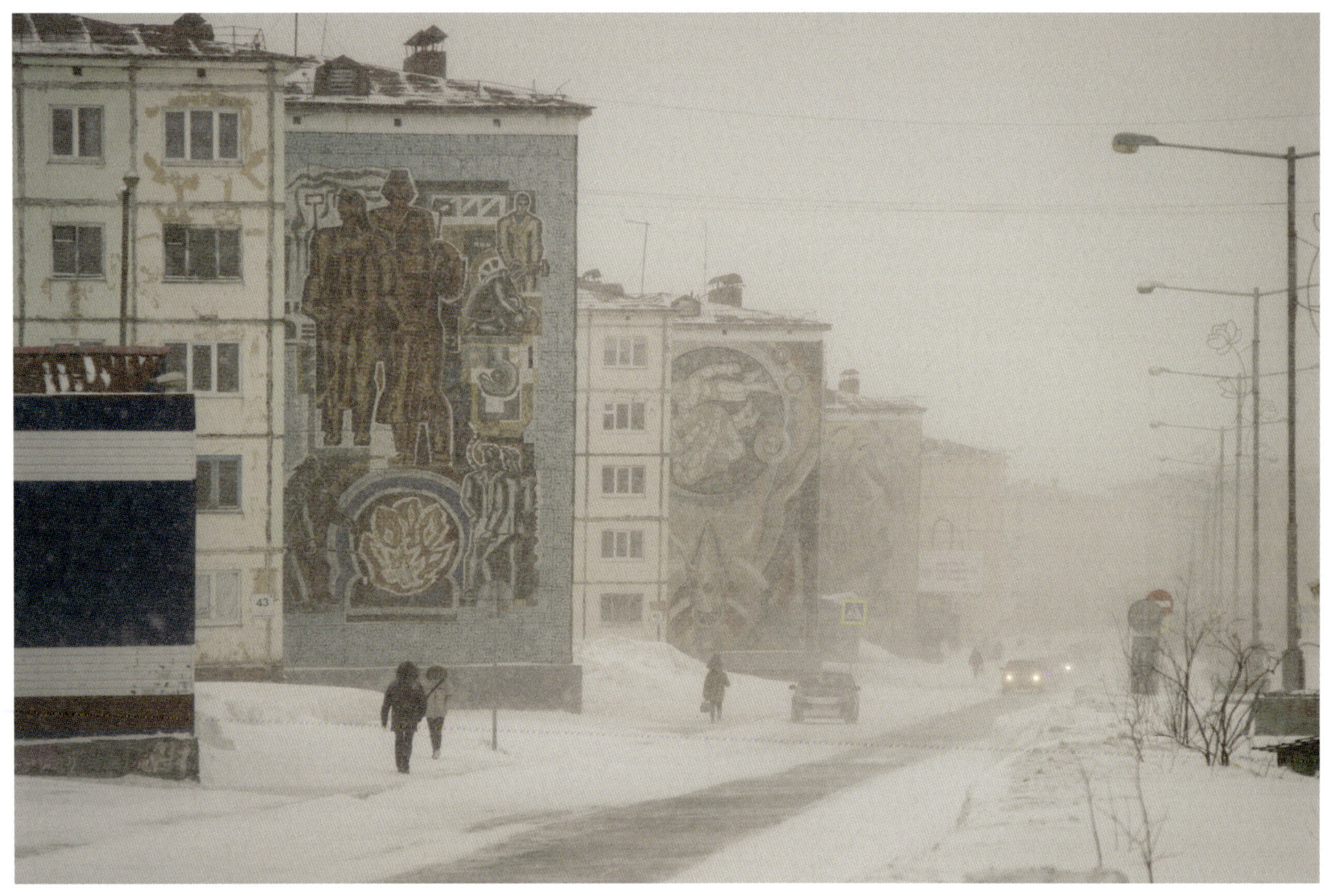

Mosaics on Komsomolskaya Street
NORILSK, RUSSIA
Created in 1973

These moasics were designed by a group of Norilsk artists led by the painter Nikolay Loy. They immortalise stories from the life of the Komsomol (the All-Union Leninist Young Communist League), whose members helped in the construction of this part of the city.

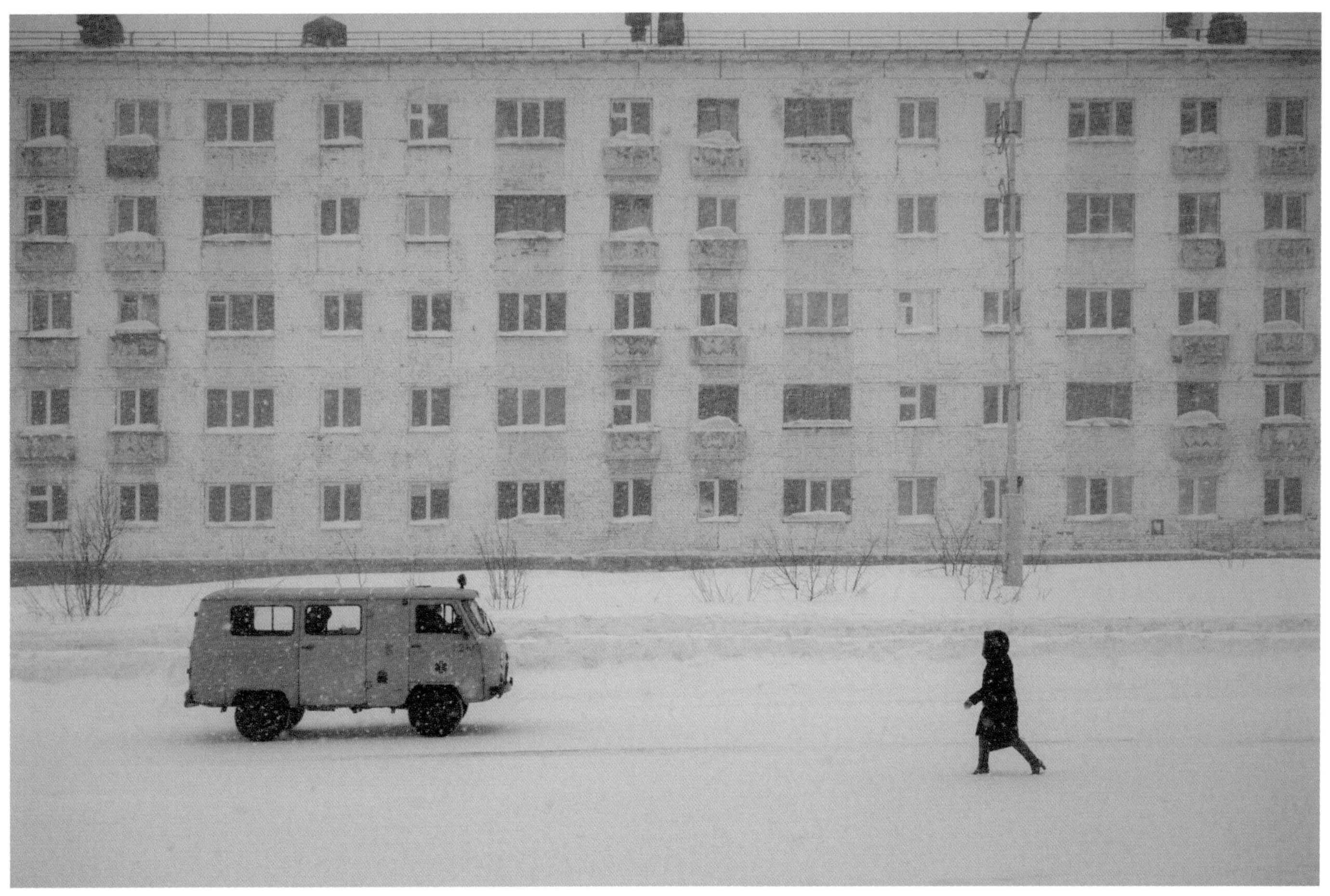

UAZ-452 medical vehicle on Ordzhonikidze Street
NORILSK, RUSSIA

This street is named after Sergo Ordzhonikidze, a Soviet statesman and political figure, under whose leadership a plan was developed for the construction of the Norilsk Combine. The street is the location of the last residential block to be built in Norilsk, in 2002.

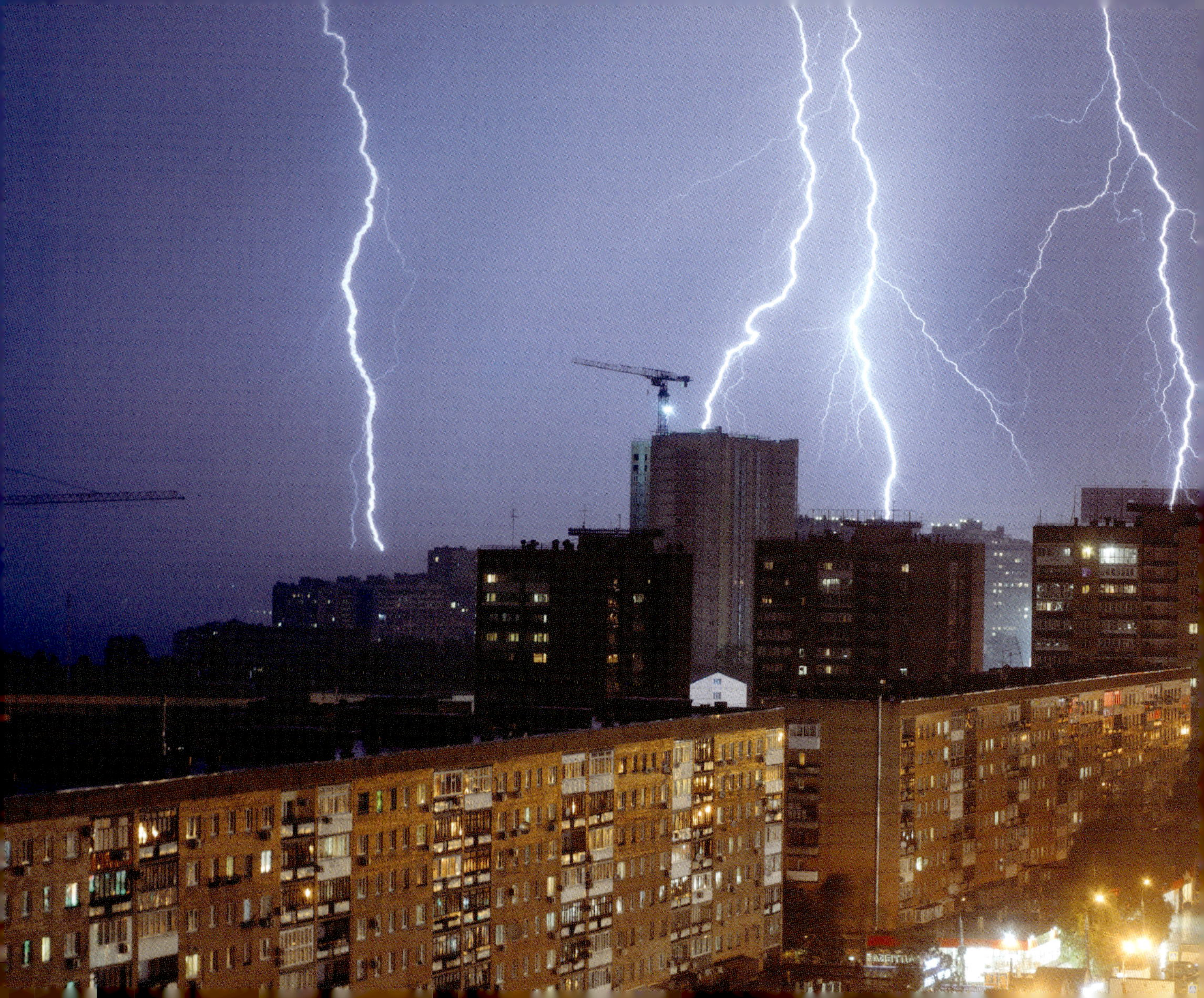

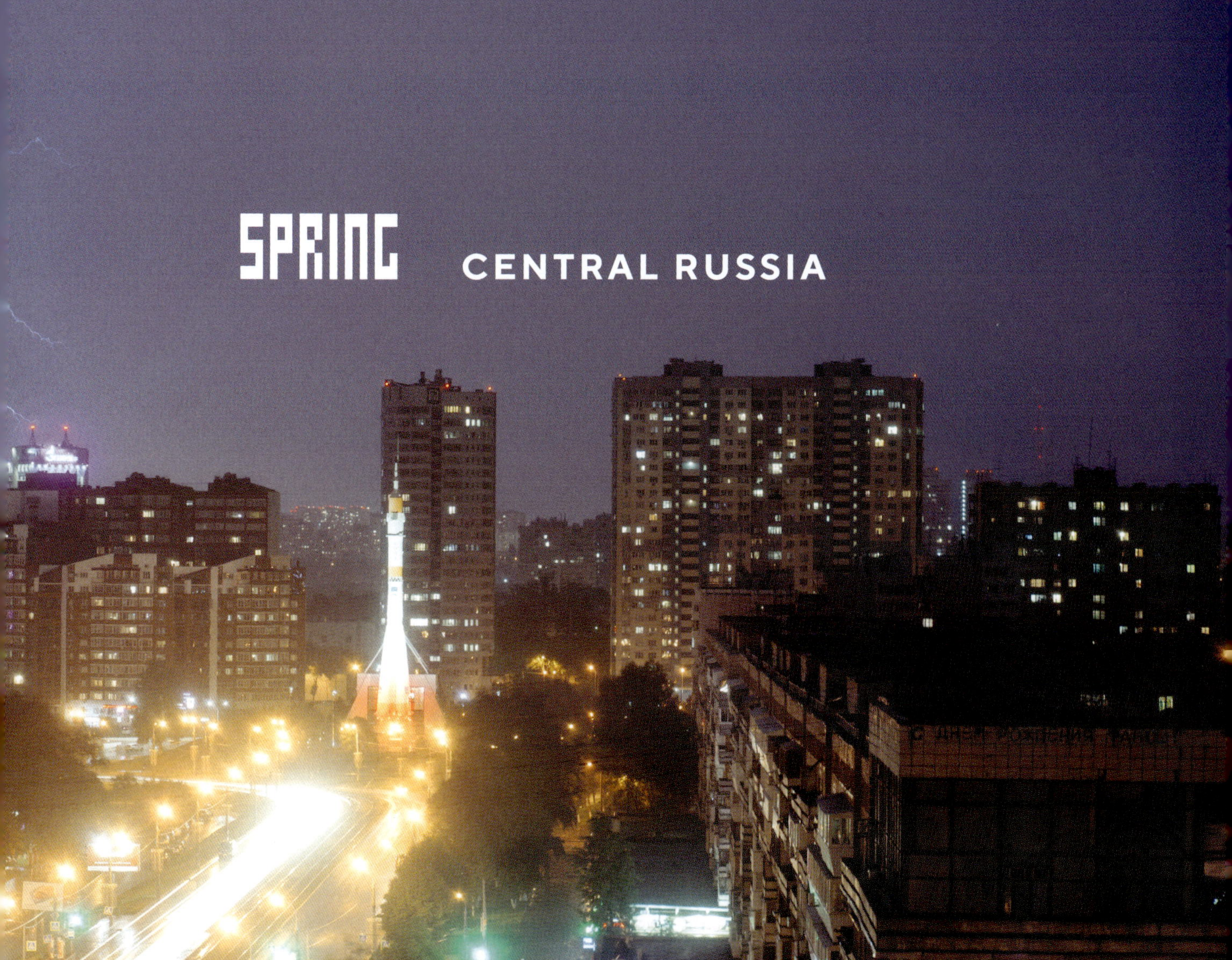

SPRING
CENTRAL RUSSIA

CENTRAL RUSSIA

Most of Central Russia is located within the East European Plain. Russians settled in this area long ago; it is where the nucleus of the Russian state was formed. To the south of the Plain lie the foothills of the Caucasus, rich in natural resources. To the east are the Ural Mountains, a natural border between Europe and Asia. Even in the time of ancient Russia, the area was already crossed by important trade routes, crafts were developing rapidly and cities were growing.

Central Russia is mostly forest – coniferous, deciduous and mixed. Hills, low ridges, ravines, reservoirs, rivers, streams, large and small lakes: all lend a peculiar charm to the area and are depicted in the works of many of the writers, poets and artists of our Motherland. People have happily settled here since ancient times. A moderate climate with sufficient rainfall, a flat terrain, comparatively good soil, fertile meadows and pastures – all favour the development of agriculture and the breeding of cattle. The numerous rivers and lakes were rich in fish, the dense forests rich in birds and beasts. Forests and swamps served as a reliable defence against enemies.

For centuries, Central Russia has been an important area within our country. From here, Russian people moved to the outer regions, settling the southern steppes, the northern forests, the Siberian taiga. It was here that one of the country's oldest industrial complexes developed, and its importance is still great today, even though many others have sprung up. Dozens of cities, including Moscow, capital of the Soviet Union, are concentrated in a relatively small area.

Today, this region is not at all what it was before the Revolution, when it mainly produced textiles, earning Moscow the nickname 'chintz'. Over years of Soviet rule, factories that had existed before the Revolution were largely rebuilt, transforming the area into a powerful network of industries including mechanical engineering, light engineering, chemicals and food. The hundreds of factories produce so many types of machines, mechanisms and devices it would be impossible to list them all: they include automobiles, diesel locomotives and wagons, radioelectronic devices, electrotechnical and optical devices, radio receivers, TV sets, electronic machines, radio components, measuring instruments, electric motors of different sizes, photographic cameras and many, many other products. The steel tracks of the electrified highways radiate from the capital to all corners of the country, like a multi-pointed star. Thanks to them, Central Russia both receives raw materials and semi-finished items and is able to dispatch finished goods across the Soviet Union.

'Native Land', V. I. Orlov (editor), *Prosveshcheniye*, 1976

previous page
May thunderstorm on Lenina Avenue
SAMARA, RUSSIA

Garages on Pervomaiskaya Street
SAMARA, RUSSIA

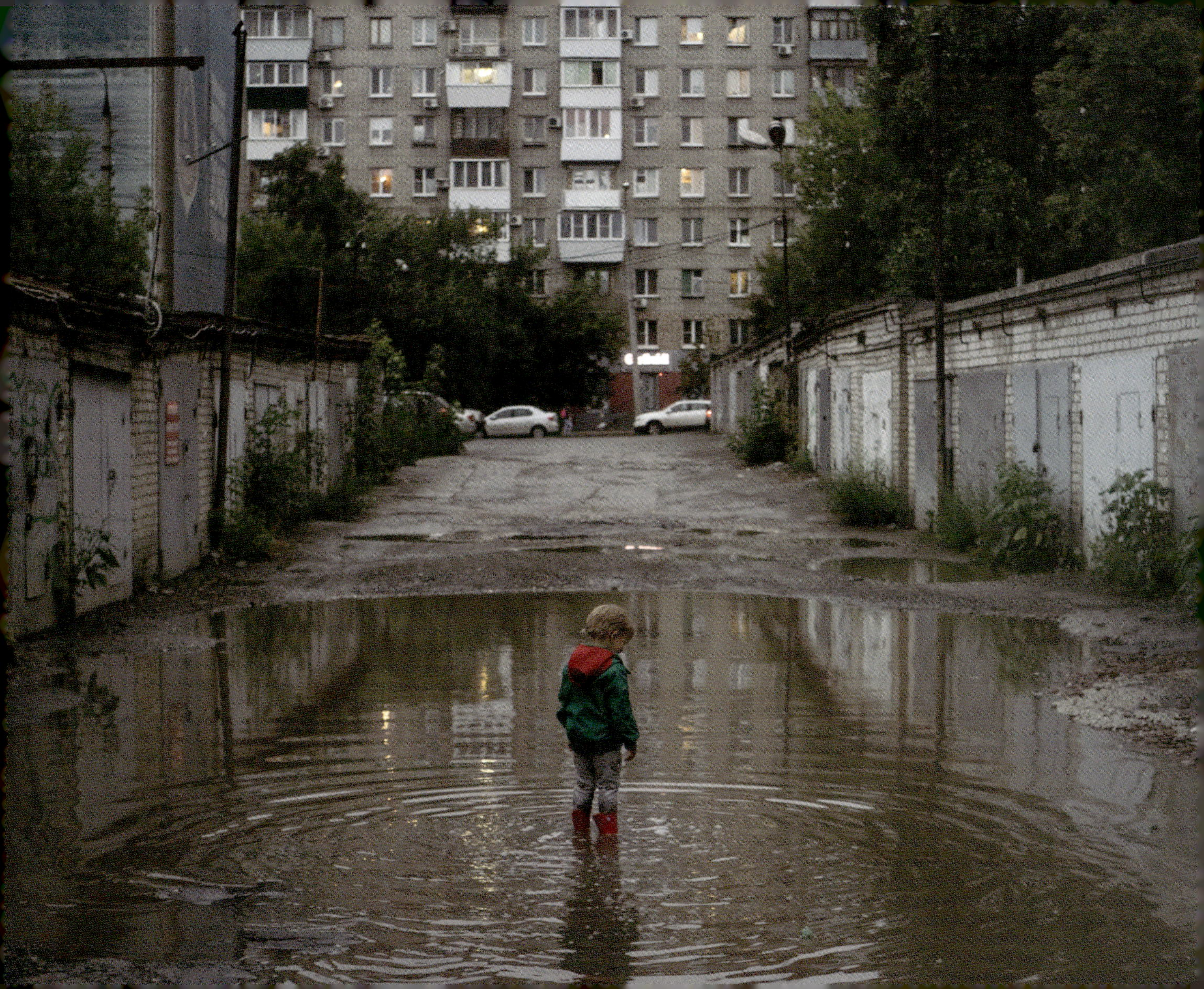

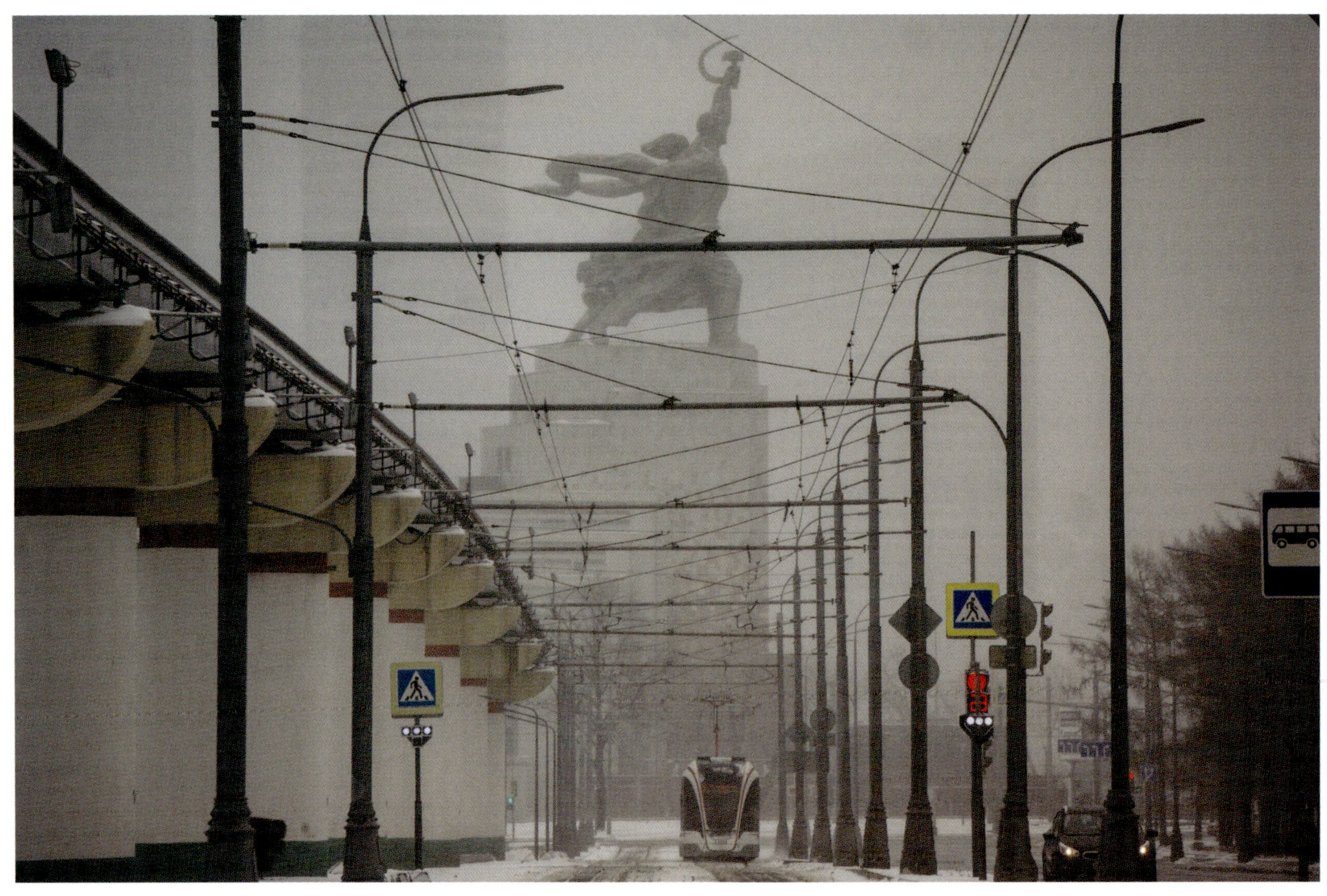

'Worker and Kolkhoz Woman'
MOSCOW, RUSSIA
Erected in 1937
Designer: V. Mukhina

This stainless-steel monument was made by Vera Mukhina, the 'Queen of Soviet sculpture'. It was built in 1937 for the World's Fair in Paris and is recognised as an exceptional example of Socialist Realism, emplying an Art Deco aesthetic to embody the ideals of the USSR.

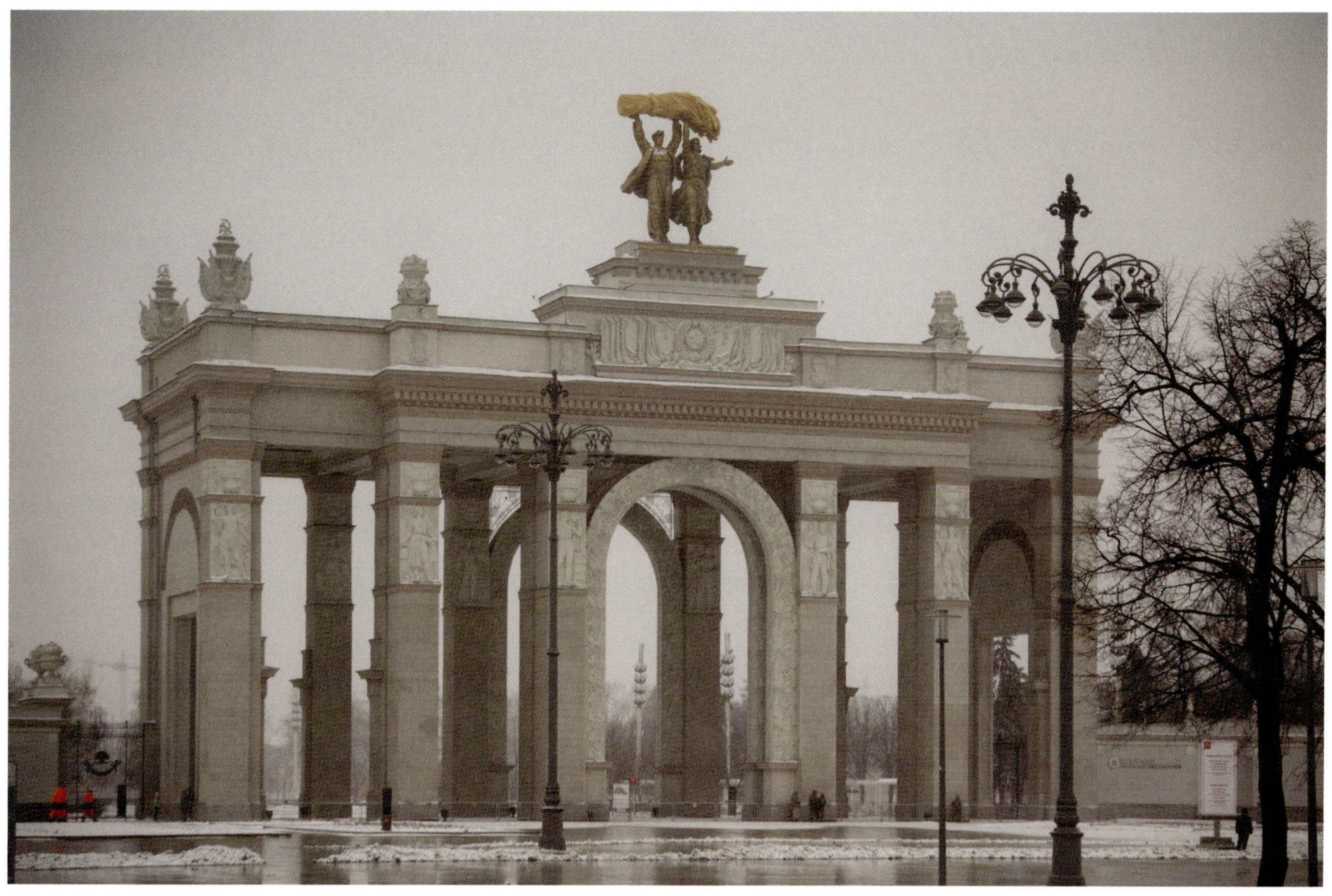

Arch of the Main Entrance to VDNKh
MOSCOW, RUSSIA
Built in 1984
Architect: I. Melchakov

The arch is designed in the Stalinist style, with six pairs of columns decorated in bas-relief, depicting various agricultural occupations. Crowning the arch is the sculpture 'Tractor Driver and Collective Farm Girl', embodying both industry and agriculture.

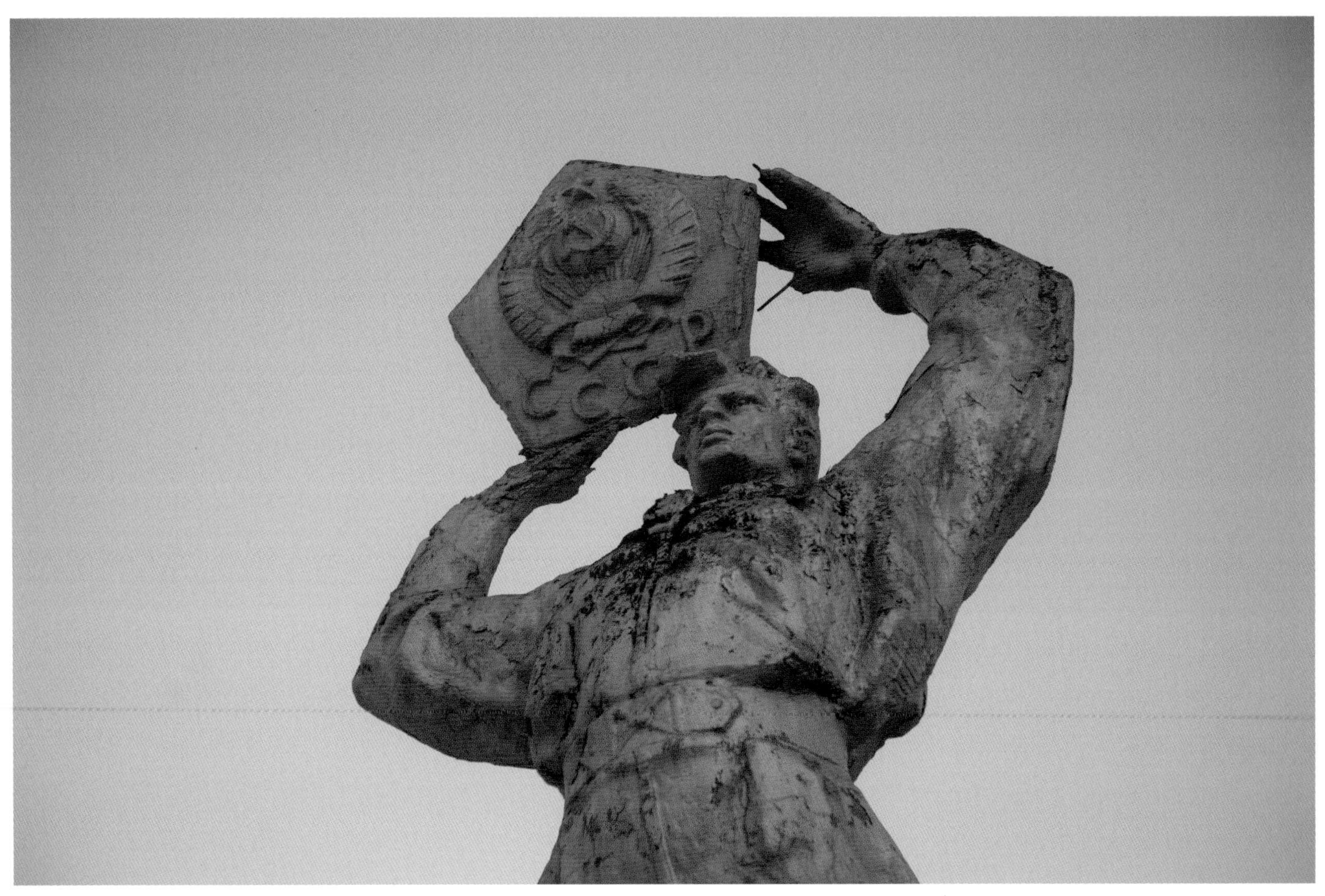

Monument at Light Workers Square
SARANSK, RUSSIA

The figure holds a pentagon symbol similar to those carried by Soviet spacecraft to the Moon, Venus and Mars. From 1958 to 1965, metal pentagons bearing the emblem of the USSR were made for more than 30 launches.

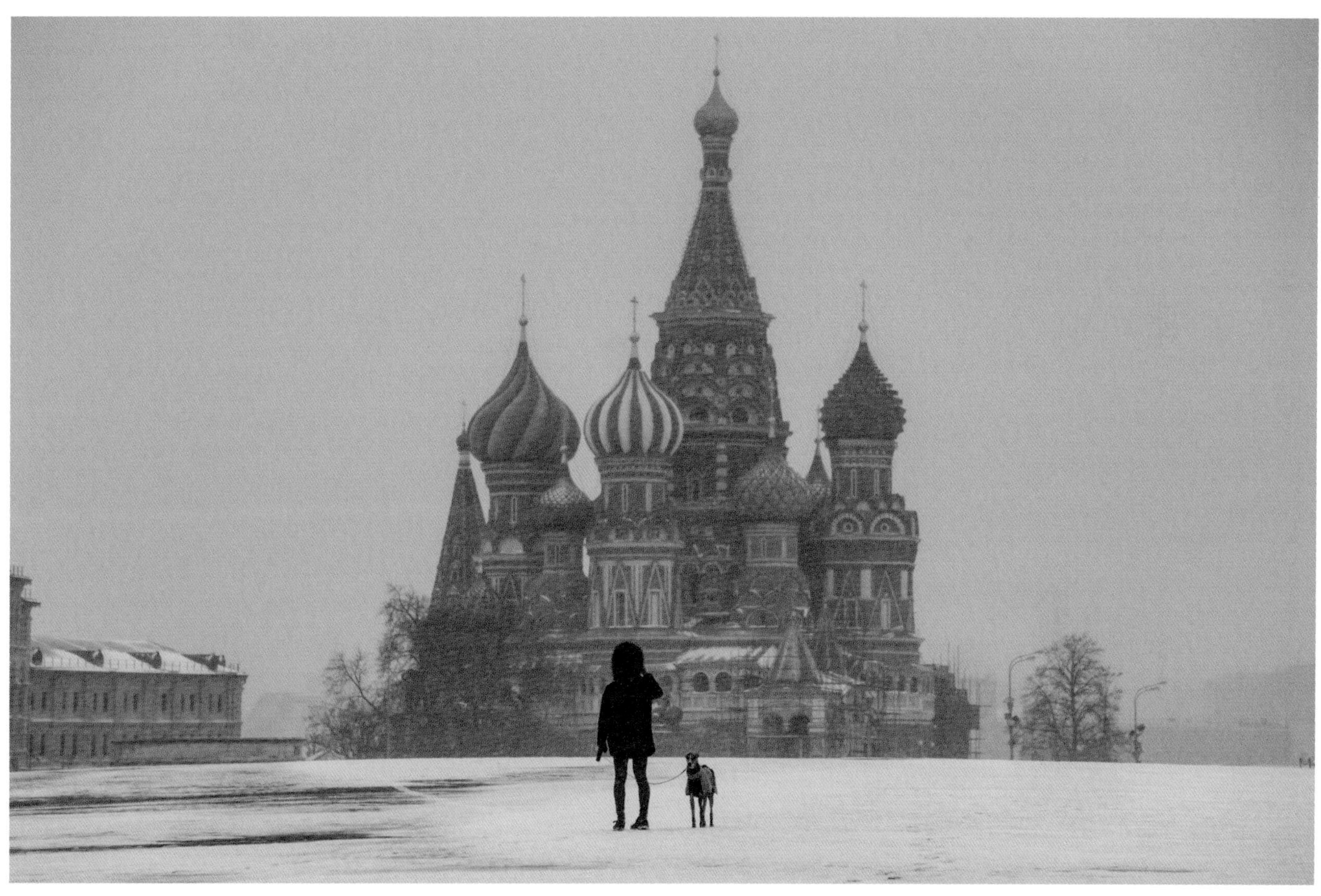

Saint Basil's Cathedral
Red Square
MOSCOW, RUSSIA

Red Square, where Vladimir Lenin addressed the people, was a main site for the Revolutionary events of 1917. The Soviet regime gave Red Square a new status, making it the location for official parades, as well as a memorial to Revolutionary heroes, and later to its leader.

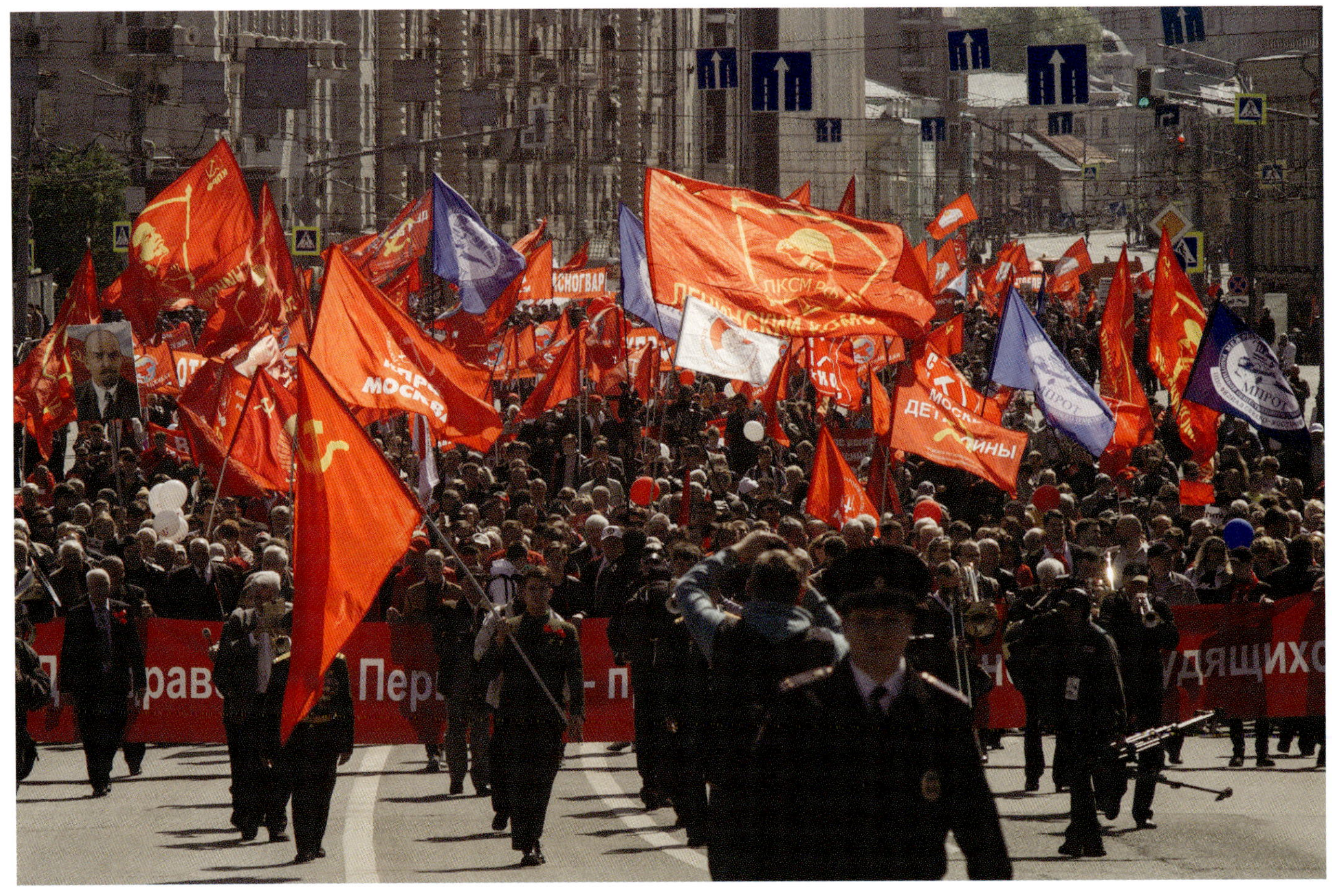

May Day Parade, 2019
MOSCOW, RUSSIA
right: SAMARA, RUSSIA

In the USSR, May Day was a workers' holiday. According to Lenin, on this day workers celebrated 'their awakening to light and knowledge, their unification into one fraternal union for the struggle against all oppression… [and] the socialist organisation of society.' Since the

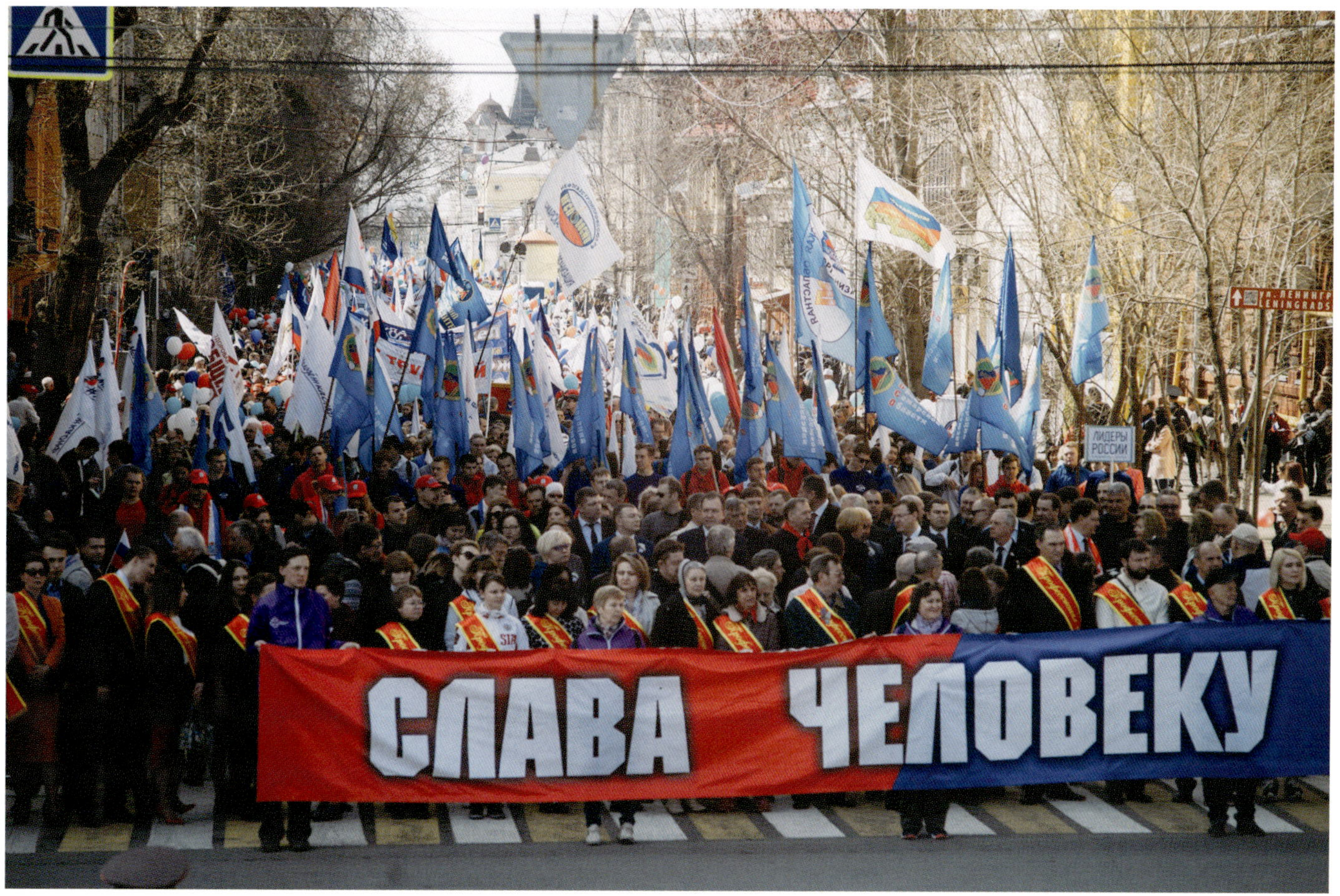

1960s, May Day in the Soviet Union has carried a different meaning. Workers began demonstrating to 'express their solidarity with the revolutionary struggle of workers in the capitalist countries and with the national liberation movement, to express their determination to give their all to the struggle for peace, and for the construction of a Communist society'. Today the holiday has lost its political origins. According to some media reports, the majority of Russians view it simply as an extra day off and the start of the dacha gardening season.

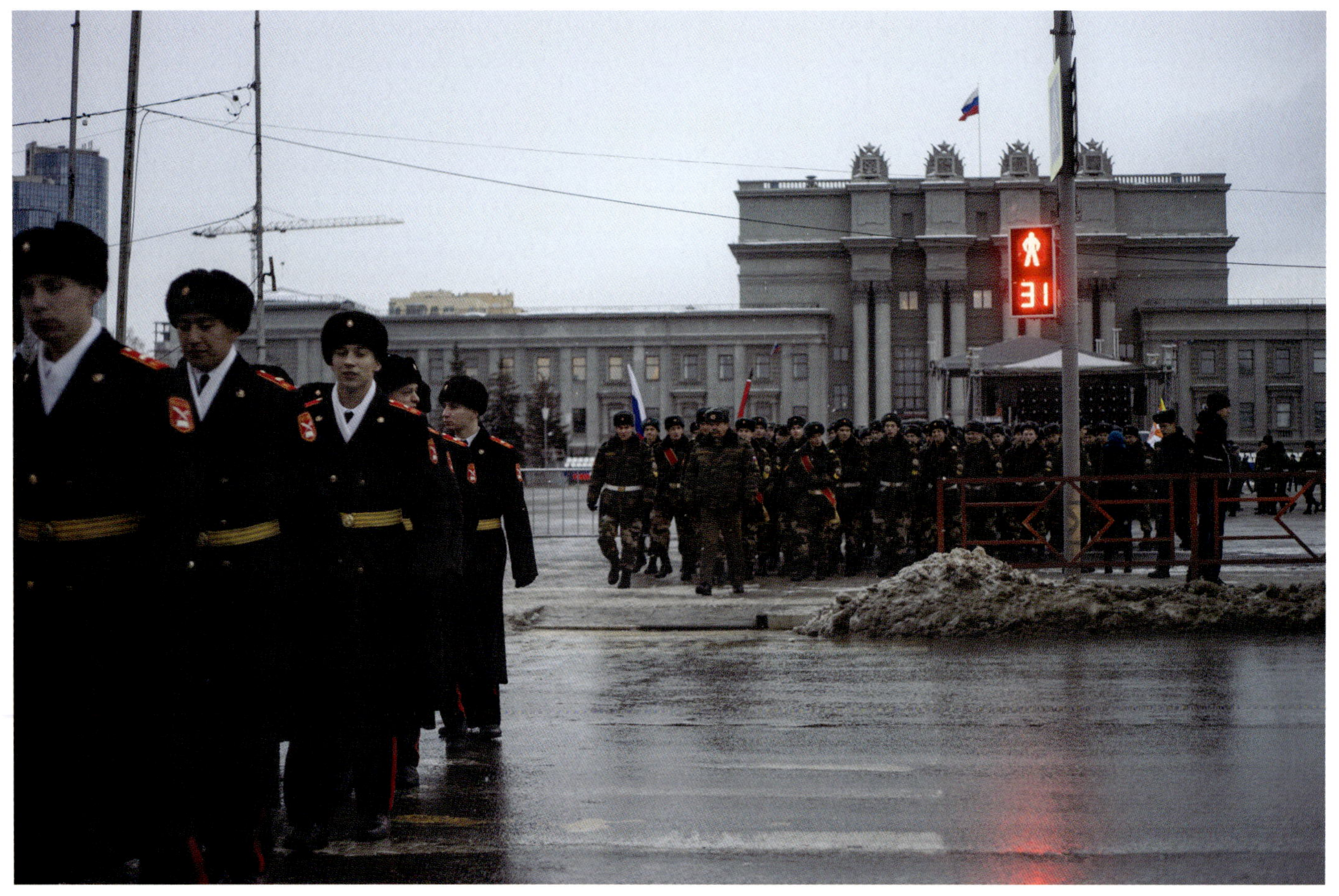

Victory Day Parade, 2019
SAMARA, RUSSIA
right: MOSCOW, RUSSIA

Victory Day (9 May) marks the greatest achievement of the Soviet people during the 20th century – victory over Nazi Germany (an accomplishment that can be compared only to sending the first man into space). However in 1948, because of the dire economic situation

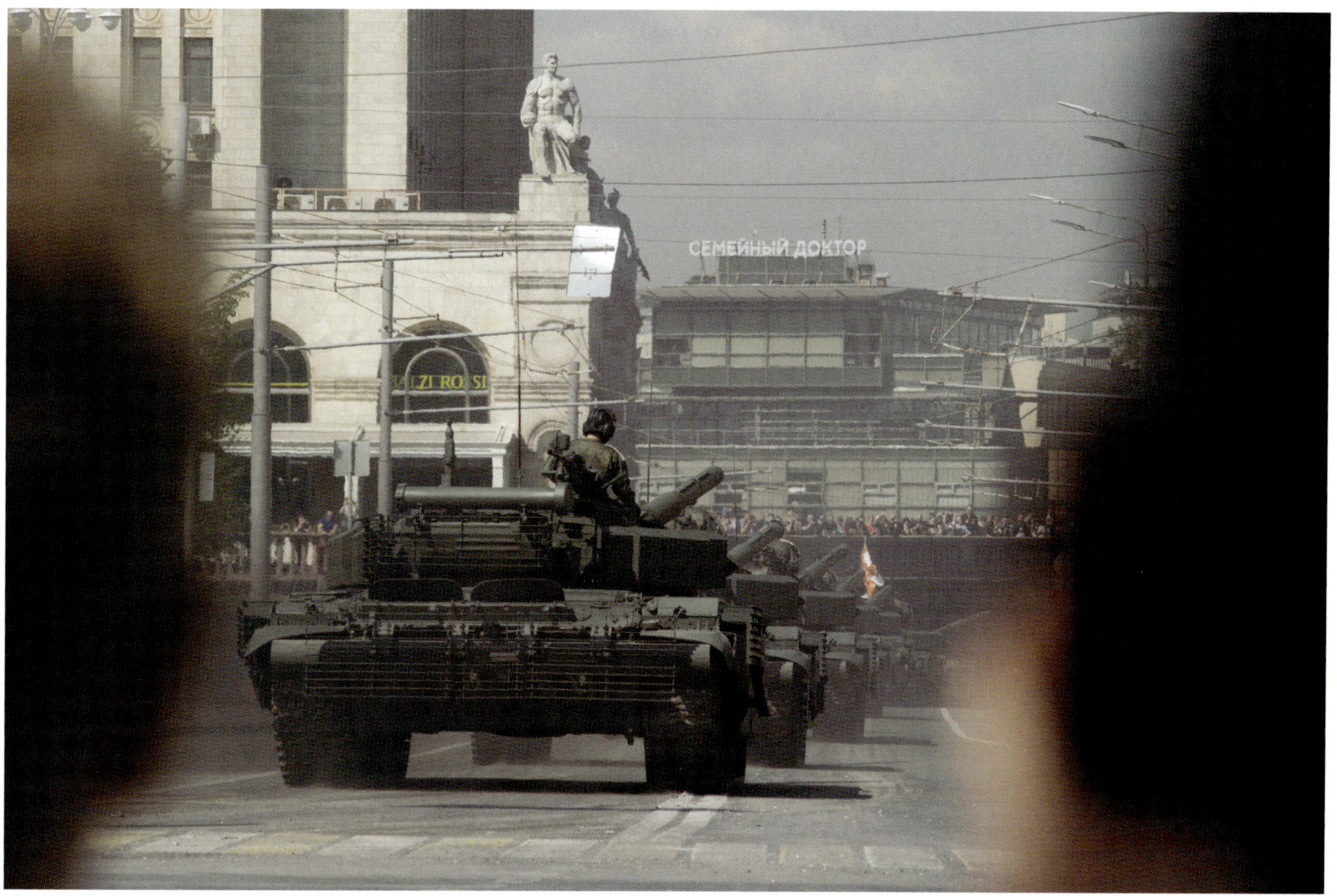

following the war, it was designated an ordinary working day. In 1965, Victory Day was once again declared a holiday, and military parades were held in many cities. However, unlike the annual October Revolution parades, Victory Day parades were held only once every ten years. During the Soviet era, they took place in 1965, 1975, 1985 and 1990. From 1995, following the collapse of the Soviet Union, the tradition of large-scale celebrations was resumed and now parades take place every year.

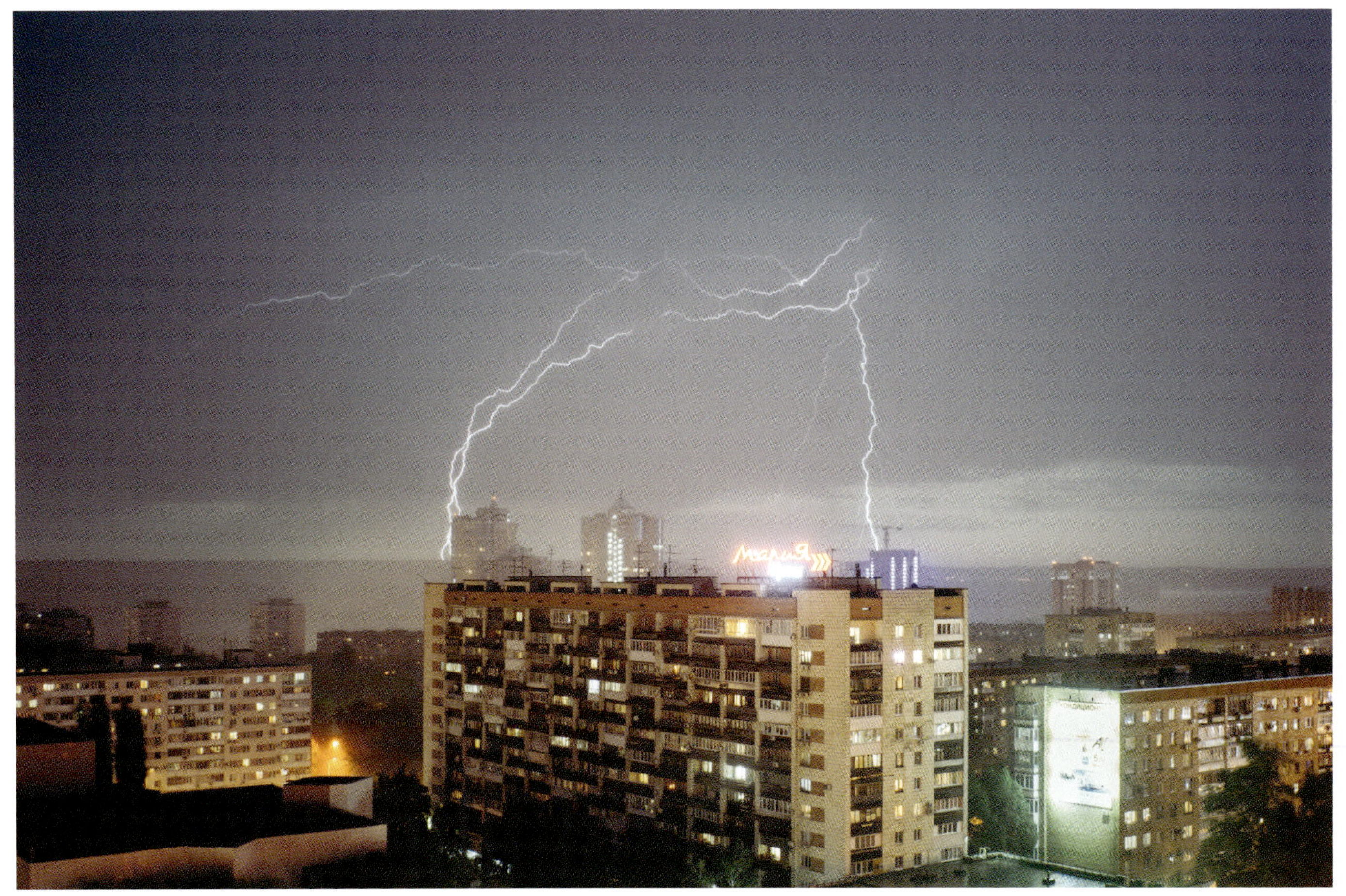

May thunderstorm over Lenina Avenue
SAMARA, RUSSIA

From the end of April to the end of May, Central Russia and Northern Europe are affected by a collision of massive air fronts. These lead to particularly powerful spring thunderstorms, accompanied by heavy rainfall.

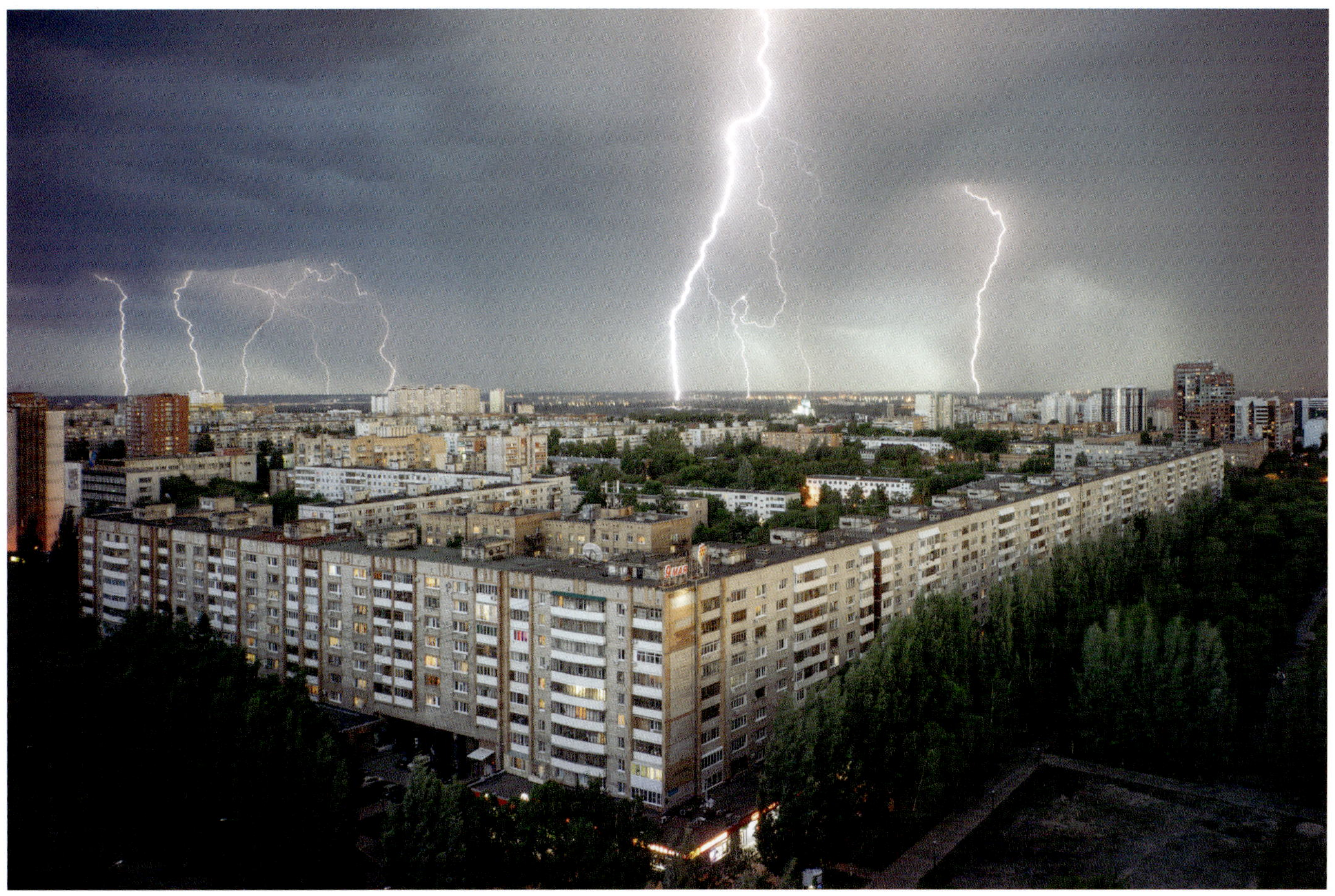

May thunderstorm over Lenina Avenue
SAMARA, RUSSIA
Built in the 1970s

This apartment block on Lenina Avenue is the second longest in Samara. It was built for employees of the design department of the Progress Rocket and Space Plant. The area has large green spaces, children's playgrounds and sports facilities.

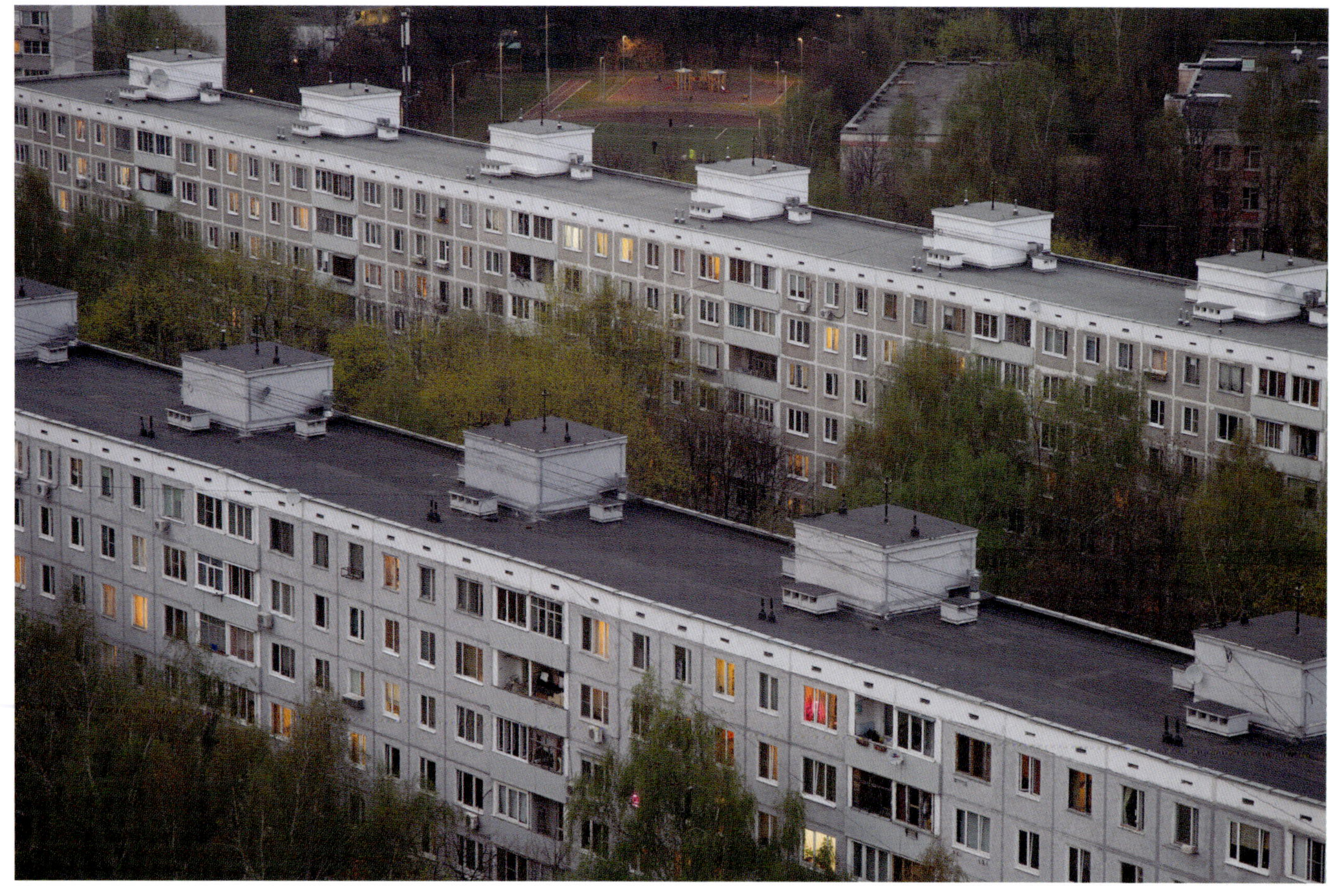

1605-AM/9 Series residential blocks
South Chertanovo District
MOSCOW, RUSSIA
Built in 1971

Between 1966 and 1972, 9-storey apartment blocks using this series
of prefabricated panelling were built in Moscow and Togliatti.

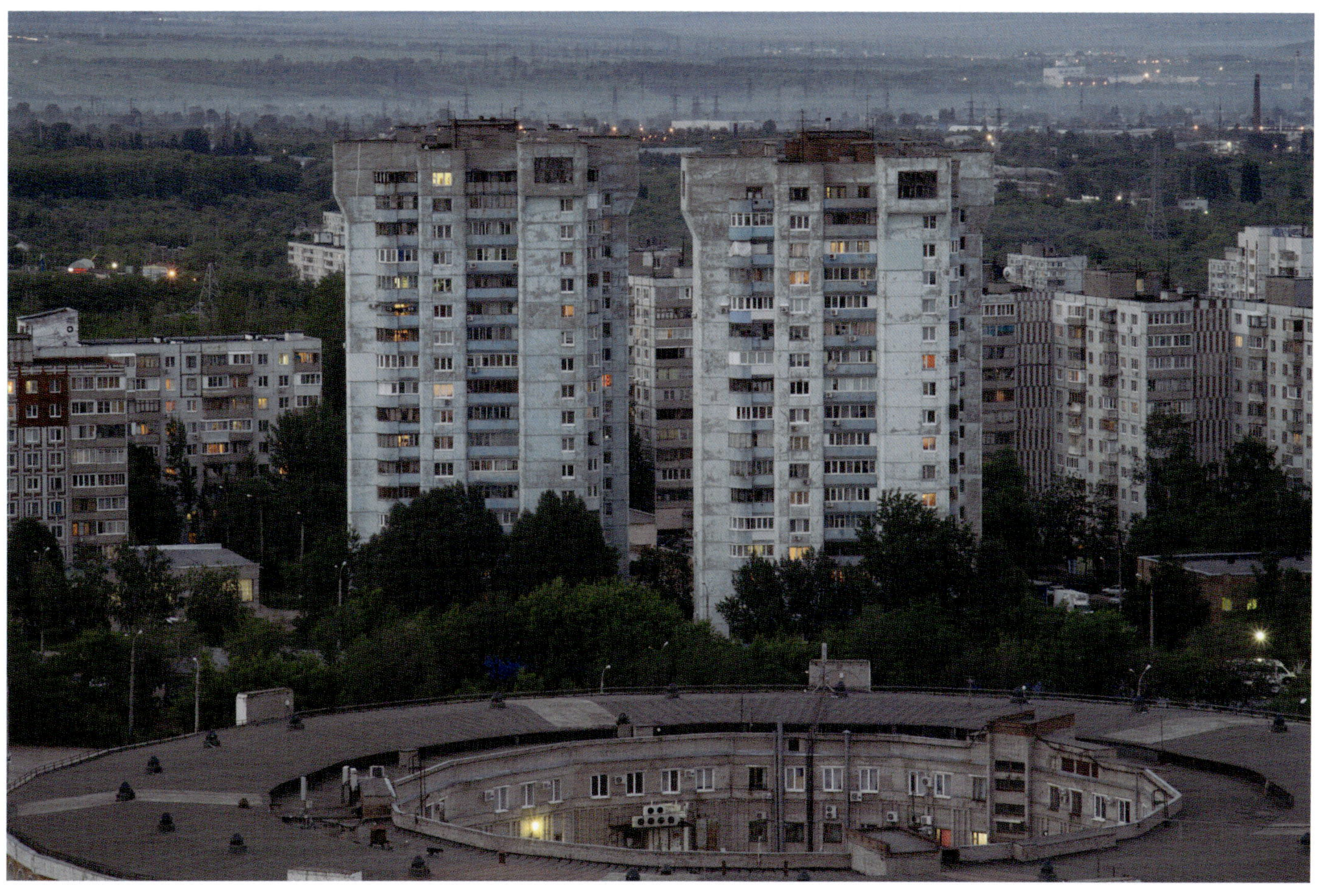

Colosseum Shopping Mall and 3086/85 Series towers
SAMARA, RUSSIA
Built in the 1980s

This type of construction was regularly used towards the end of the Soviet period and beyond. Similar monolithic 17-storey buildings in reinforced concrete were erected between the 1980s and 2000s in cities across Russia and Ukraine.

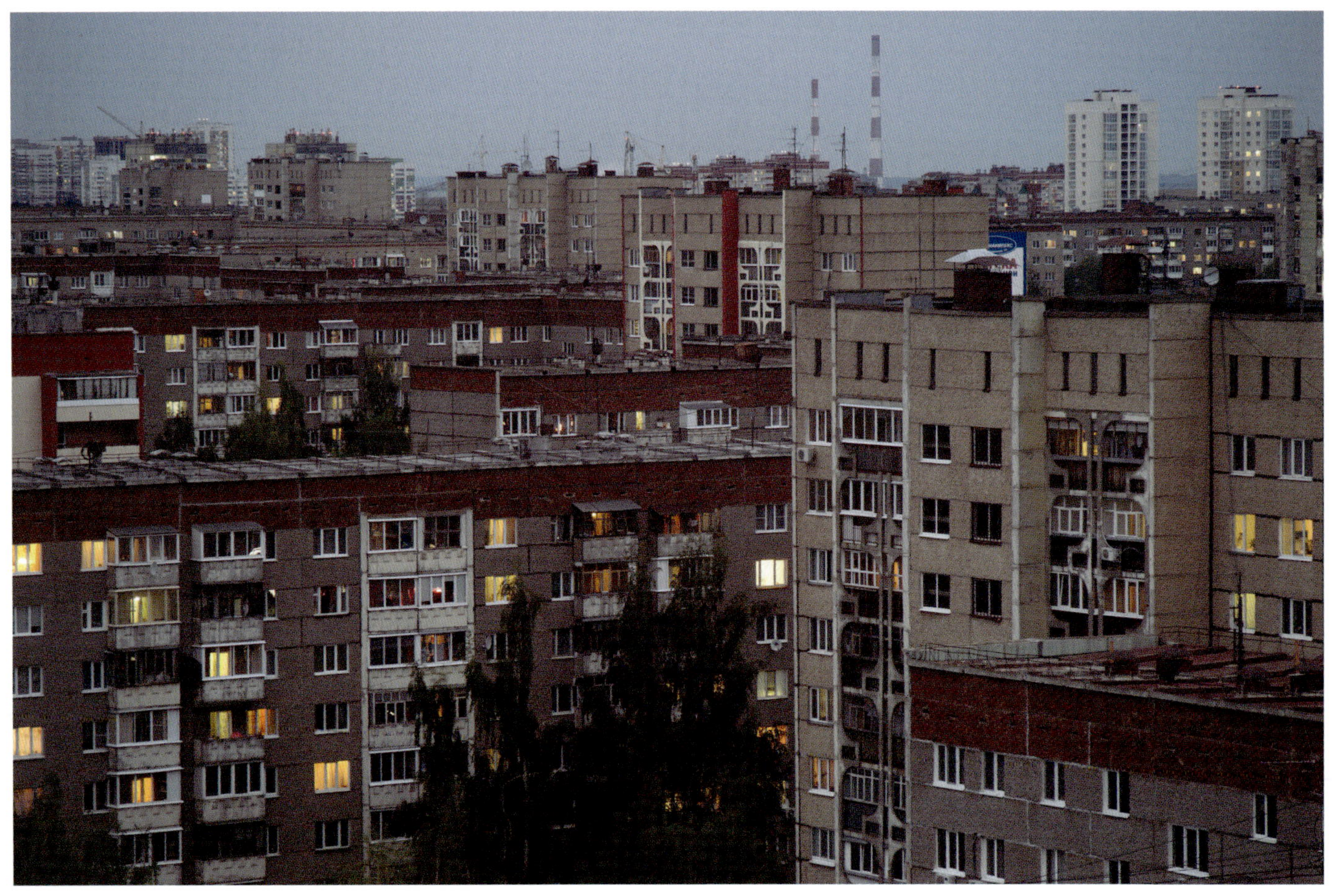

Ustinovskiy District
IZHEVSK, RUSSIA
Built in the 1970s

The construction of large-scale industrial enterprises to the north of Izhevsk's modern district began in the 1970s. Simultaneously, the building of panel-type, multi-apartment blocks for workers commenced on adjacent land.

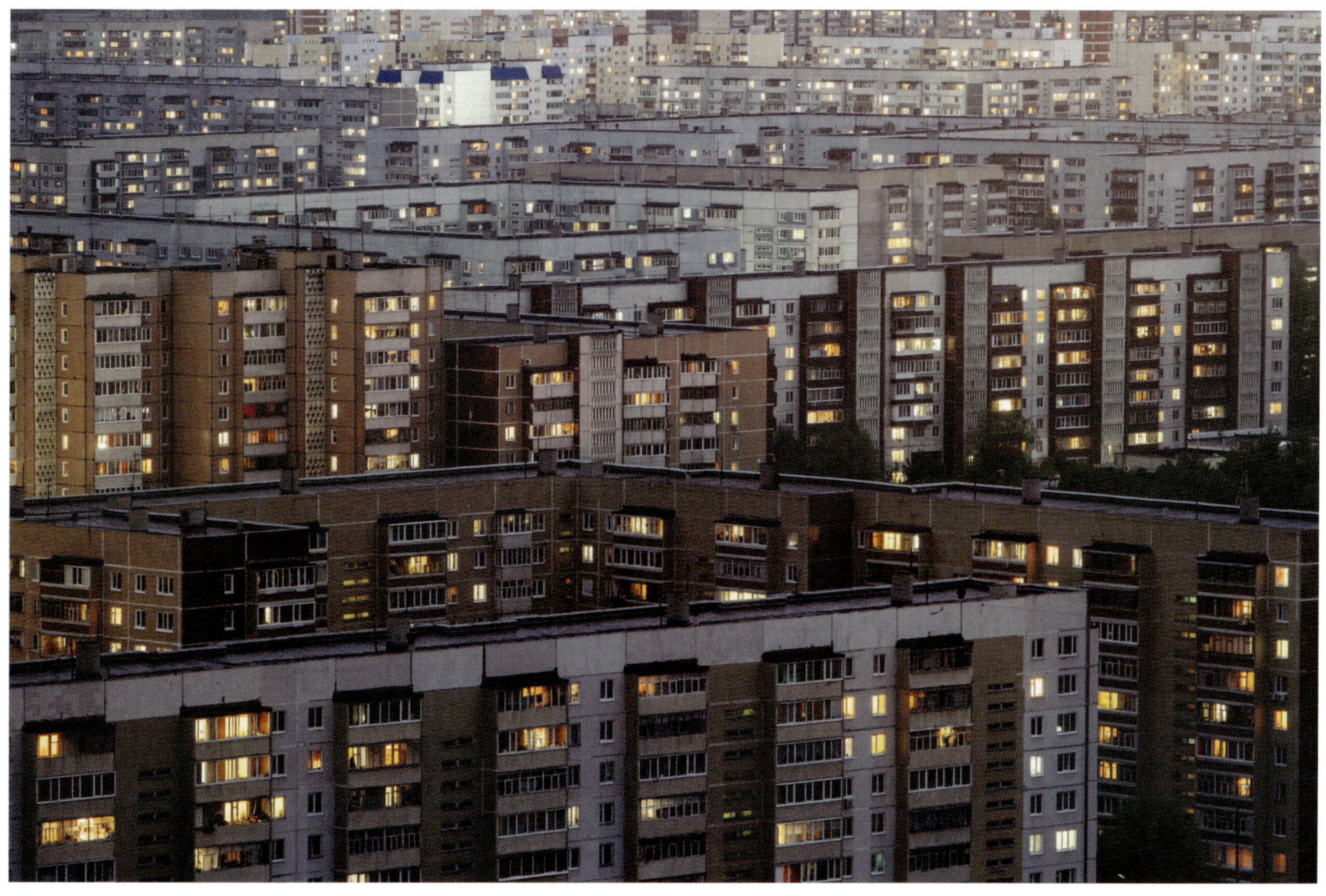

Sviyaga Microdistrict
ULYANOVSK, RUSSIA

Initially, this neighbourhood in Ulyanovsk (known as the birthplace of Lenin) was inhabited by workers from the numerous factories located nearby. Since the mid-1960s, it has been developed using 9-storey panel buildings.

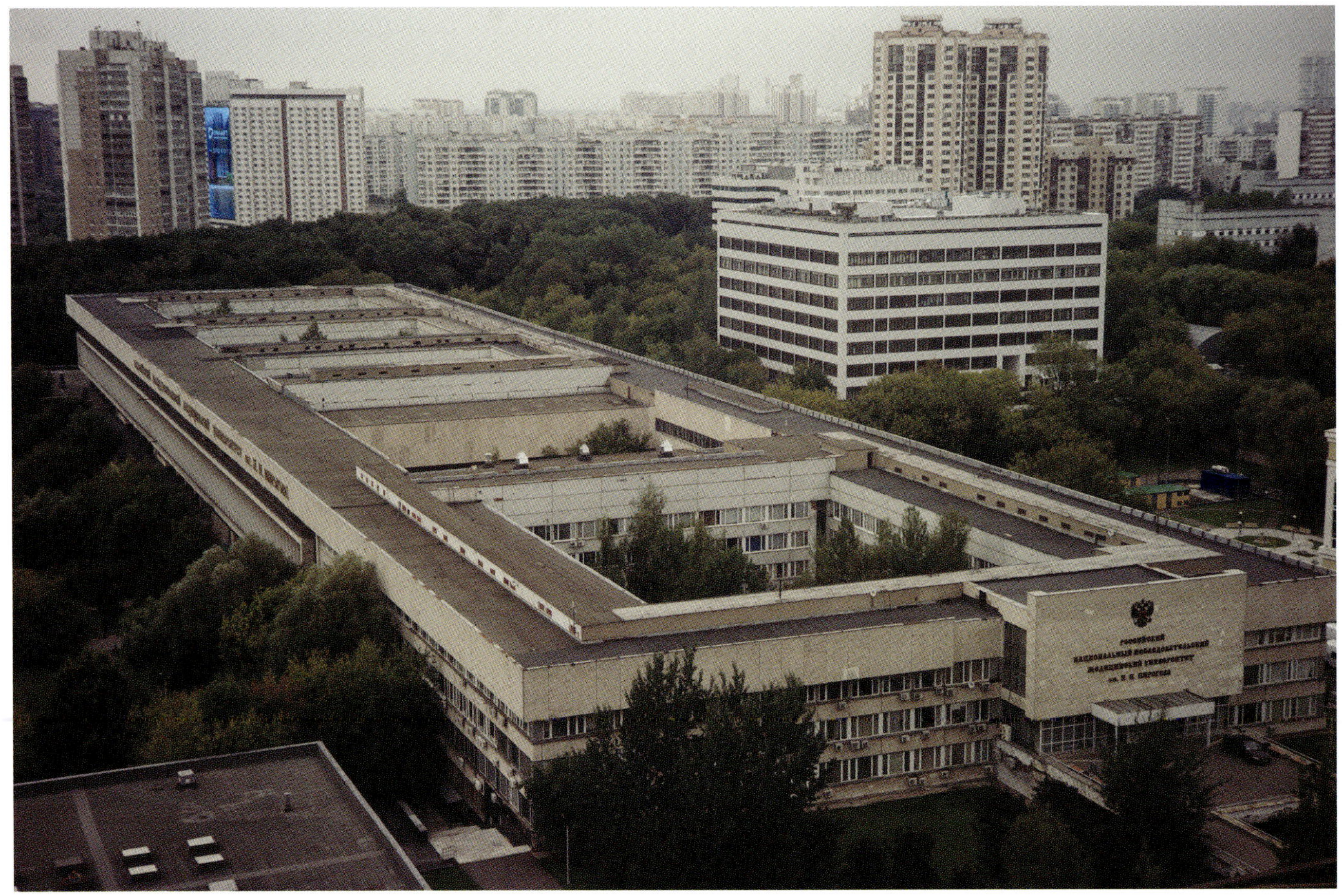

Pirogov State Medical University
MOSCOW, RUSSIA
Built in 1984
Architects: V. Fursov, E. Afanasiev et al.

This is one of the largest medical universities in Russia, with more than 9,000 students across 135 departments. A new institute and laboratory were built on the right bank of the Ochakovka river, on the site of the former Bogorodskoye estate.

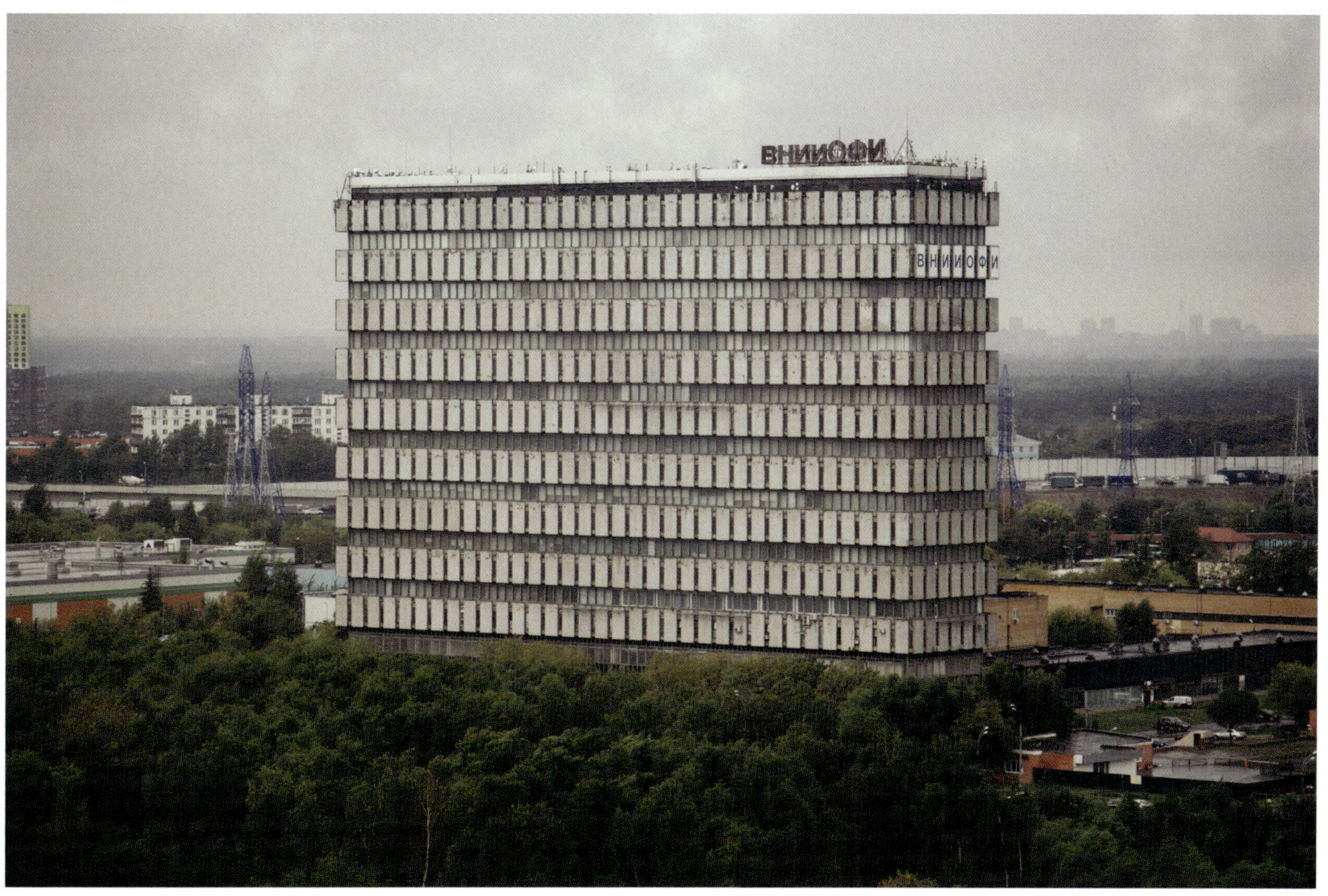

VNIIOFI Building
MOSCOW, RUSSIA

VNIIOFI, the All-Union Research Institute of Optical and Physical Measurements, has created a state system for ensuring the uniformity of measurements in photometry, radiometry, optical radiation and the parameters of pulsed electromagnetic fields.

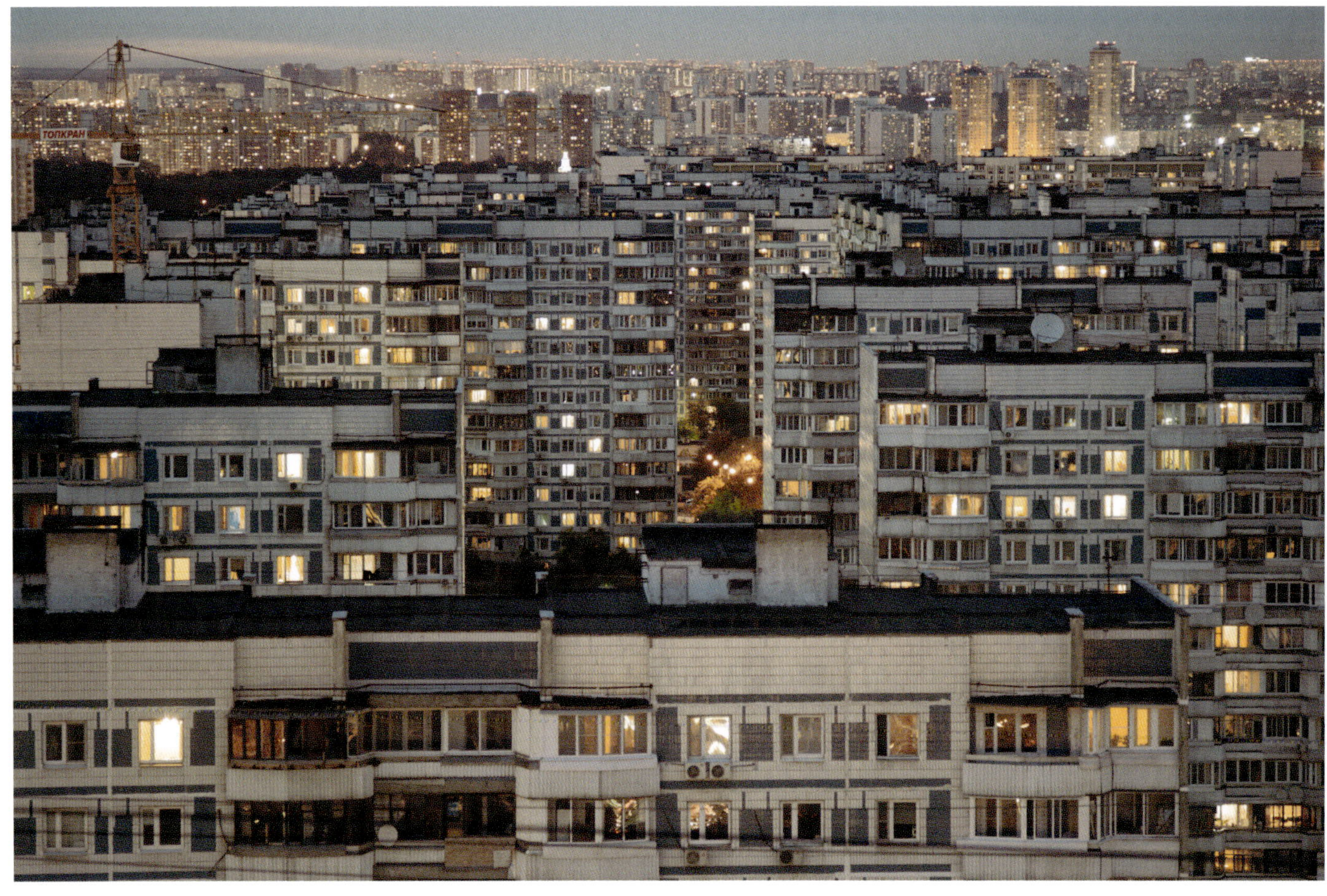

Housing development in the Krylatskoye District
MOSCOW, RUSSIA
Built in the 1980s

Krylatskoye is a district in the west of Moscow with a population of 83,000. This massive housing development was initiated in 1982.

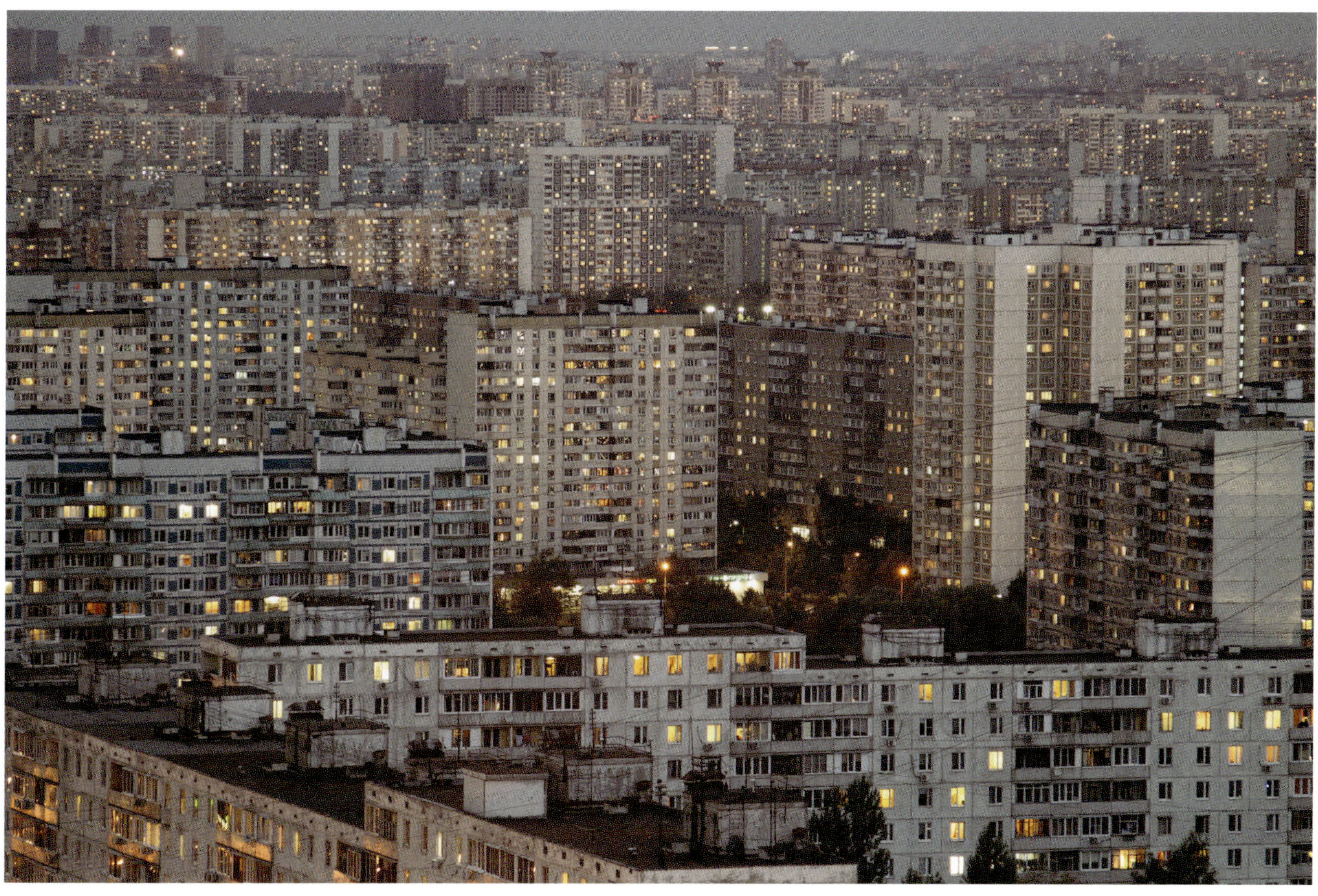

Zyablikovo District
MOSCOW, RUSSIA
Built between 1960 and 1990

This district, with a population of 133,000, has been developed using multi-apartment panel buildings of various series since the 1960s. The area was once a flood plain, occupied by the villages of Zyablikovo and Borisovo.

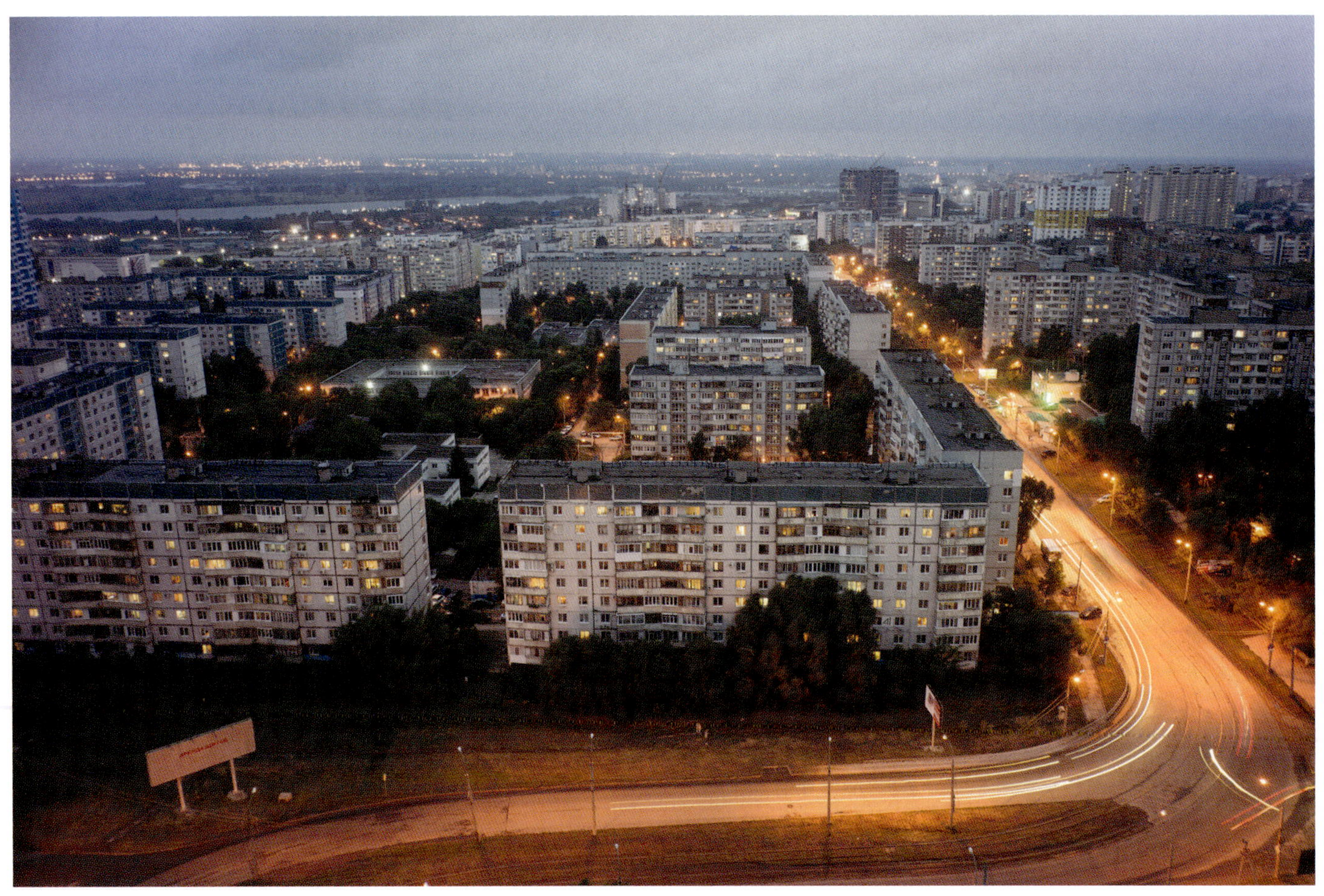

3rd Microdistrict
SAMARA, RUSSIA
Built in the 1980s

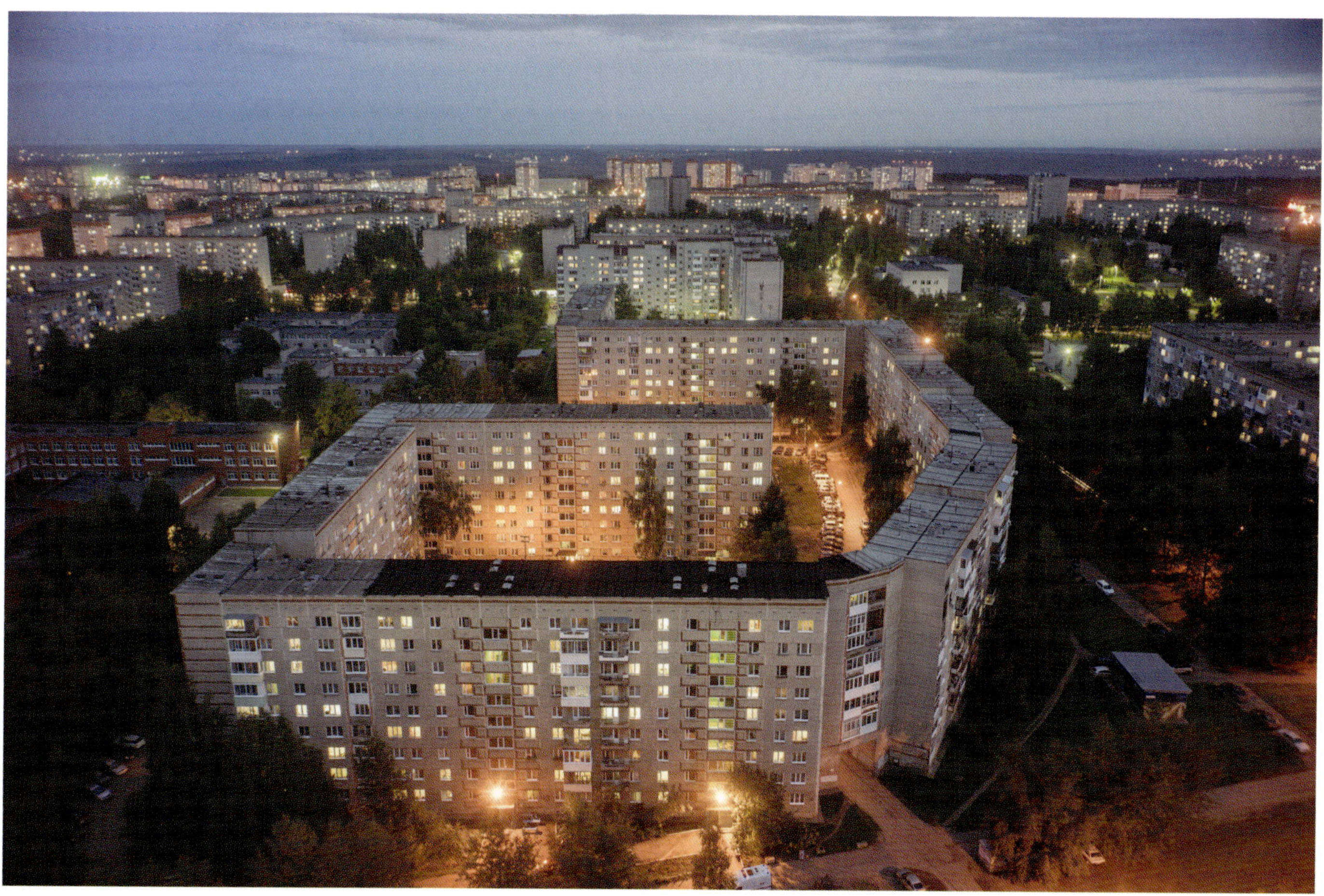

Ustinovskiy District
IZHEVSK, RUSSIA
Built in the 1980s

Izhevsk is the capital of the Udmurt Republic. A large industrial, scientific, educational and cultural centre for the Volga and Ural regions, it is renowned for its defence and engineering industries. The famous Kalashnikov assault rifle is produced here.

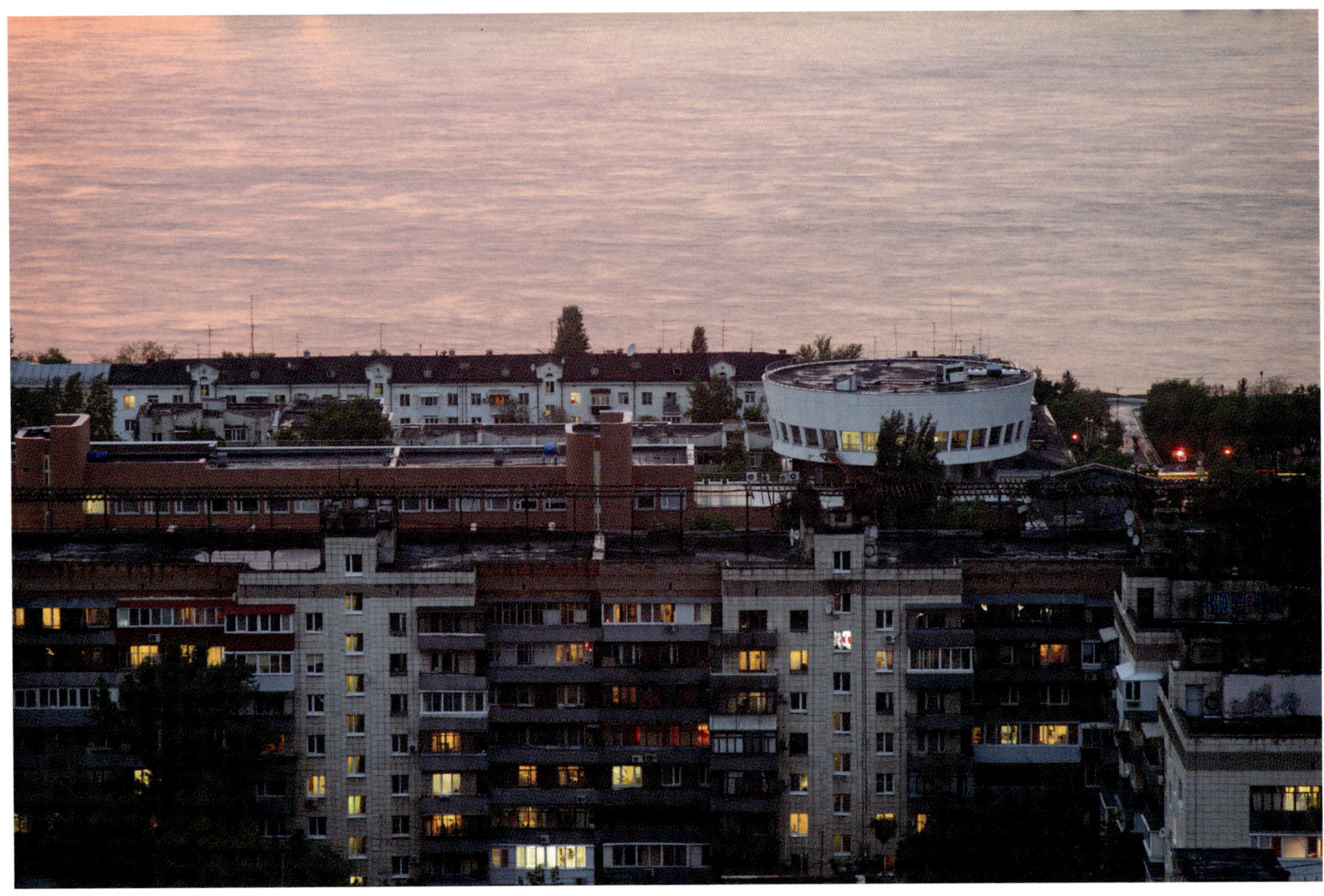

Zonal Computing Centre and Volga River
SAMARA, RUSSIA
Built in 1980
Architects: A. Gerasimov, A. Morgun

The Zonal Computing Centre for the Regional Dispatch Control of Electrical Systems in the Middle Volga managed local energy systems. It housed a circular control panel that dictated its form. Today the panel has been removed and the building is used as office space.

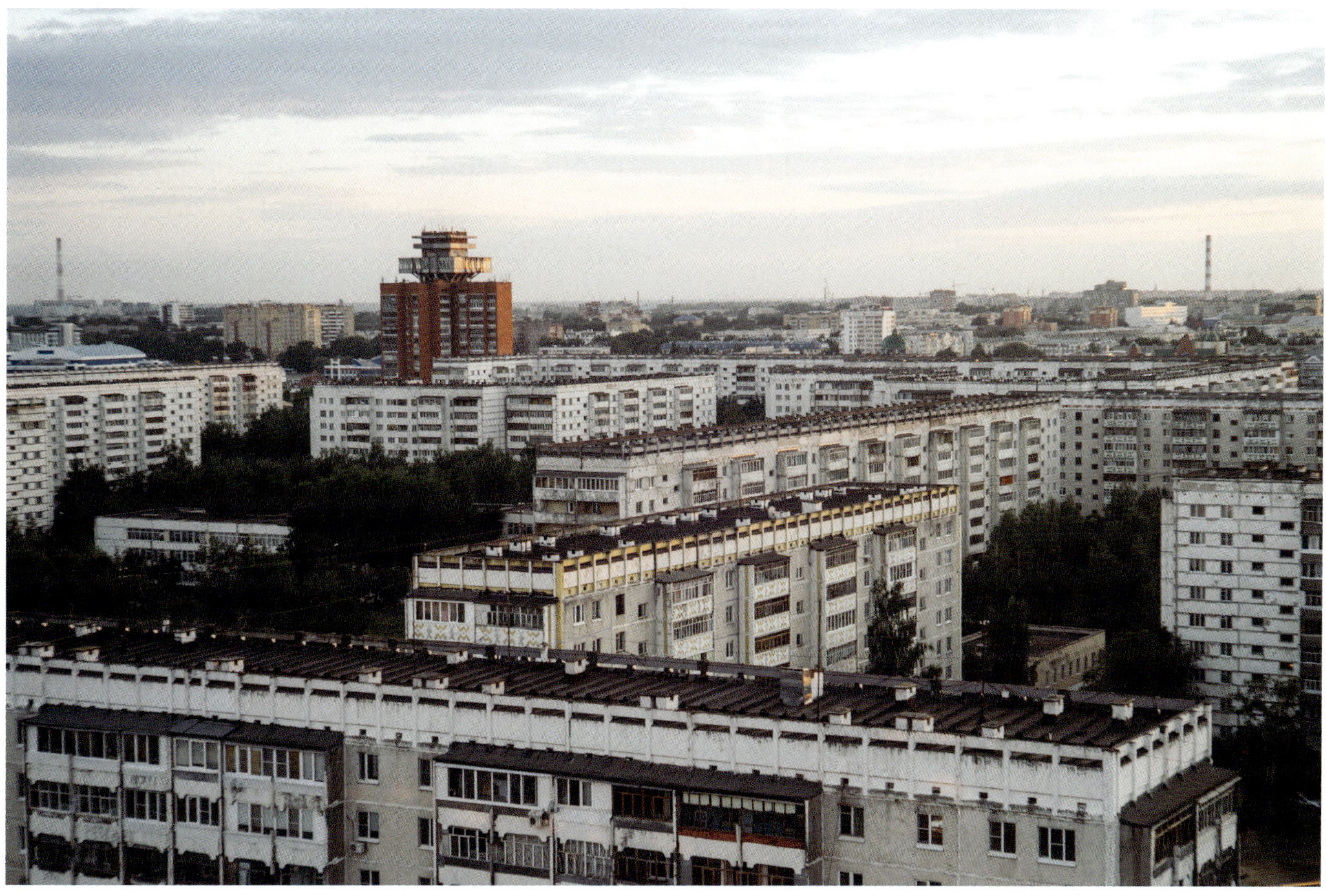

The 'Cologne-building' and left bank neighbourhood
YOSHKAR−OLA, RUSSIA
Built in 1992
Architect: A. Galitsky

The Seventh Sky Café was planned for the 17th floor of this building, but in June 1992, the café equipment was vandalised. The building remained uncompleted because of the economic crisis of the time. Eventually, the vacated premises were converted to office space.

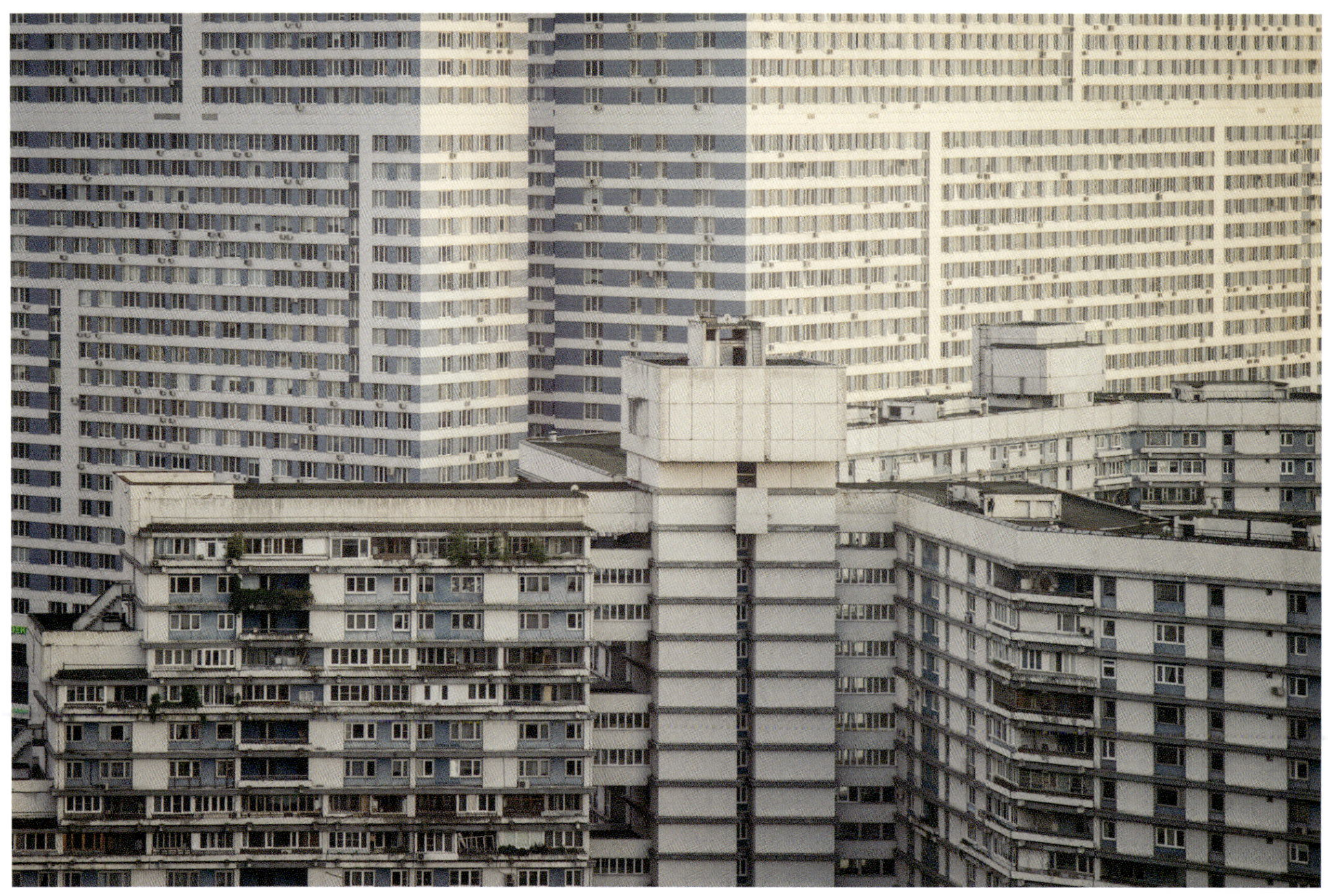

North Chertanovo District
MOSCOW, RUSSIA

In the foreground stands Severnoe Chertanovo (North Chertanovo). This exemplary residential district, built in the 1970s, was architecturally the most modern of its time. In the background stands a 45-storey residential complex, built in 2005, the era of infill development.

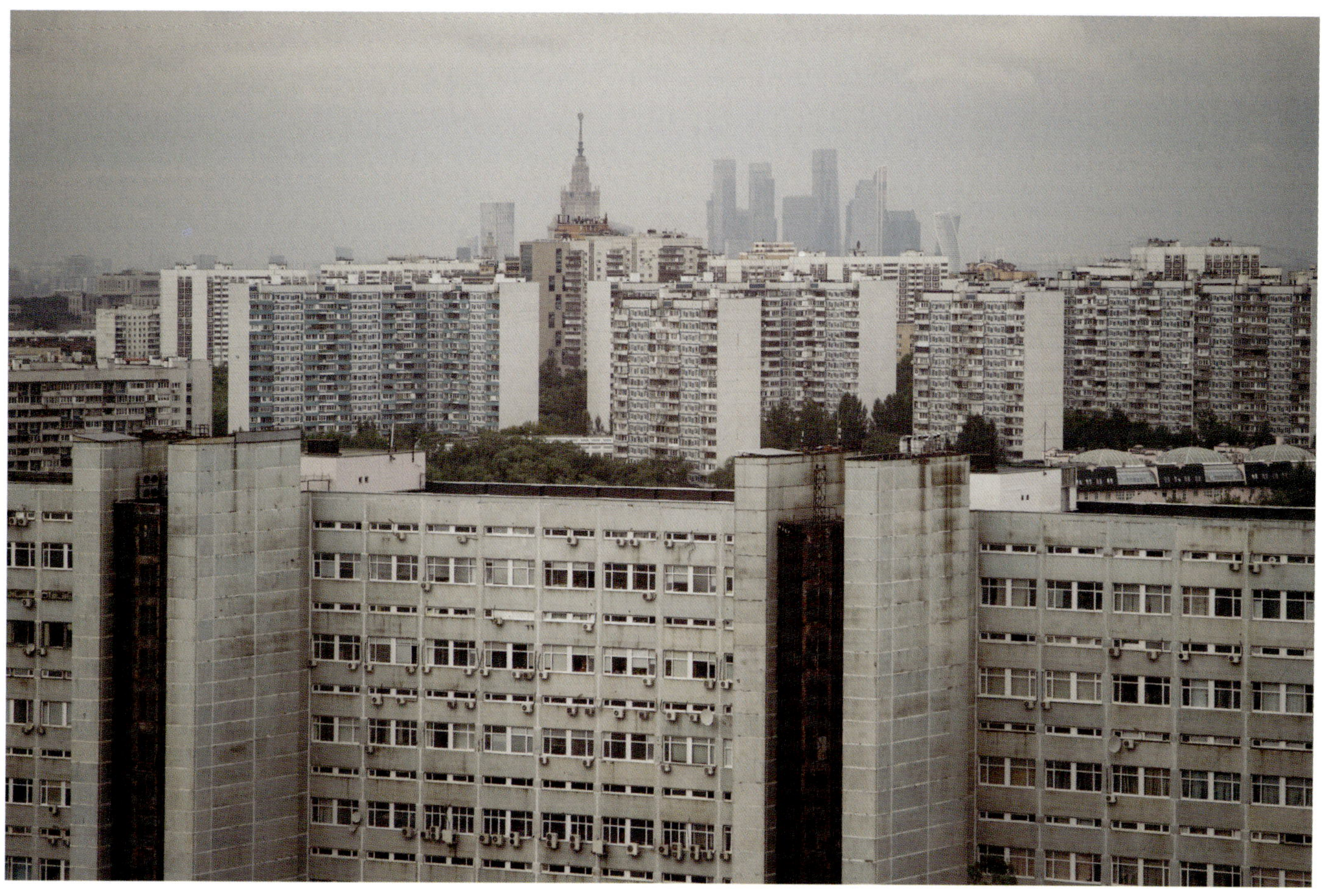

Space Research Institute
MOSCOW, RUSSIA
Built in 1978
Architect: Y. Platonov

The institute conducts experimental research in astrophysics, planets, physics of the Sun, space plasma, and nonlinear geophysics. It also prepares programmes in space research and the development and the testing of scientific equipment.

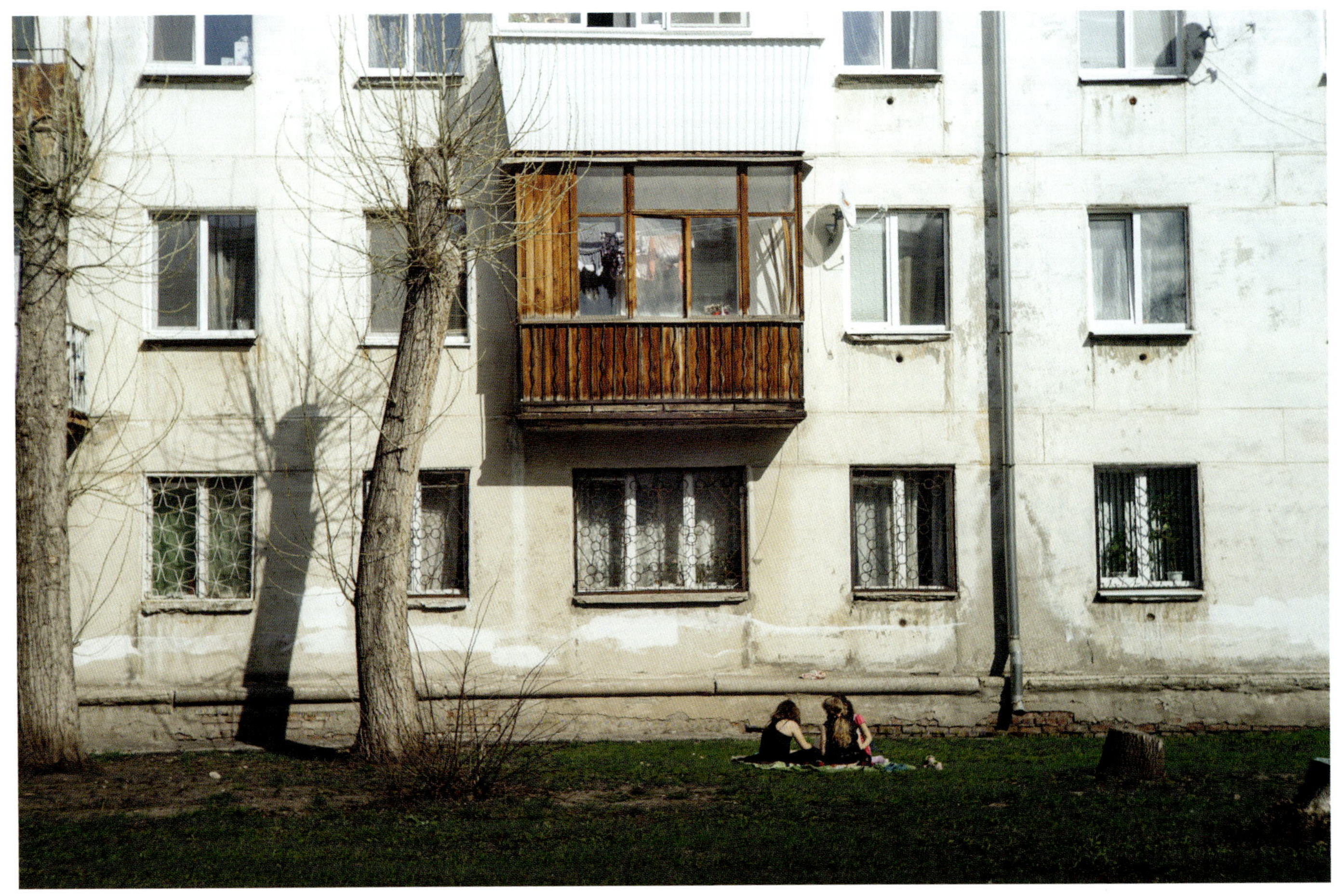

Girls picnic in front of a 1-335 Series building
NOVOKUYBUSHEVSK, RUSSIA

1-335 is the most common series of predominantly 5-storey panel residential blocks throughout the former Soviet Union. Produced by the Leningrad branch of the State Design Institute (Gorstroyproekt), buildings using this series were constructed between 1956 and 1968.

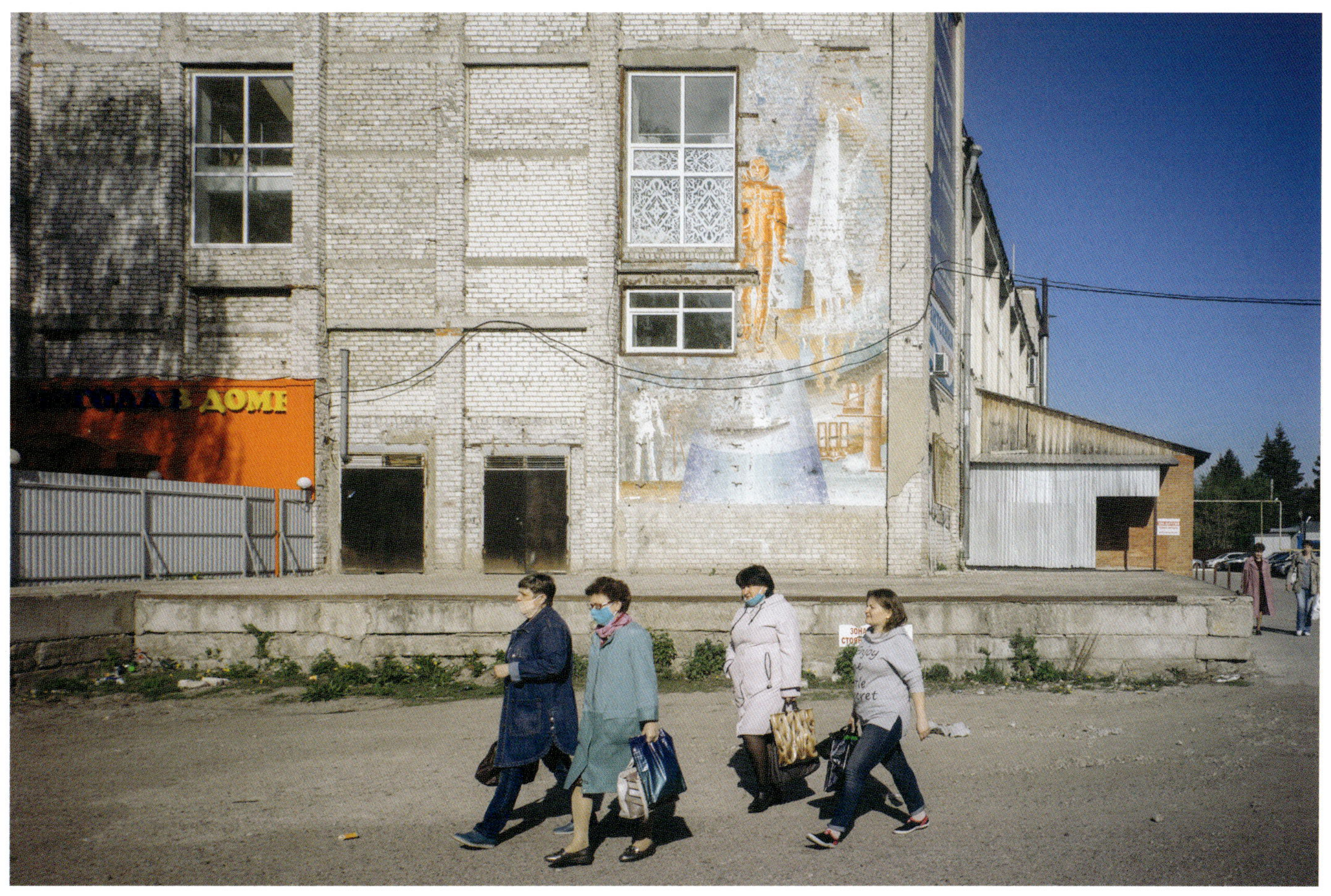

Soviet-era space-themed mural
Signal Sports Centre
ULYANOVSK, RUSSIA

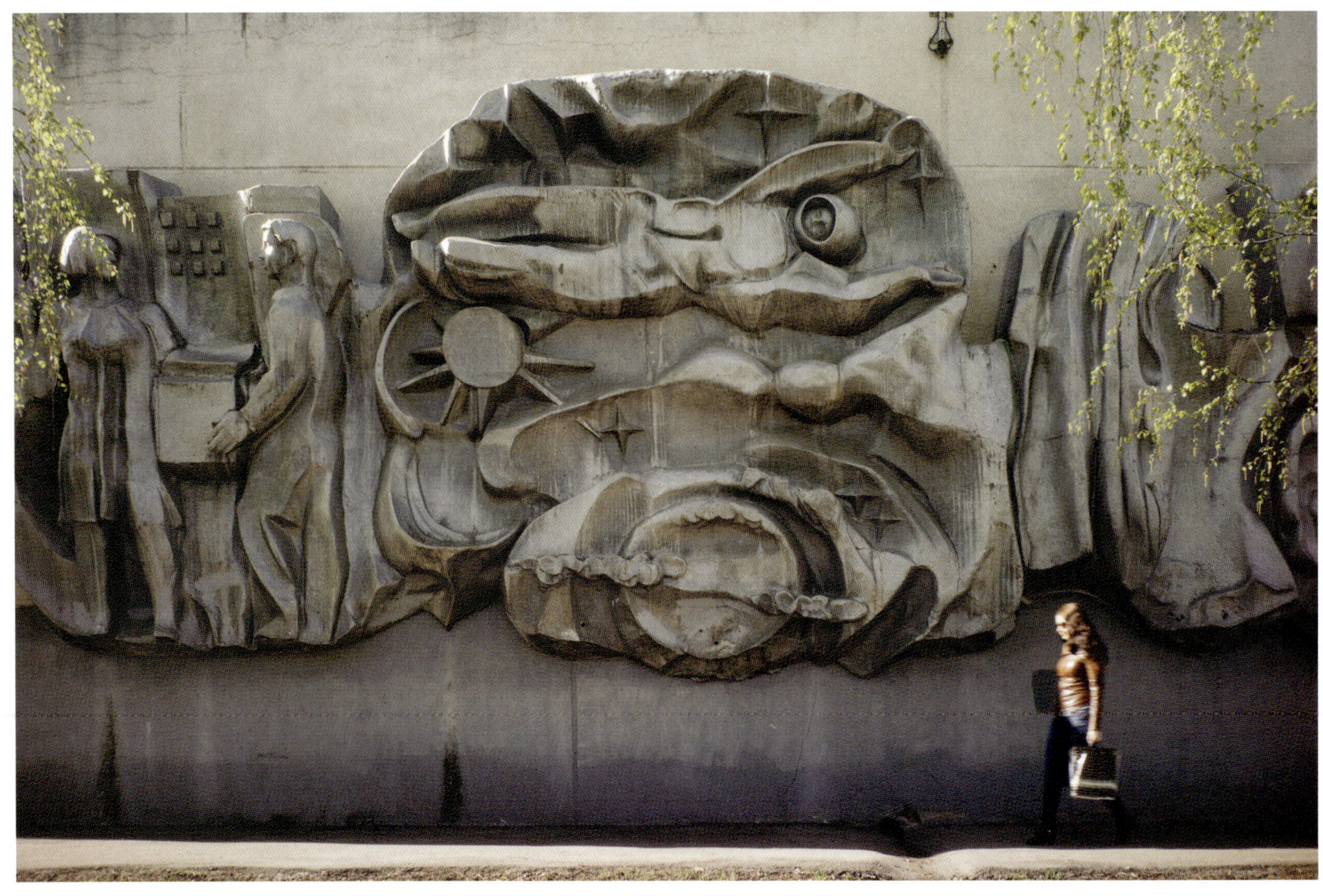

Bas-relief, School No.40
TOGLIATTI, RUSSIA

In 1967, as the Volga Automotive Plant (VAZ) was under construction, so was a residential area for its workers. The town, named Togliatti after the Italian Communist Party leader, was created from scratch. This allowed planners to position the streets to take advantage of

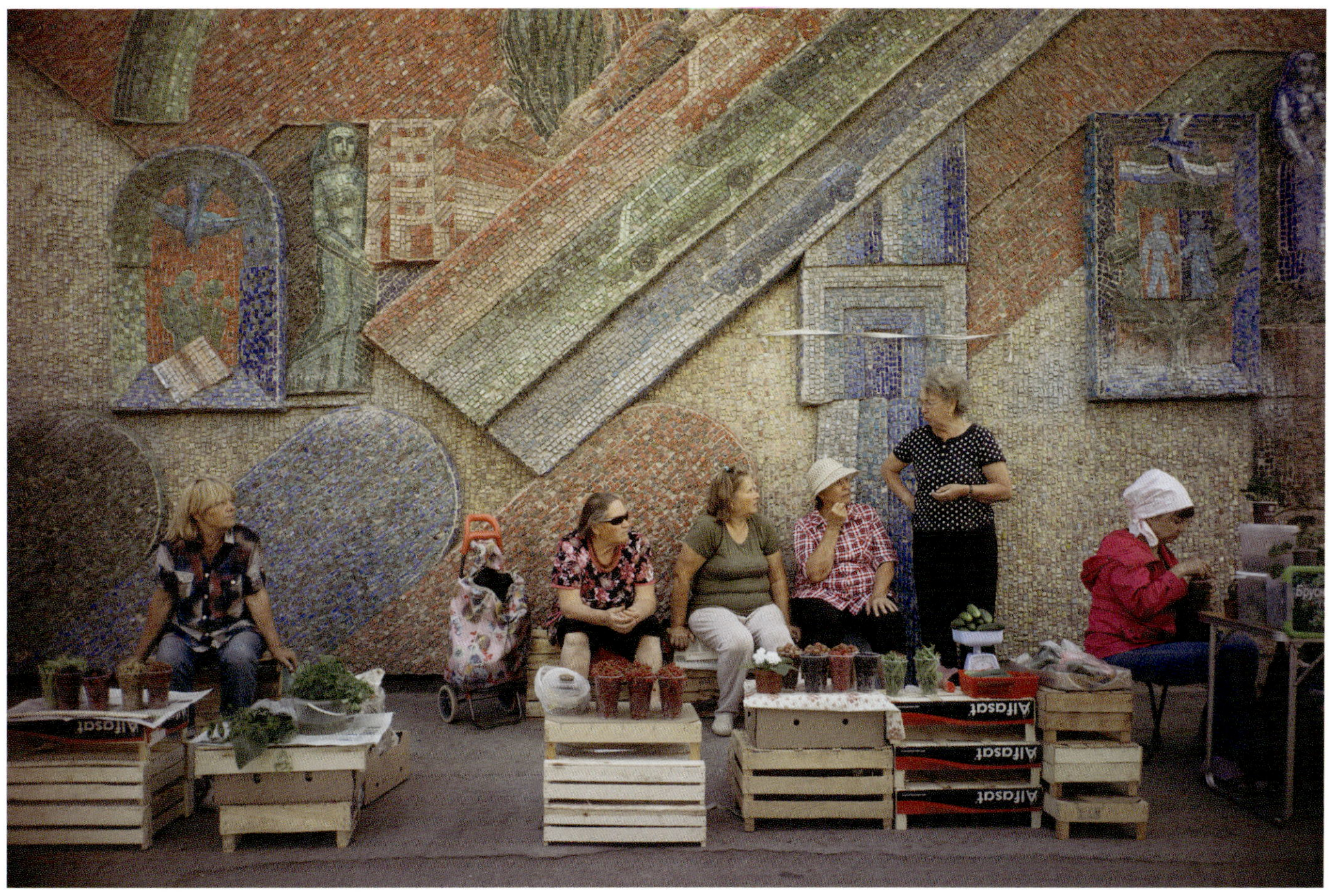

'Peaceful Labour' mosaic, Post Office No.36
TOGLIATTI, RUSSIA

the temperate winds from the Volga river. Many public buildings
in the Avtozavodsky District are decorated with monumental art
produced by artists from Moscow, Leningrad and elsewhere.

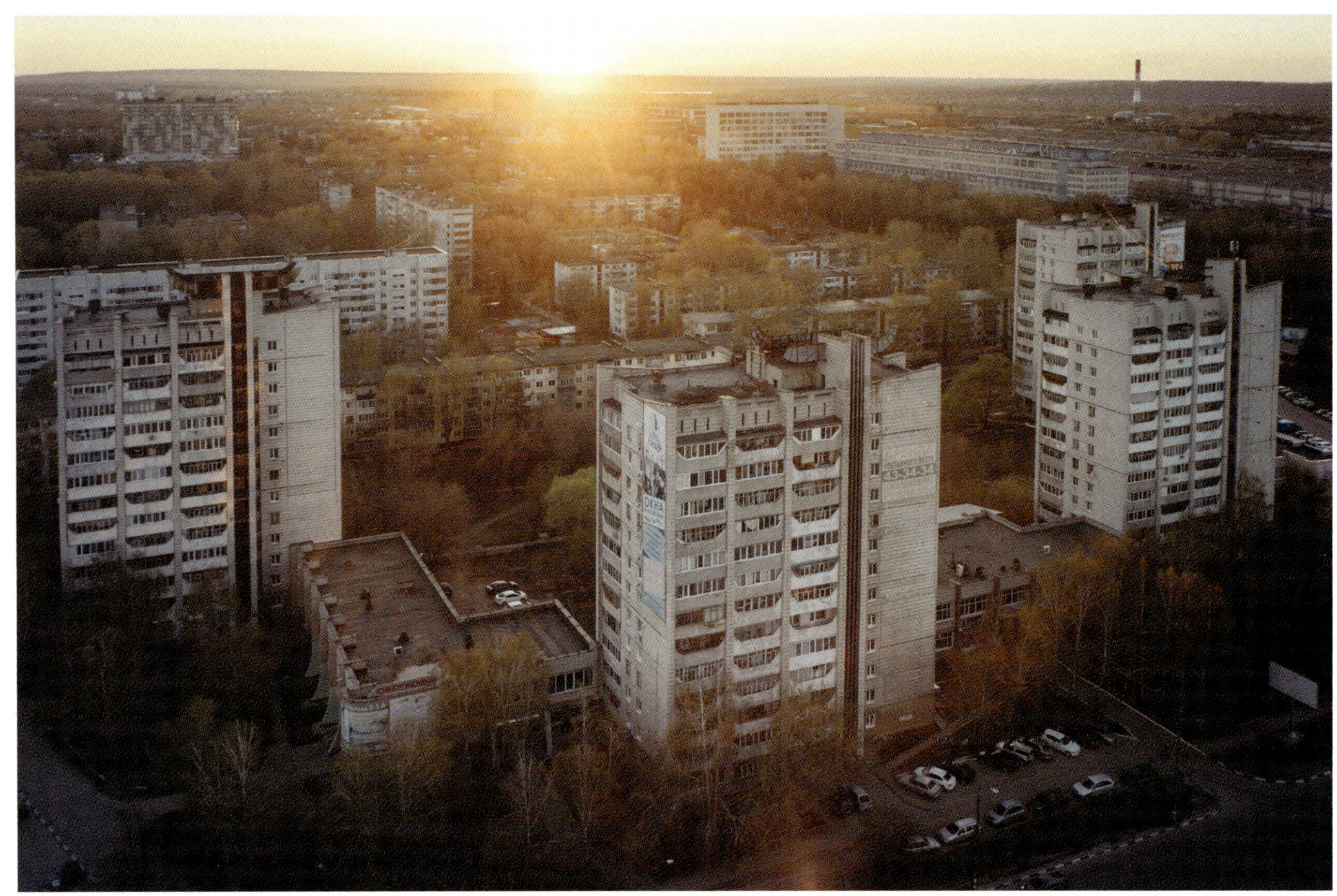

Tower-type houses with 'horns', 15th Quarter
ULYANOVSK, RUSSIA
Built in the 1980s

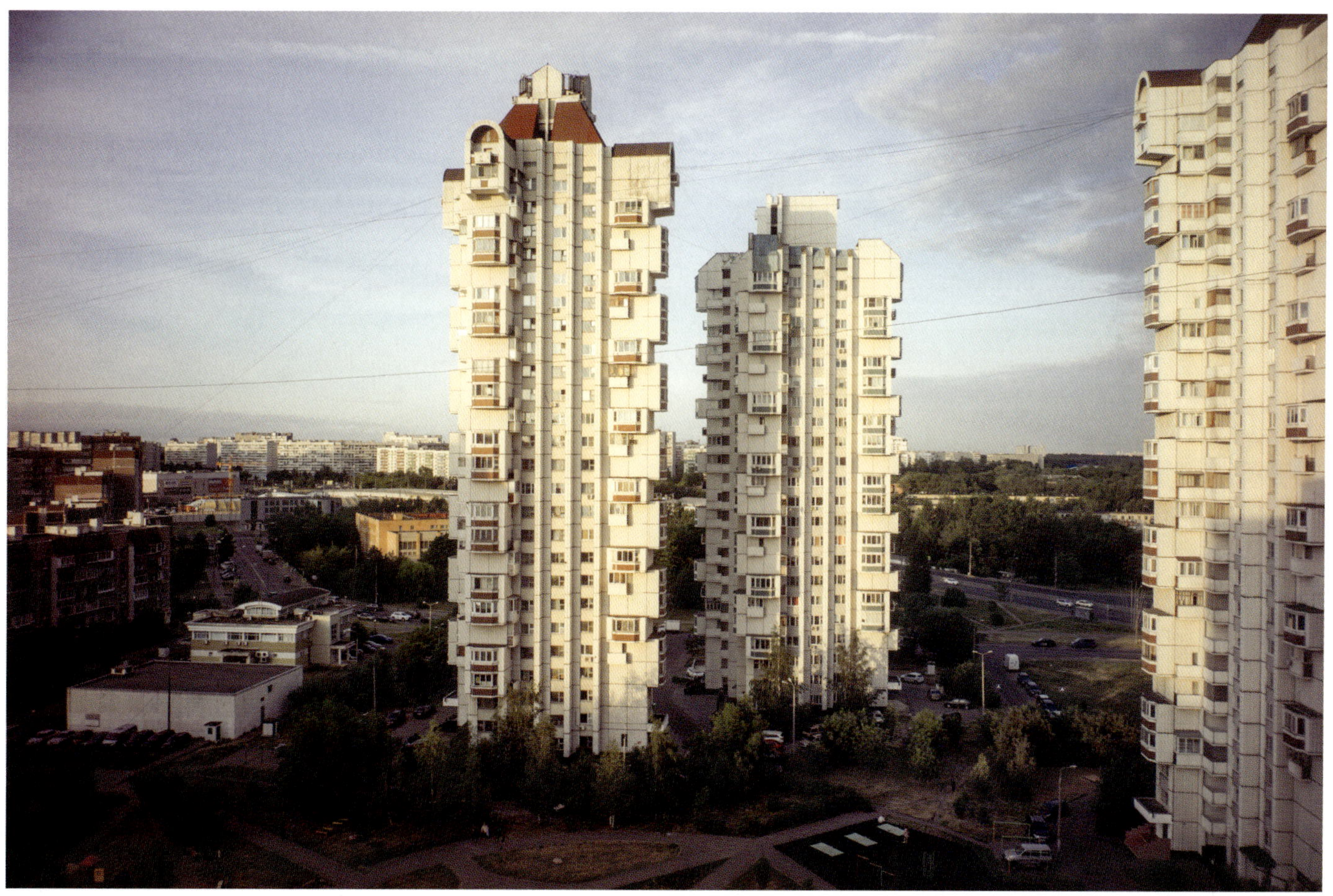

18th Microdistrict, Zelenograd
MOSCOW, RUSSIA

These monolithic apartment buildings stand 22 storeys high. Built using the E-187 Series of prefabricated construction, the four towers were erected between 1999 and 2003. They are the last work of prominent Soviet architect Alexander Belokon.

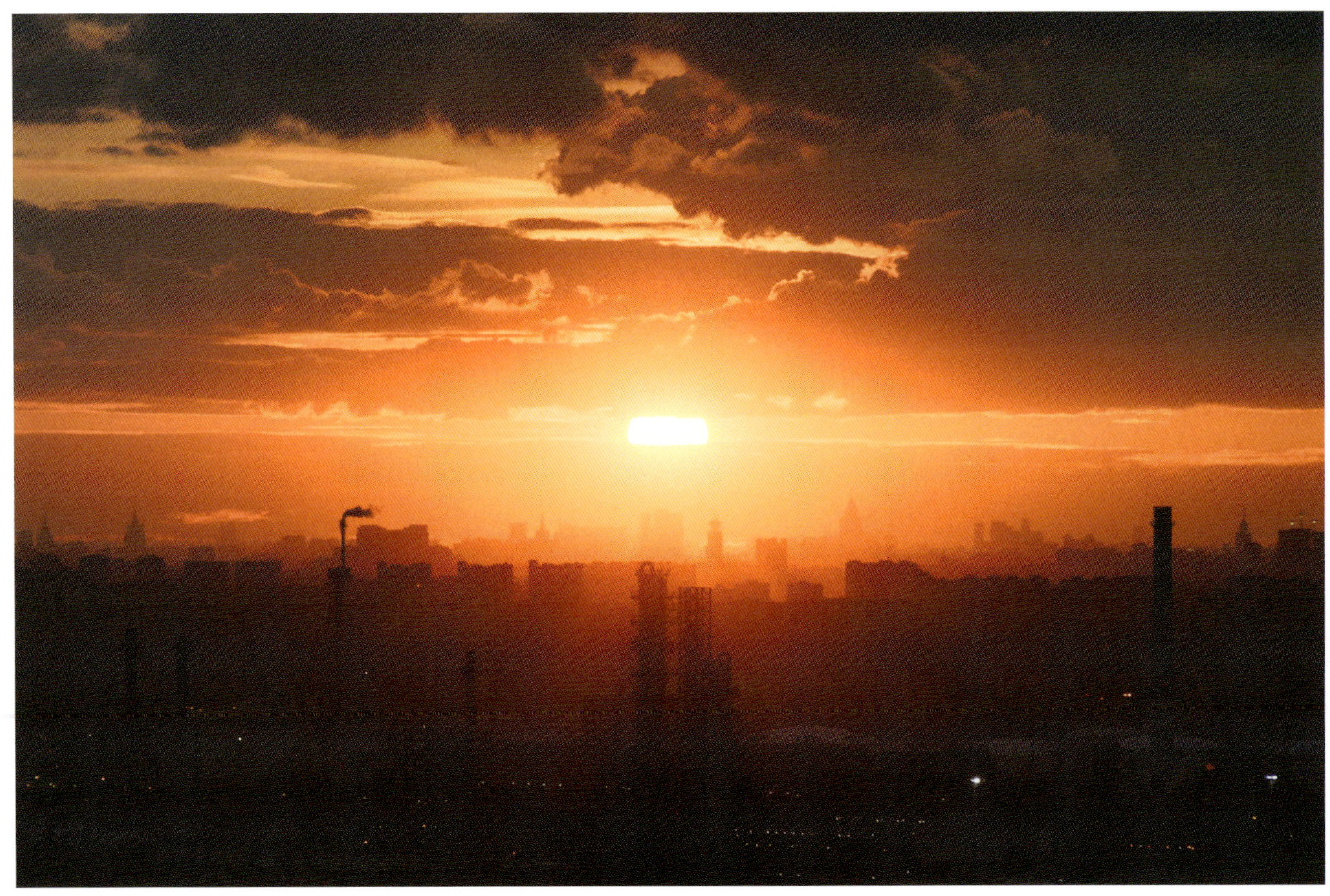

Oil Refinery
Kapotnya District
MOSCOW, RUSSIA
Built in 1938

The rapid industrialisation of the 1930s led to demand for an oil refinery near Moscow. At that time, there were only five refineries operating in Soviet Russia, all located in oil-producing areas. Today, this is one of the last large industrial enterprises in the capital.

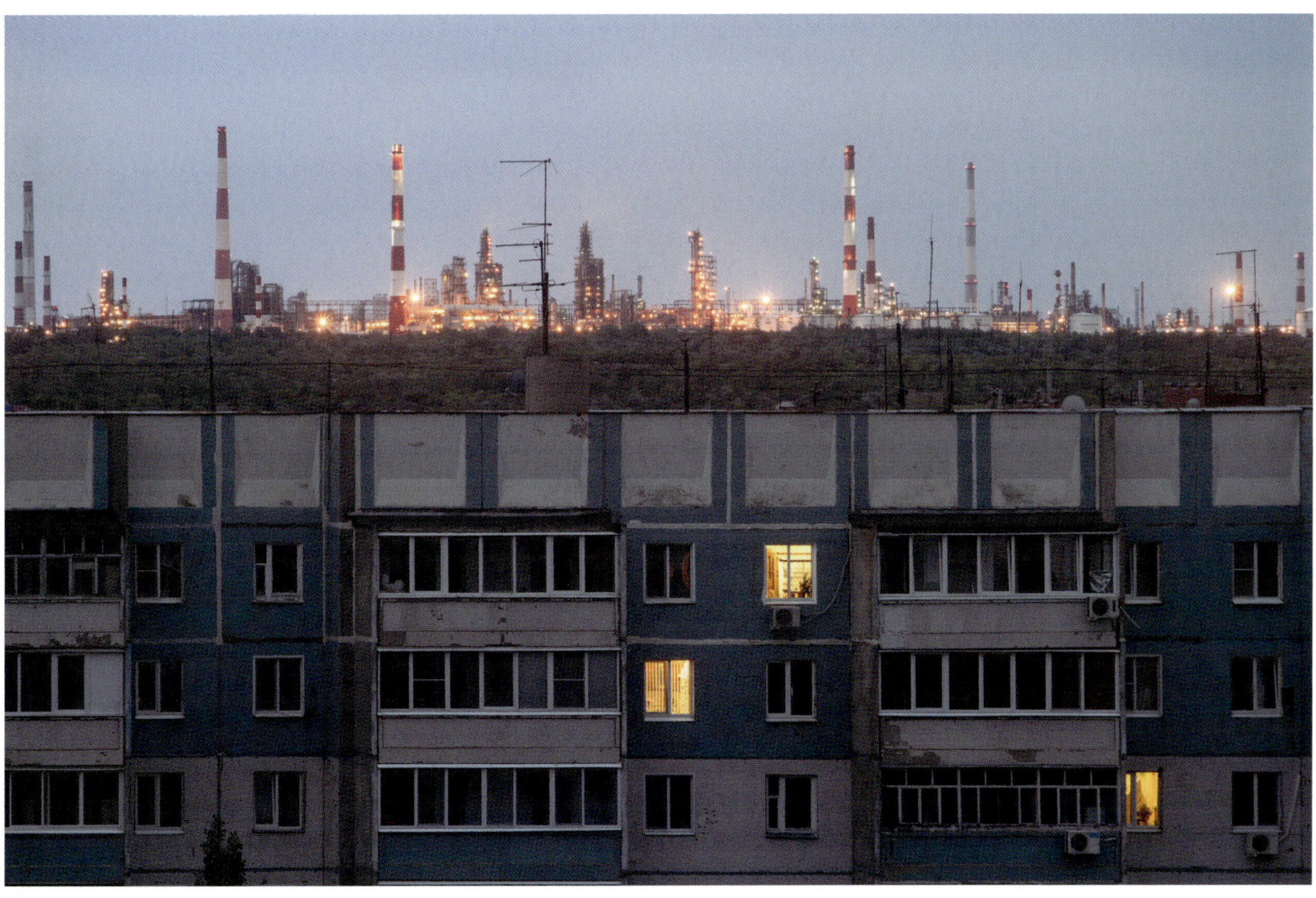

Oil Refinery
SYZRAN, RUSSIA

In 1939, work began on the construction of an oil refinery with a capacity of one million tonnes a year. The plant served local oil fields and benefitted from good transportation links, being located on a major waterway and at a railway junction. It was fully operational by 1942.

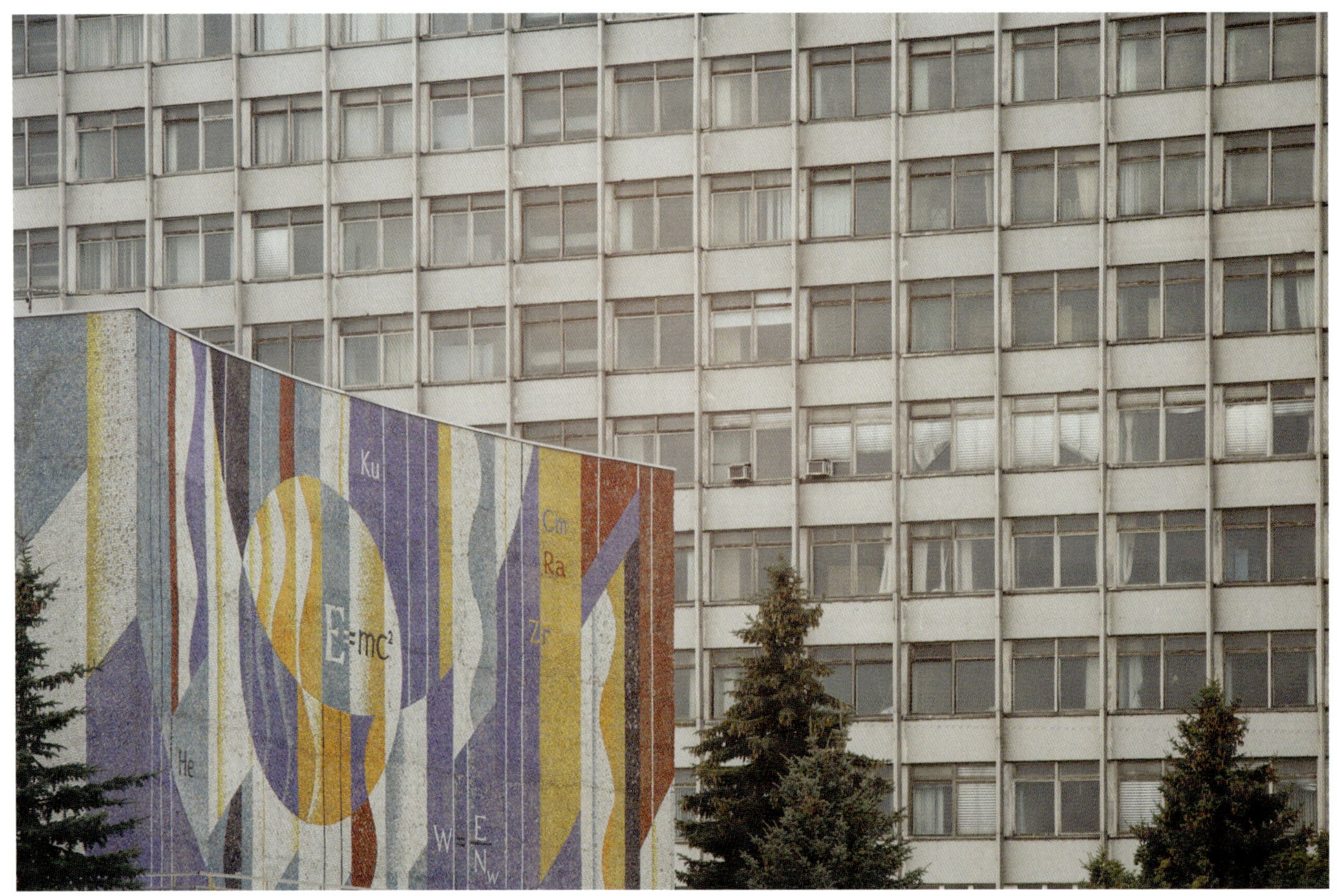

Mosaic at Signal Instrument Plant
OBNINSK, RUSSIA
Built in the 1970s

Obninsk is famous as the location of the first experimental nuclear power plant in 1954, and the city is still centred on the nuclear industry today. This building is part of the Rosatom company, producing radiochemical and nuclear power-plant equipment.

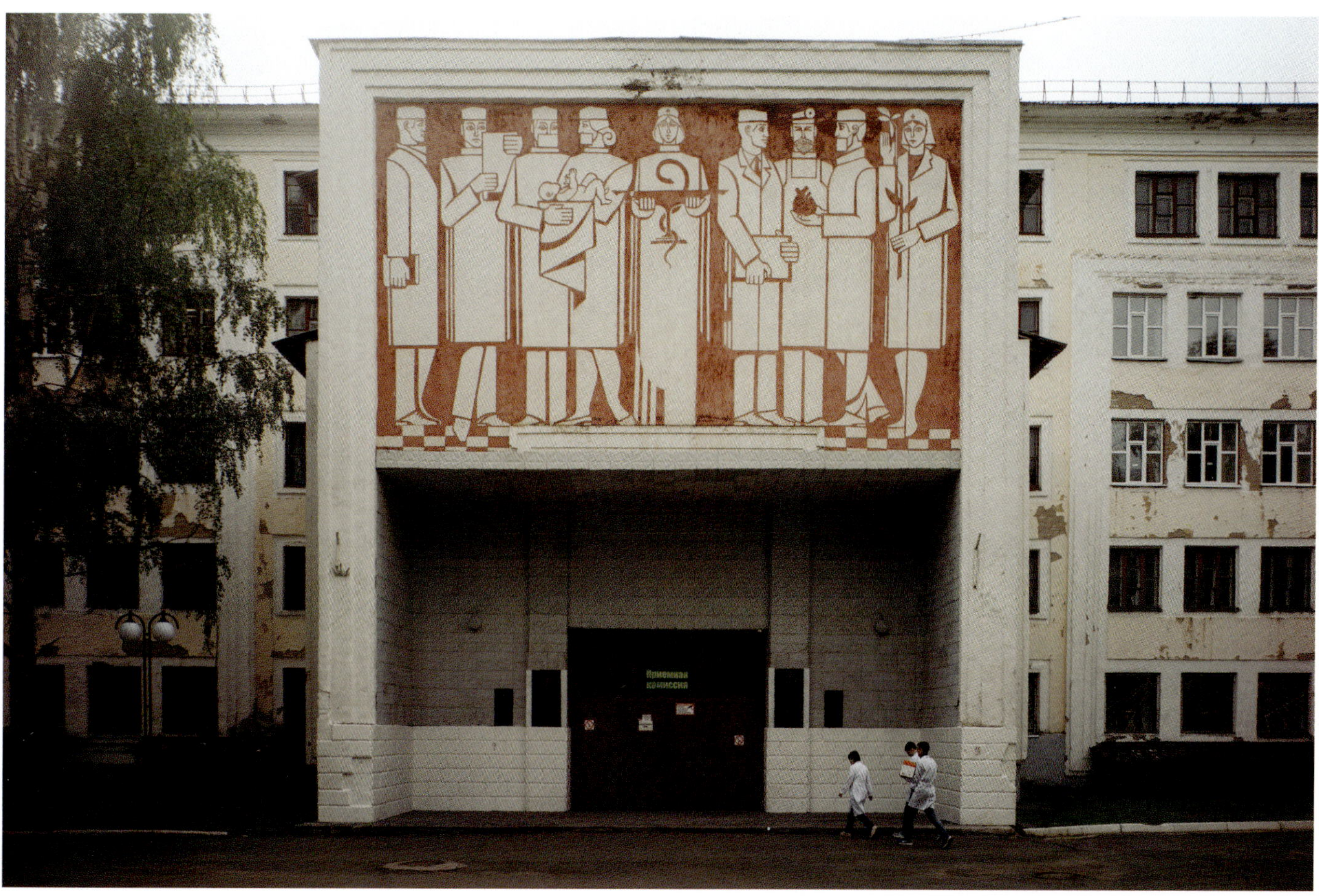

State Medical Academy
IZHEVSK, RUSSIA
Built in the 1960s

The panel above the entrance is decorated with a spectacular sgraffito mural depicting various medical specialists: cardiologists, obstetrician-gynecologists and otorhinolaryngologists. The central figure holds a snake wrapped around a bowl, the symbol of the medical profession.

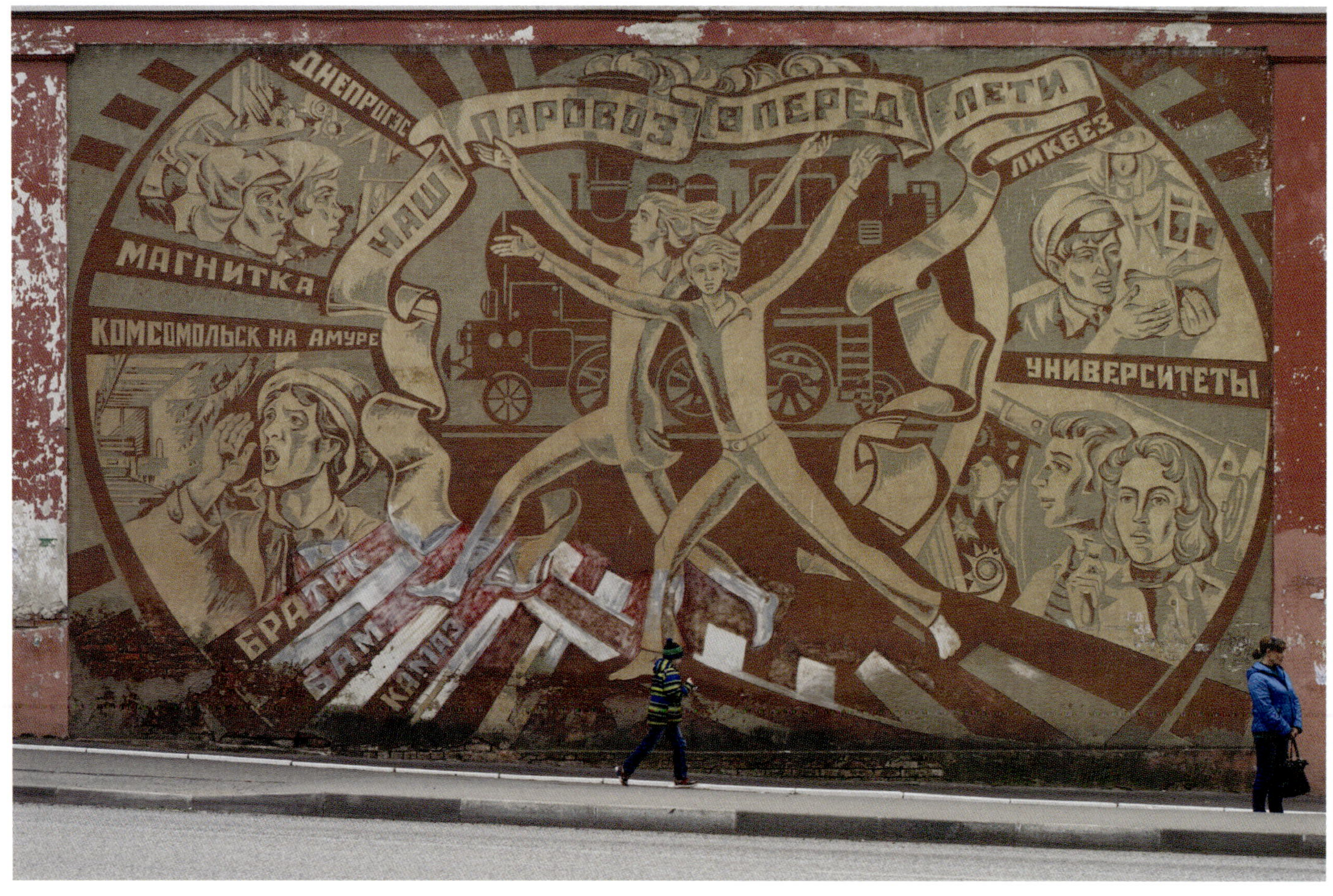

'Our steam train, fly forward!', School No.48
IZHEVSK, RUSSIA
Created in the 1980s
Designers: G. Repin, S. Kuzmin and B. Postnikov

This wall-panel mural uses the technique of sgraffito to glorify Soviet 'construction sites of the century', such as the Kamskiy Avtomobilny Zavod (KAMAZ auto factory), Baikal-Amur Mainline (BAM), Magnitogorsk, Dnepro Hydroelectric Power Plant, and so on.

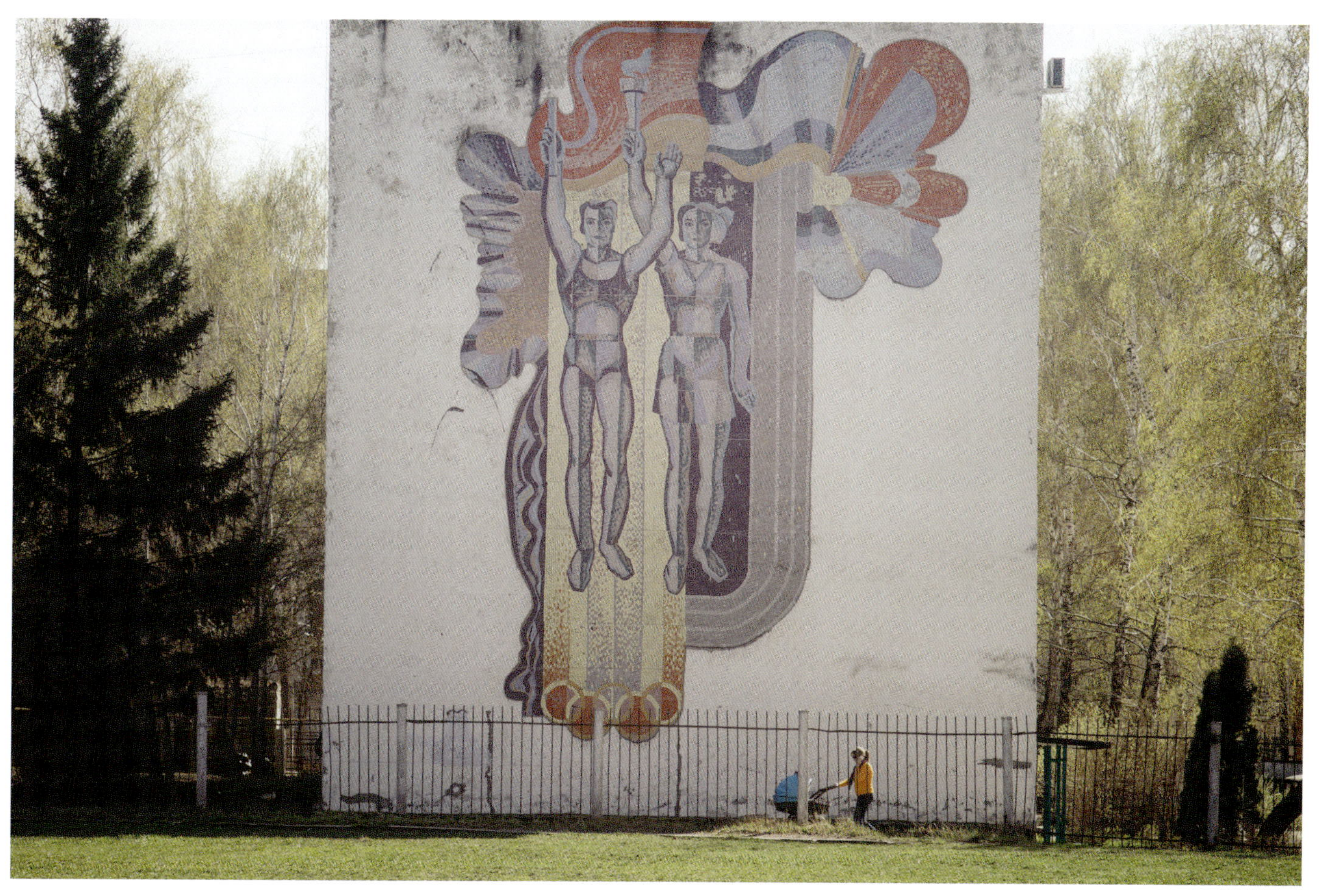

Moscow Olympic Games mosaic
Stadium of the Military-Technical School
ULYANOVSK, RUSSIA
Created in the late 1970s

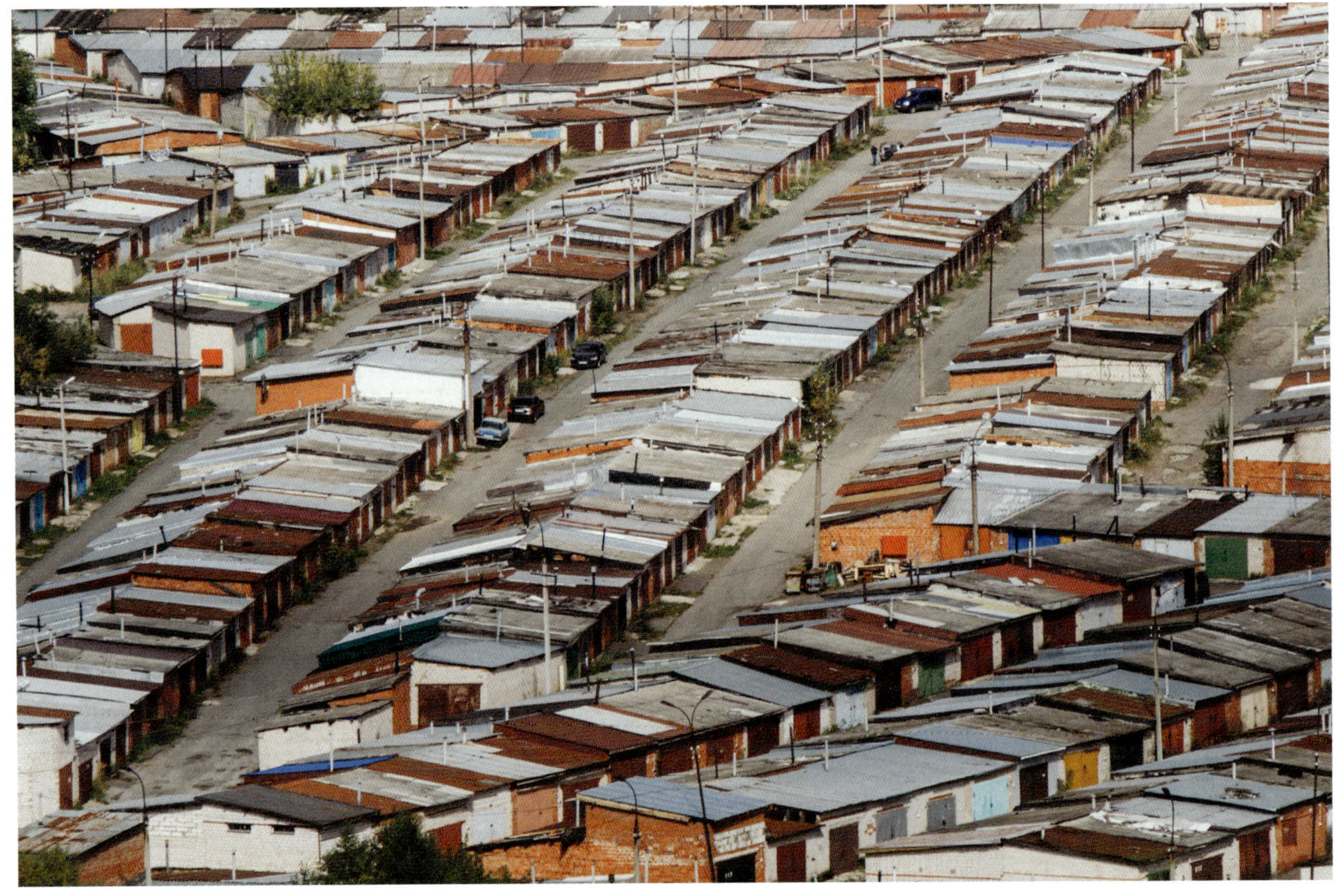

Luch garage area
IZHEVSK, RUSSIA

In the Soviet era, a garage meant much more than car storage. Often used as workshops to repair household items, they were also where men would drink, eat and socialise. Even those who did not own a car or motorcycle tried to obtain a garage as a place for escape.

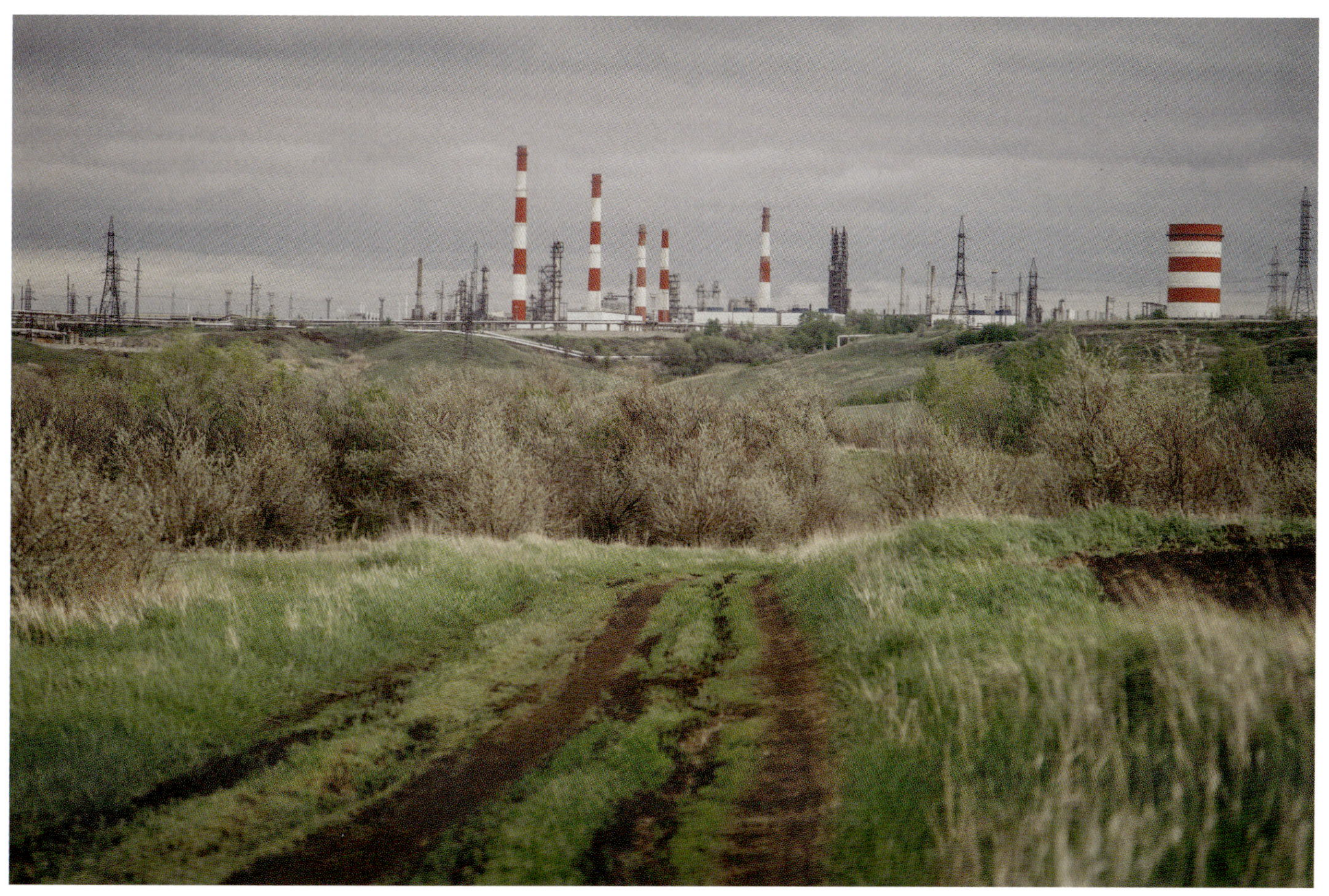

Oil Refinery
SYZRAN, RUSSIA
(see page 103)

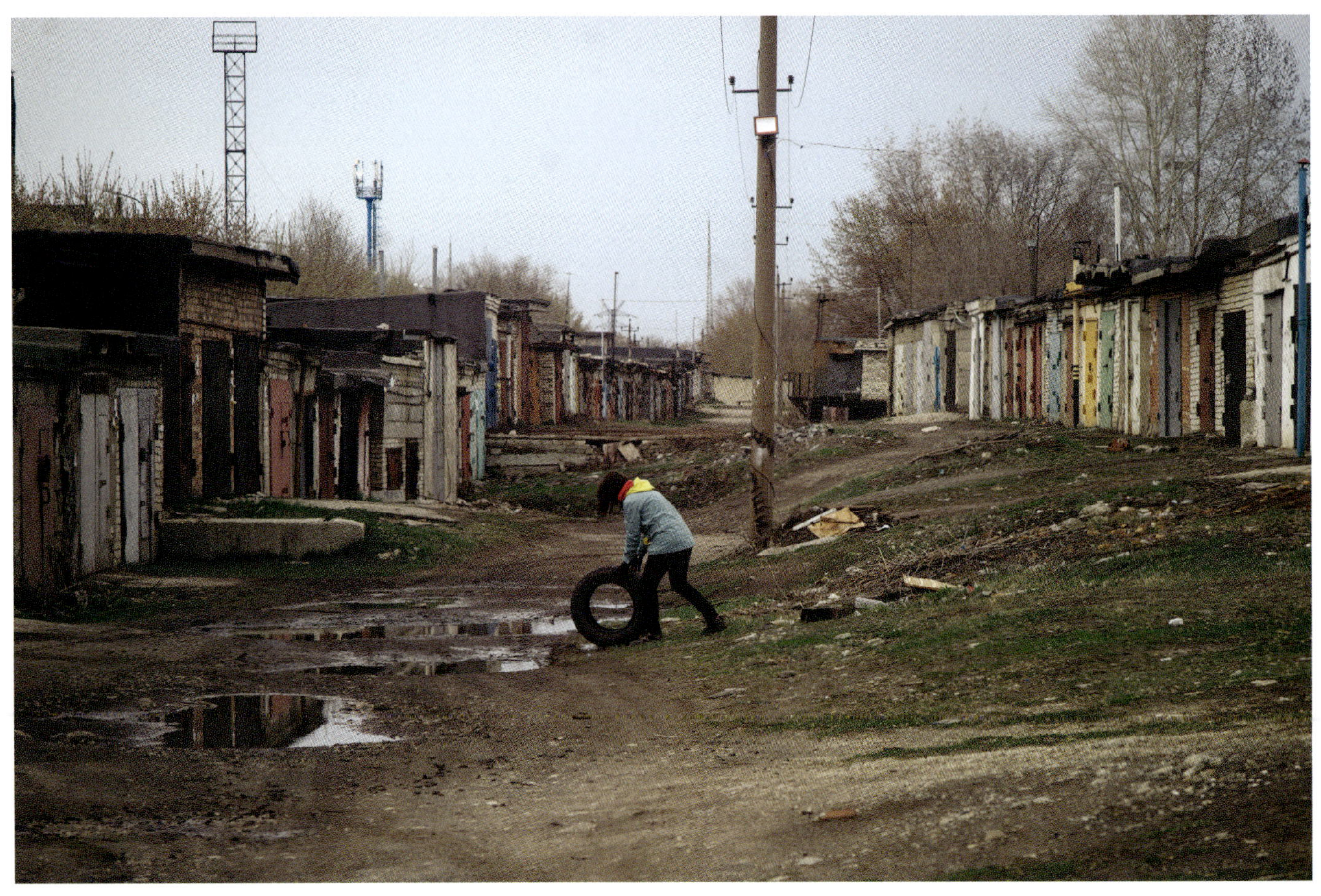

GSK-412 garage area
Kuybushevskiy District
SAMARA, RUSSIA

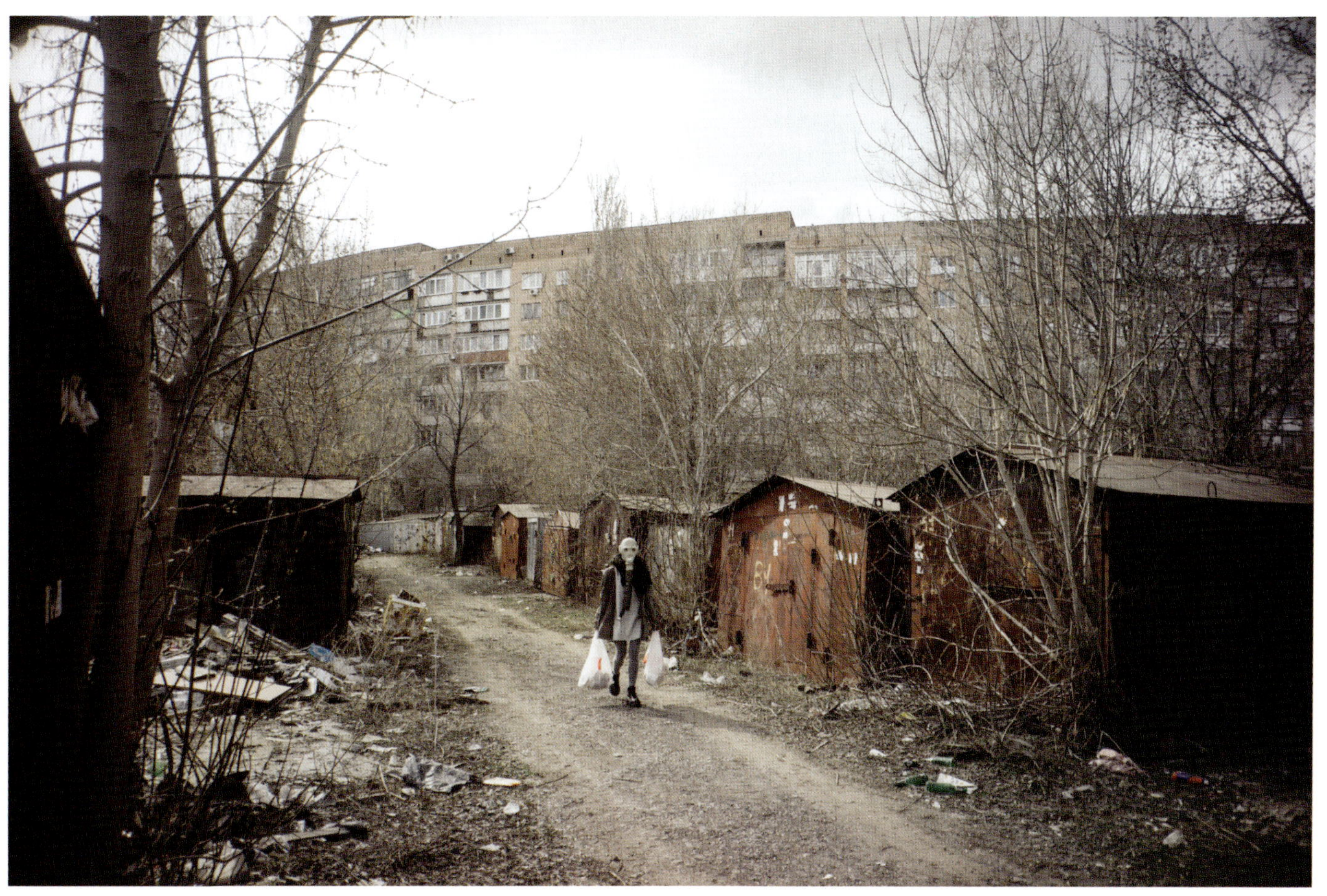

During the coronavirus pandemic
Michurinsky garage area
SAMARA, RUSSIA

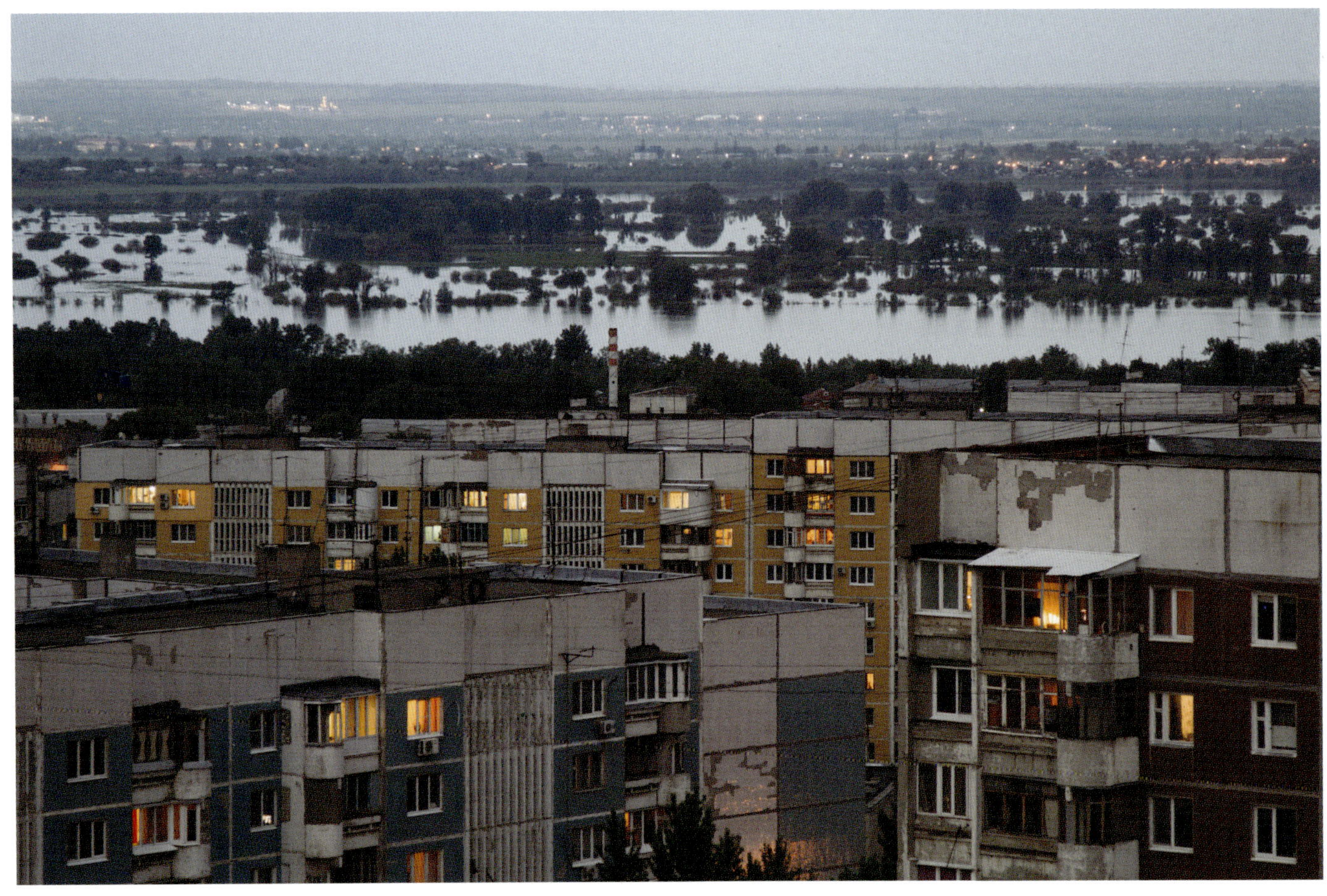

Samarka river, spring flood
Zheleznodorozhny District
SAMARA, RUSSIA

Each spring, melting snow produces a significant rise in river water levels. On the Volga, safe levels are maintained by a system of large hydroelectric power plants that open their floodgates to prevent the rivers overflowing their banks.

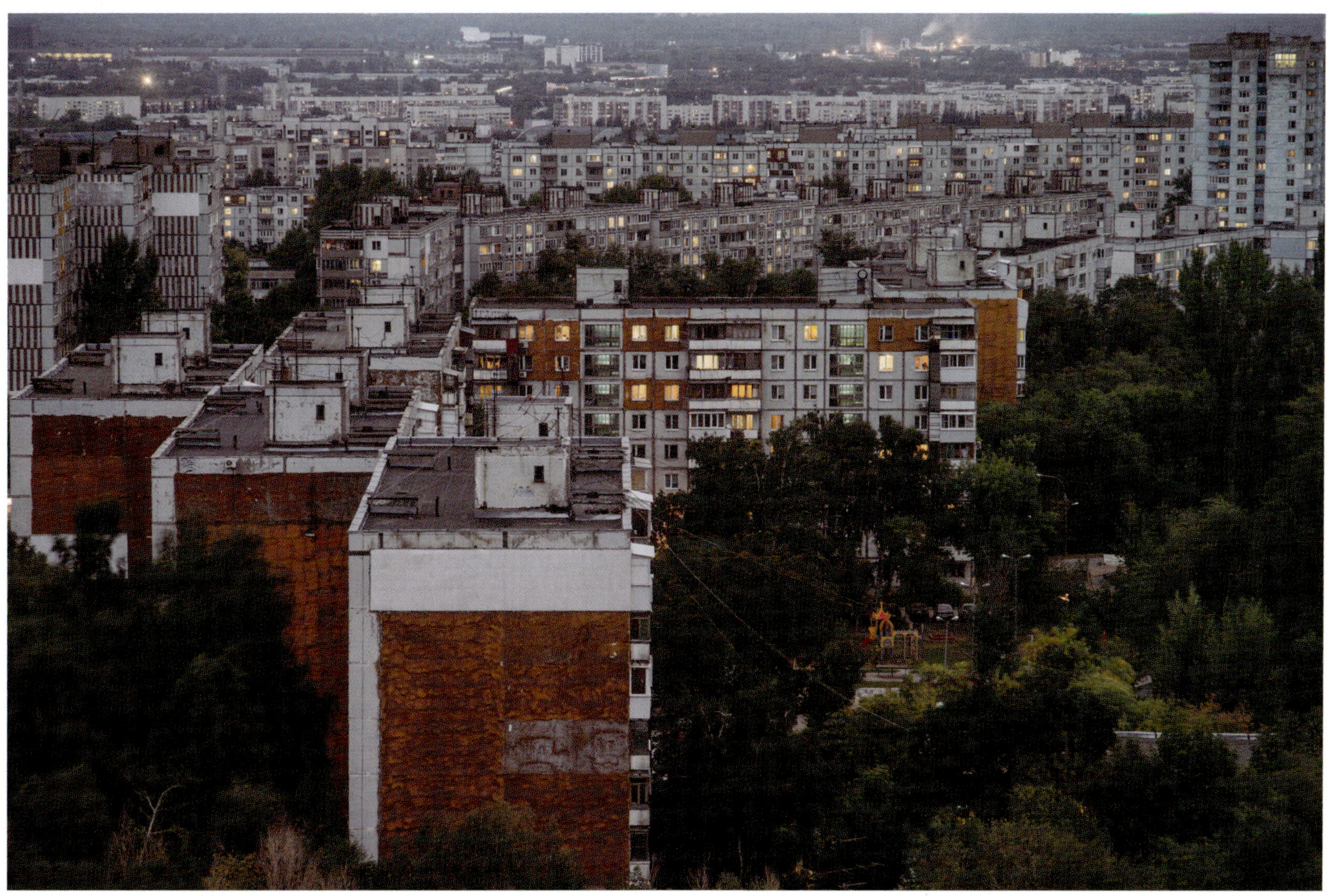

14th Microdistrict
SAMARA, RUSSIA
Built in the 1970s

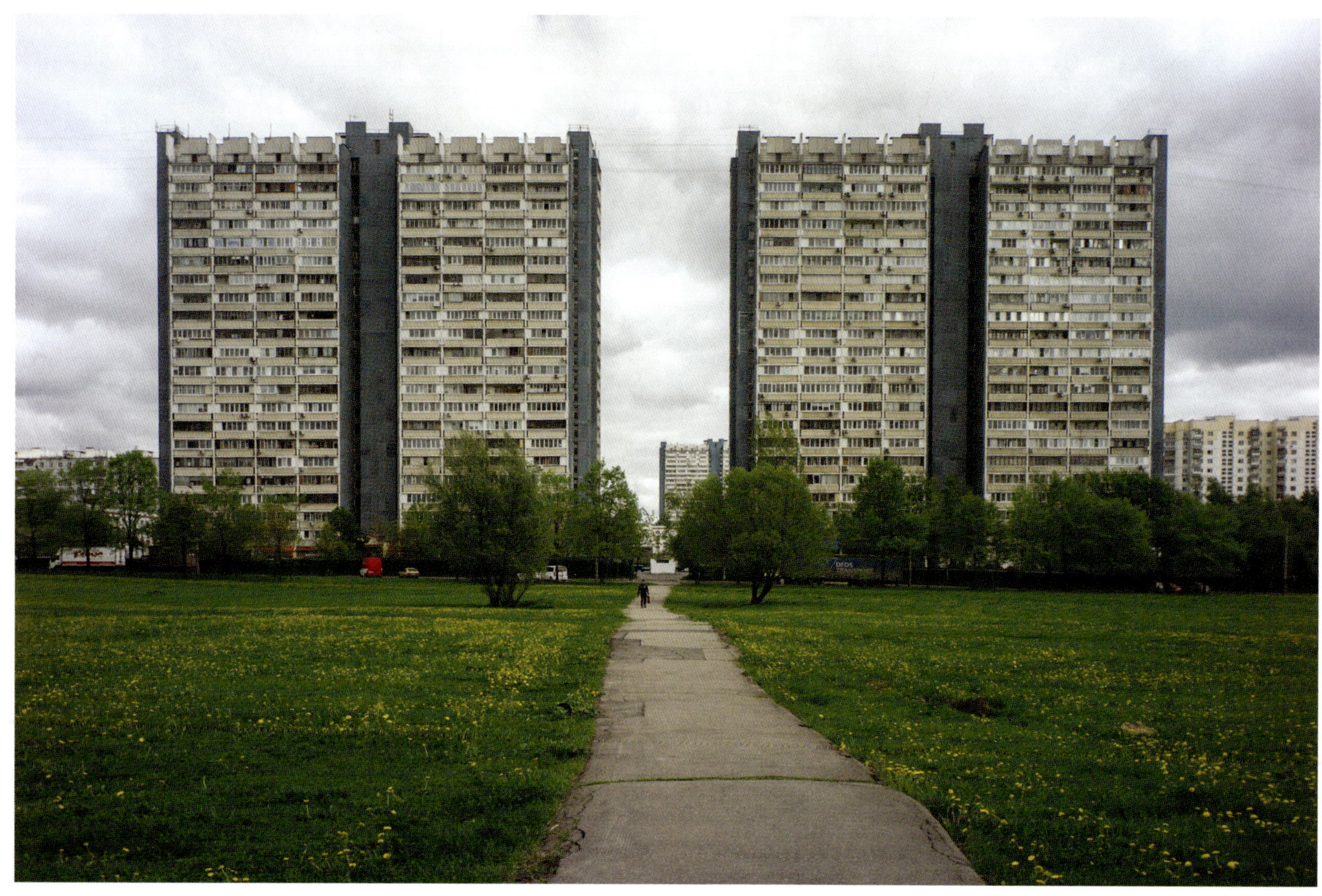

II-68/22-2 Yasenevo Towers
MOSCOW, RUSSIA
Built between 1982 and 1988
Architect: Y. Belopolsky

The completion of the Moscow Ring Road incorporated outlying districts into the city. In the mid-1970s, mass housing and social facilities were built in these areas. The Yasenevsky Microdistricts are some of the finest examples of urban planning on the outskirts of the capital.

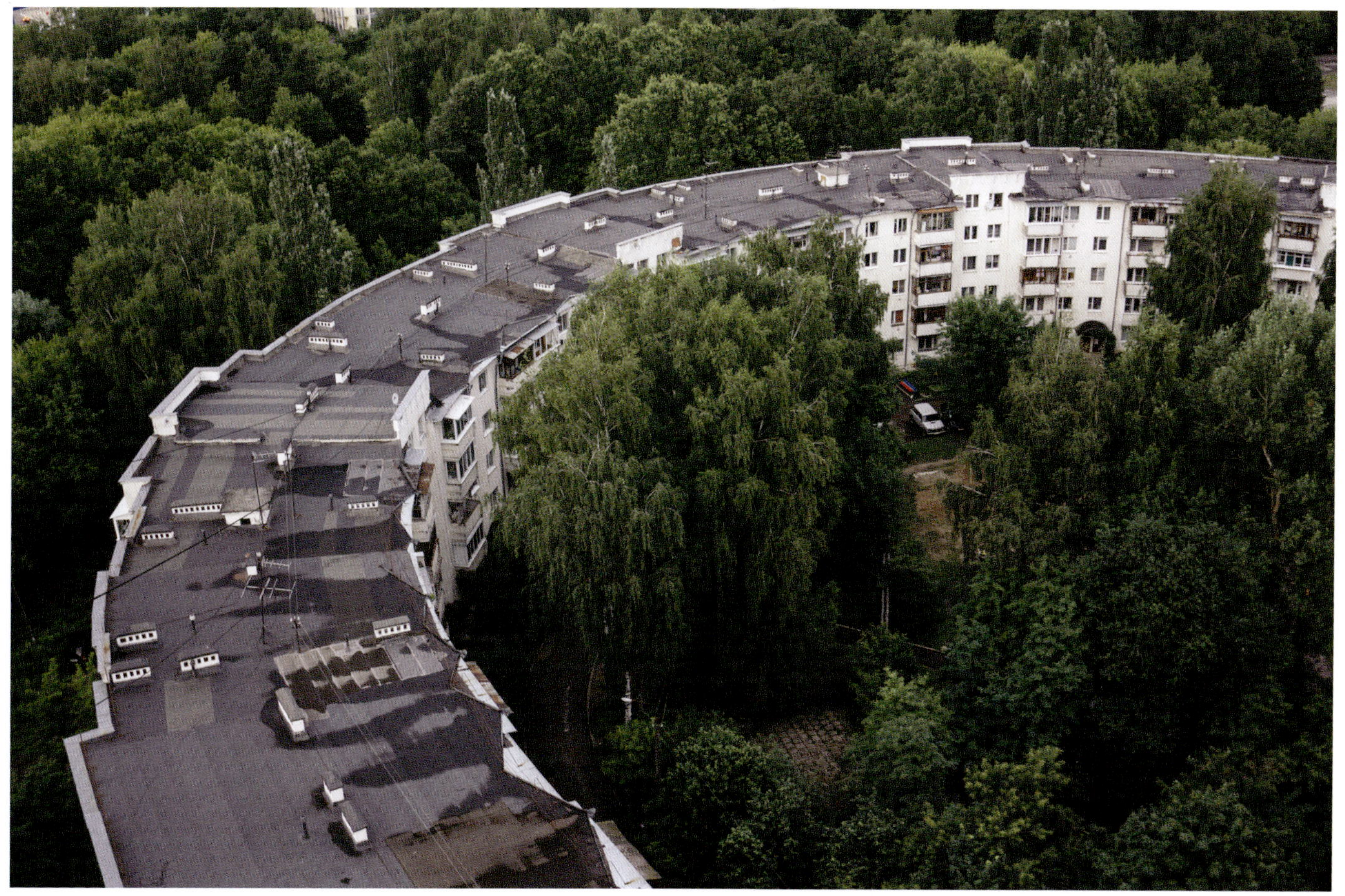

Horseshoe Building
Dobroye District
VLADIMIR, RUSSIA
Built in 1979

The first Khrushchev buildings were erected here in the 1960s and the first 9-storey building in 1973. Designed for 100,000 inhabitants, the district included schools, kindergartens, a library, hospital, cinema, communications centre and a culture and leisure park.

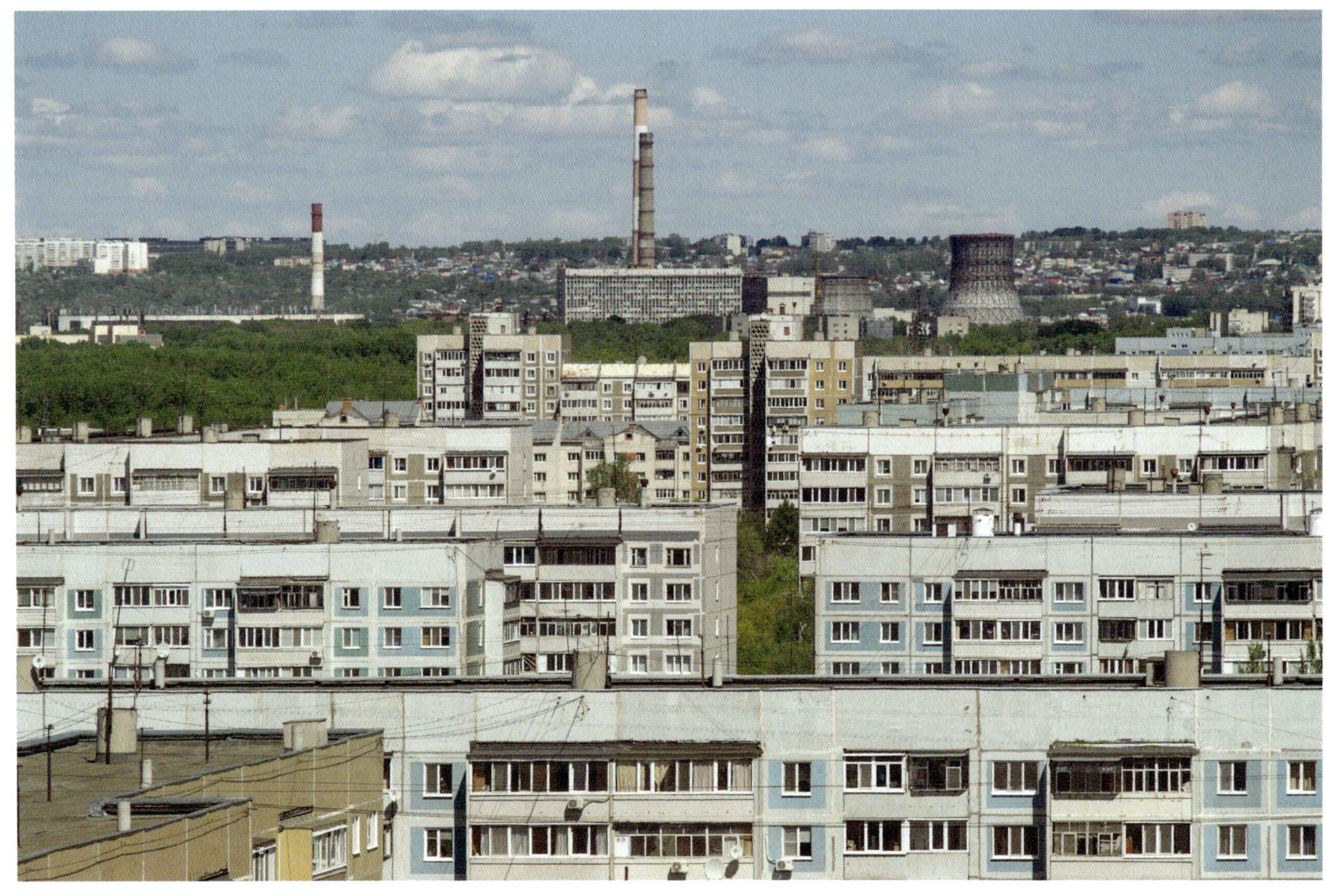

2nd Microdistrict UZTS
ULYANOVSK, RUSSIA
Built in the 1960s

This residential area is named after the UZTS (Ulyanovsk Plant of Heavy and Unique Machines) and was built to house its workers. The plant produced machines requiring foundations. It was closed following the collapse of the USSR.

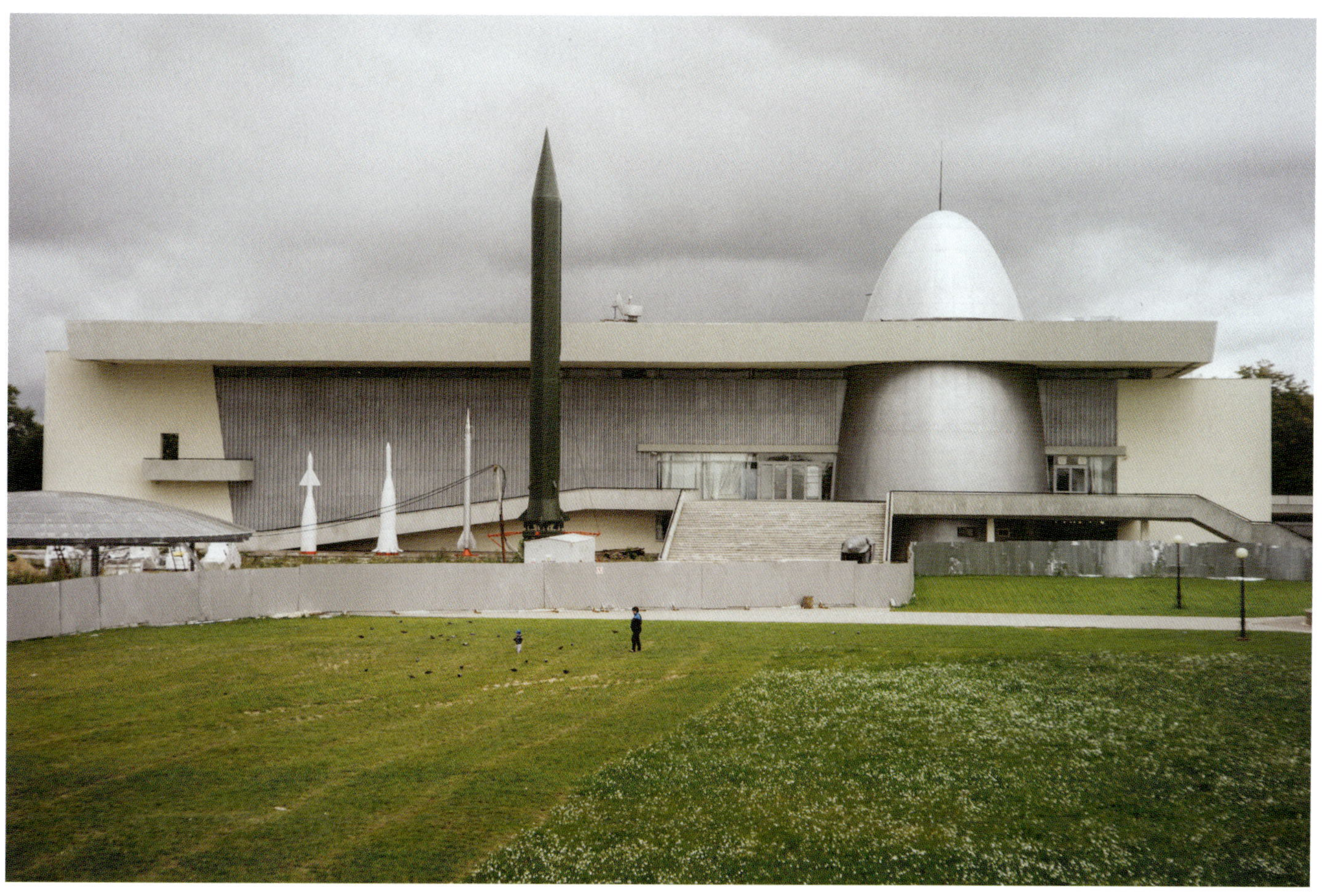

Tsiolkovsky Museum of the History of Cosmonautics
KALUGA, RUSSIA
Built in 1967
Architects: B. Barkhin, E. Kireev, N. Orlova

The museum presents the national history of cosmonautics, from the first artificial earth satellite to modern long-term orbital stations. The scientific heritage of Konstantin Eduardovich Tsiolkovsky, founder of theoretical cosmonautics, is exhibited in detail.

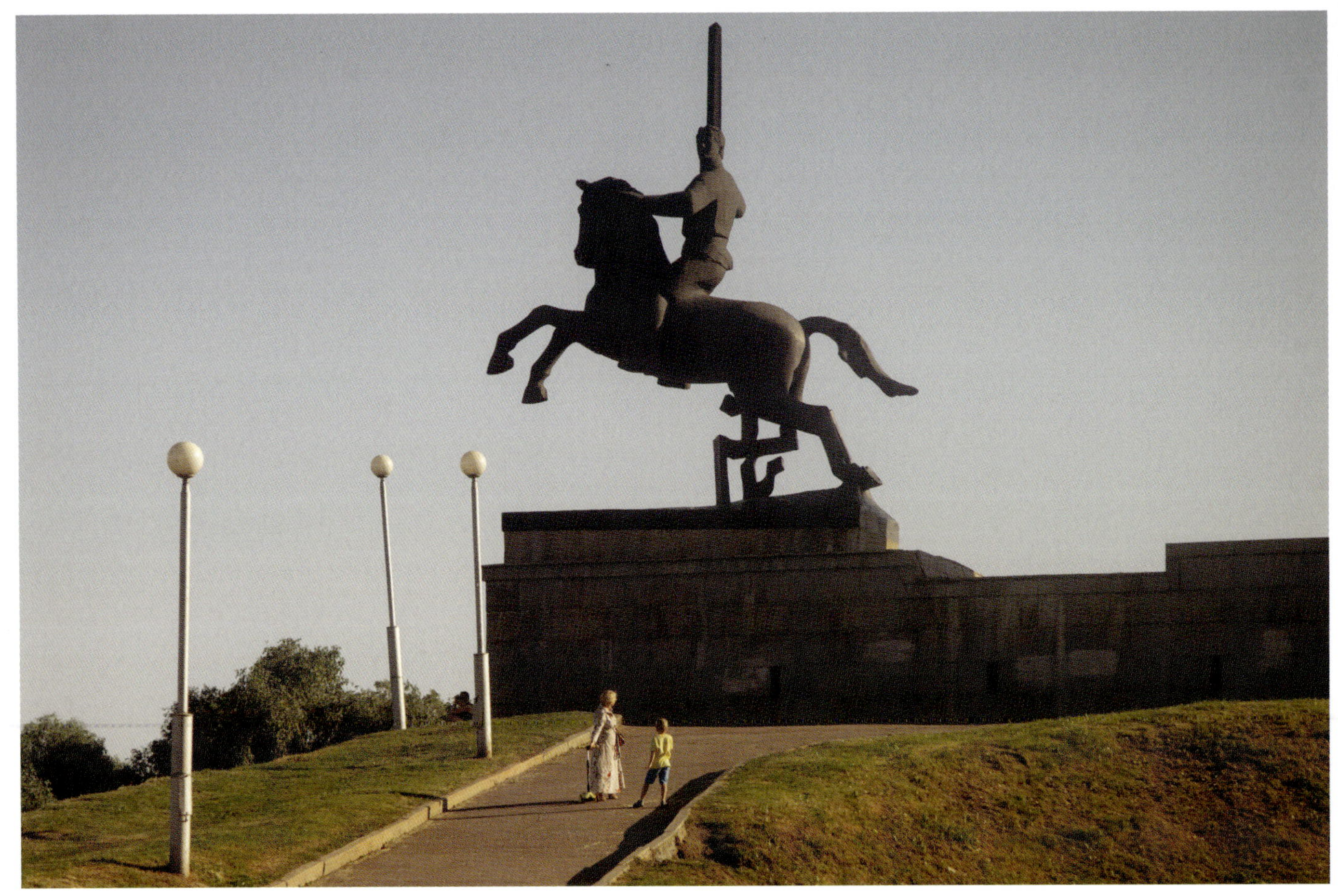

Victory Monument
VELIKY NOVGOROD, RUSSIA
Erected in 1974
Designers: G. Neroda, A. Dushkin

The monument was inaugurated on 20 January 1974, the 30th anniversary of the liberation of Novgorod from the Nazi occupation. The monument is intended to represent the great power of the Soviet state and the accomplishment of its people in the defeat of Germany.

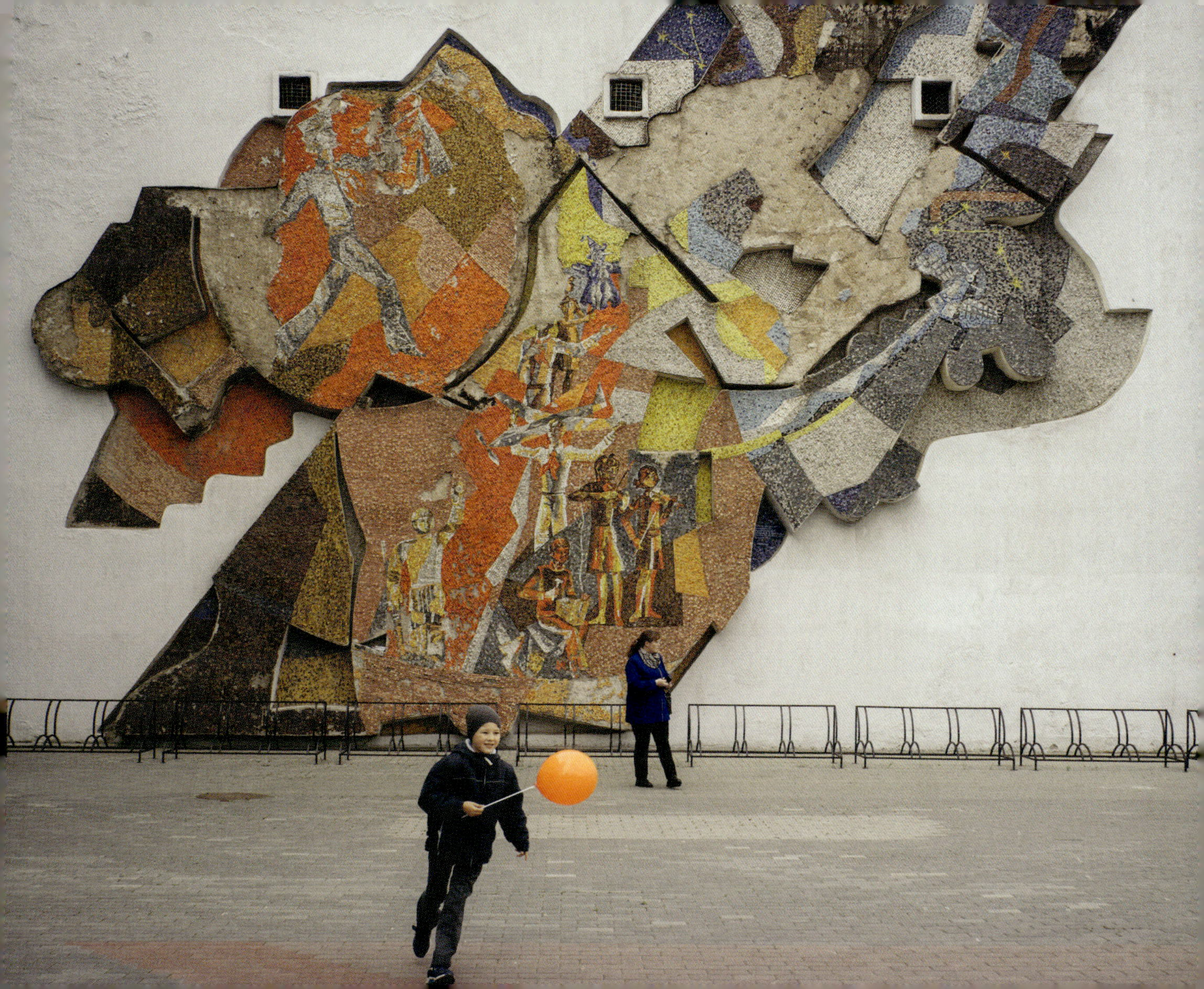

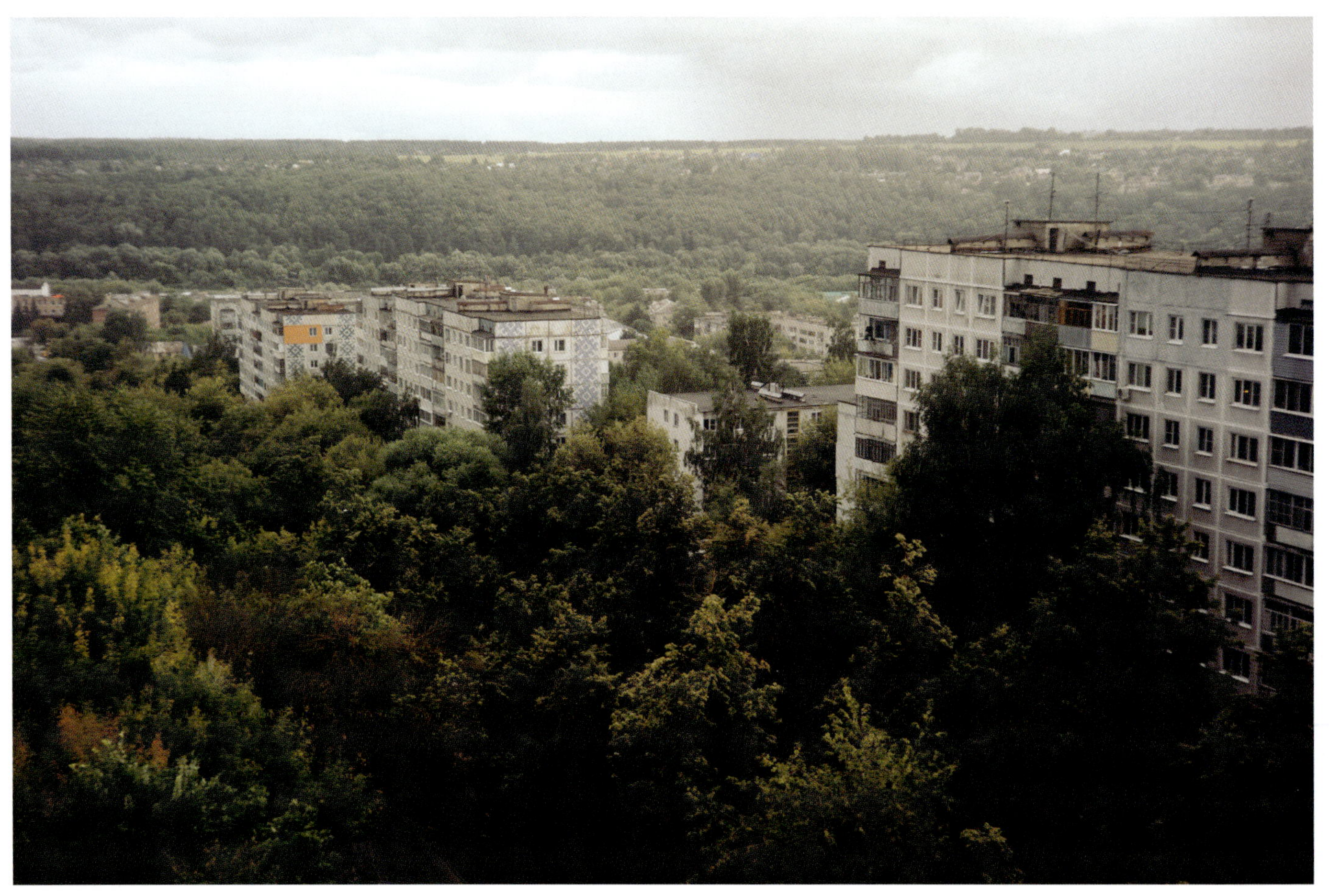

9-storey buildings, Stepana Razina Street
KALUGA, RUSSIA

previous page
Mosaic on the façade of the Palace of Young People's Art
IZHEVSK, RUSSIA
Created in 1981
Designer: S. Medvedev

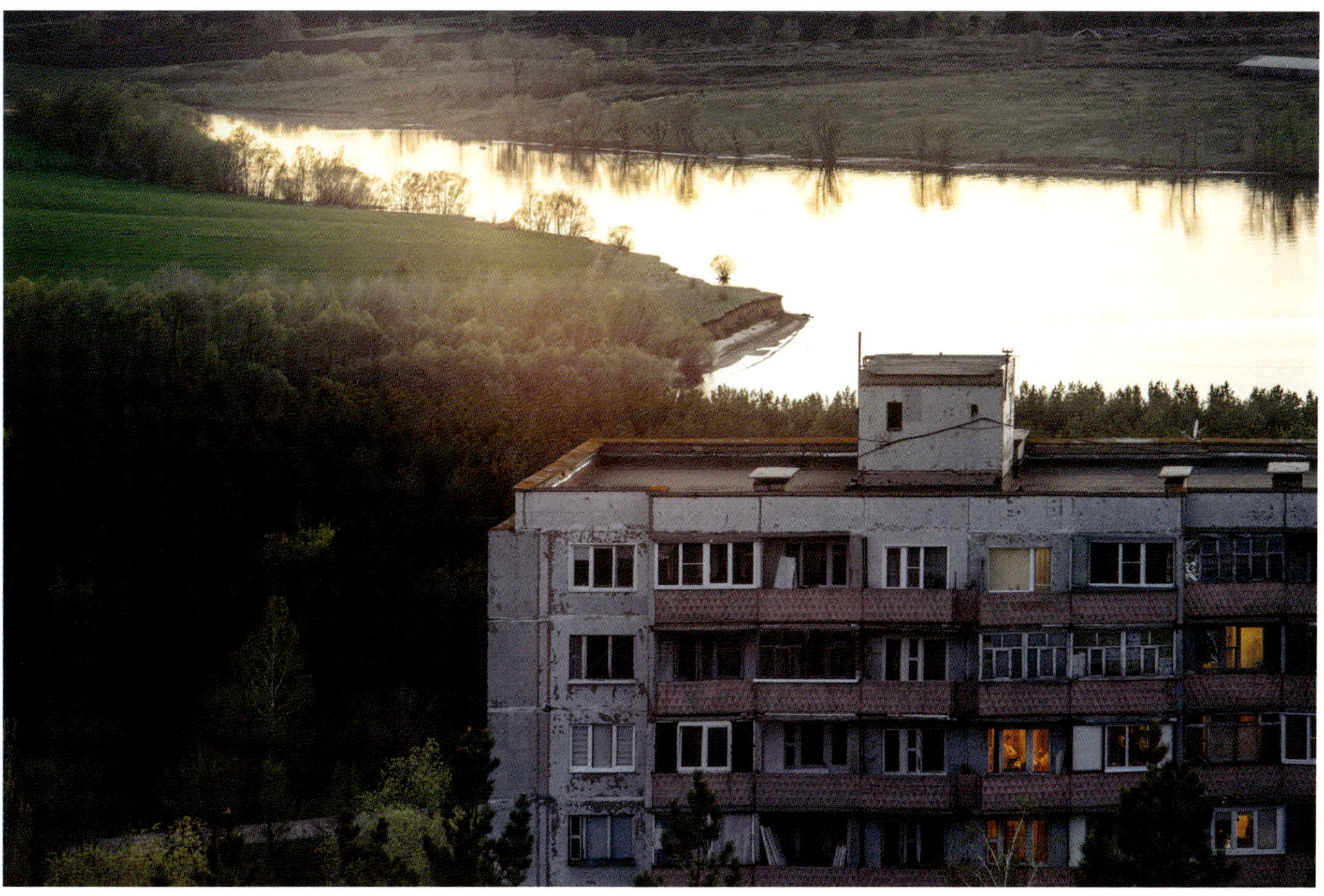

9-storey building
VOLZHSKIY UTYOS, RUSSIA
Built in the late 1970s

Standing on the banks of the Volga, Volzhskiy Utyos is a small village built for employees of the nearby sanitorium. It consists of one street, lined with 5- and 9-storey panel houses. Today it has a population of around 1,900.

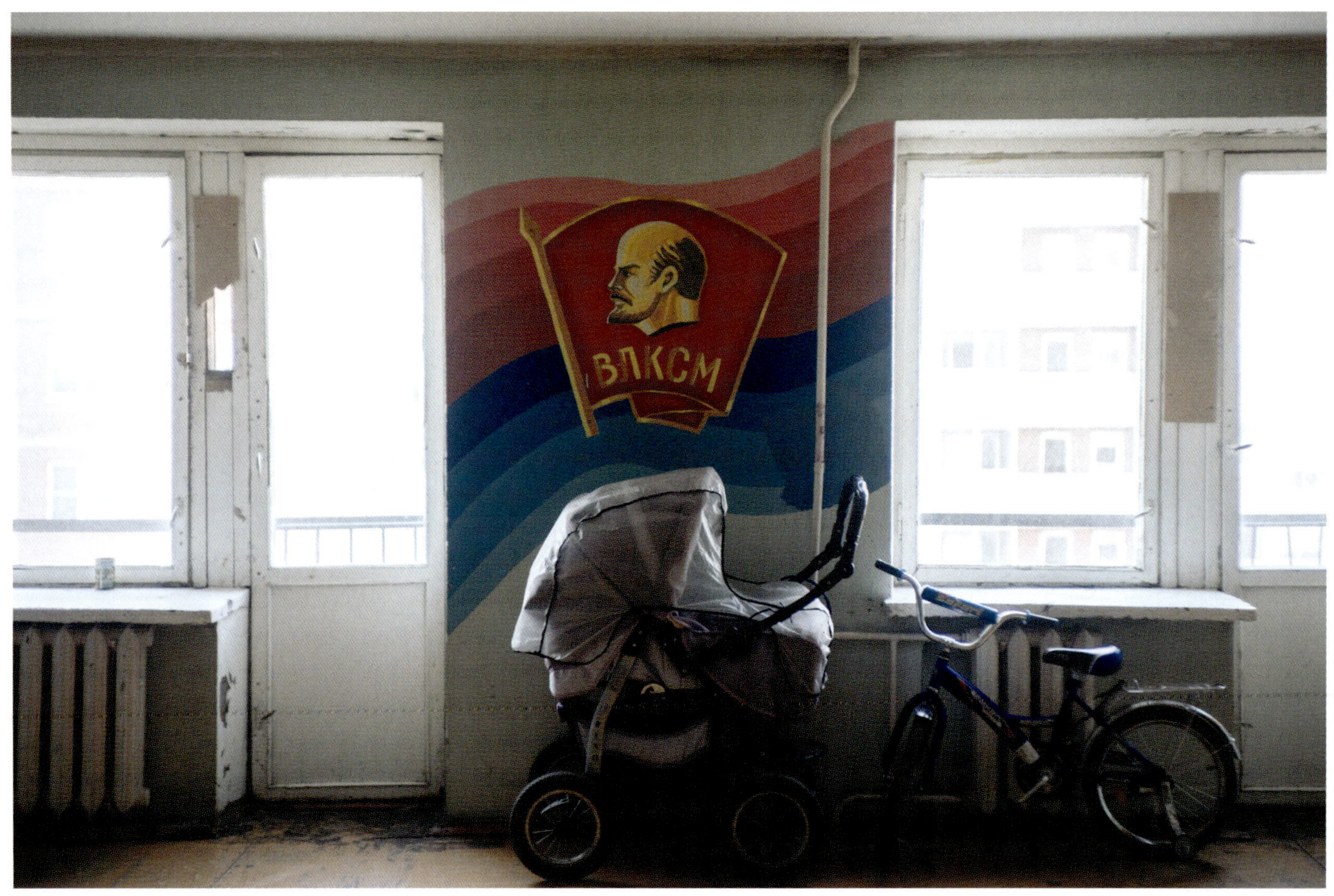

Dormitory hallway in the 4th Quarter
Avtozavodskiy District
TOGLIATTI, RUSSIA

Like many public buildings, housing block interiors were often decorated with murals created by professional artists. However, it is likely that a simple Komsomol sign such as this one was painted by a local amateur.

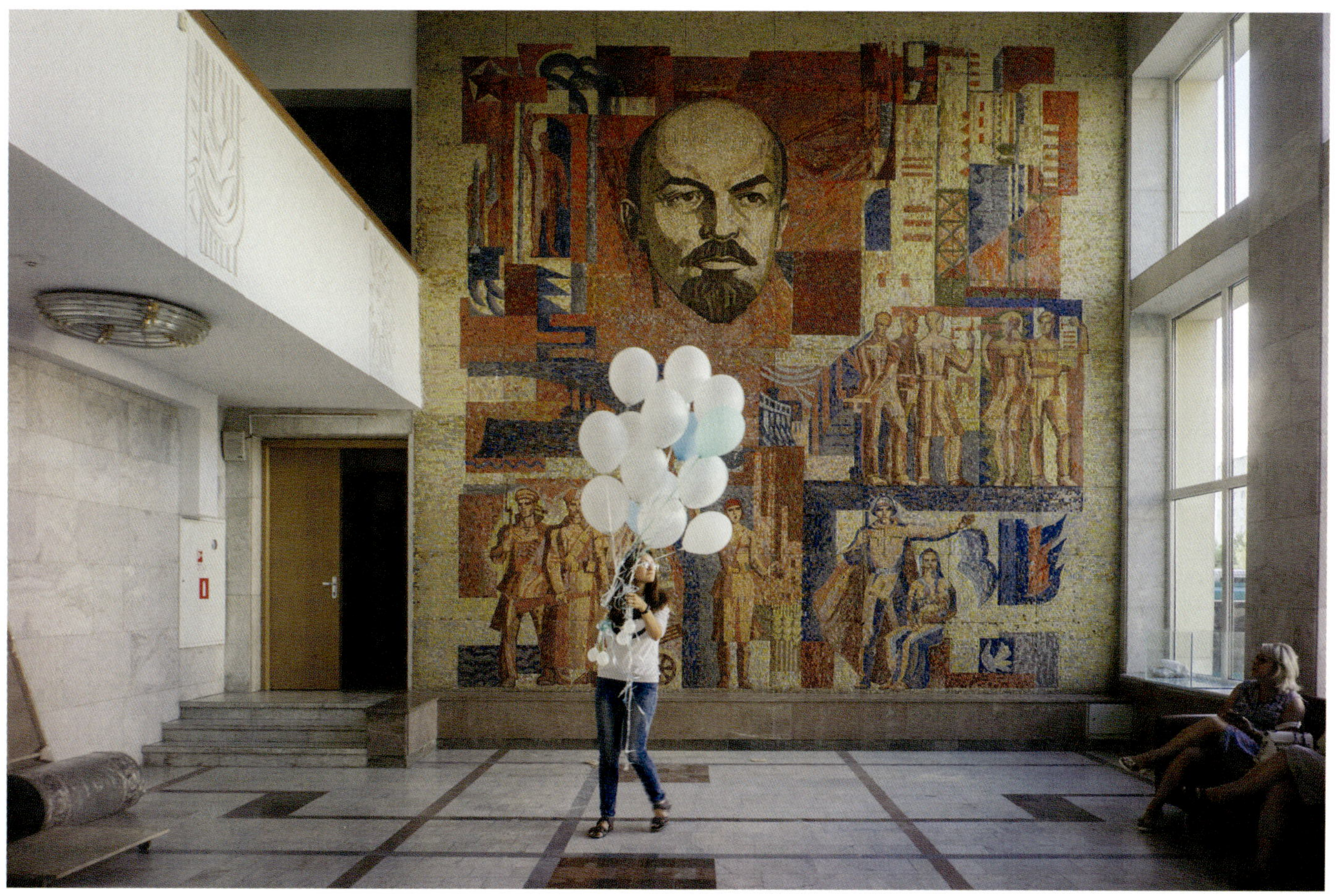

Mosaic in the interior of Oktyabr House of Culture
PODOLSK, RUSSIA
Built in 1975

Built for employees of the Podolsk Electromechanical Plant, this House of Culture was used for public events and celebrations. After the plant went bankrupt and was destroyed, the House of Culture was gifted to the city.

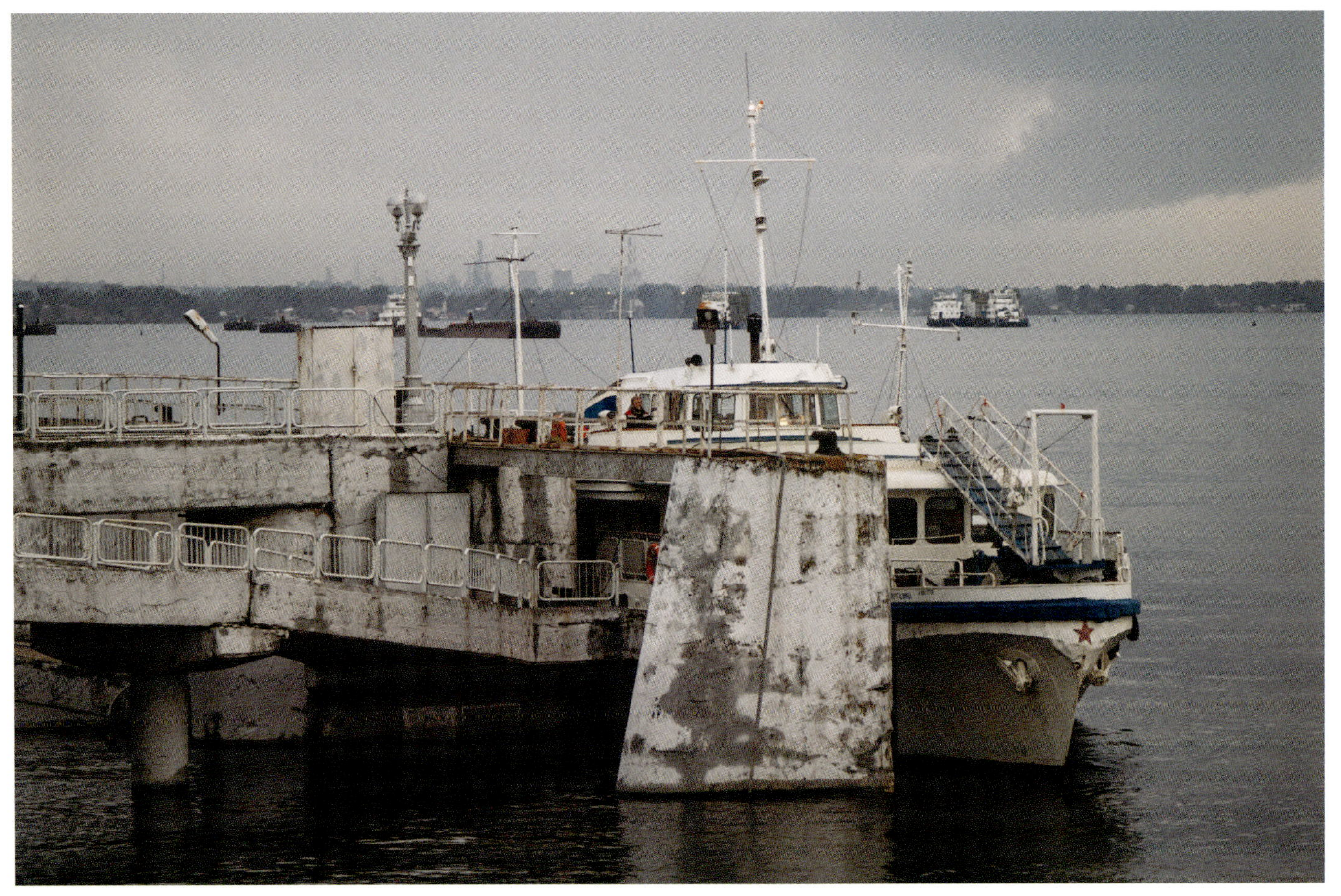

River Station Pier
SAMARA, RUSSIA
Built in 1971
Architect: Yu. Kogan

The Samara River Station is a popular stopping place for numerous tourist cruise ships that sail the Volga. There are also several routes used by passenger ferries to connect Samara with villages on the other side of the river.

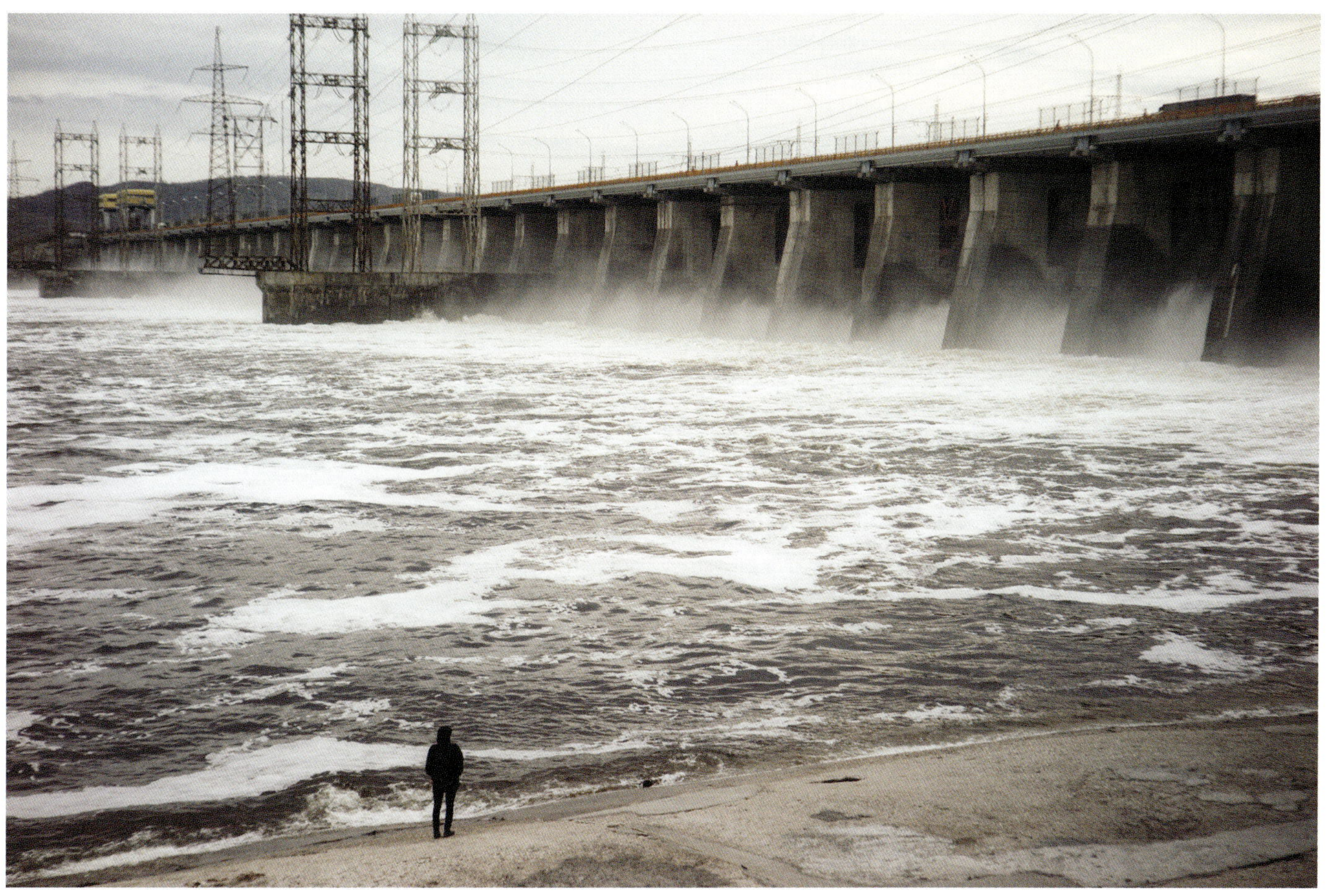

Kuibyshevskaya Hydropower Plant
SAMARA REGION, RUSSIA
Built in 1955

Zhigulyovskaya (formerly Kuibyshevskaya) Hydropower Plant, is situated on the Volga river between Zhigulyovsk and Togliatti and is part of the Volga-Kama Hydropower Plant Cascade. Between 1957 and 1960 it was the largest hydropower plant in the world.

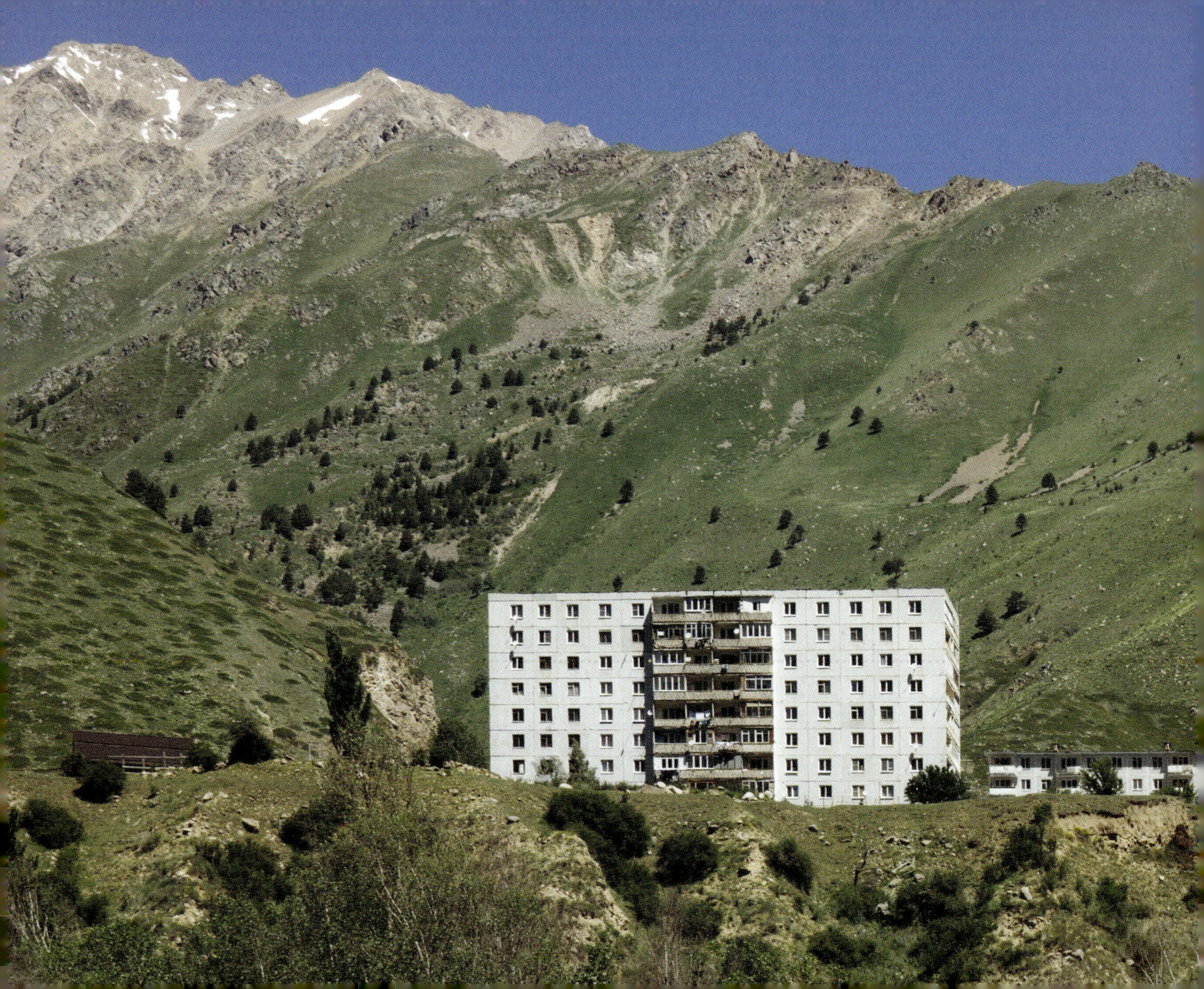

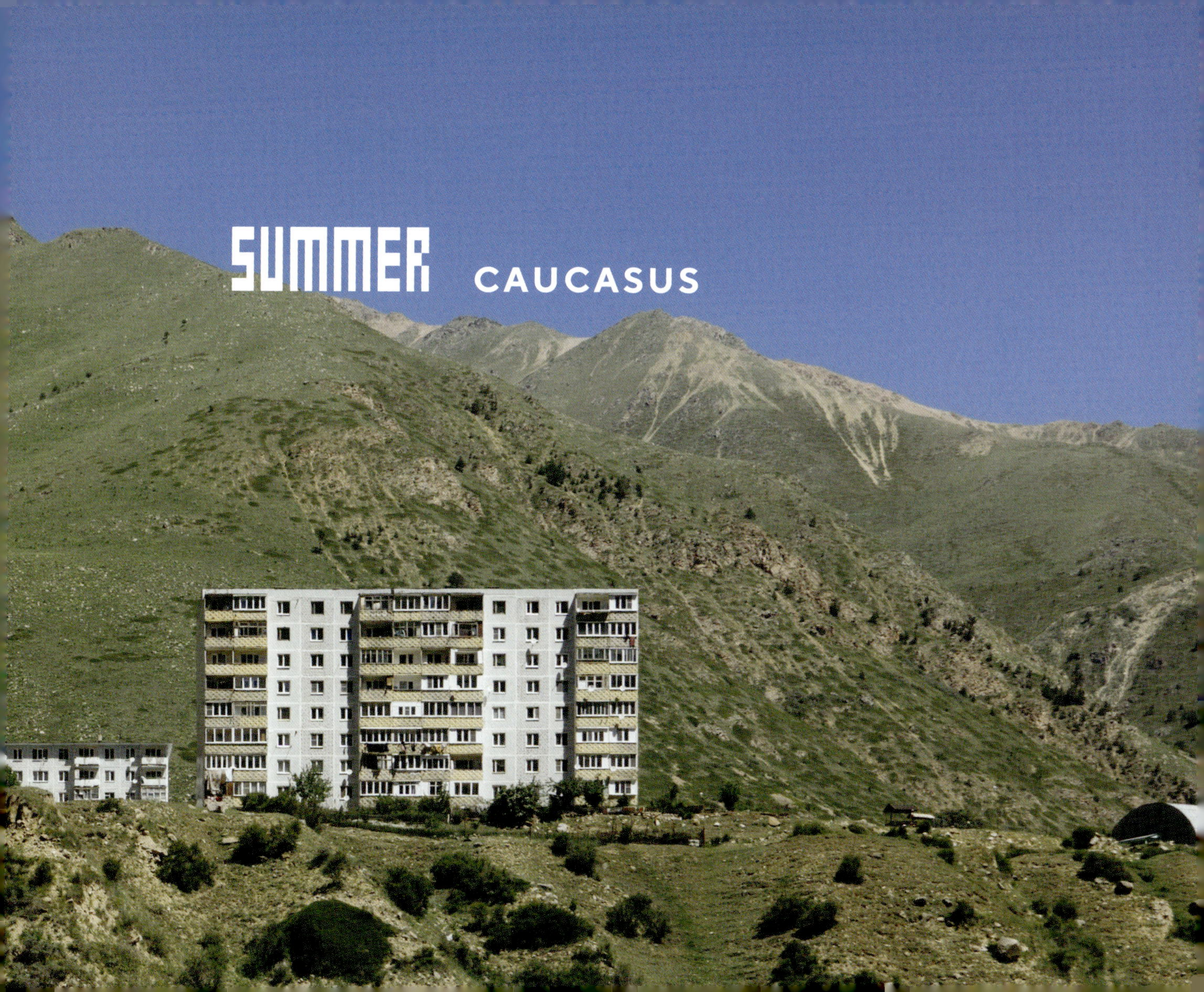

SUMMER
CAUCASUS

CAUCASUS

The snow-capped peaks of the Greater Caucasus, up to 5,000 metres high; the spurs of the Lesser Caucasus, with deep gorges along which mountain rivers rush; alpine meadows bordering eternal snow; mountain slopes covered with forests; green valleys filled with orchards and vineyards; surf rumbling and crashing with a roar on coastal cliffs: such is the nature of the Caucasus, one of the most picturesque places within our country.

A variety of natural environments can be found across a relatively small area, from arid semi-desert through lush alpine meadows to the unmelting snow of the highest ground. The characteristics of this nature are largely determined by vertical zones: climate, vegetation, crops and fauna all change according to the altitude. Nature has generously endowed the Caucasus with underground riches and resources. Fast-flowing mountain rivers deliver hydropower, with huge power plants supplying the area's towns and settlements.

Around 40 nationalities live in the densely populated North Caucasus, most of them Russians, Chechens, Ukrainians, Armenians, Ossetians, Kabardins, Dargins, Karachais, Avars, Kumyks, Lezgins and Ingush. The population is particularly diverse in the mountain regions, where different linguistic groups often share the same valley.

The Transcaucasus, which lies to the south of the Caucasus range, is made up of three national republics: Georgia, Azerbaijan and Armenia. Under our socialist system, with the brotherly help of the peoples of the USSR, this backward outpost of the Russian Empire has developed into an industrial and agricultural powerhouse.

In Georgia, heavy industry – involving energy, metallurgy, chemicals and machines – has been established. In Tkibuli and Tkvarcheli, coalmines have been reconstructed and fully mechanised and new oil and copper-ore mining enterprises created. Azerbaijan's economy was primarily built on oil extraction, petrochemicals and the production of cotton and grapes. A powerful industrial base was established in Soviet Armenia, with engineering plants in Yerevan, Kirovakan, Leninakan and other cities producing transformers, generators, small water turbines, electric meters, cables, metal-cutting machines, equipment for the food industry and much more.

In general, the economies of these three republics, which make up the single large Transcaucasian economic zone of the USSR, are developing comprehensively. There are close ties between the regions: Georgia supplies Azerbaijan and Armenia with ferrous metals, pipes, cars, textiles and tea; Azerbaijan provides Georgia with oil and oil products, gas, iron ore, cotton and tyres; Armenia supplies Georgia with copper, cable products, sulphuric acid and refractory materials.

Based on *The Great Soviet Encyclopaedia*, 1970

previous page
These blocks were built in 1977 for employees of the first neutrino observatory in the USSR, located underneath the nearby mountain.
BASKAN, RUSSIA

Gldani District
TBILISI, GEORGIA

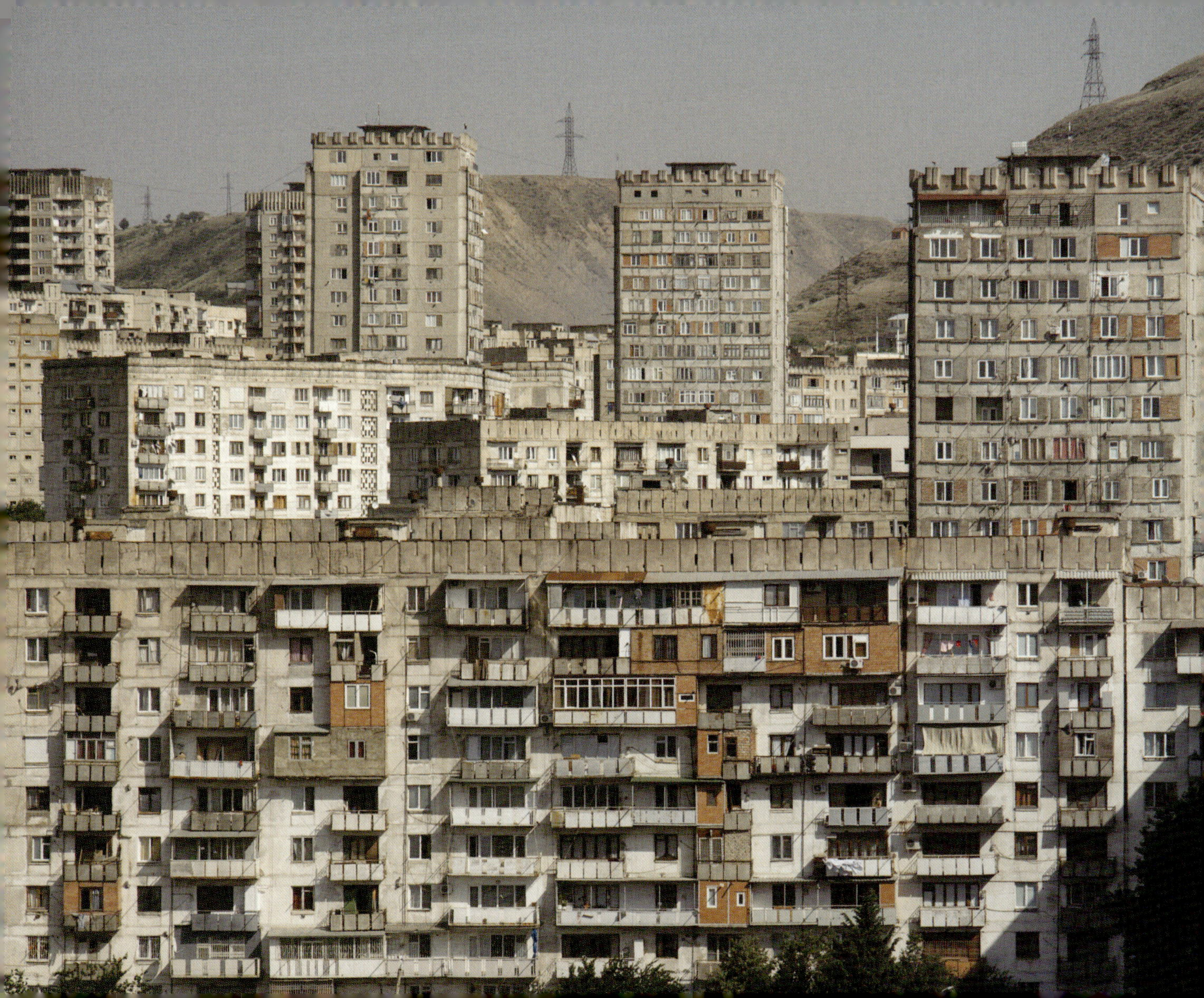

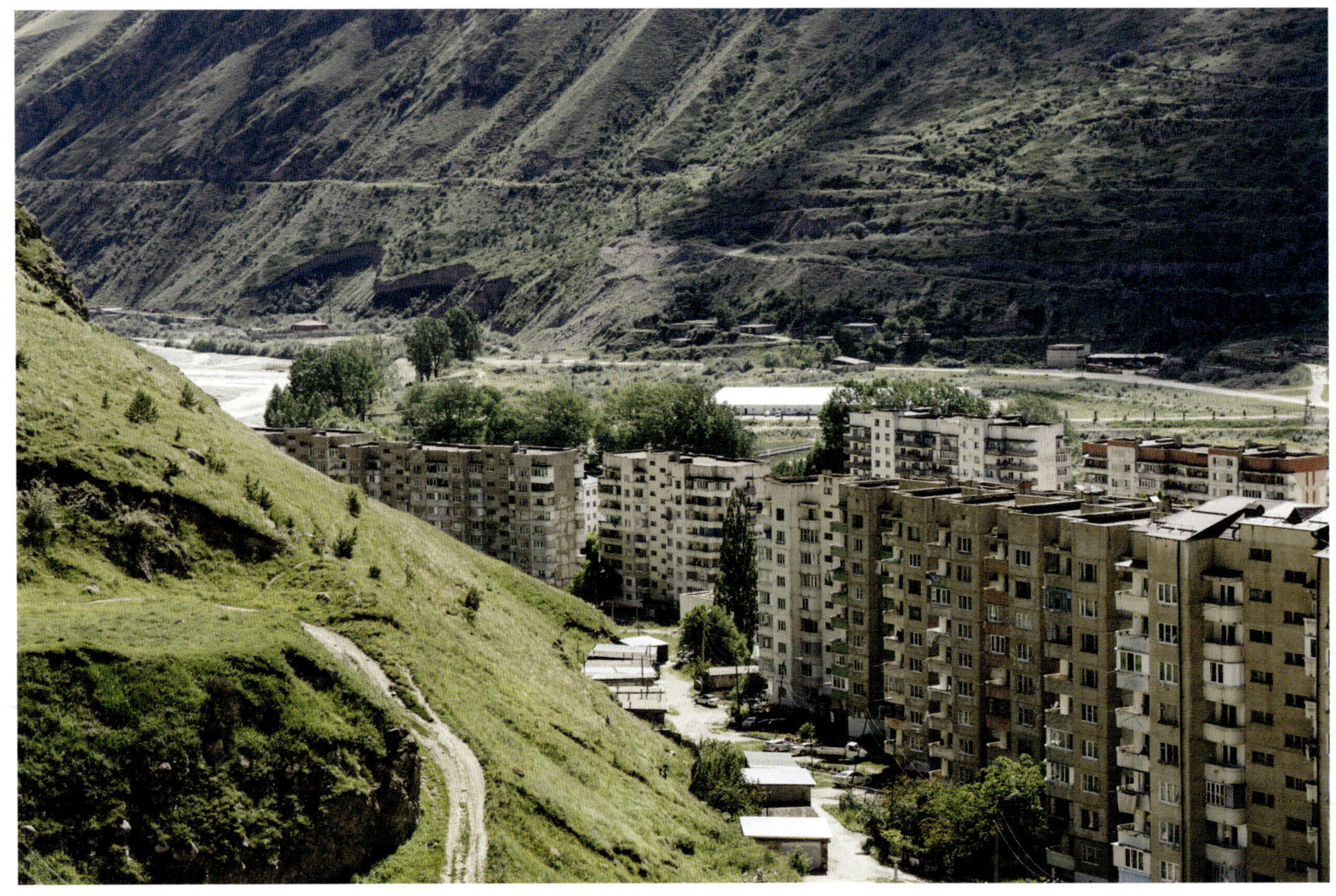

Typical 9-storey panel buildings
TYRNYAUZ, RUSSIA
Built in the 1980s

The town of Tyrnyauz is the administrative centre of the Elbrussky District of the Kabardino-Balkarian Republic. Situated in the mountainous Baksan Gorge at an altitude of more than 1,300 metres above sea level, it is one of the highest towns in Russia.

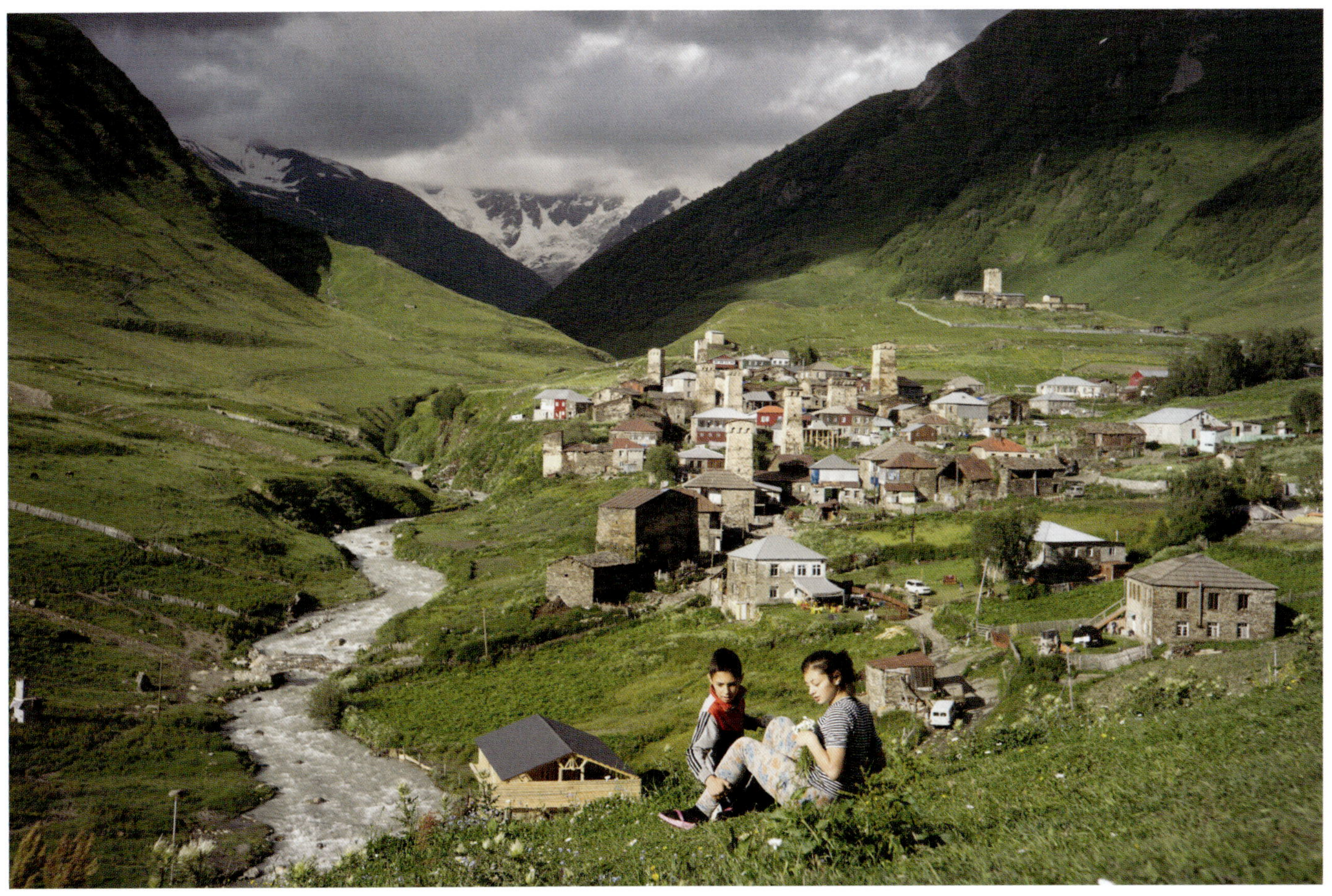

Svan tower houses
USHGULI, RUSSIA

This Svan village is located on the banks of the Inguri River. At 2,200 metres above sea level, it is the highest permanent settlement in the Caucasus. The traditional Svanetian tower houses are of considerable historical interest, and the area is a UNESCO World Heritage site.

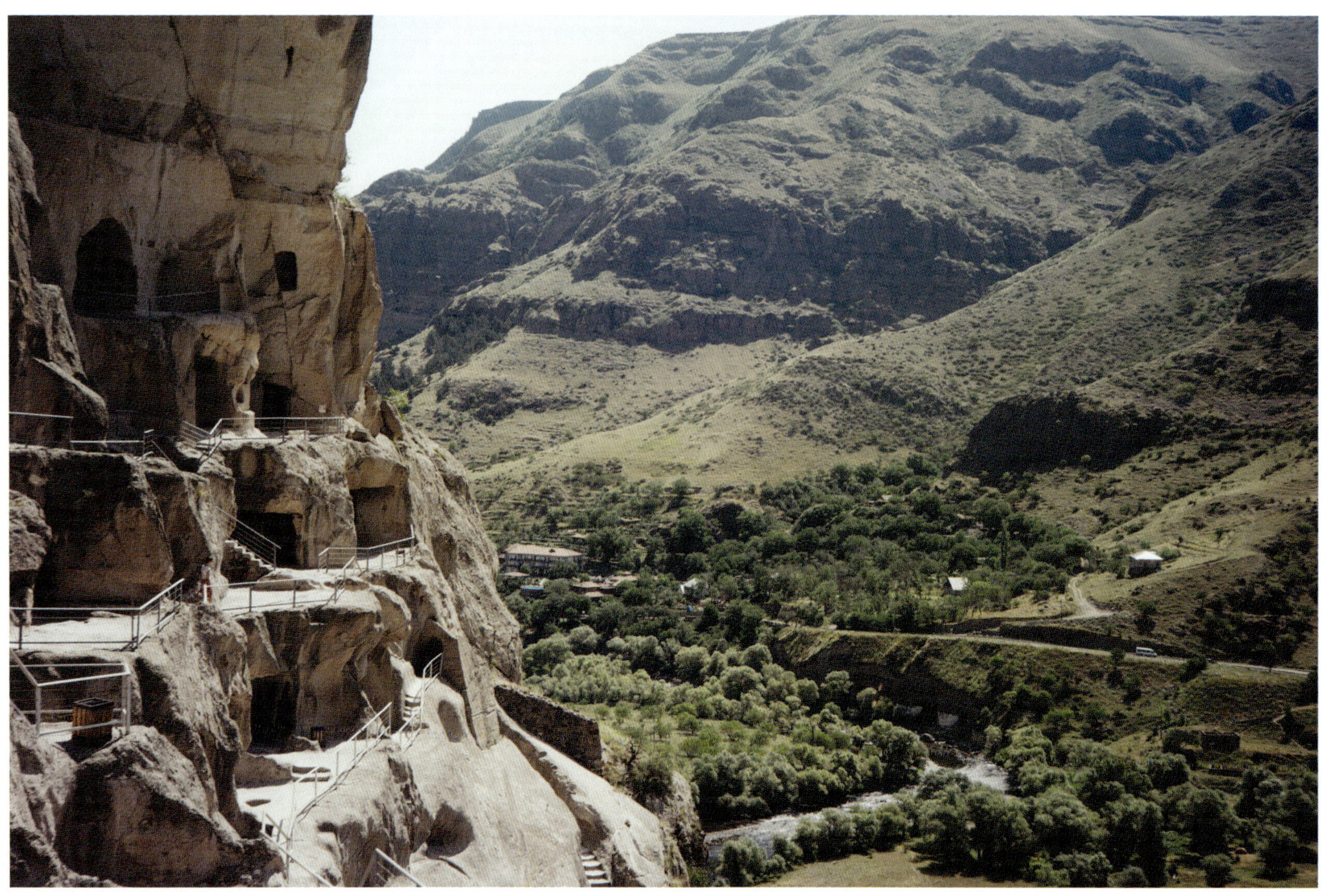

Vardzia cave complex
JAVAKHETI, GEORGIA
Built between the 12th and 13th centuries

Used as both a monastery and a fortress, this system of caves prevented invasion from the gorge of the River Kura. Underground passages connected to the surface allowed large detachments of warriors to appear in unxpected places, taking the enemy by surprise.

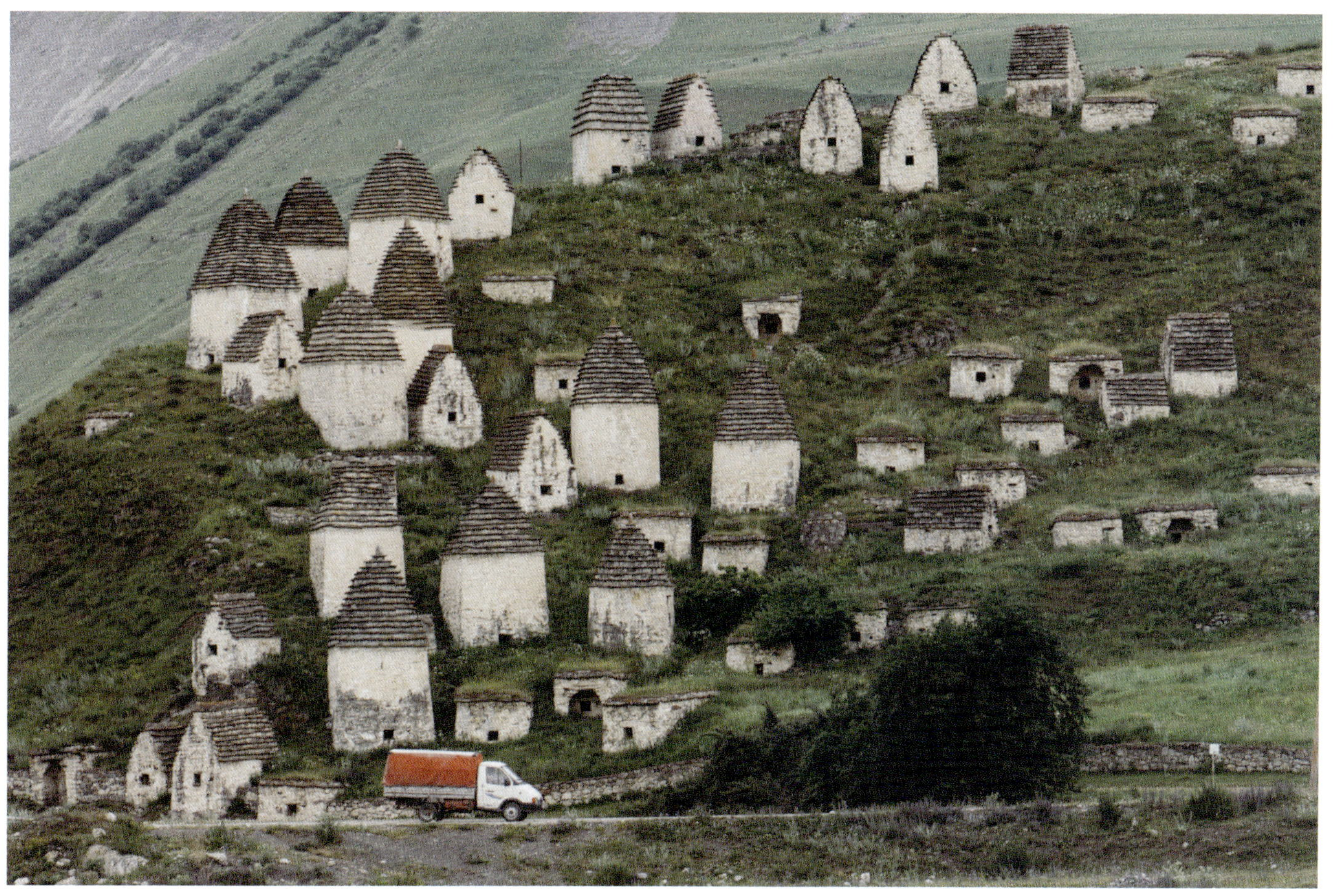

City of the Dead
DARGAVS, RUSSIA
Built between the 14th and 18th centuries

These tomb structures in North Ossetia are constructed from large, roughly hewn stones, held together with lime mortar. Open burials took place here, with the corpses passed through a hole and left on wooden planks or on top of previously abandoned bodies.

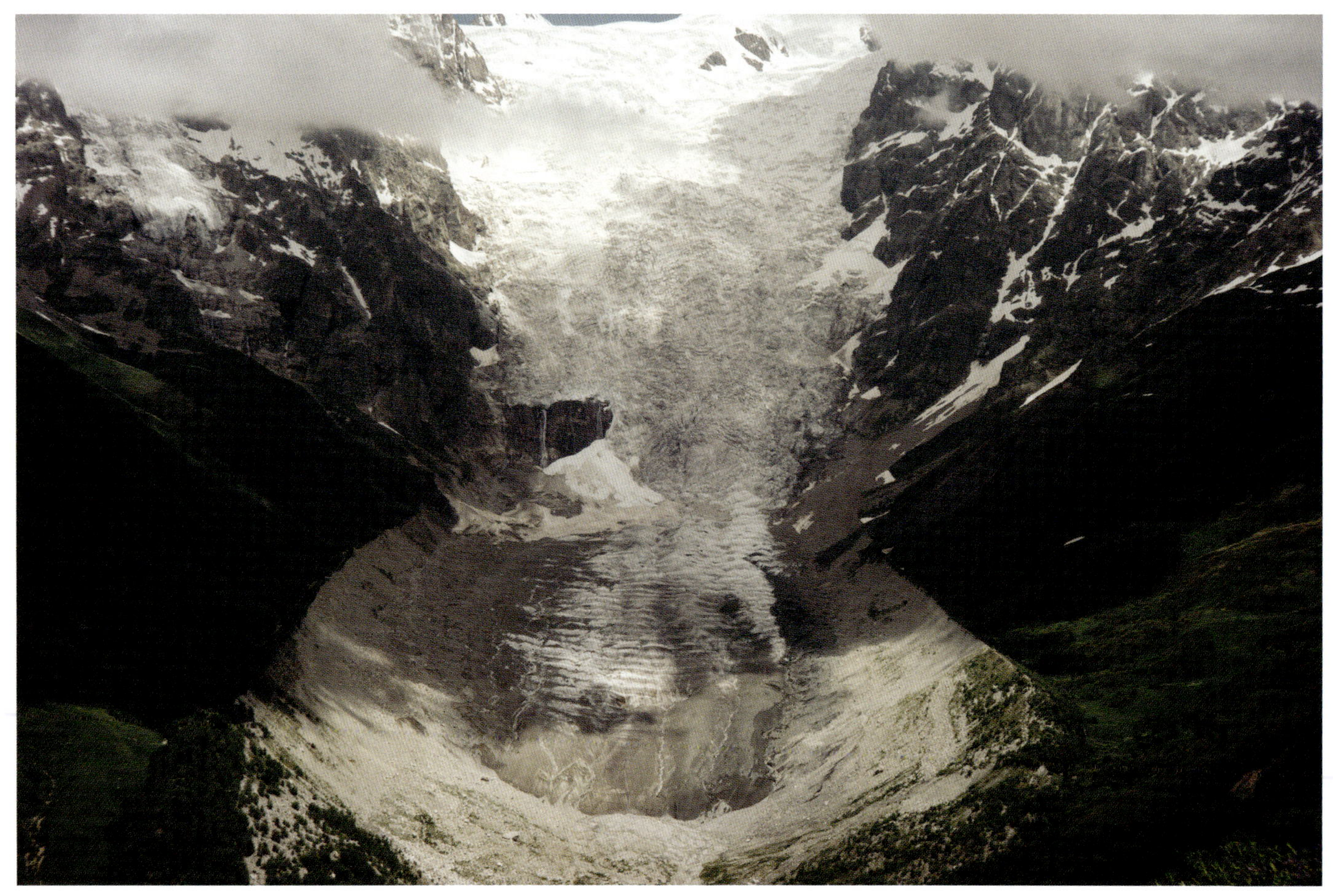

Lardaad Glacier
UPPER SVANETIA, GEORGIA

There are about 3,000 glaciers in the Caucasus. It is estimated that since the 1960s, as a result of global warming, the total area of the Caucasus mountains covered by glaciers has declined by about 30 per cent.

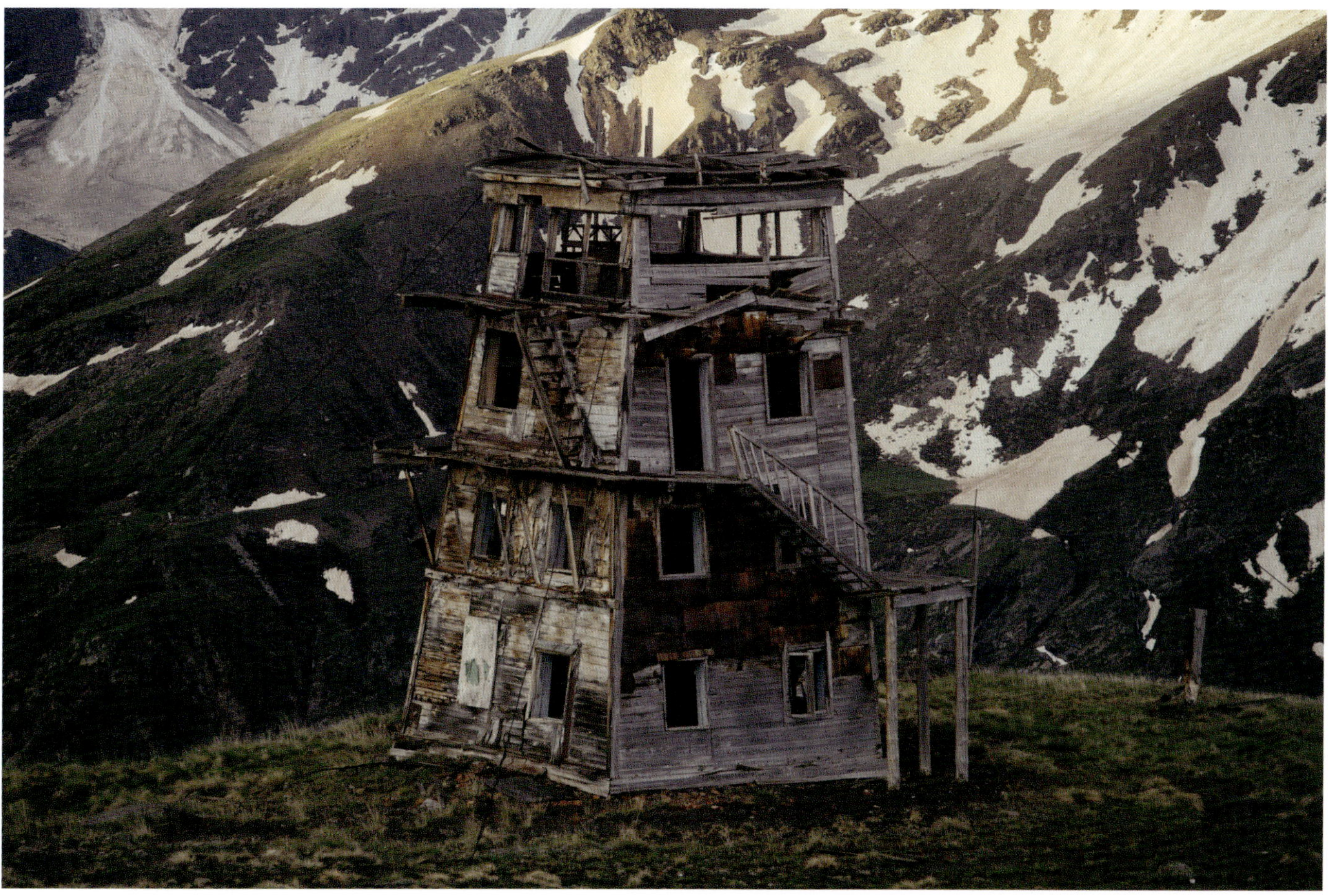

Abandoned meteorological station
KABARDINO–BALKARIA, RUSSIA

Wooden walls and a ruined stove are all that remain of this building, located on the slopes of Mount Elbrus, about 200 metres from the Mount Terskol Observatory. Visitors to the region walk the mountains to acclimatise and the route to the observatory is very popular.

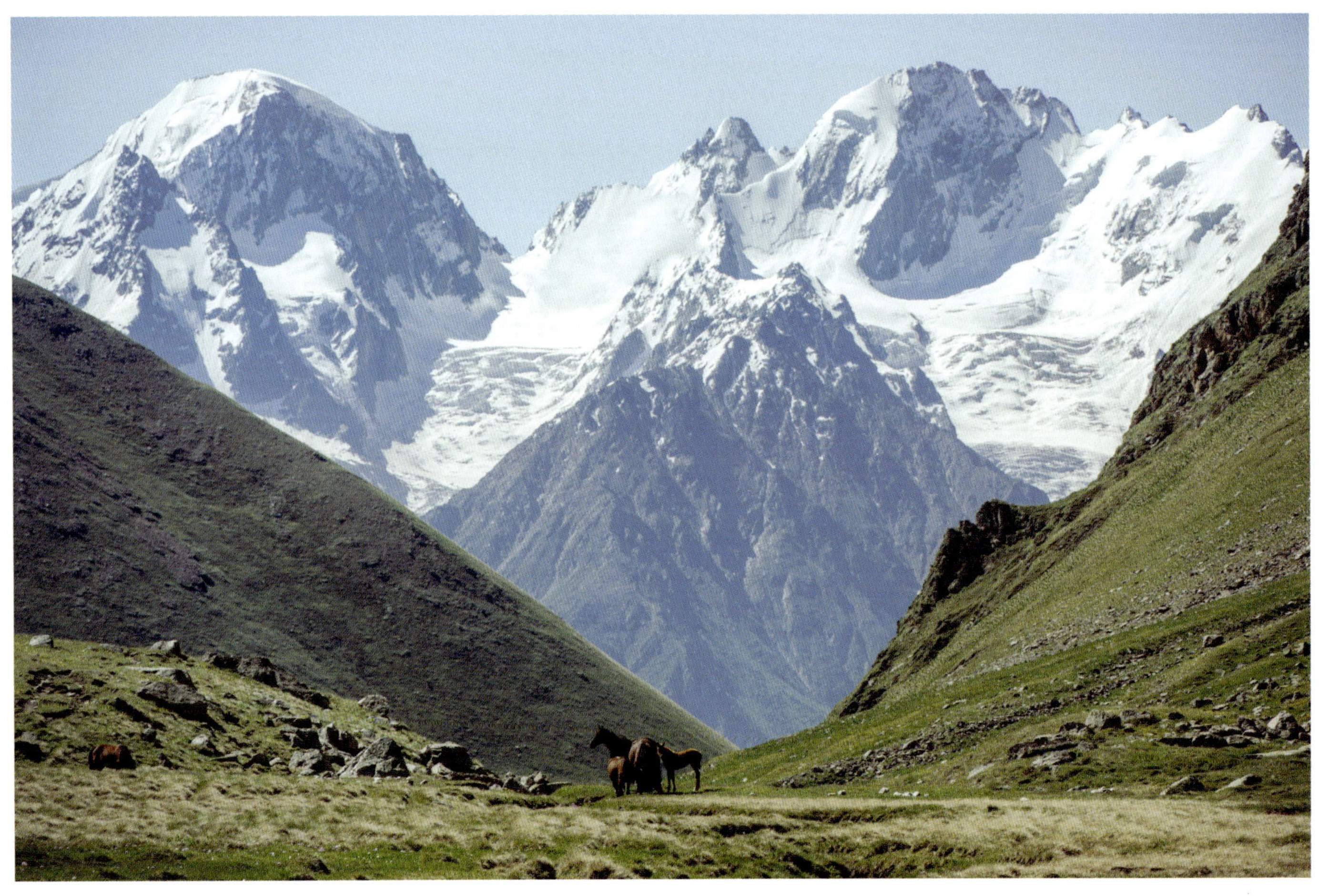

Irick river valley
KABARDINO–BALKARIA, RUSSIA

overleaf
Towers of Mestia
UPPER SVANETIA, GEORGIA

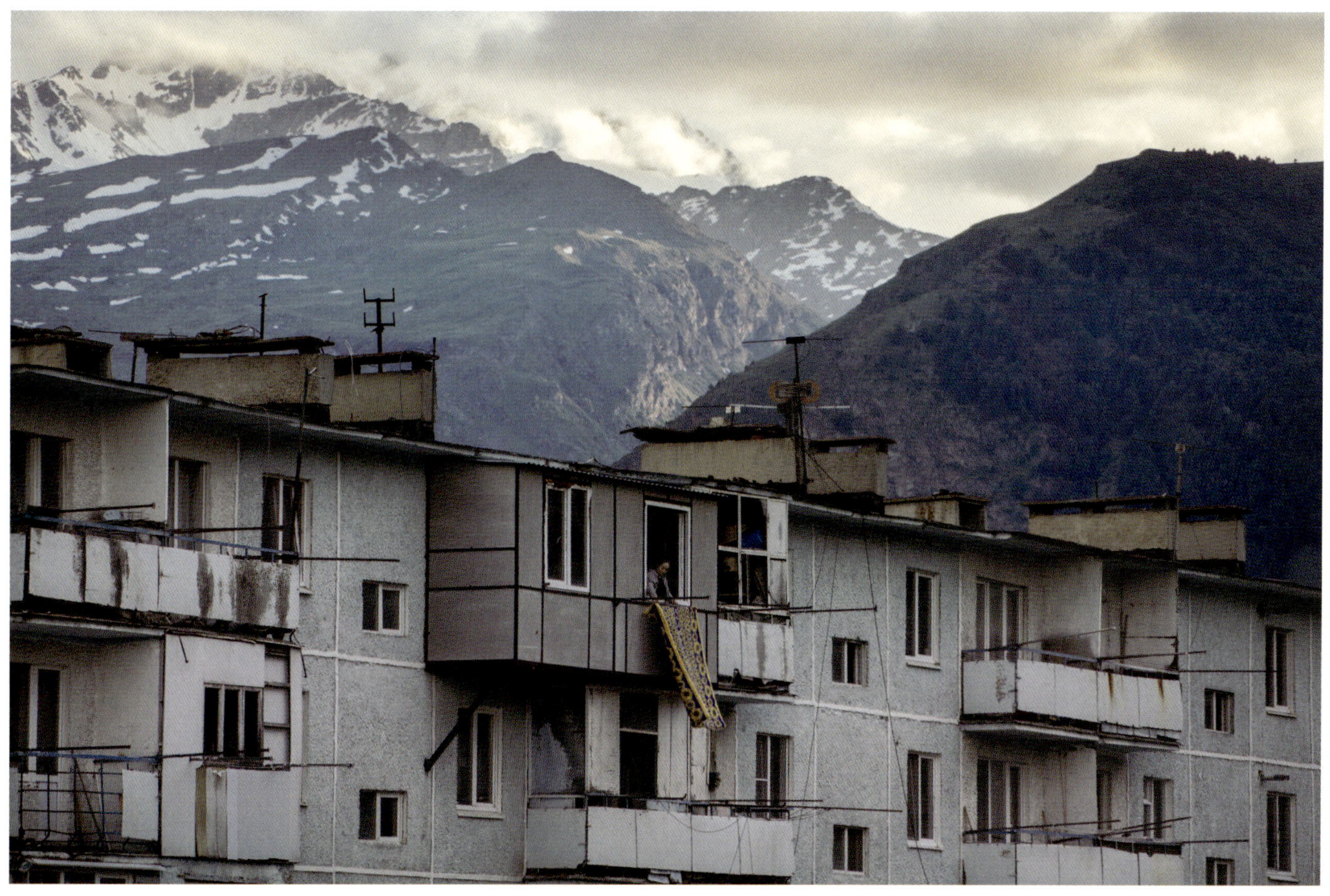

Neutrino village
KABARDINO-BALKARIA, RUSSIA
Built in the 1970s

The majority of villagers live in two 9-storey buildings on the bank of the Baksan River. Built for scientists at the nearby underground observatory, the settlement once housed 800 but now has only 370 inhabitants, a third of whom work at the Baksan Neutrino Observatory.

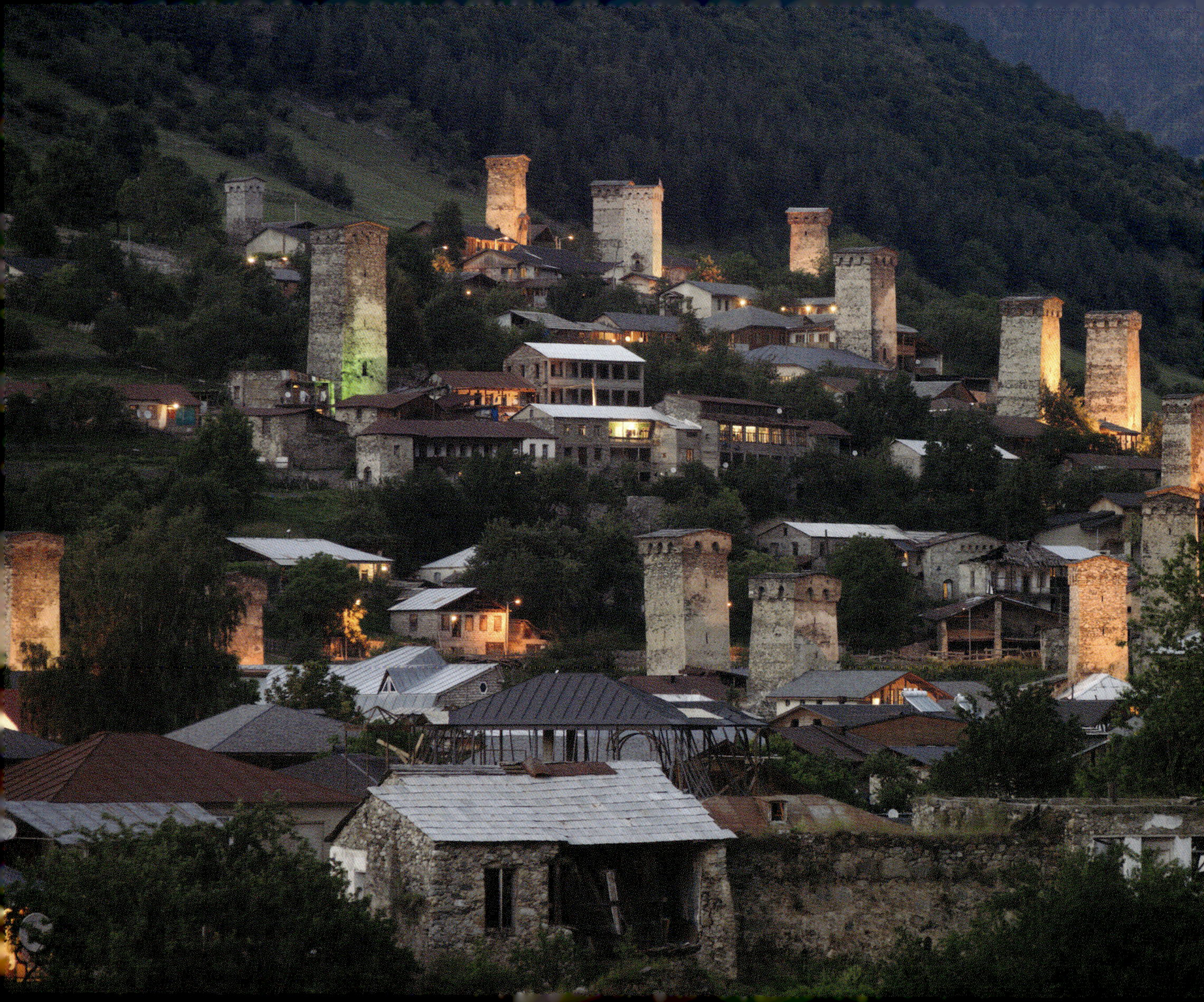

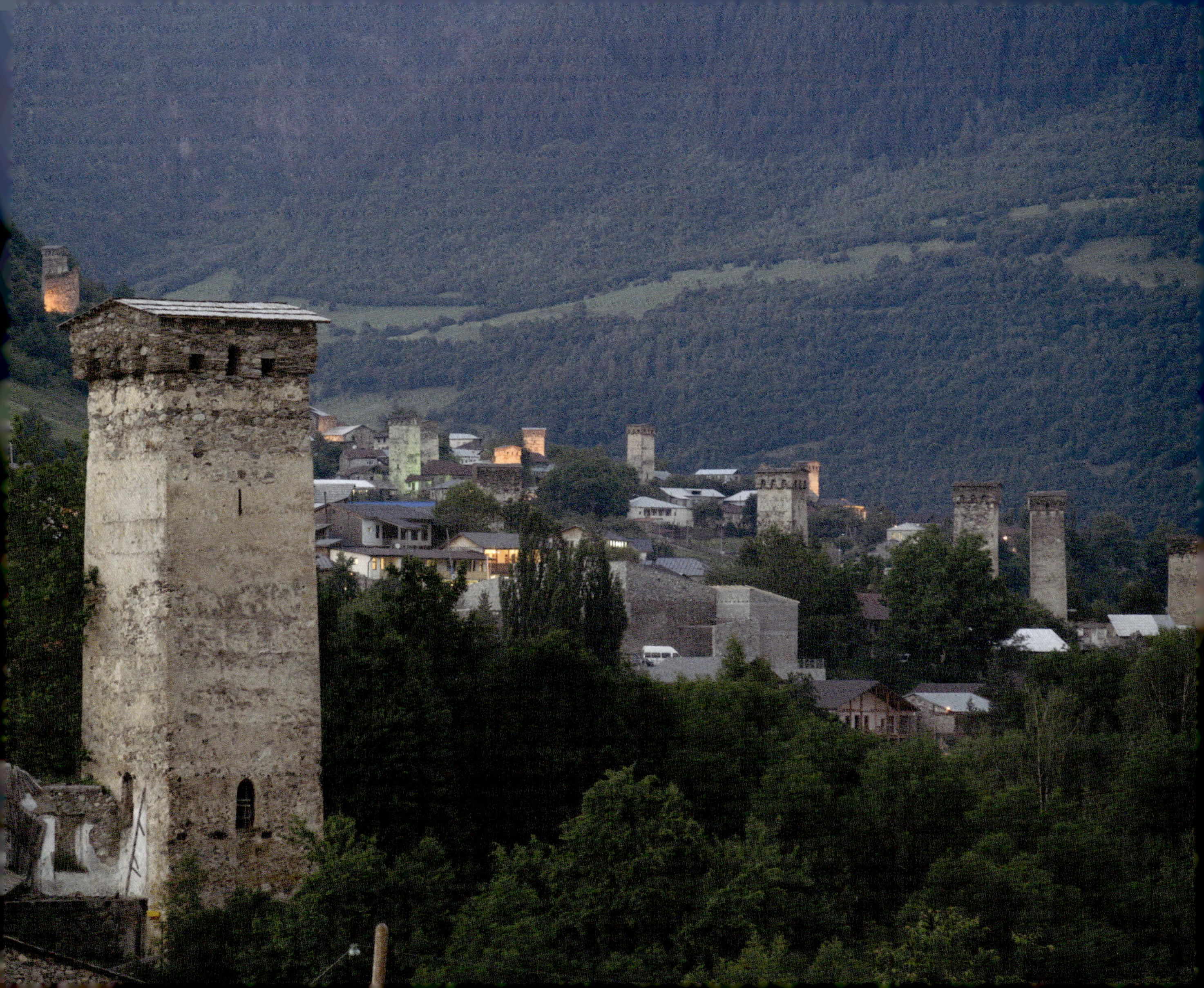

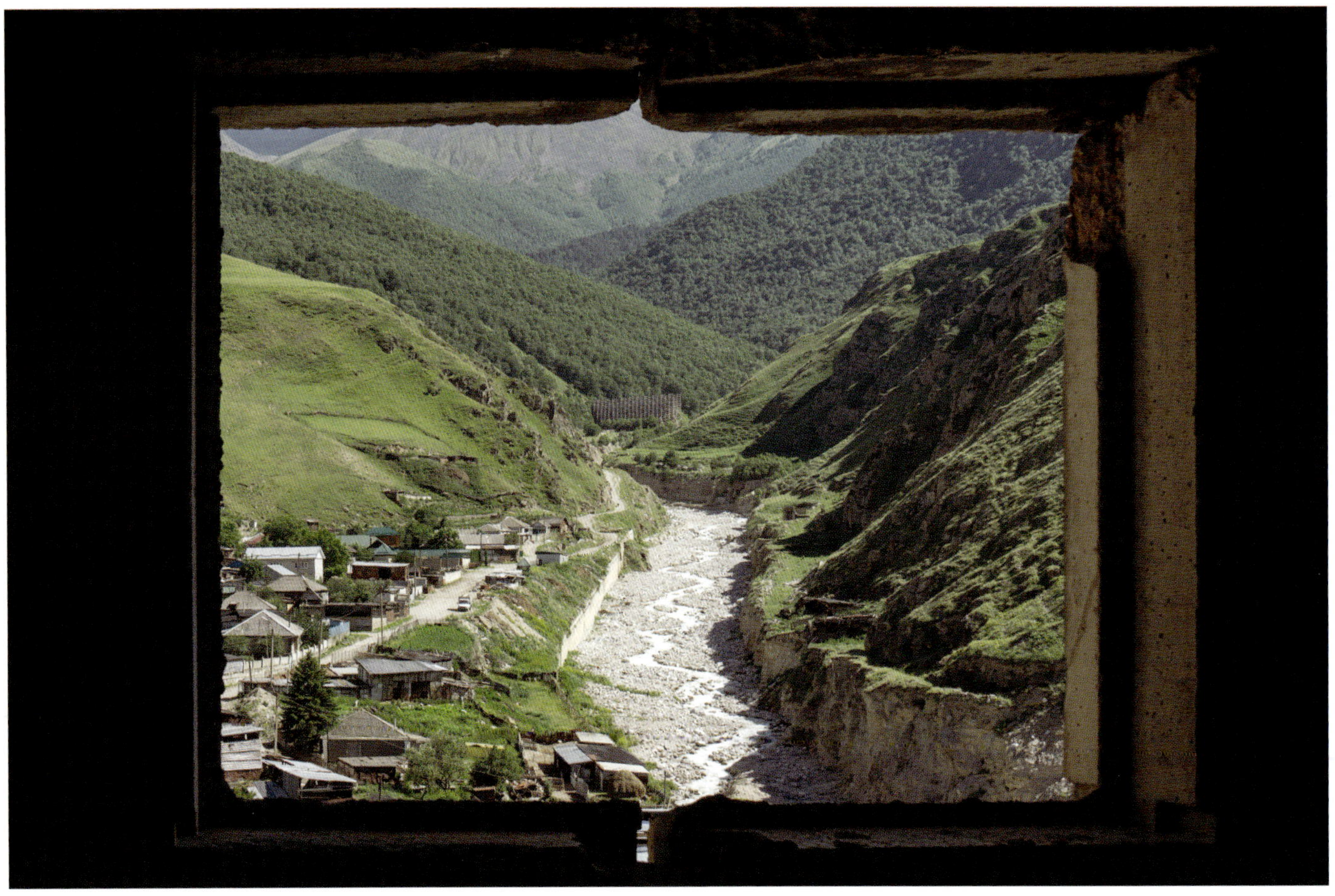

View from an unfinished 16-storey building
Gerhozhansu river valley
TYRNYAUZ, RUSSIA

An increase in the mining of wolfram–molybdenum ores in the 1980s marked this area for expansion, with new high-rise apartment buildings planned. However, as the USSR collapsed, the ore mining proved unprofitable, so construction was halted and industy stopped.

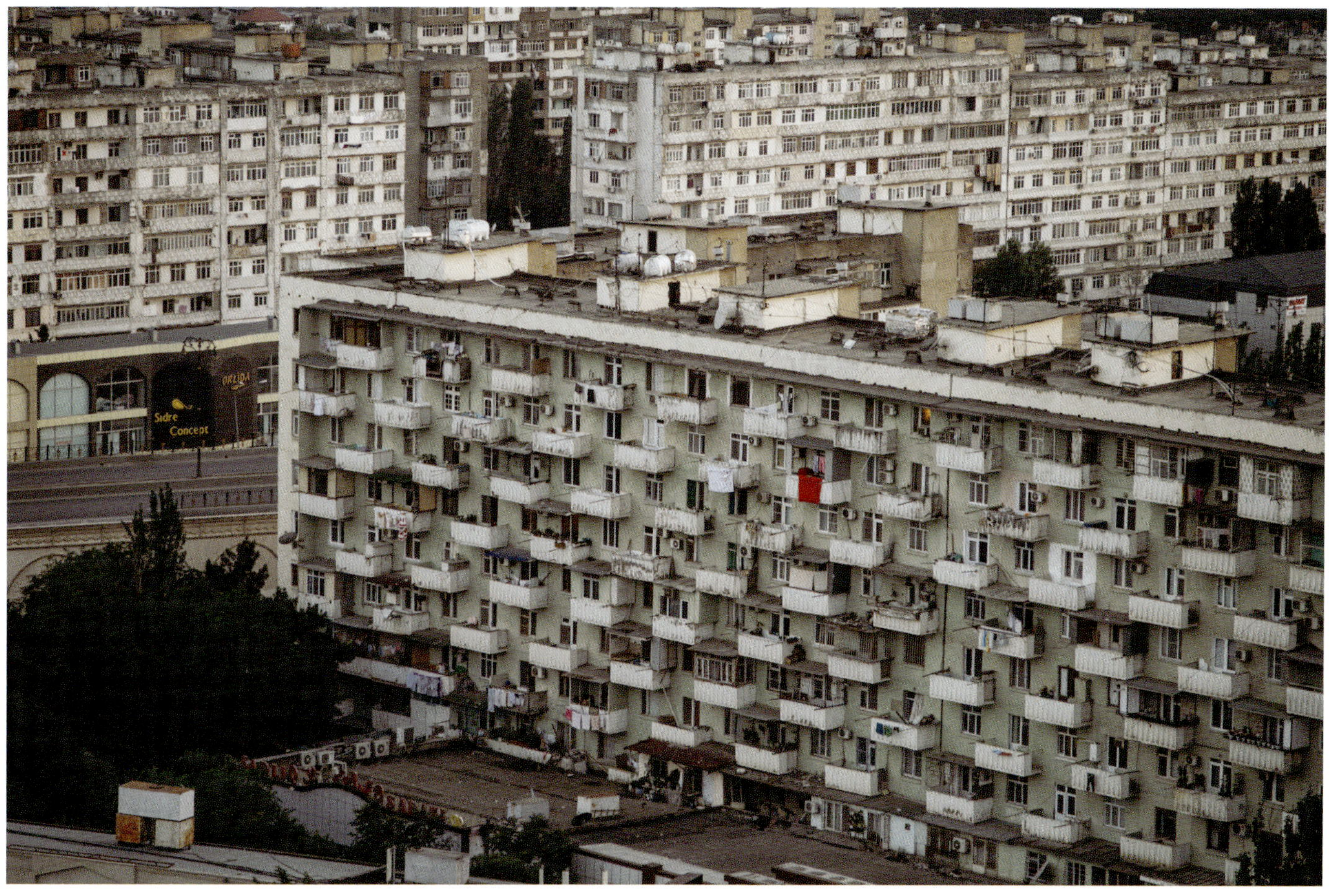

Hatainskiy District
BAKU, AZERBAIJAN

From the 1960s to the 1980s, the widespread use of concrete, metal and glass saw the development of new architectural forms based on these materials. This was reflected in housing and cultural buildings, transport systems and the landscaping of the city.

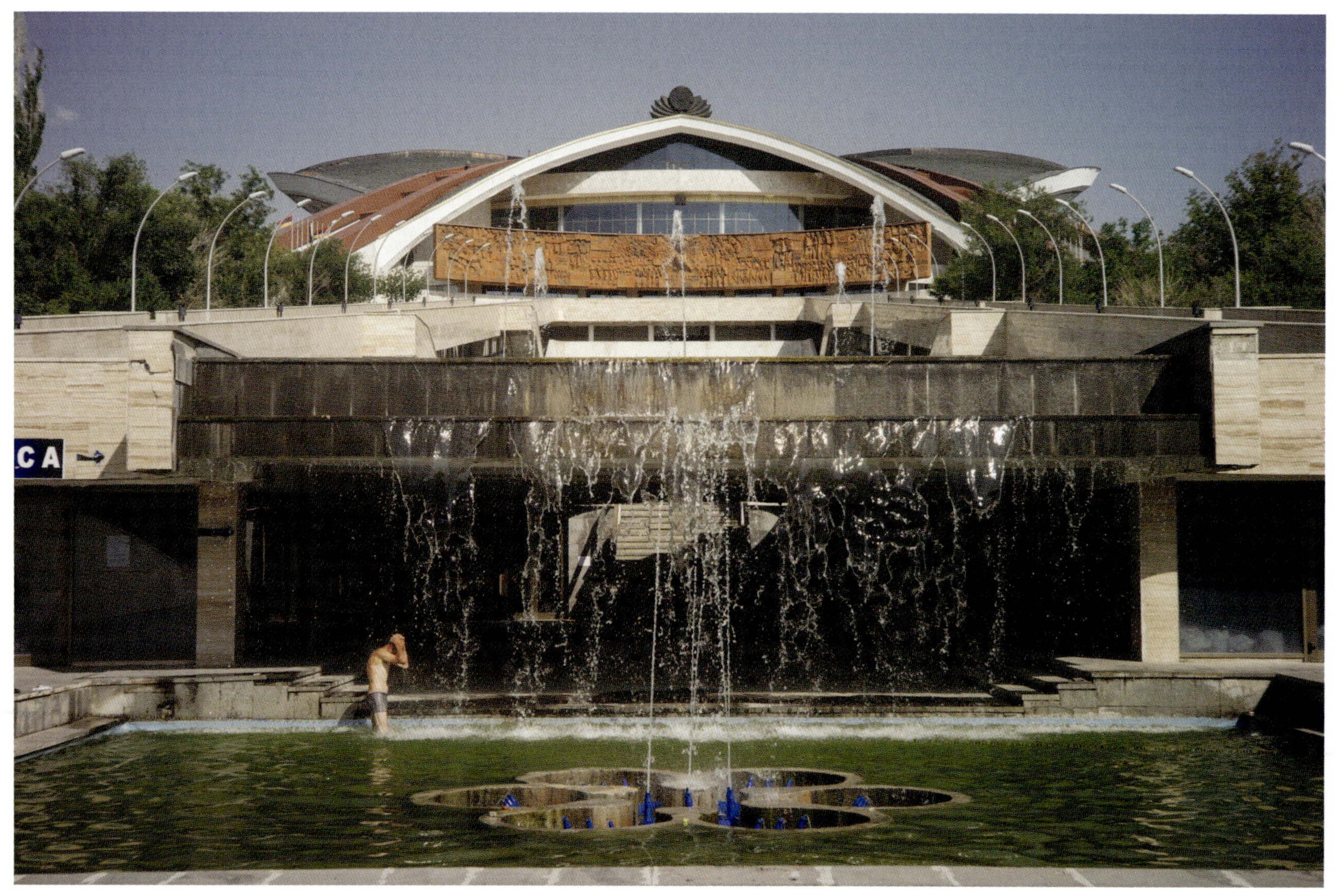

Sport and Concert Complex
YEREVAN, ARMENIA
Built in 1983
Architects: A. Tarhanyan, S. Khachikyan et al.

This multi-purpose facility consists of a concert and sports hall, both equipped with revolving stages, with a total capacity of 12,000. The front entrance is decorated with a huge high relief (6 by 60 metres) depicting Armenia and its revival.

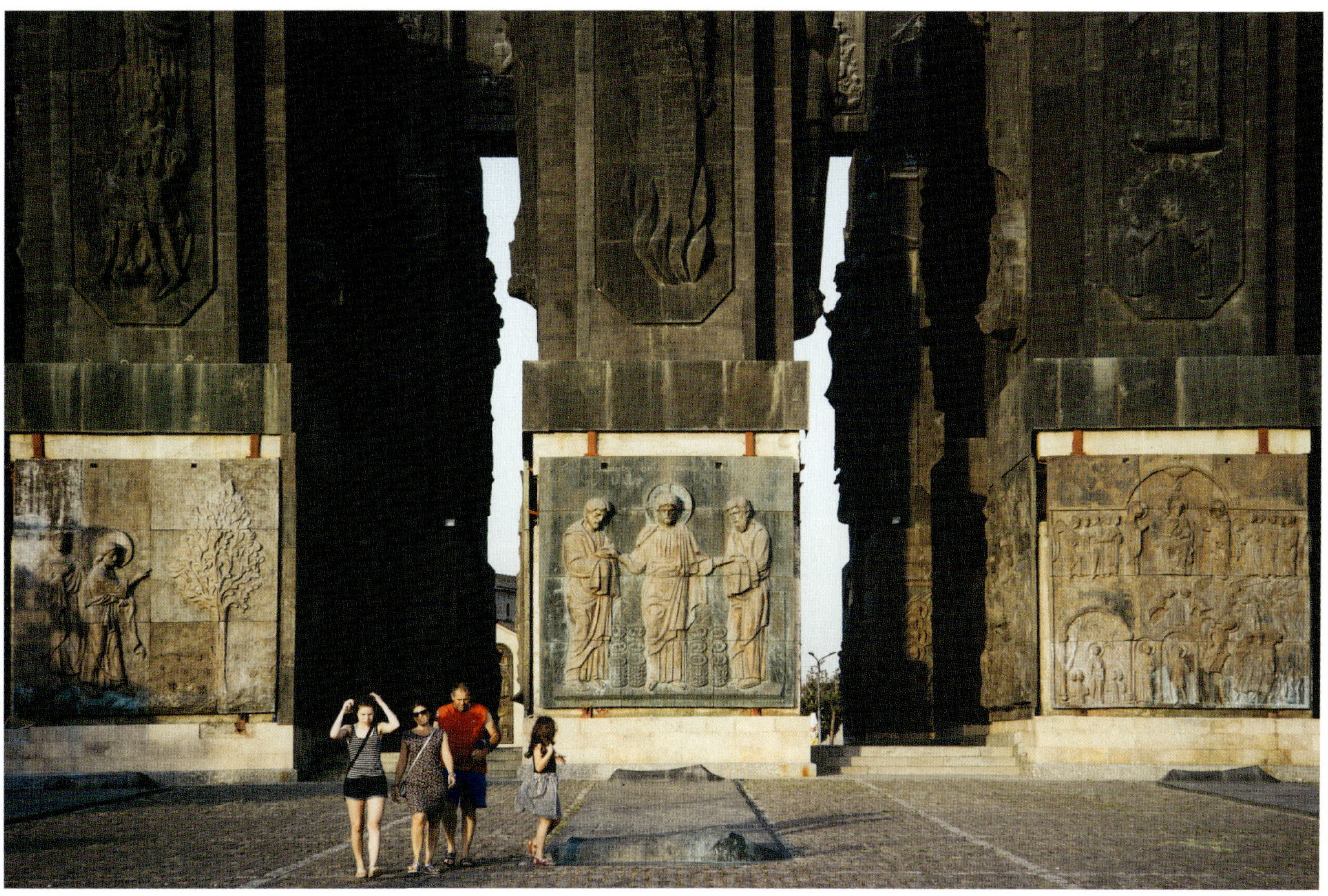

'Chronicle of Georgia' monument
TBILISI, GEORGIA
Erected in 1985 (unfinished)
Architect: Z. Tsereteli

The complex consists of sixteen columns decorated with bas-reliefs. These are divided into three: biblical stories (bottom), prominent national figures (middle), everyday scenes (top). As aspects of Georgian history remain contentious, the monument has not yet been completed.

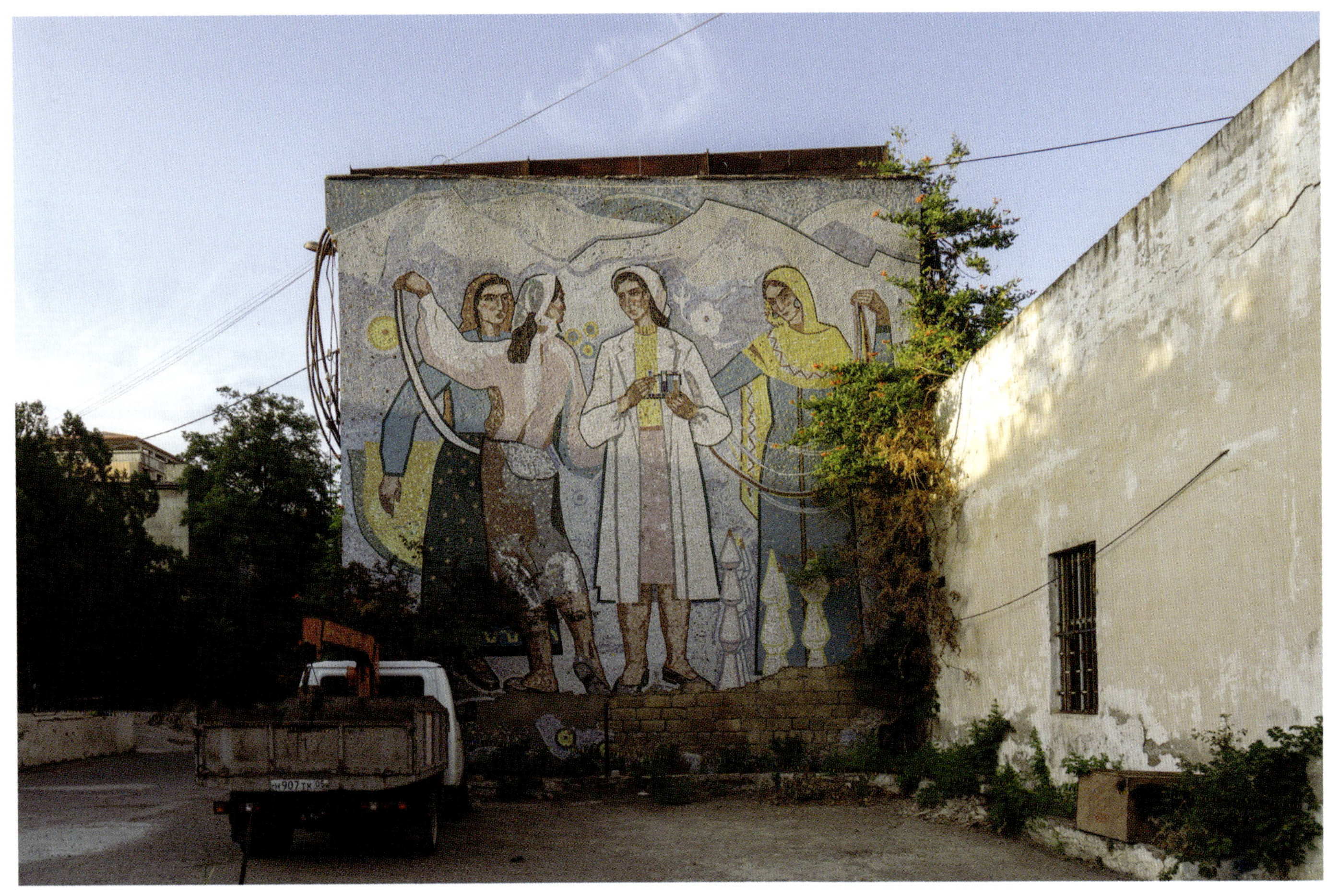

Glass Factory mosaic
MAKHACHKALA, RUSSIA

Wall mosaics help to trace the evolution of an ideology – from elements of everyday life, to the dreams and aspirations of a society (the conquest of space, visions of a bright Communist future). Mosaics also often reflect the function of the building on which they are sited.

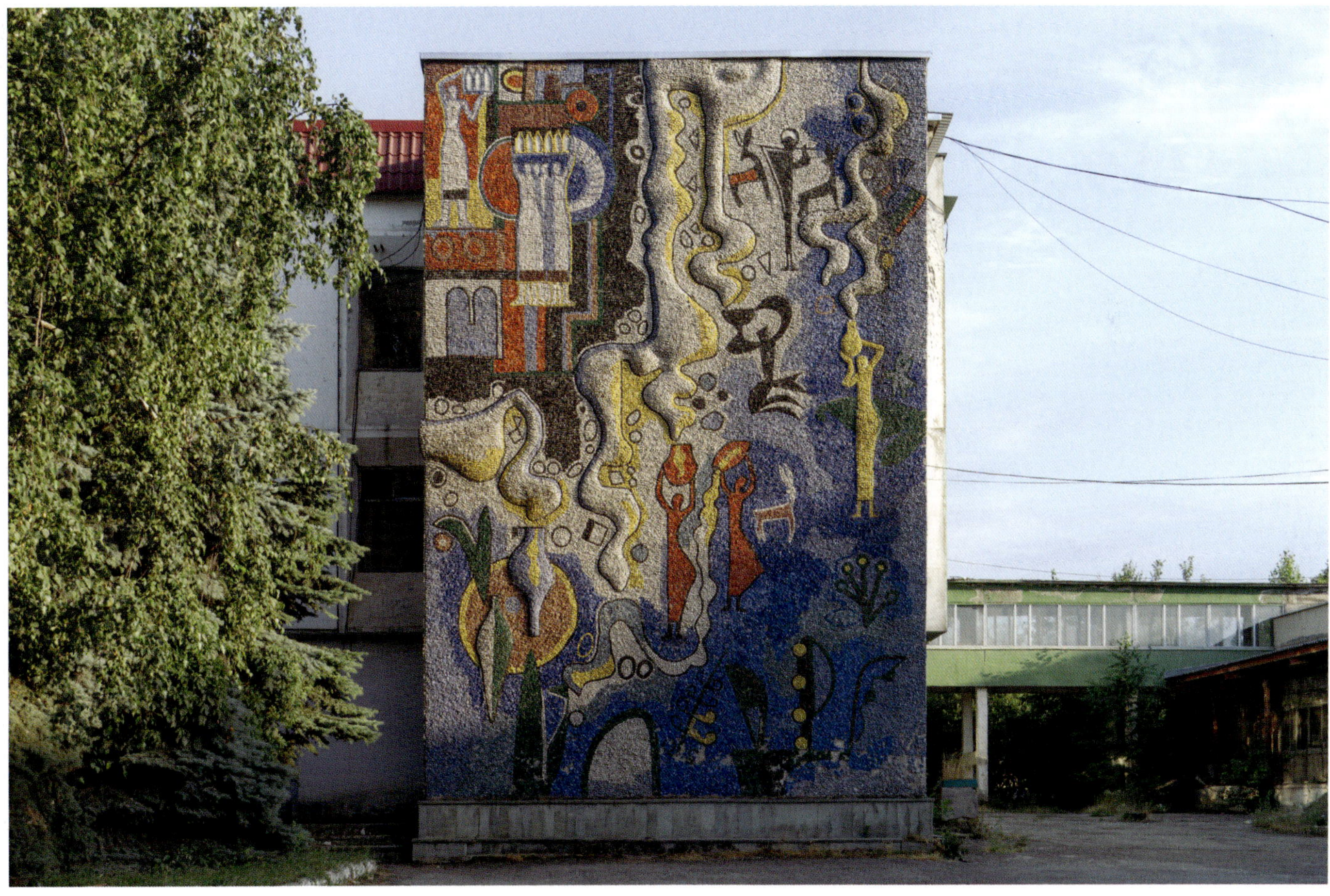

Milk Factory mosaic
NALCHIK, RUSSIA

The 1960s and 1970s were the high point for Soviet mosaics, a time when the USSR had a message for its citizens and the world. Designs depicted the conquest of space, the development of nuclear energy, advances in science and the heroic builders of industies and cities.

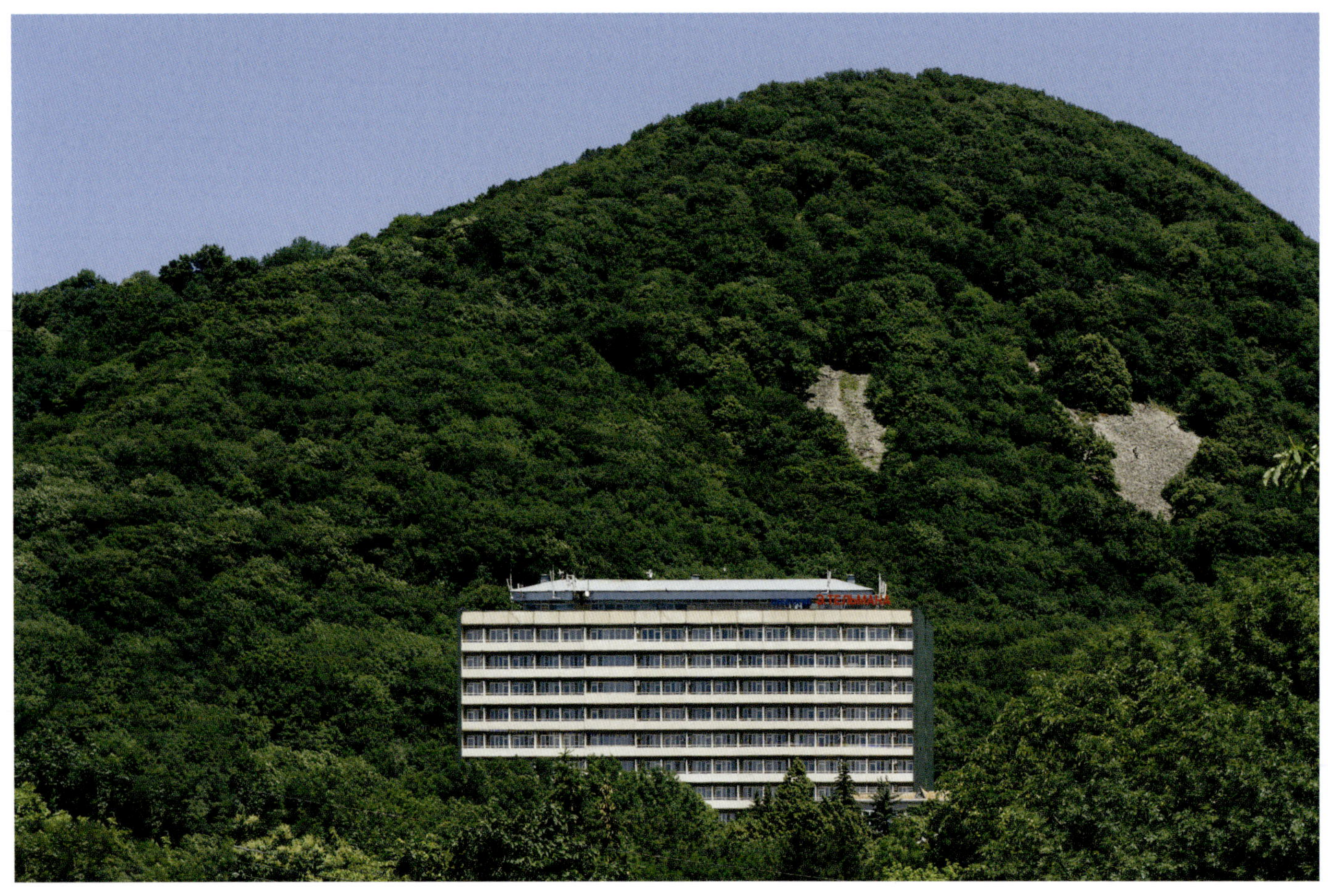

E. Telman Sanatorium
ZHELEZNOVODSK, RUSSIA

The building is named after Ernst Thälmann, leader of the Communist Party of Germany from 1925 to 1933 (when he was arrested by the Gestapo). In August 1944, after more than eleven years in solitary confinement, he was executed on direct orders from Adolf Hitler.

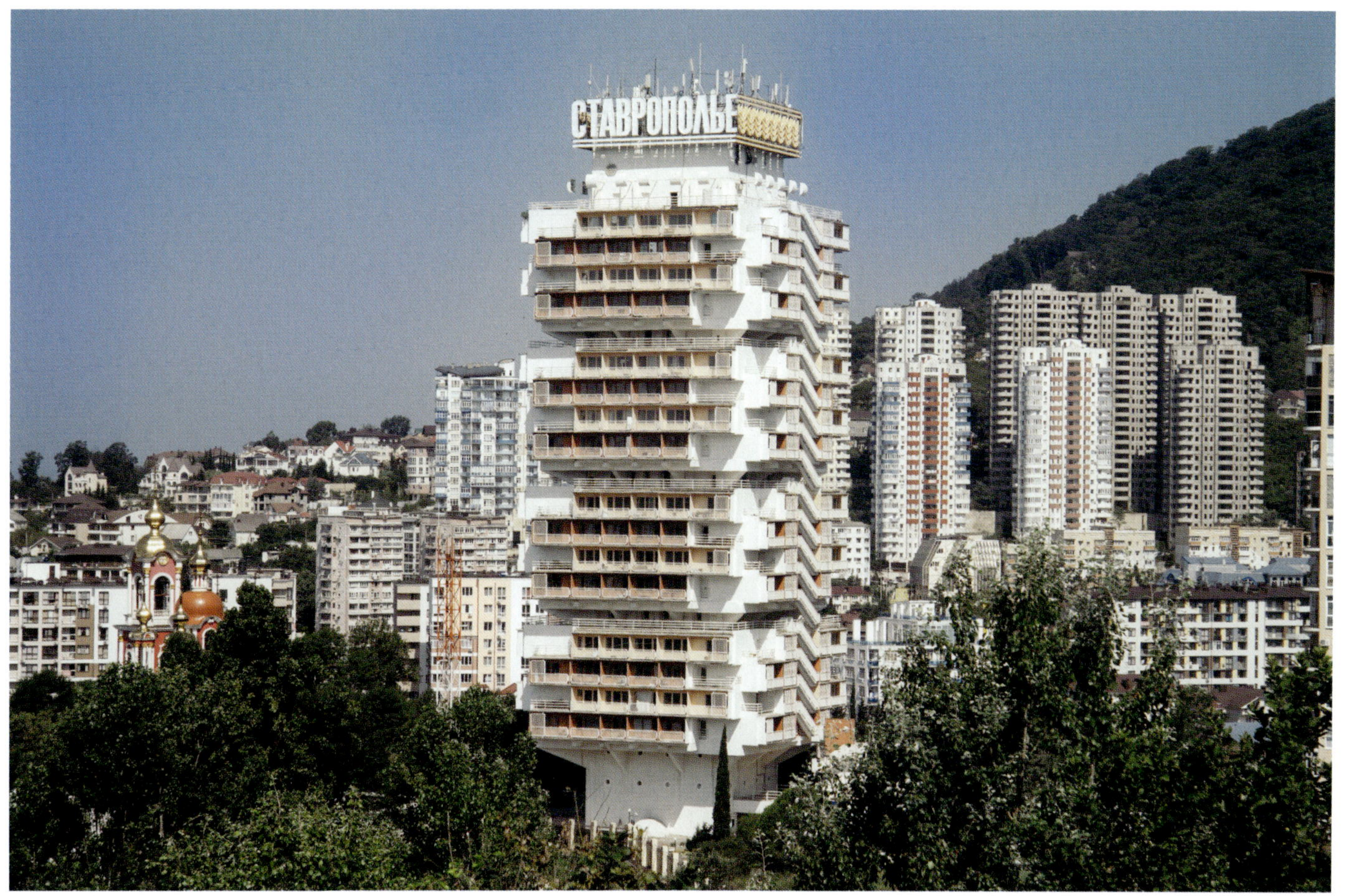

Stavropol Sanatorium
SOCHI, RUSSIA
Built in 1974
Architect: T. Sotskaya

This abandoned 24-storey sanatorium is known as the 'Corn' because of its resemblance to a corn cob. Once able to accommodate 1,100 guests, it offered two dormitories, a treatment centre, cinema, sports grounds, tennis courts, indoor and outdoor pools and a private beach.

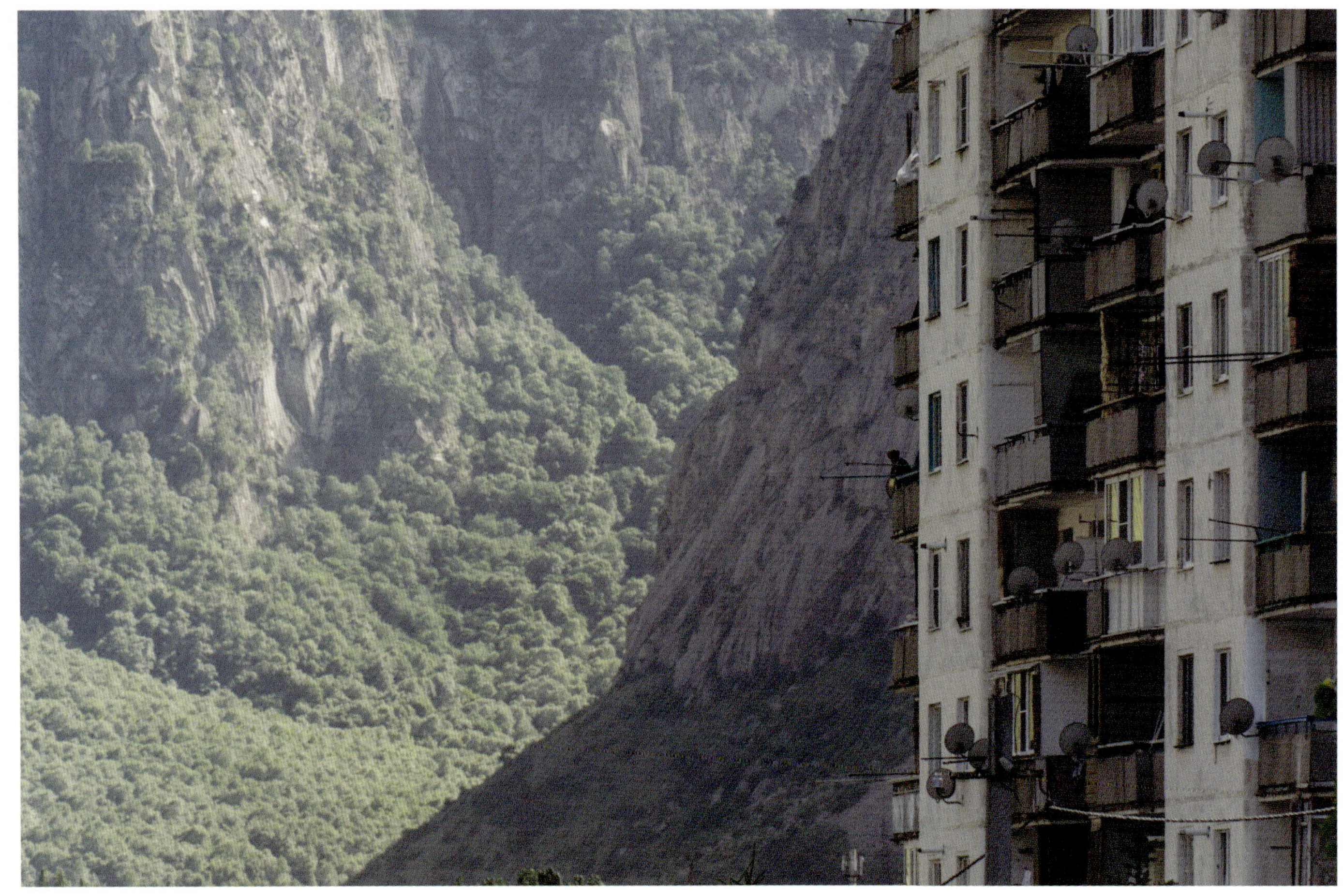

9-storey building
TYRNYAUZ, RUSSIA

Located on the upper Baksan river, the town of Tyrnyauz has a population of around 20,000. It was founded in the 1930s after the discovery of a rich tungsten-molybdenum ore deposit and the subsequent construction of a mining and metallurgical plant.

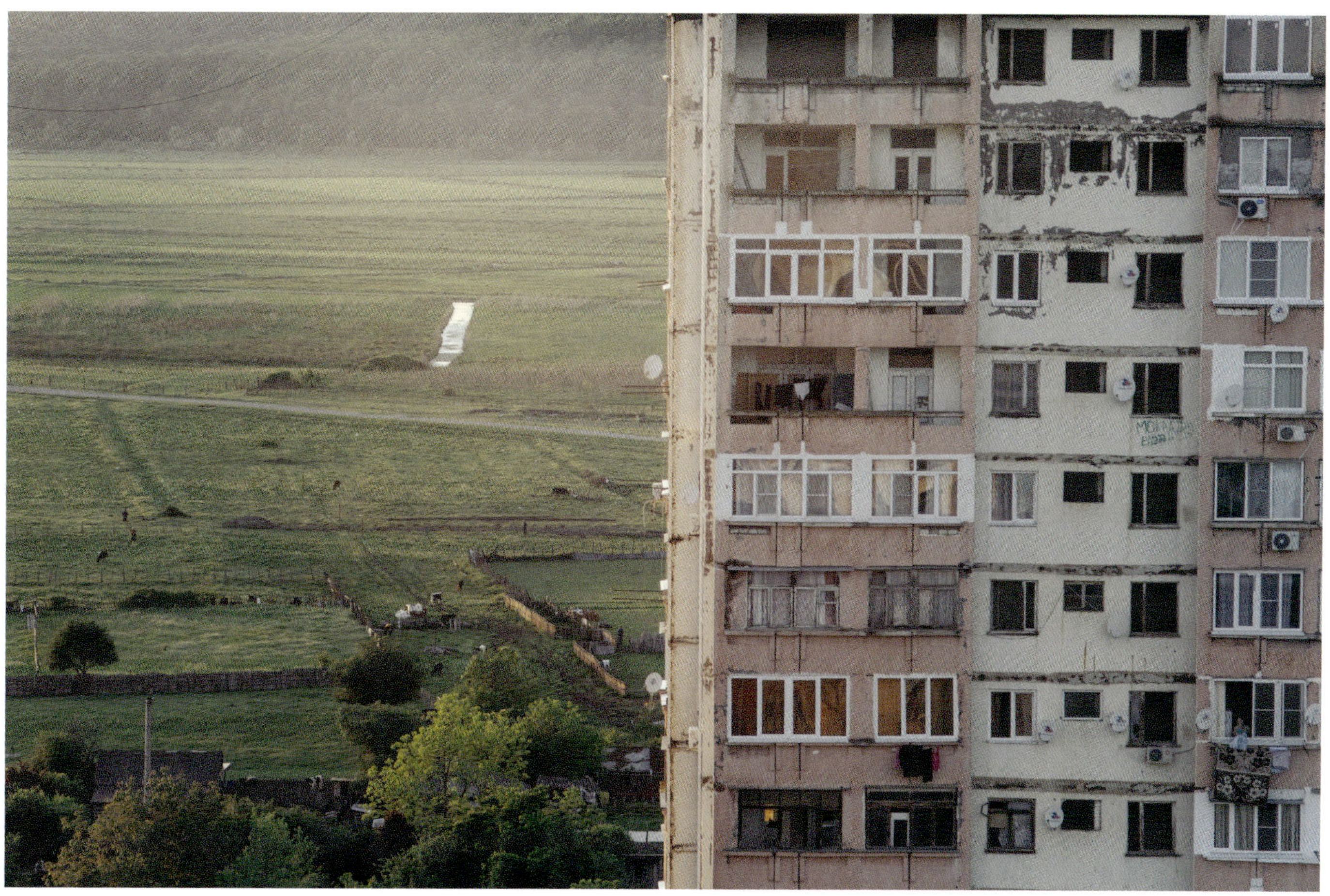

16-storey apartment building
PITSUNDA, ABKHAZIA
Built in the 1980s

Pitsunda is a resort town in Abkhazia with a population of 4,200. One of the largest Soviet sanatorium complexes on the Black Sea was built here. After the collapse of the USSR and subsequent civil war in Georgia, the region remains in a deep social and economic crisis.

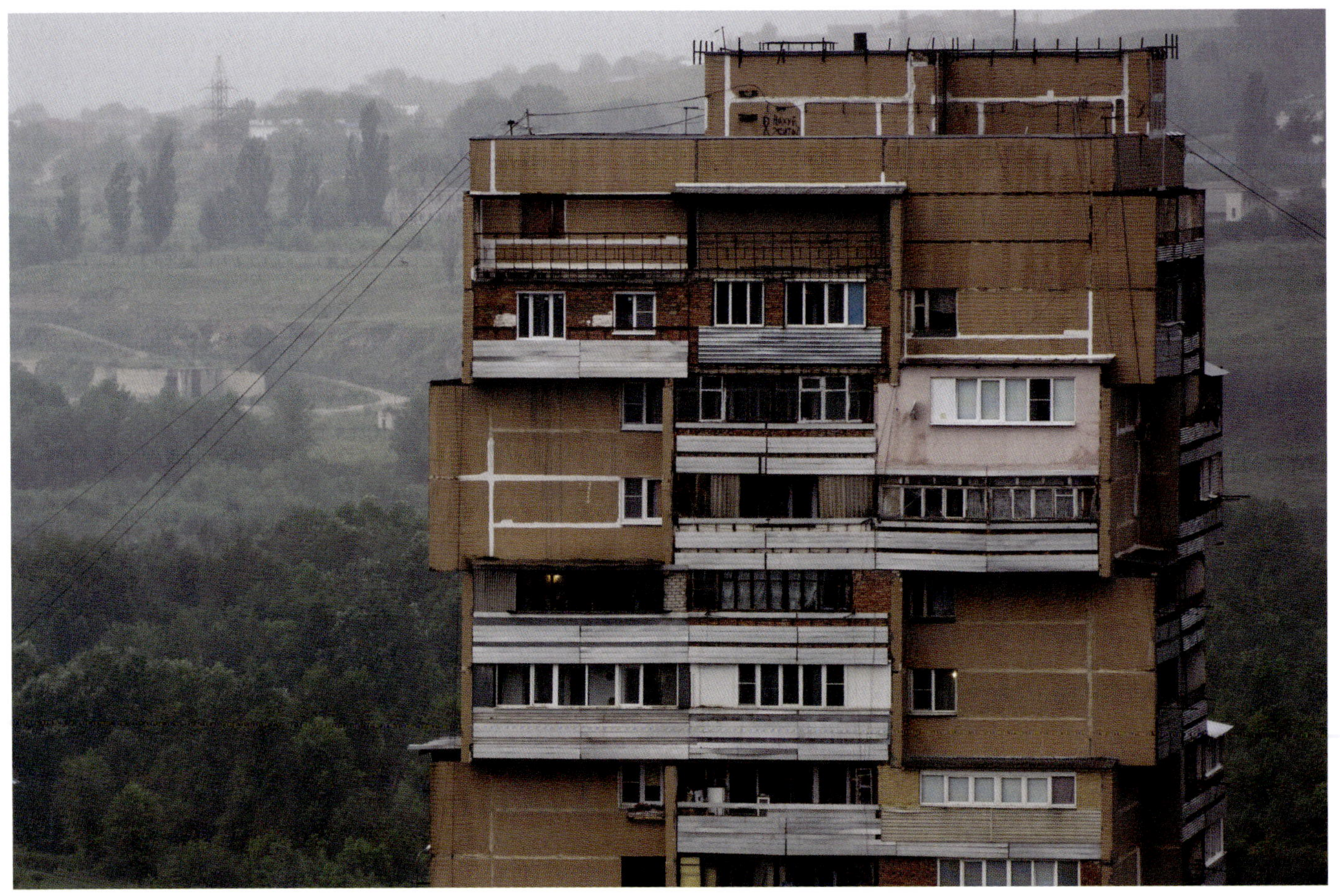

Apartment building
KISLOVODSK, RUSSIA
Built in the 1980s

In the 20th century, the spa city of Kislovodsk (meaning 'sour waters') was fully developed into a resort. Today it comprises about 60 sanatoriums, boarding houses and hotels. Half of its 125,000 population is involved in the service industries.

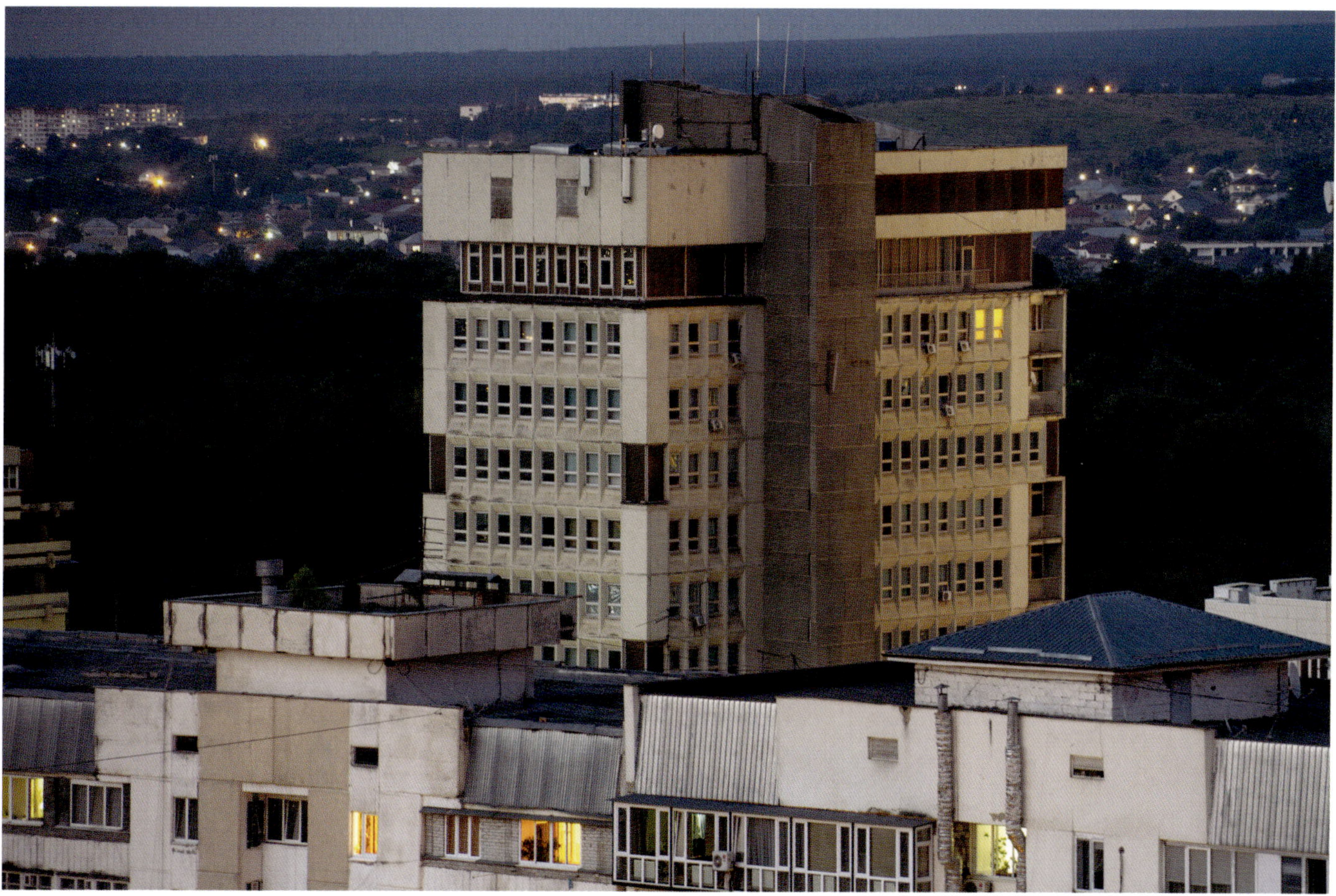

Press House
NALCHIK, RUSSIA
Built in the 1980s
Architects: A. Kiryazev, Y. Logovatovsky

This 12-storey building located on Lenin Avenue houses the editorial offices of many regional newspapers and magazines. The various publications produced here include the government newspaper *Kabardino-Balkarskaya Pravda*, established in 1921.

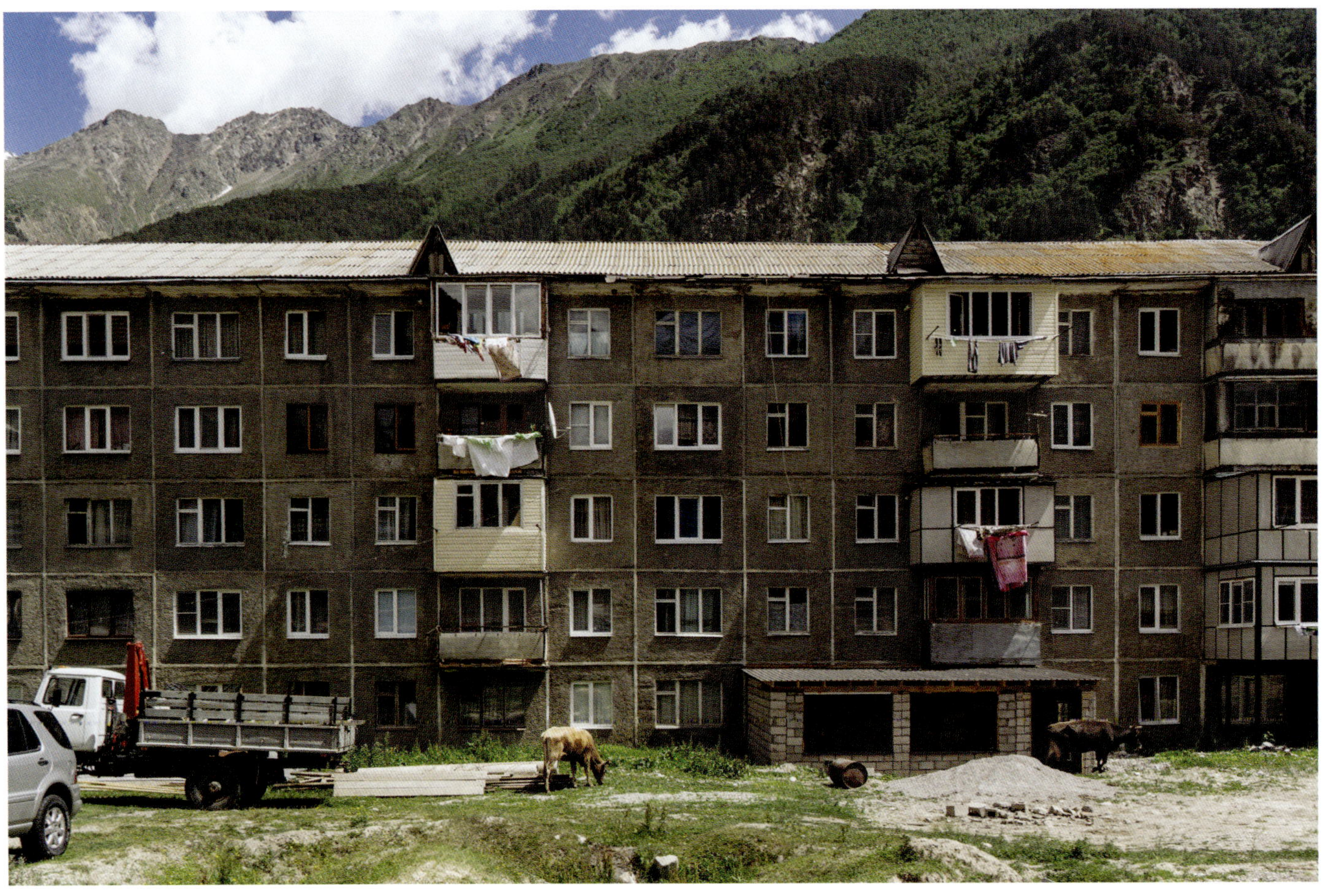

Series 1–464 panel building
ELBRUS, RUSSIA
Built in 1985

These typical panel blocks (known as 'Khrushchyovka' as they were developed when Nikita Khrushchev was leader of the Soviet government) were erected across the USSR. Various modified versions of the panels were in production from the late 1950s to the 1990s.

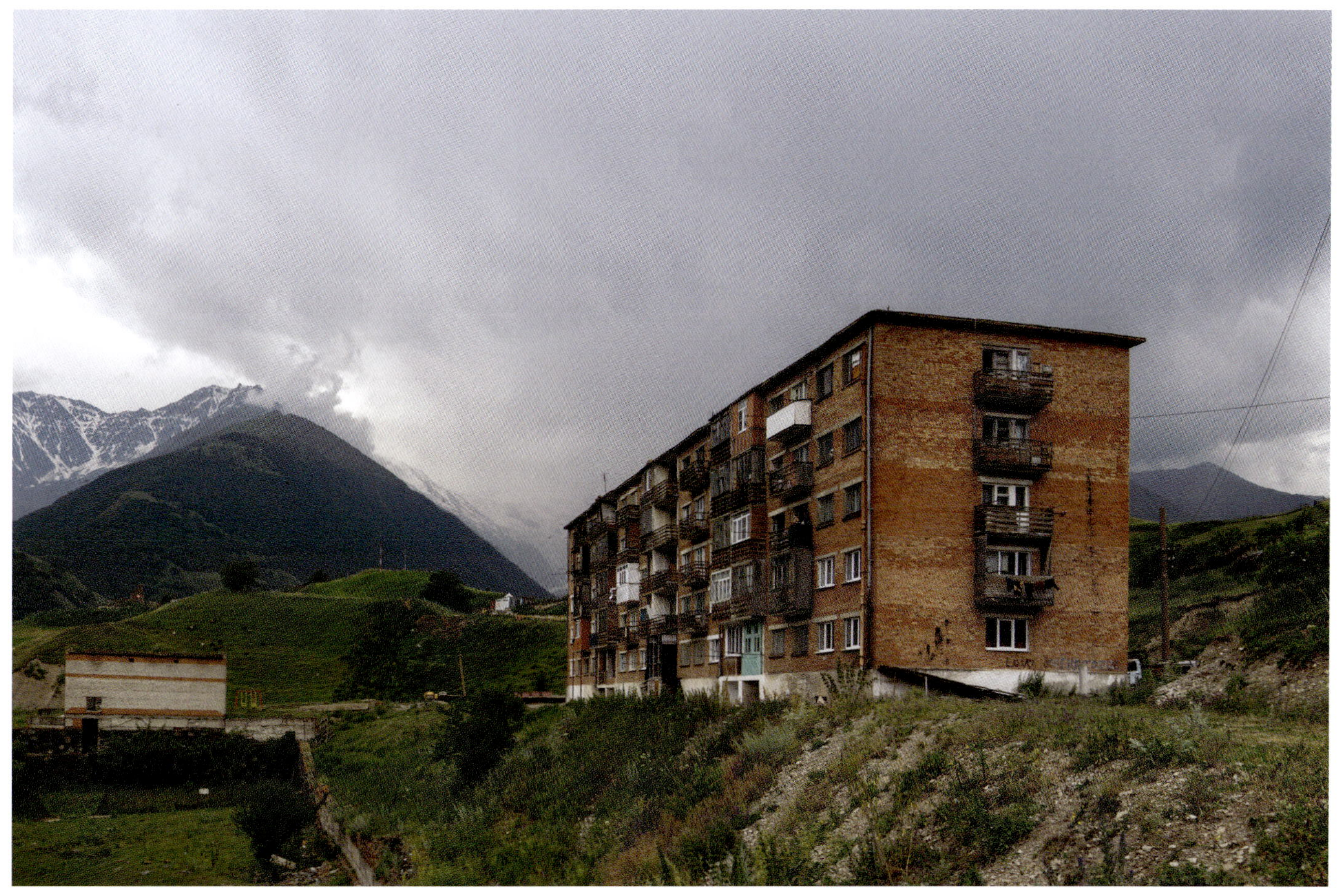

Apartment building
KARMADON, RUSSIA

Karmadon is a village in the mountains of North Ossetia with a population of less than 100. Until the 2000s, a sanatorium and health resort operated here and this single apartment building was constructed to provide its employees with housing.

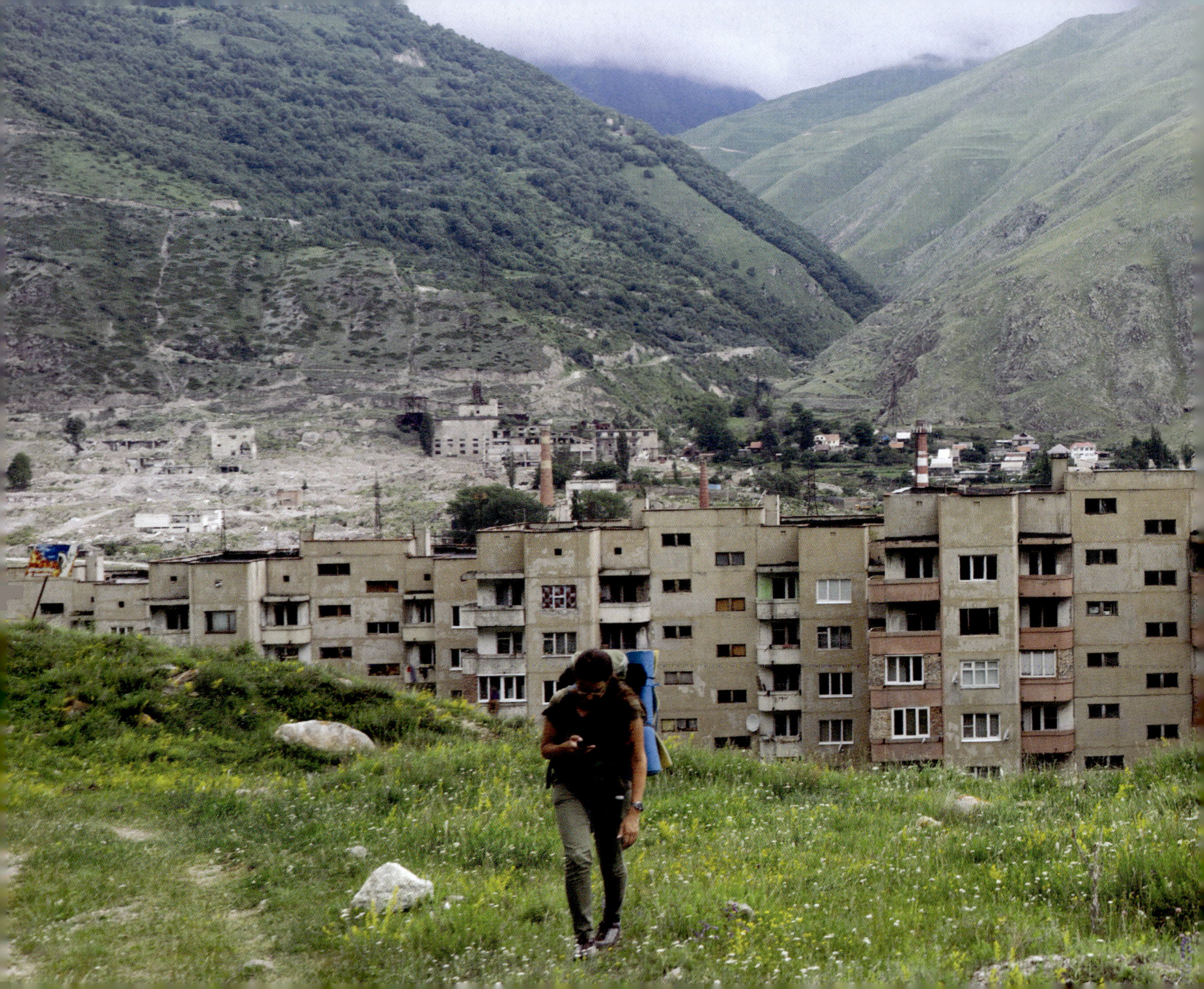

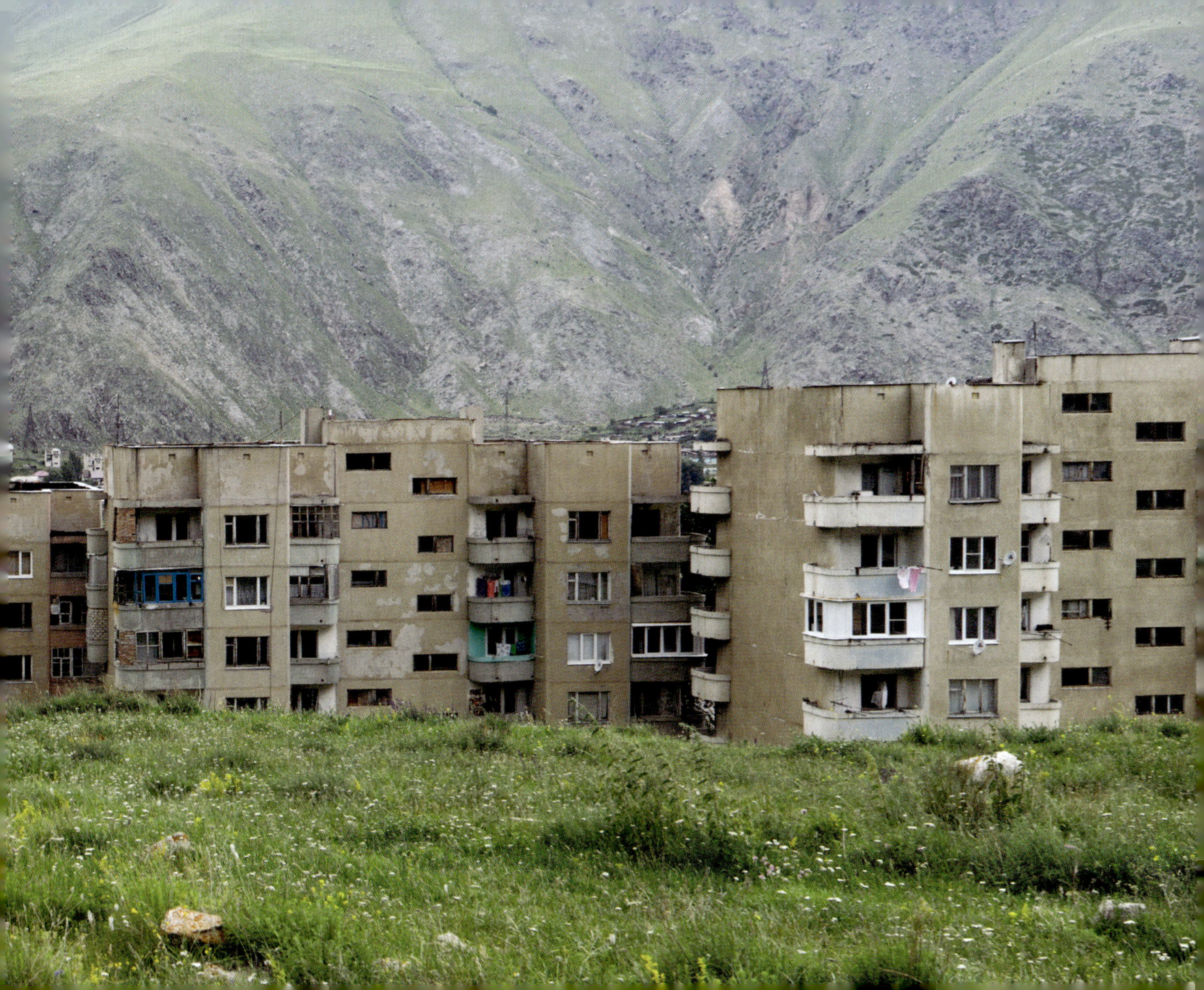

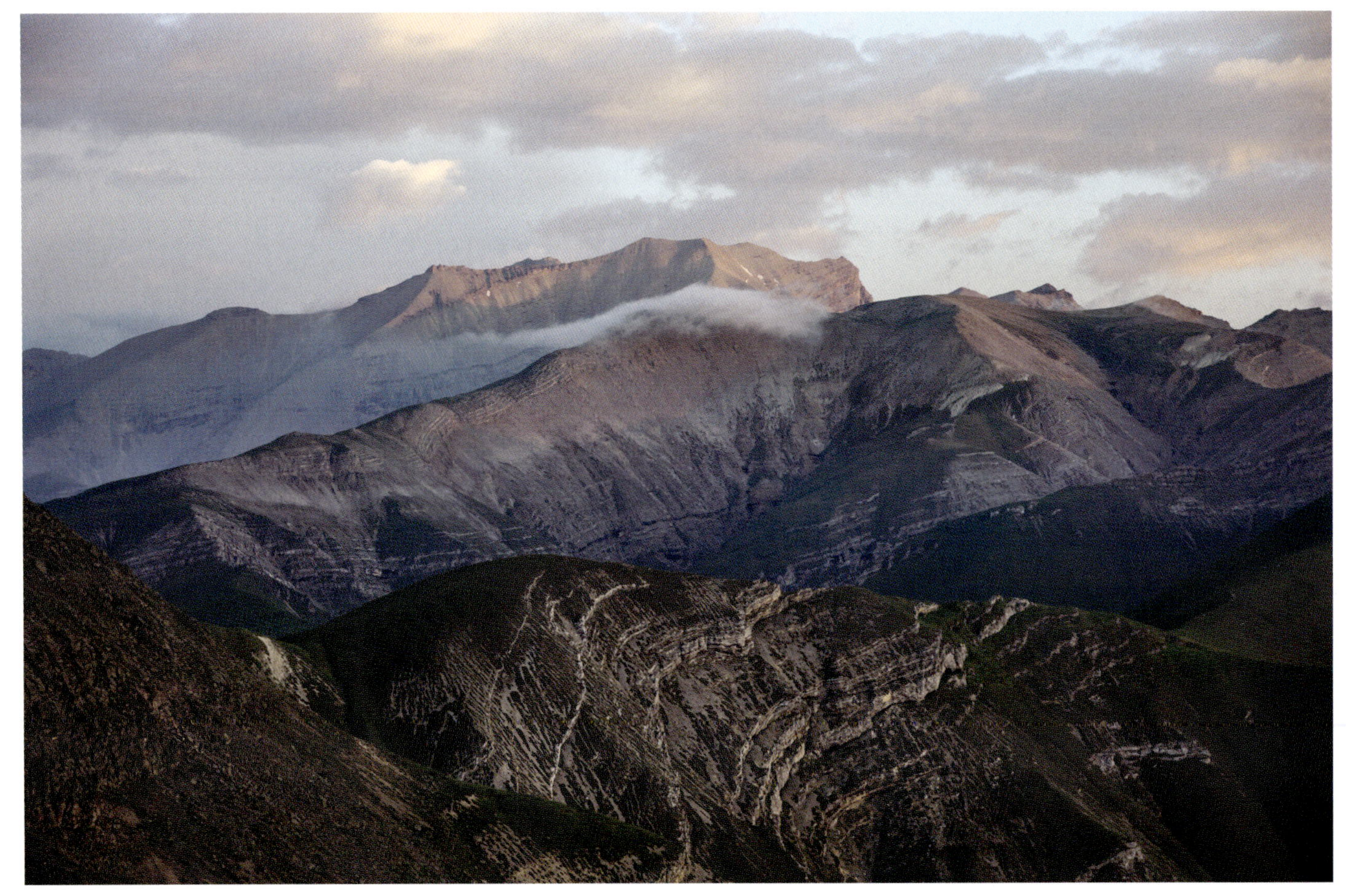

Chegem Gorge
KABARDINO-BALKARIA, RUSSIA

previous page
Hiker in the mountains
TYRNYAUZ, RUSSIA

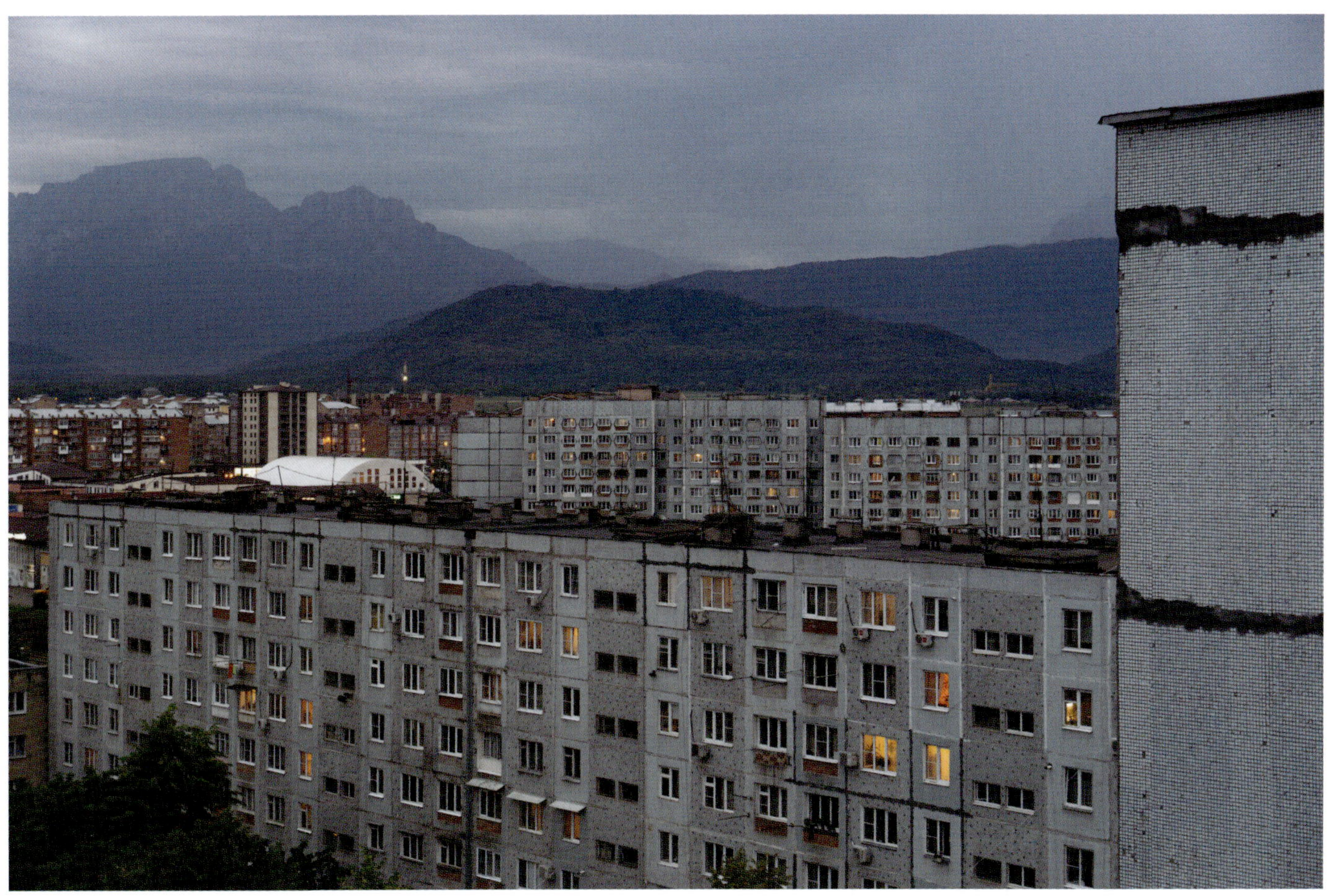

10th Microdistrict
VLADIKAVKAZ, RUSSIA
Built in the 1970s

Vladikavkaz is the capital city of the Republic of North Ossetia-Alania.
About 300,000 people live here, making it one of the most populous
cities of the North Caucasus. During the Soviet period, the city was a
major industrial centre.

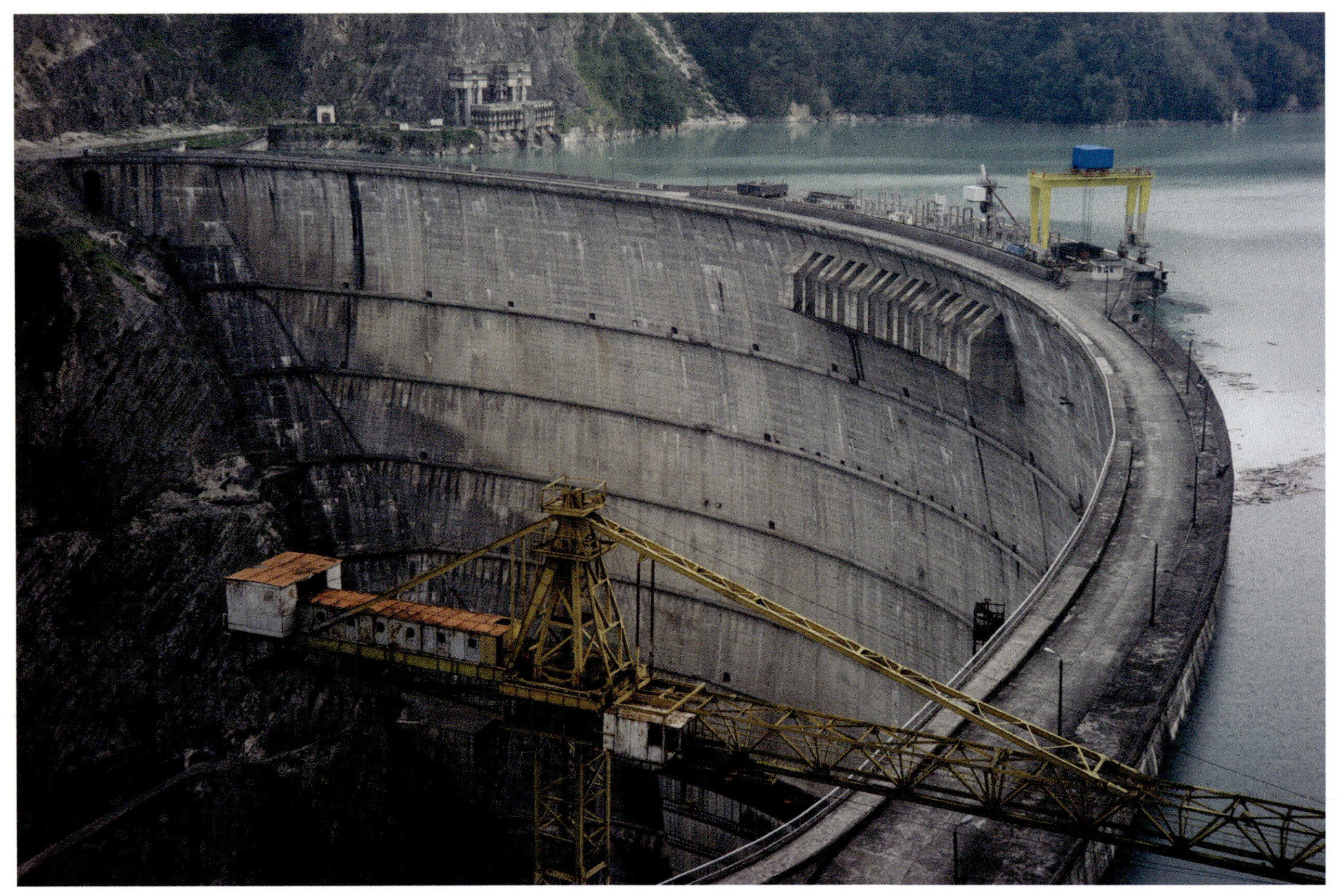

Enguri Hydropower Plant
SVANETIA, GEORGIA
Built in 1978

Key facilities of this hydropower plant (the largest in the Caucasus) are located on territory controlled by the unrecognised Republic of Abkhazia as well as on territory controlled by Georgia. Its operation is only possible with the cooperation of both parties.

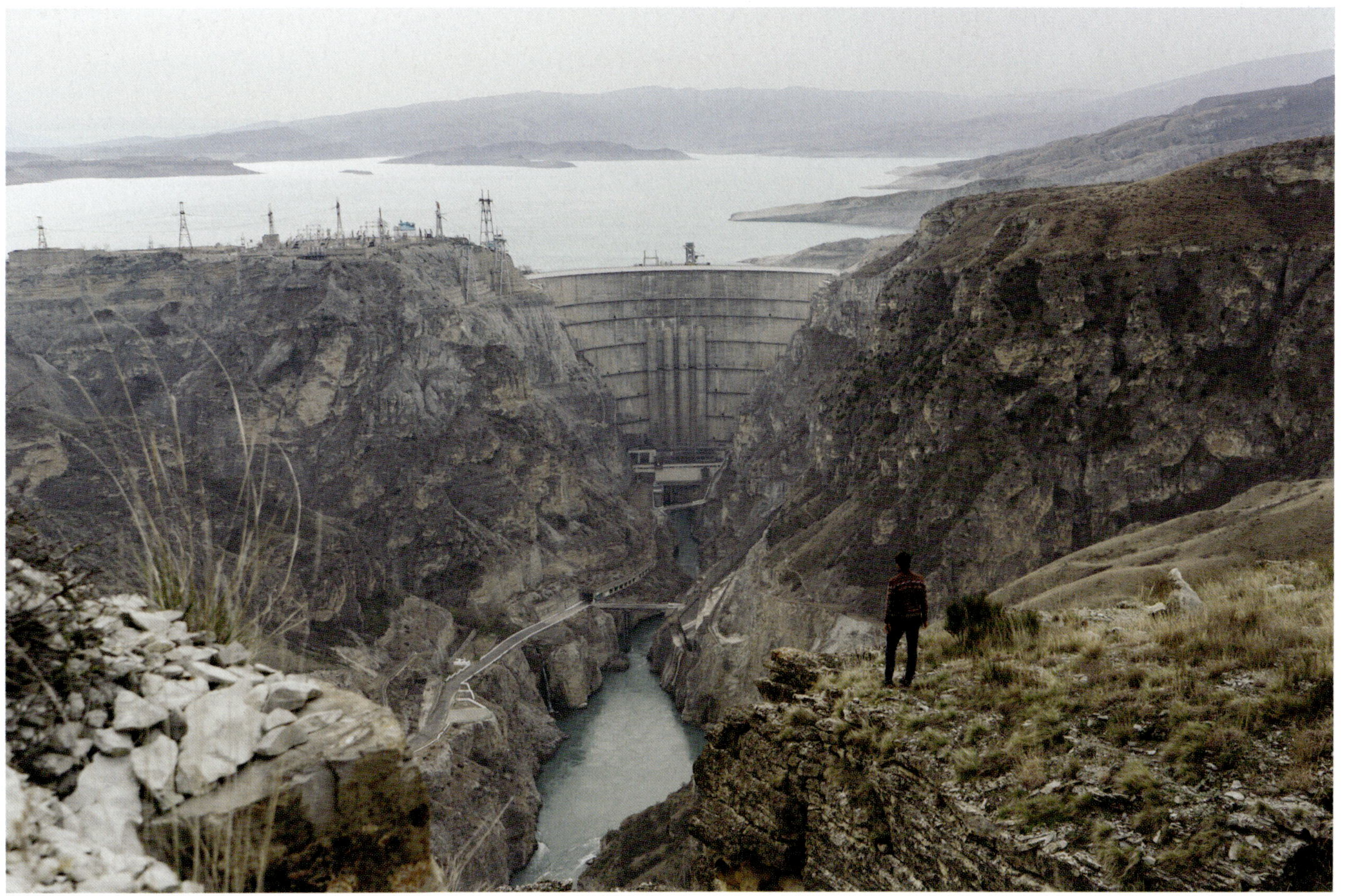

Chirkey Hydropower Plant
DAGESTAN, RUSSIA
Built in 1974

With a capacity of 1,000 MW, this plant on the river Sulak, near the village of Dubki in Dagestan, is the most powerful in the North Caucasus. It has the second-highest dam in Russia and is situated first in the Sulak Hydropower Plant cascade.

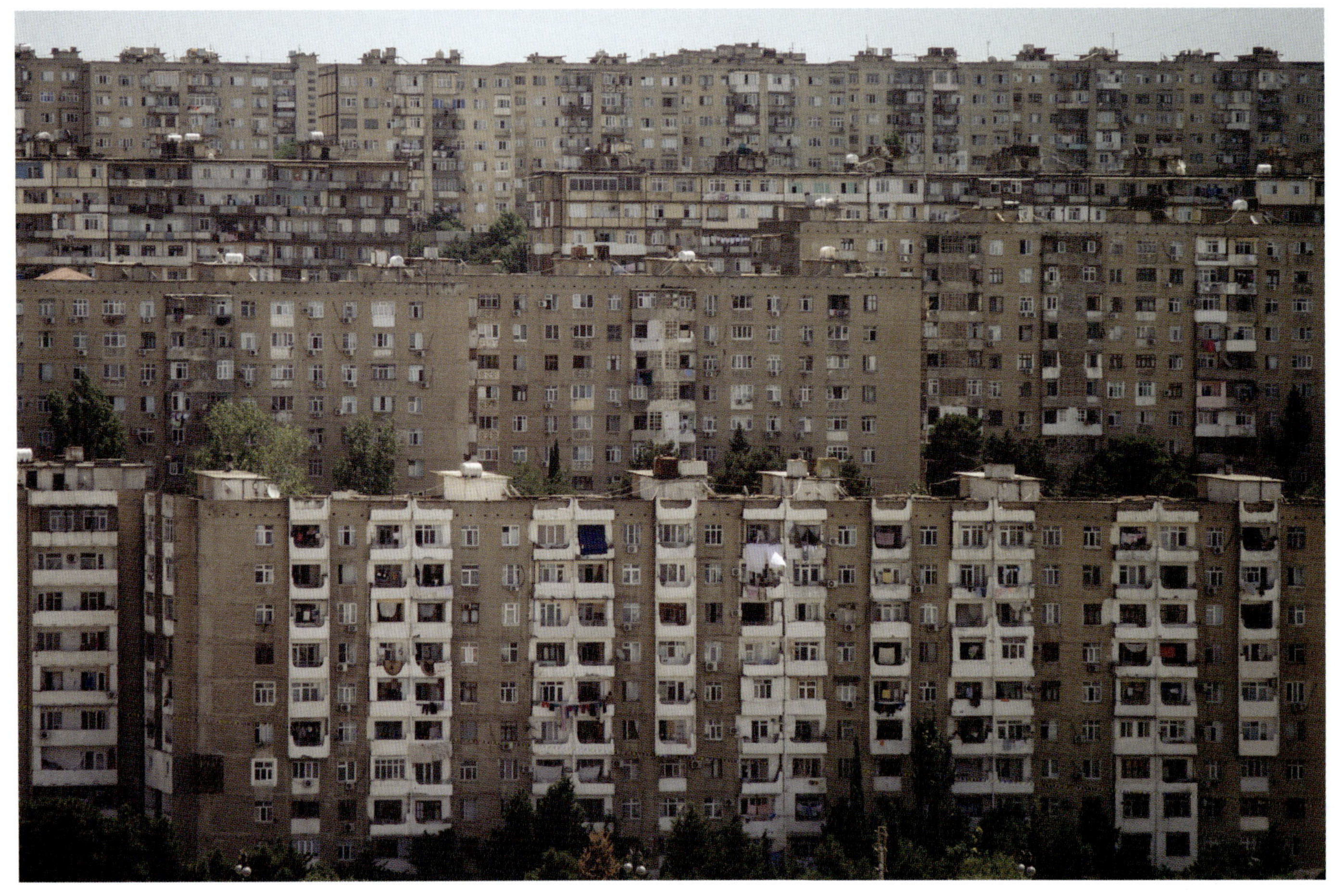

Hatainskiy District
BAKU, AZERBAIJAN
Built in the 1970s

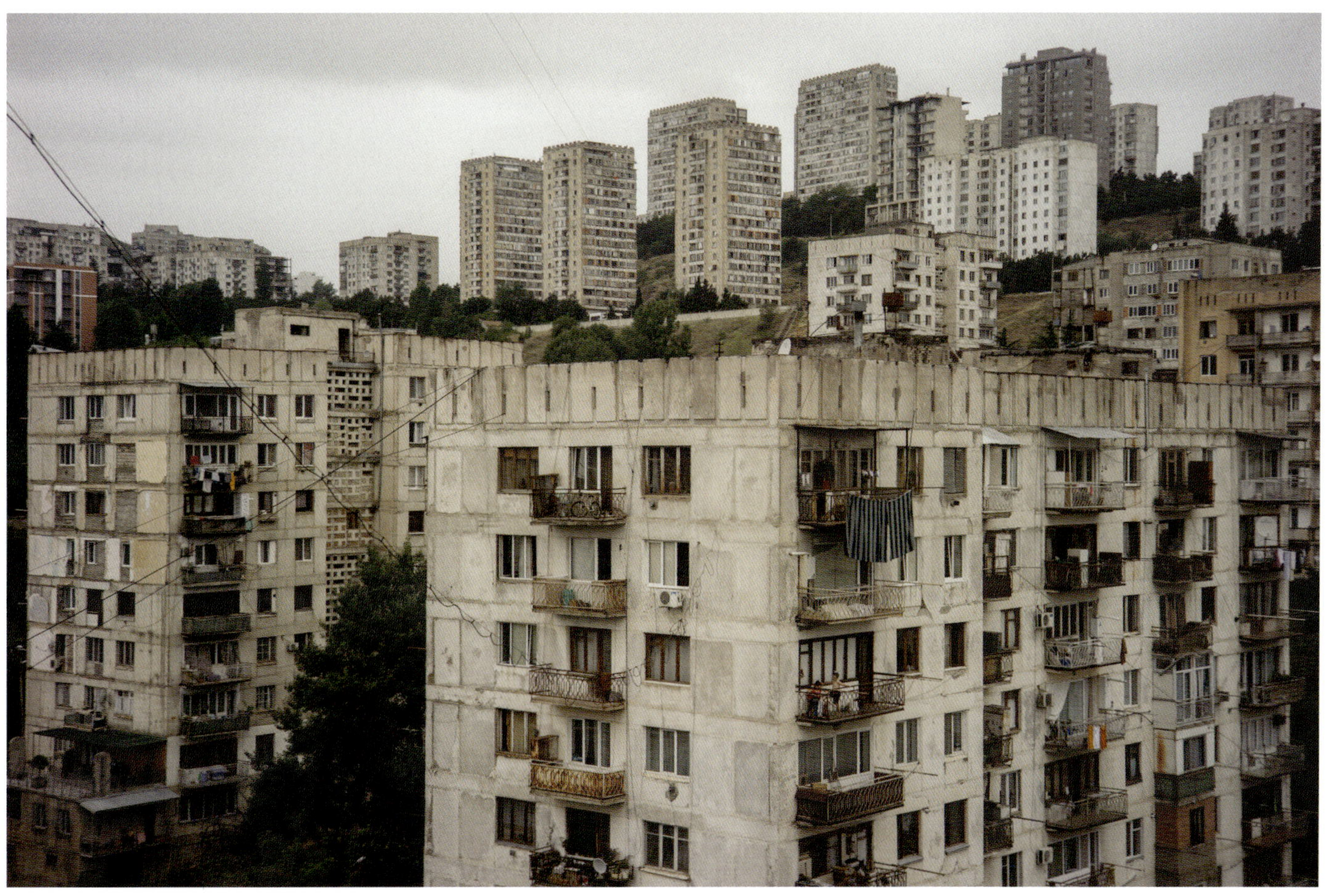

Nutsubidze Plateau development

Built in the 1970s

The Nutsubidze Plateau is a major residential area of Tbilisi, located on the terraces of a steep mountain slope. Relatively flat areas have clusters of panel buildings connected by a serpentine street, along which cars and, with some difficulty, public transport scramble.

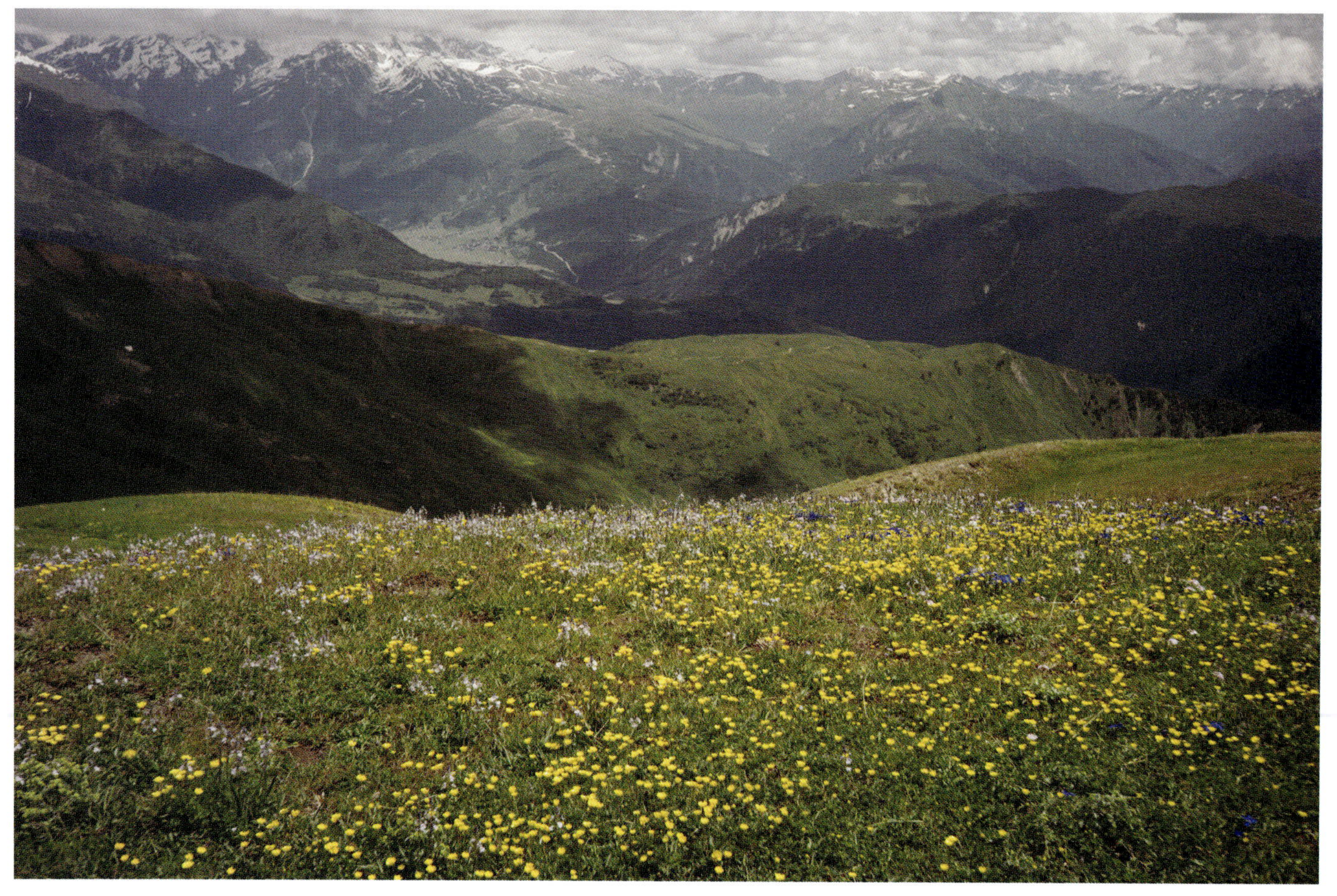

Alpine meadows and wild flowers
SVANETIA, GEORGIA

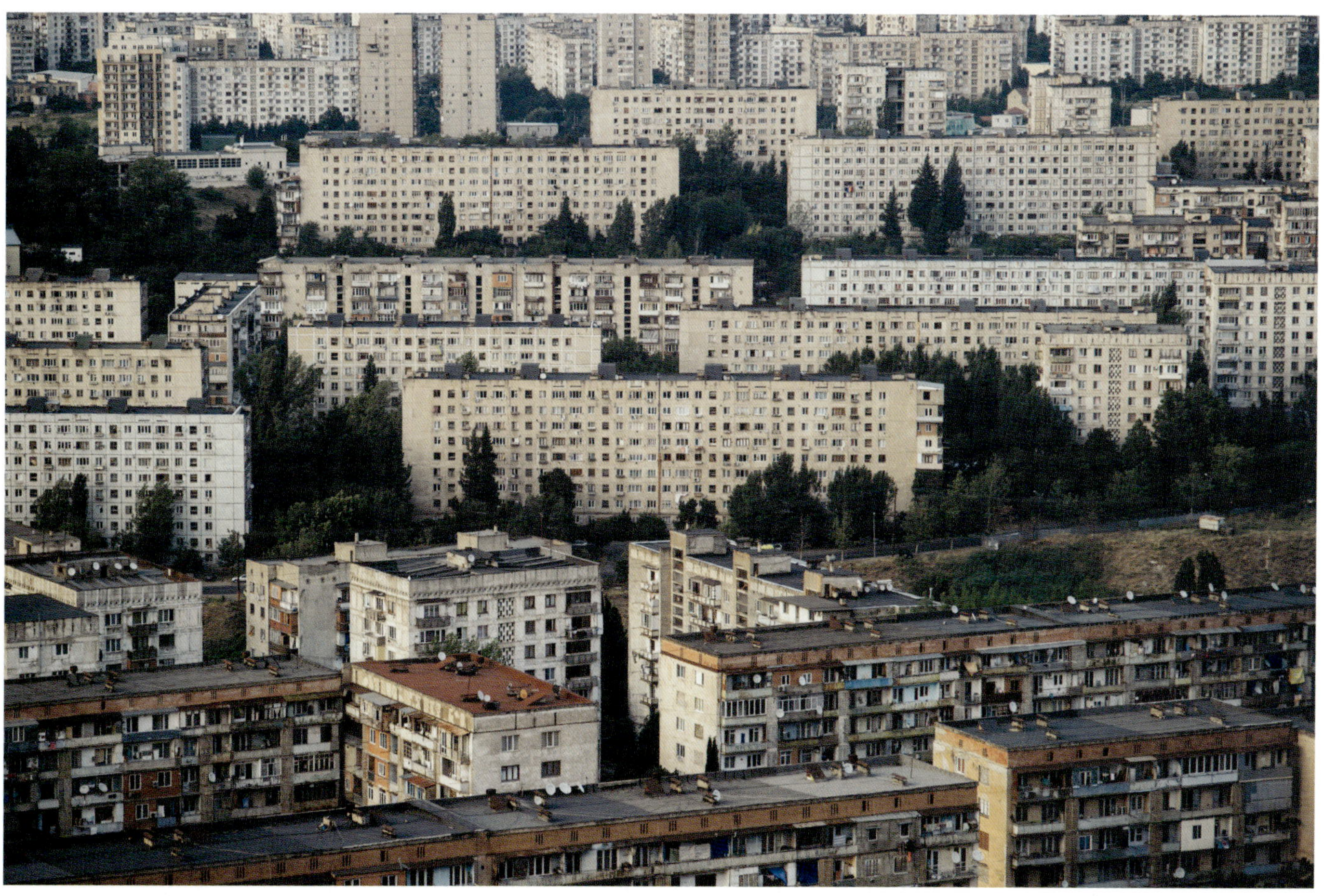

The largest residential neighbourhood in Georgia
GLDANI, GEORGIA
Built in the 1960s

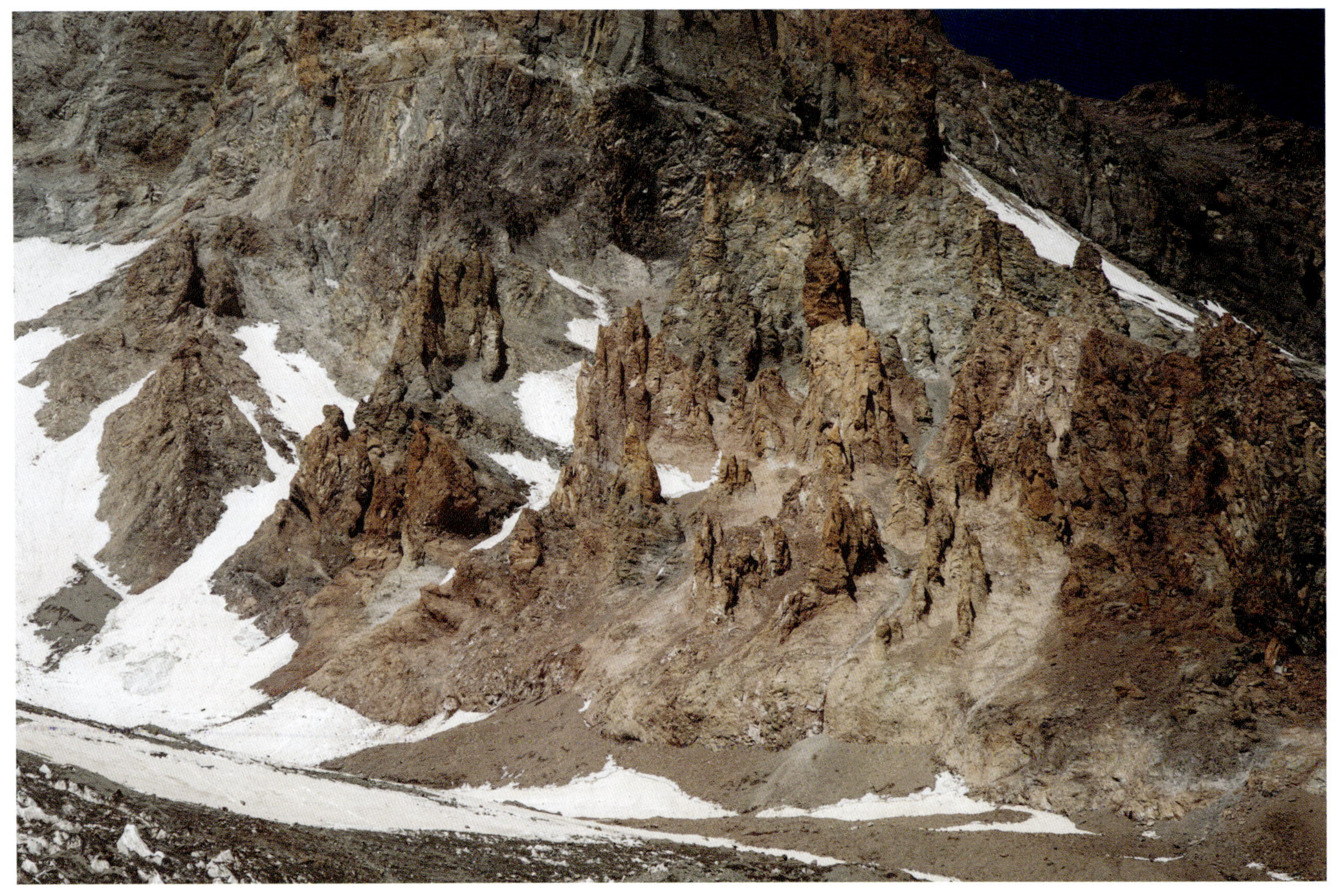

Slopes of Mount Kazbek
MTSKHETA–MTIANETI, GEORGIA

Kazbek is a dormant stratovolcano. Legend has it that Amirani (the Georgian version of Prometheus) was chained to the mountain for stealing fire from the gods. The area surrounding this easternmost peak of the Caucasus was designated a nature reserve in 1979.

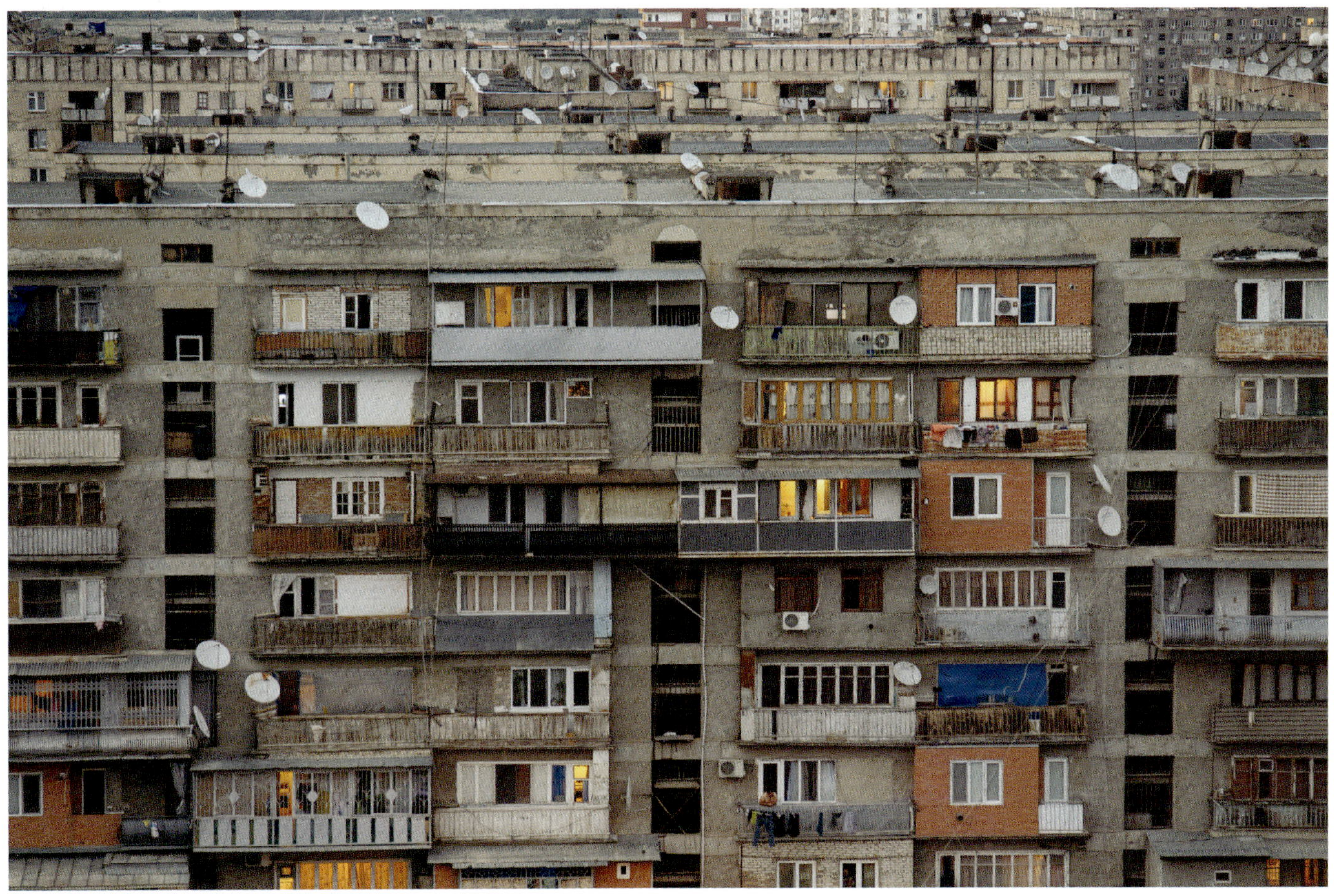

Typical residential development
RUSTAVI, GEORGIA

During the Soviet era, the city's giant metallurgical plant provided jobs for most of the population. With the break-up of the USSR, integration into the Soviet economy was lost, and most local industry closed. Around 65 per cent of workers lost their jobs.

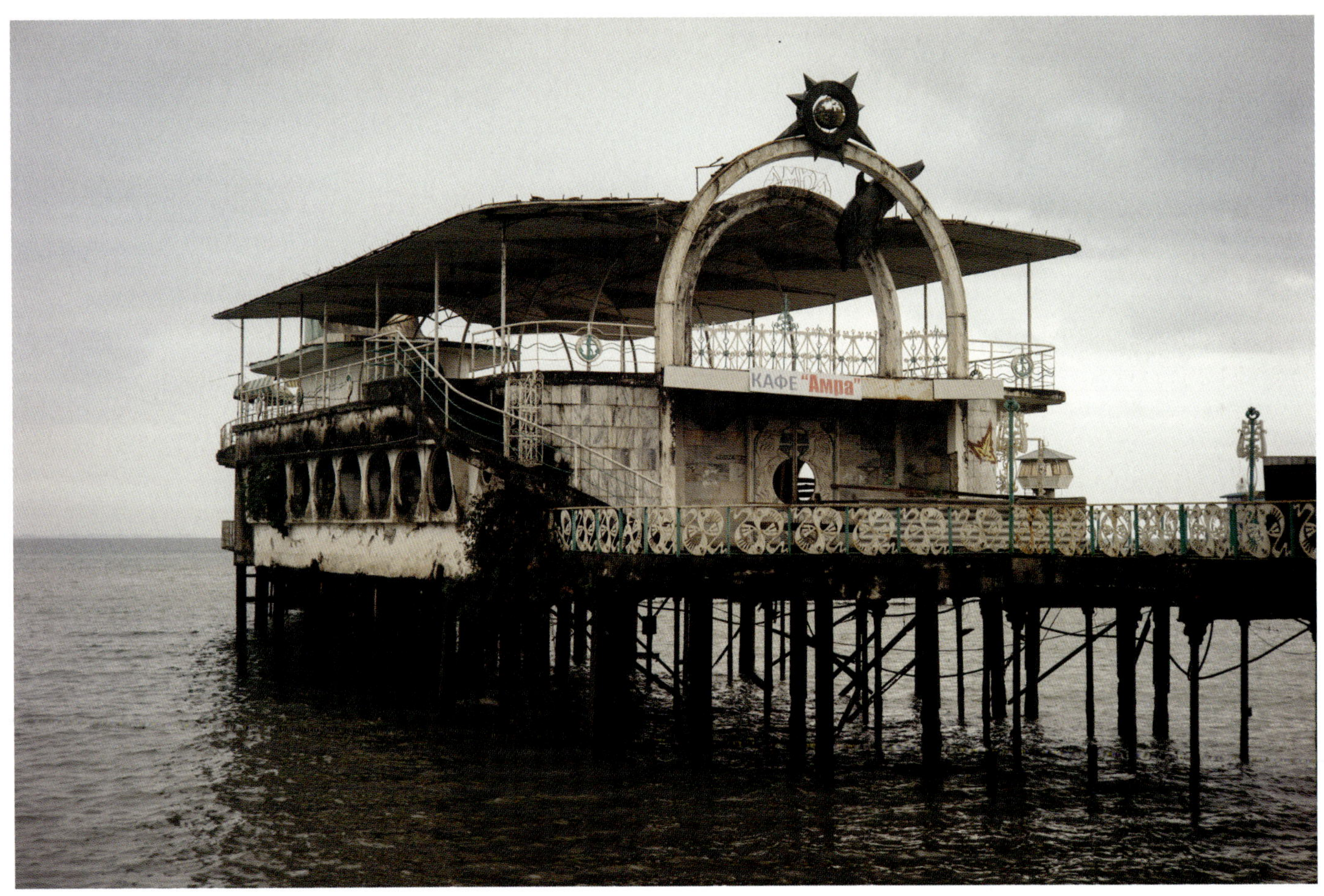

Amra Restaurant
SUKHUM, ABKHAZIA
Built in the 1960s

The Amra Restaurant on the Sukhum seafront is believed to have been founded by Communist Party leader Mikhail Bgazhba, who constructed the building on iron piles. In Soviet times, the restaurant was an iconic location, visited by the local intelligentsia.

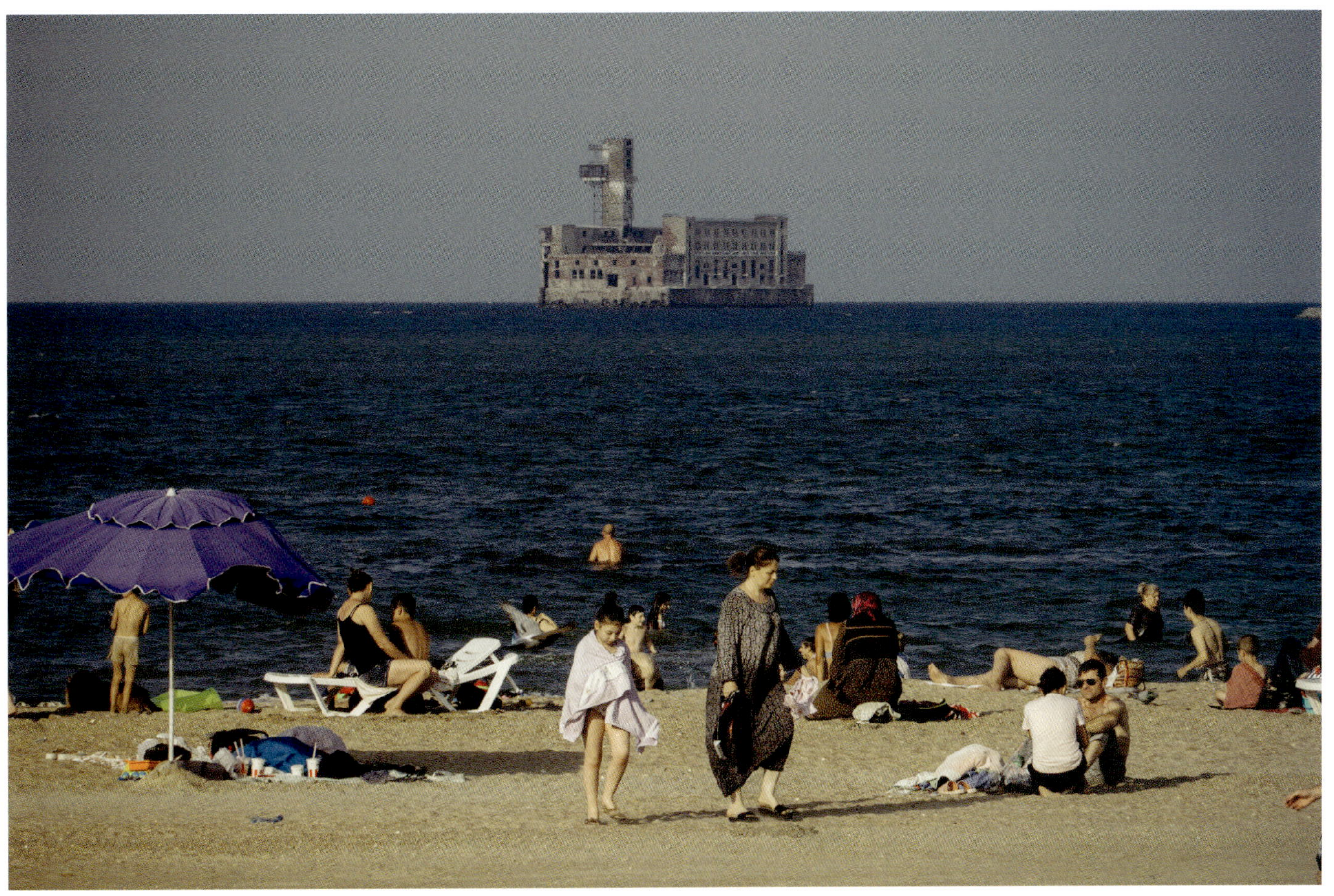

Naval Weapons Plant
(8th Workshop of the Dagdizel Plant)
KASPIYSK, RUSSIA

The decision to establish a naval weapons plant in Dagestan was made in 1931, with the plant and the village of Dvigatelstroy being constructed simultaneously. One of the torpedo workshops was built out to sea, on a stone foundation laid on the seabed.

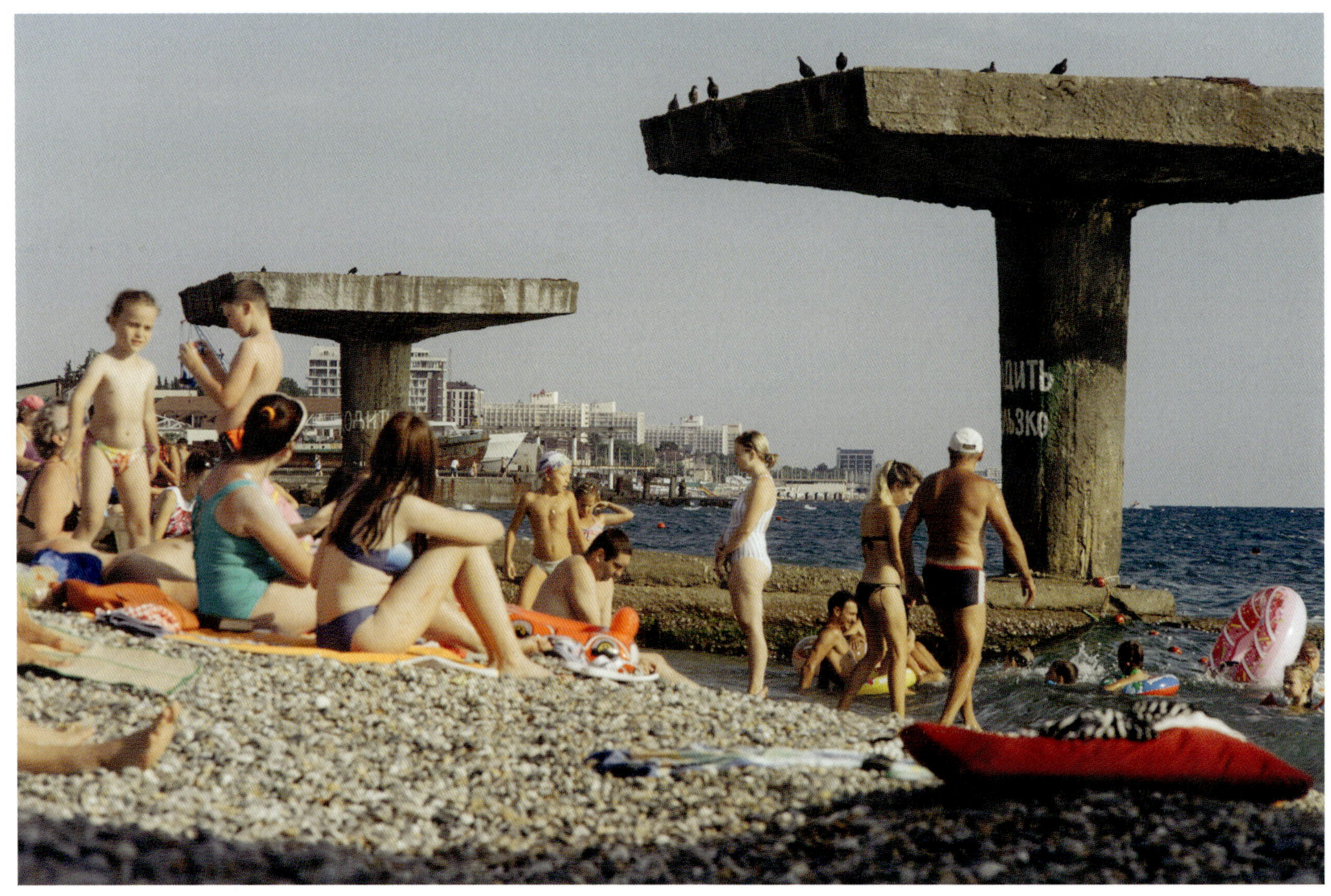

Remains of concrete pier supports
Black Sea beach
SOCHI, RUSSIA

The construction of buoys, breakwaters and other shore-protection structures began in the mid-20th century to prevent coastal erosion. The strong Black Sea currents travel clockwise along the shore, taking with them pebbles, sand and sediment.

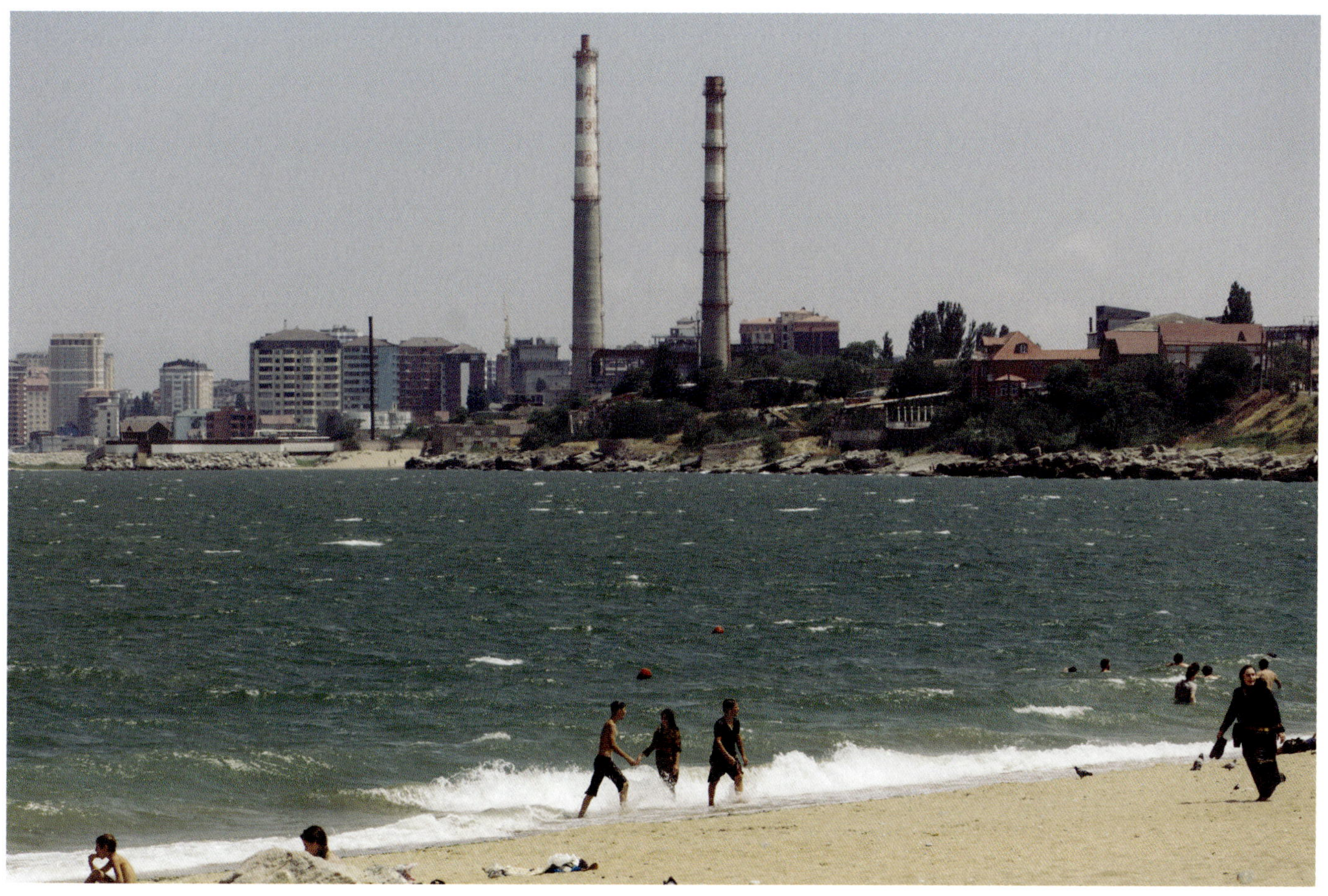

Makhachkala Combined Heat and Power Plant
Caspian Sea beach
MAKHACHKALA, RUSSIA

The Makhachkala Combined Heat and Power Plant, commissioned in December 1953, can be seen in the background. In the 1970s, the station was converted from oil to gas, and its equipment unpdated. It has an electric capacity of MW 18 and a heat capacity of 256 Gkal/h.

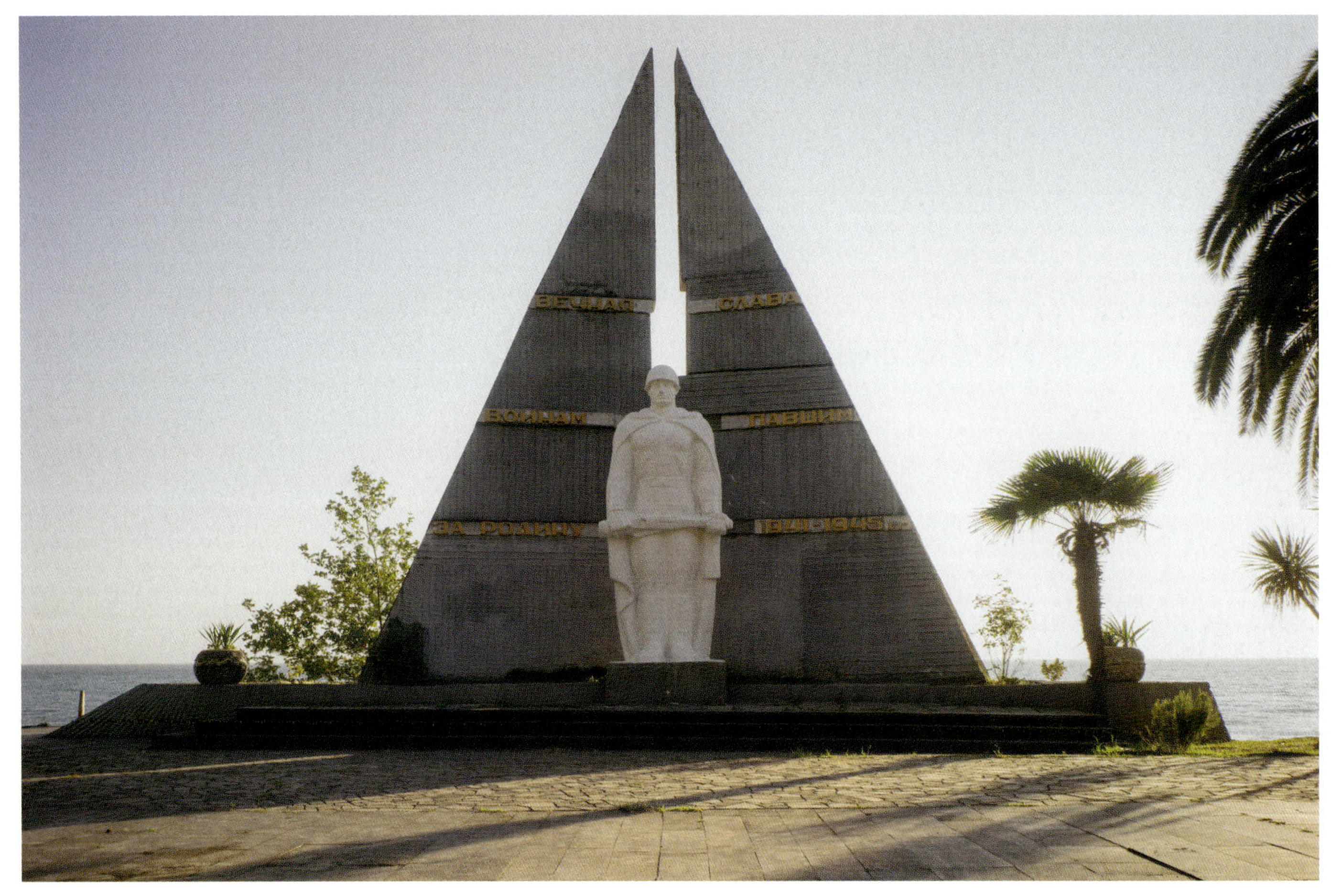

Monument to the Fallen in the Great Patriotic War
GAGRA, ABKHAZIA

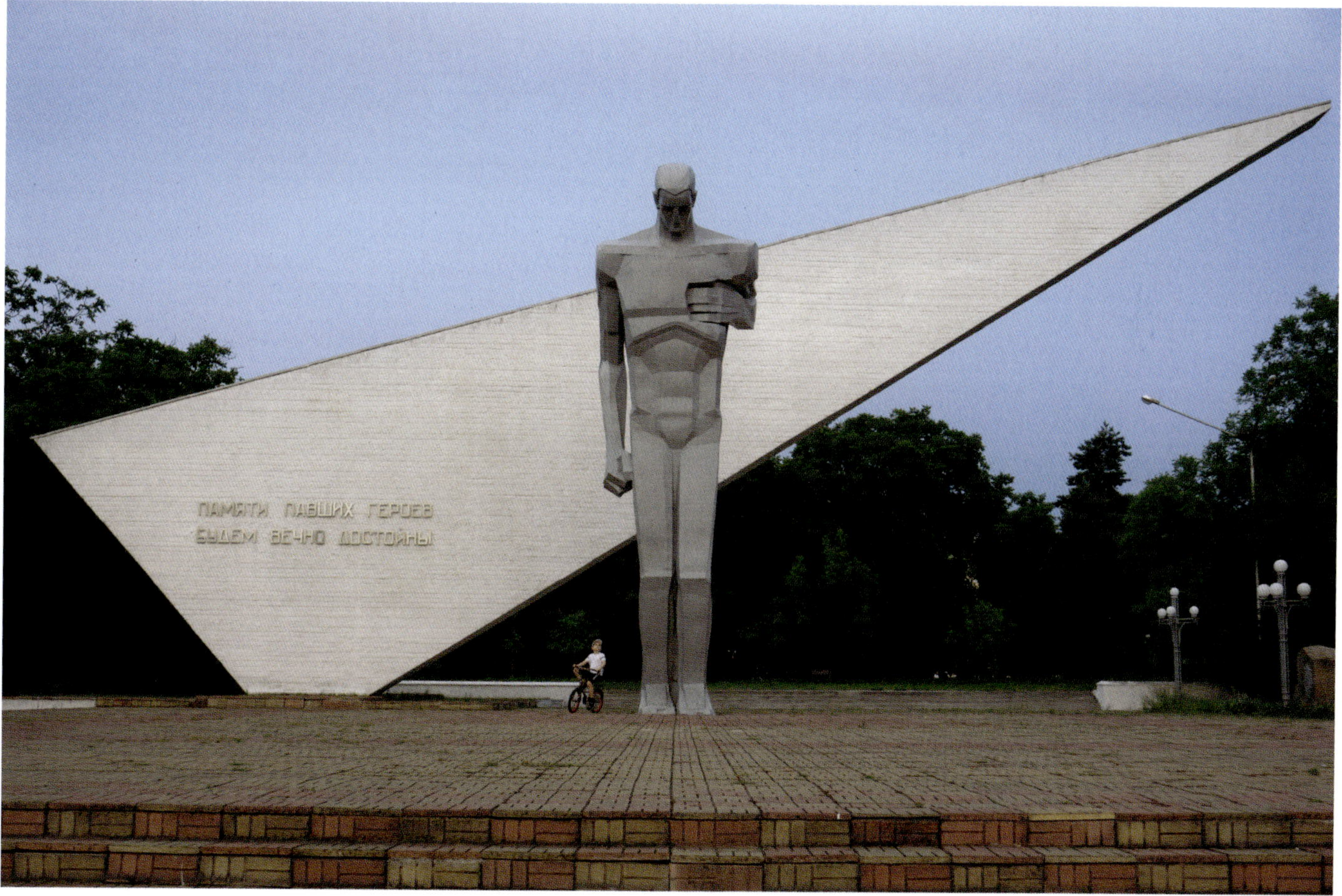

Monument to the Komsomol Who Died in the Civil War
NALCHIK, RUSSIA
Erected in 1968

Unveiled on the 50th anniversary of the Komsomol, the monument
(nicknamed 'Fantômas' after its likeness to the fictional character)
originally had a large penis. Outraged locals demanded the authorities
take action and the organ was amputated.

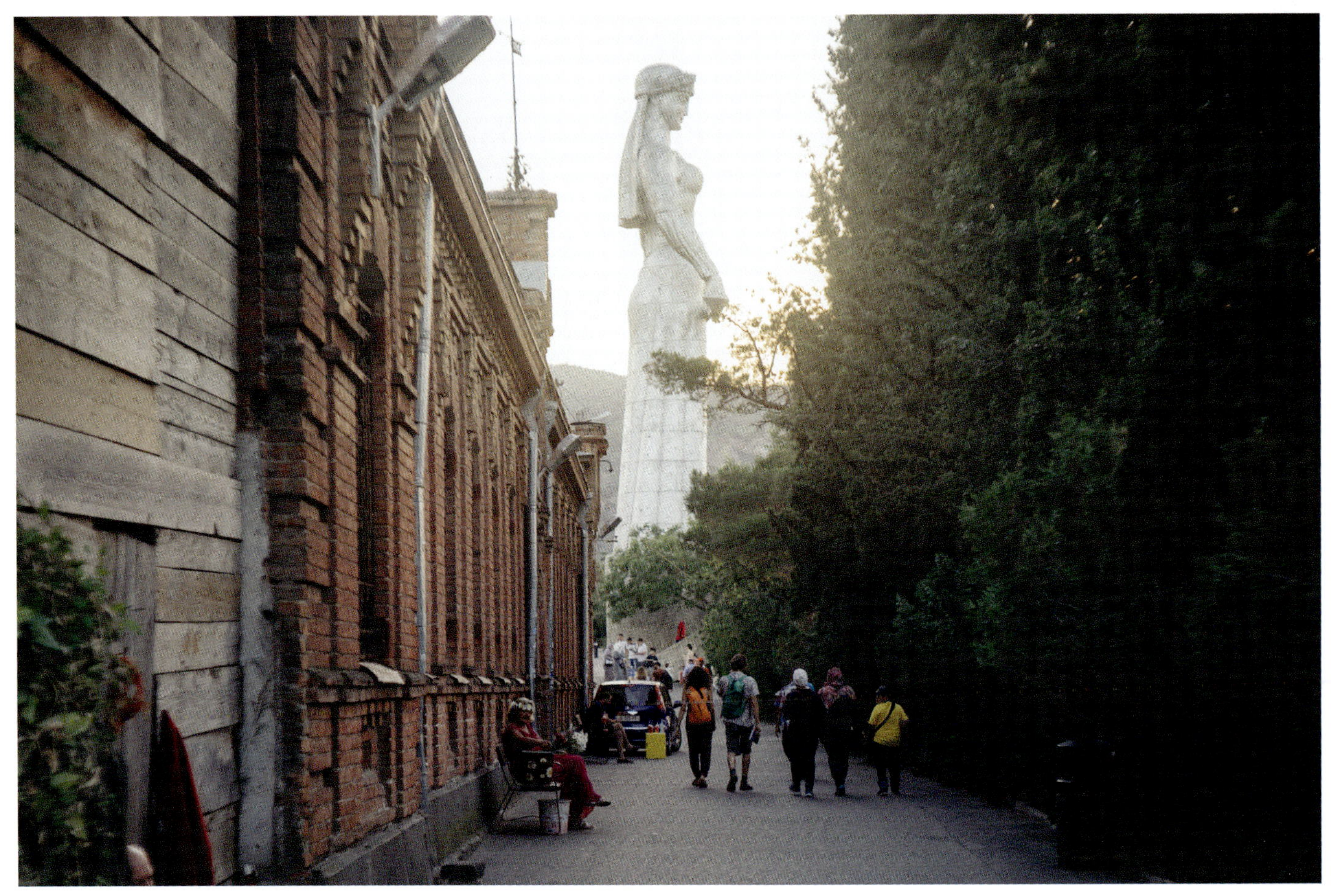

'Mother of Georgia'
TBILISI, GEORGIA
Erected in 1958
Designer: E. Amashukeli

The 'Mother of Georgia' monument on Sololaki Hill was originally made of wood. In 1963, it was covered with aluminium to prevent weather damage. In the 1990s, it was dismantled and a new version installed, complete with a modernised dress and updated kerchief.

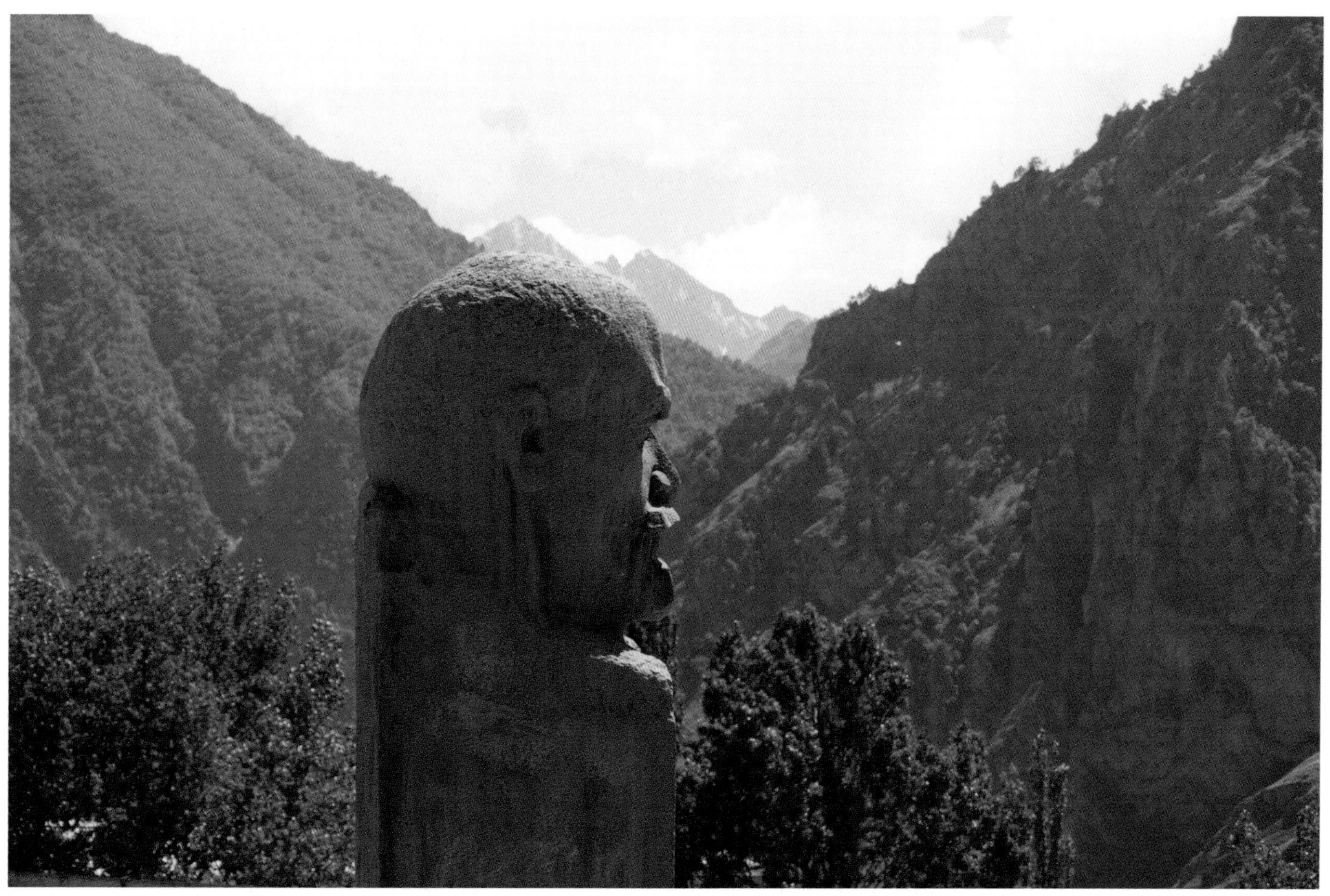

Lenin's head
TYRNYAUZ, RUSSIA

This monument to Lenin is located near the abandoned building of the Tyrnyauz tungsten mining and processing plant, around which the town was founded in 1955. In the background are the tree-covered spurs of the mountains that border the Tyryauz valley.

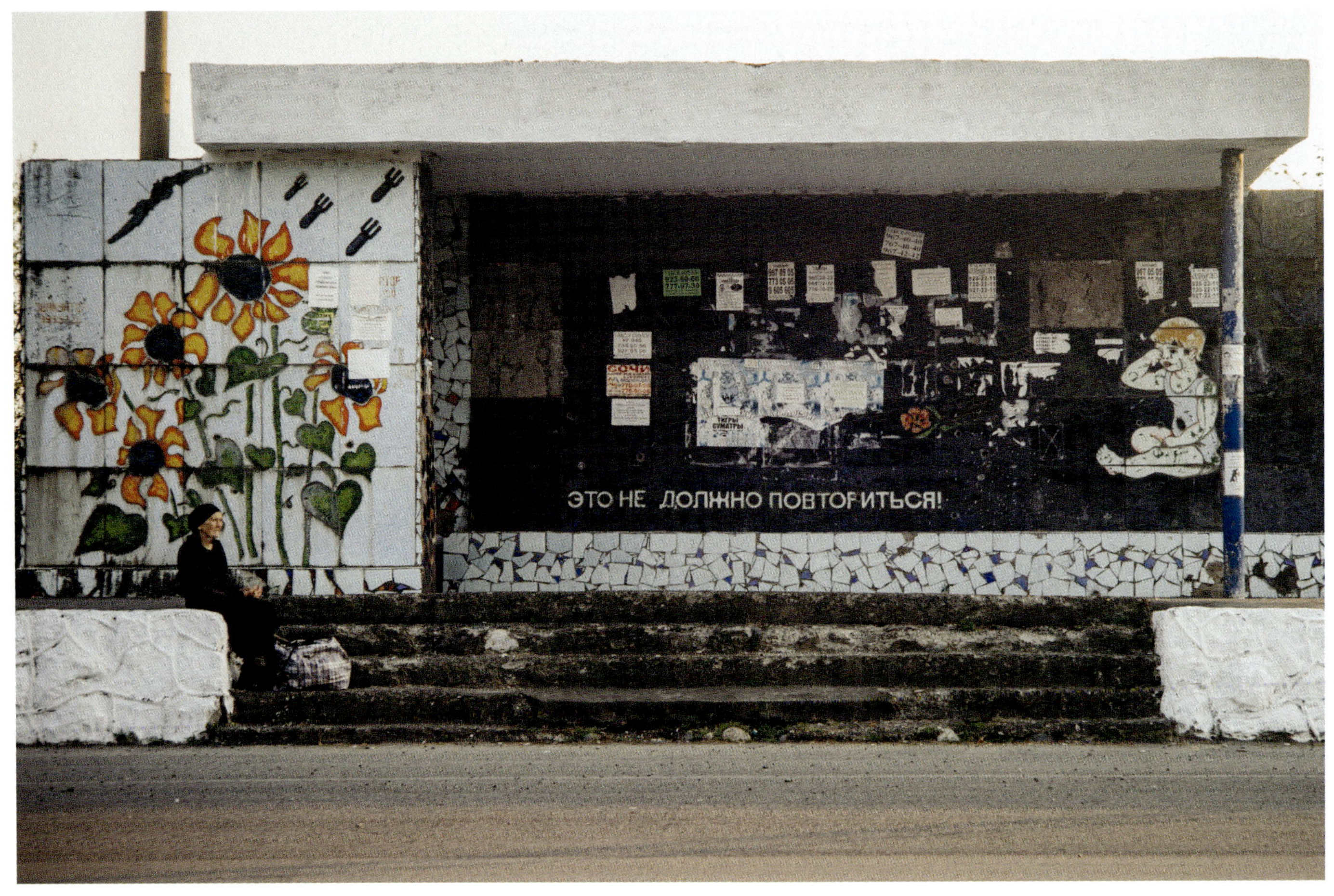

Bus stop
SUKHUM, ABKHAZIA
Built in the 1980s

The Russian text on this bus stop declares 'It must not happen again!', a reference to the Great Patriotic War (World War II), in which it is estimated that 27 million Soviets, both civilian and military, died (the exact figure is disputed).

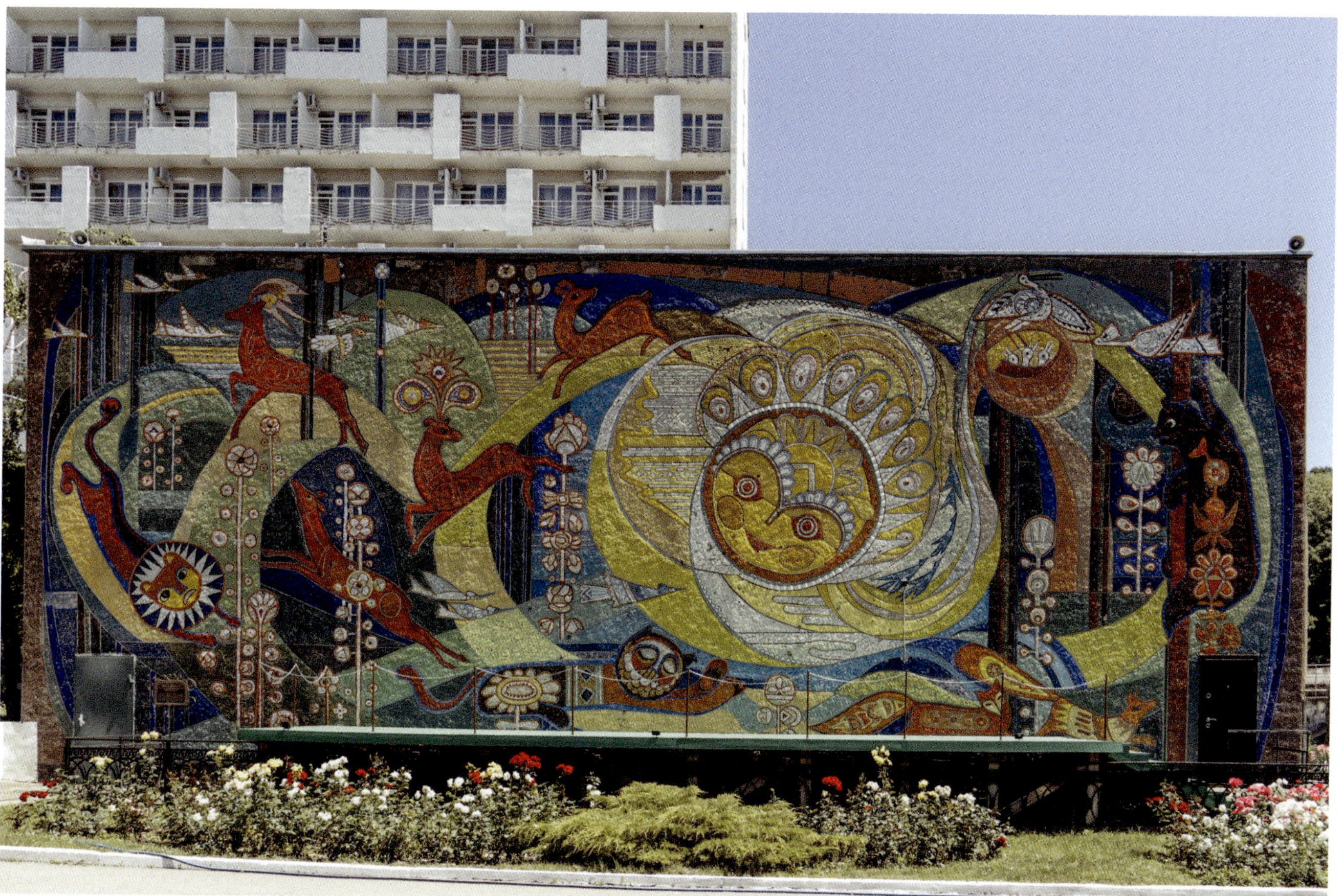

Dubrava Sanatorium mosaic
ZHELEZNOVODSK, RUSSIA
Created in 1981

Dubrava Sanatorium is an 11-storey hotel containing a dining room, cinema and concert hall. A heated, covered passage connects the main dormitory building to the 2-storey diagnostic and treatment building.

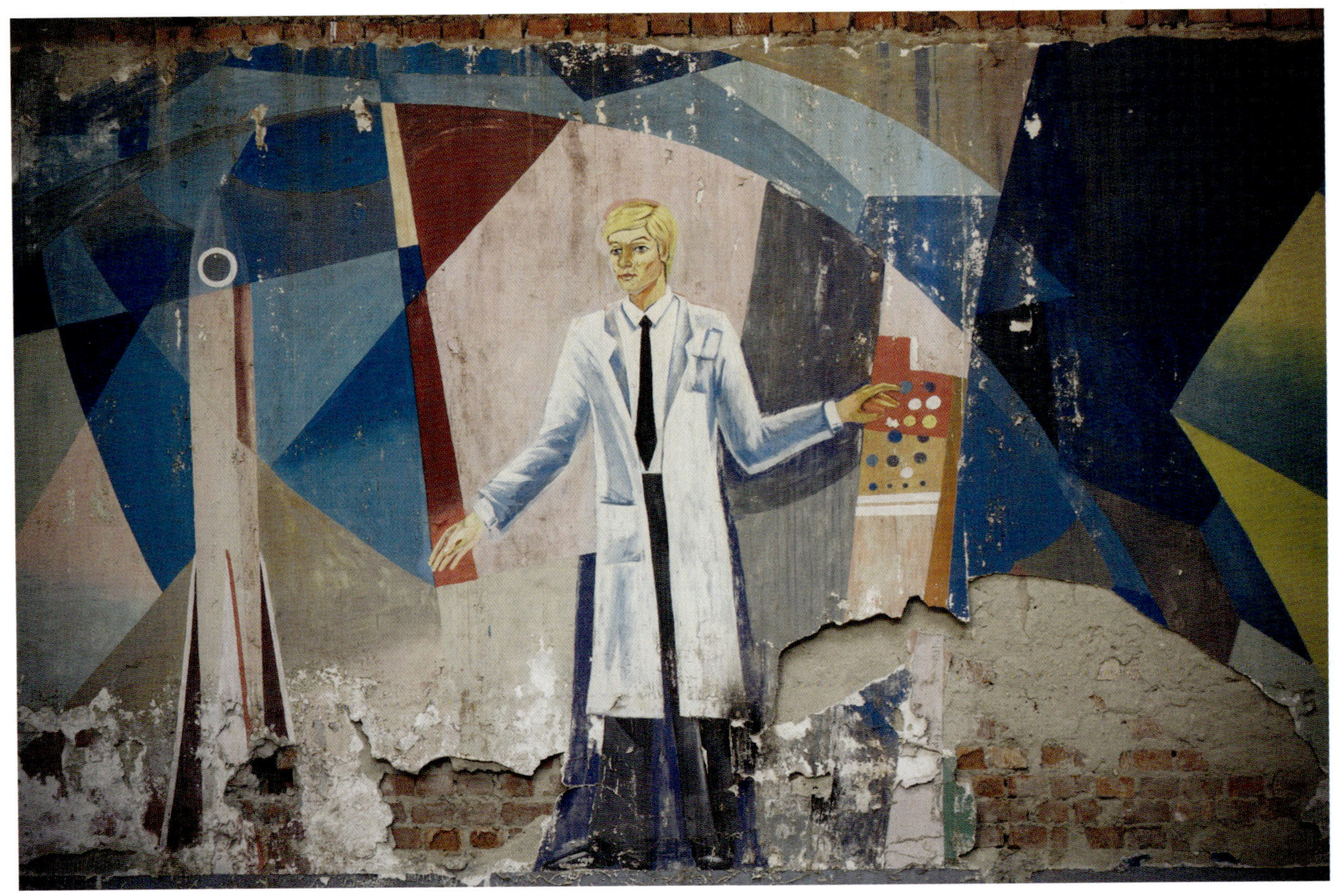

Painting in the abandoned electro-vacuum plant
NALCHIK, RUSSIA
Created in 1959

This plant, orginally a defence-industry operation, was later converted to the production of cathode-ray tubes and kinescopes for television and radio apparatus. In the Soviet era, the plant was famous and prospered, but it was abandoned after it went bankrupt in the 1990s.

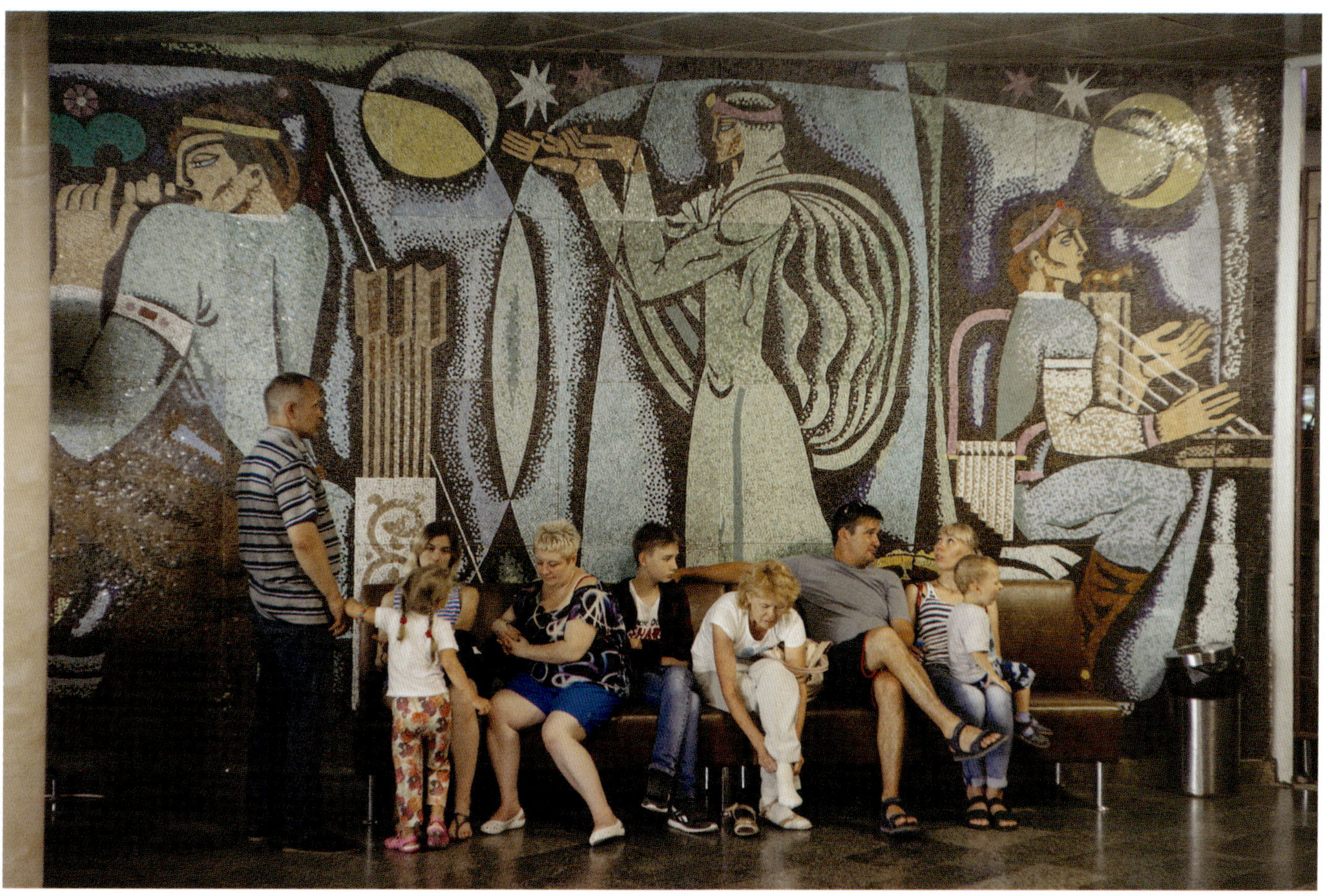

Funicular Station mosaic, New Athos Cave
NEW ATHOS, ABKHAZIA
Created in 1975

A special train takes visitors through a tunnel into the bowels of the cave, one of the largest in the world. The New Athos light metro was the first of its kind in the USSR. It consists of three stations spanning a length of 1.3 kilometres.

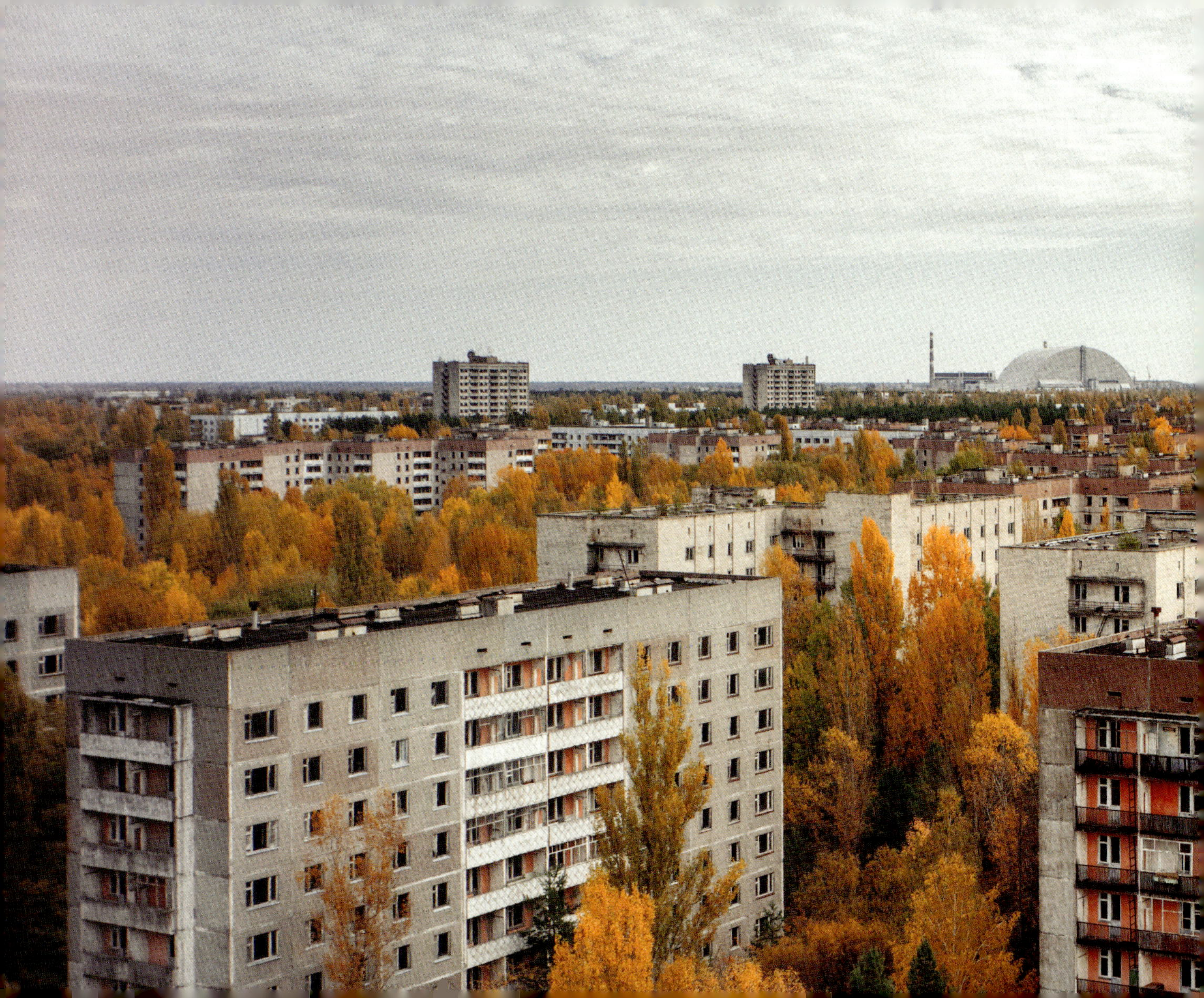

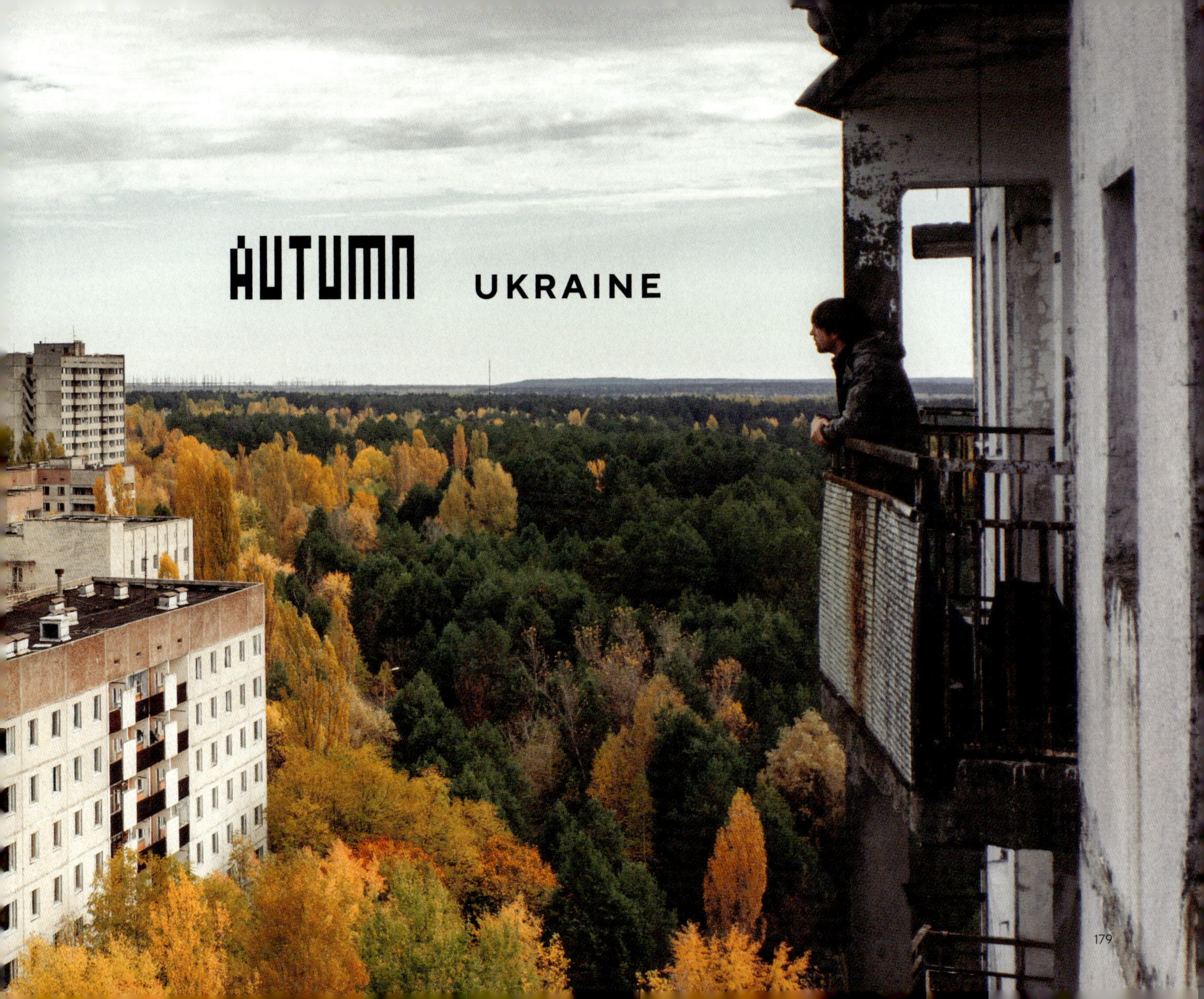
AUTUMN UKRAINE

UKRAINE

From the green Carpathian Mountains to the wide steppes of Donetsk, from the forests and meadows of Polesye to the Black and Azov seas – this is the expanse of the Ukrainian SSR. Within the family formed by our sister republics, Soviet Ukraine is second to the Russian Federation in population and economic significance. It is a republic with highly developed industry and diversified agriculture. It has the largest coal and iron-ore deposits and thriving factories, power plants, mines and blast furnaces; it has rich orchards and vineyards, alongside fields of golden wheat, sunflowers and sugar-beet. It has bright sunshine, with plains dotted with quiet lakes and crossed by blue rivers; it contains the wild mountain streams of the Carpathians, the blue expanse of the southern sea, the resorts of the Crimea. Ukraine is home to millions of Soviet people, and thanks to their work, the land is becoming richer and more beautiful.

Over a fifth of the population of the Soviet Union lives in the Ukrainian SSR. The majority are Ukrainian (75 per cent), but there are also Russians, Belarusians, Poles, Jews and other nationalities. The Ukrainians are closely linked by language, culture and history to the Russians and Belarusians. After all, Ukrainians, Russians and Belarusians descended from one ancient Russian nation that had long inhabited large areas of eastern Europe, creating a major East Slavic state – Kievan Rus – in the 9th and 10th centuries.

Ukrainians have needed to defend their independence and freedom by force of arms on many occasions. In the middle of the 17th century, the war to liberate the Ukrainian people from the oppression of feudal Poland ended with the reunification of Ukraine and Russia. This reunification was of great progressive value for Ukraine, saving the country from slavery to foreigners. Ukrainian culture, art and science developed in close connection with that of the Russian people and other Russian nations. Russian and Ukrainian workers fought together against the tsarist regime, against their class enemies – the bourgeoisie and the landlords.

The path to liberation and the means to build a new life were revealed to the people of Ukraine by the Communist Party, led by V.I. Lenin. With the victory of the Great October Socialist Revolution, a new era began for the peoples of the former Russian Empire. On 12 December 1917, the First All-Ukrainian Congress of Soviets in Kharkiv proclaimed Ukraine a Soviet Socialist Republic. The Ukrainian SSR represents an important link within the unified economic structure of the Soviet Union: it is one of the most significant coal and metallurgical bases within the All-Union division of labour. Almost half the metal and ore and a third of coal extracted and produced in the USSR comes from Ukraine. The Ukrainian SSR is closely and inextricably linked with the other republics of our Motherland and its economy is developing within the common national economic system of the Soviet Union – this is its strength and the key to success!

Children's Encyclopedia Vol. 9, 'Our Soviet Motherland', A.I. Markushevich (editor-in-chief), 1978

previous page
View from the balcony of 52 Lesi Ukrainki Street
PRIPYAT, UKRAINE

Duga-1 radar
Ceased operation on 26 April 1986 following the Chernobyl disaster
CHERNOBYL, UKRAINE

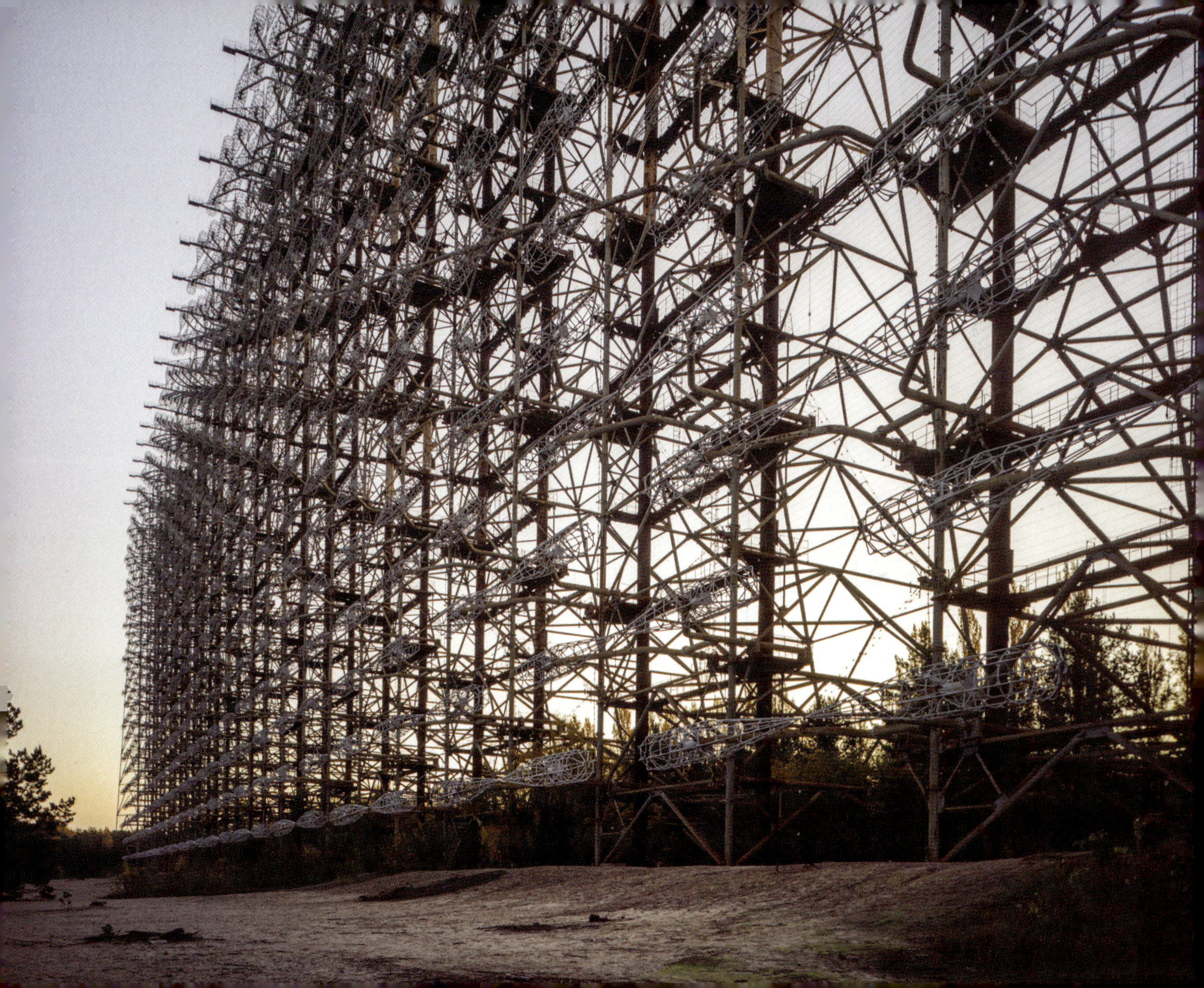

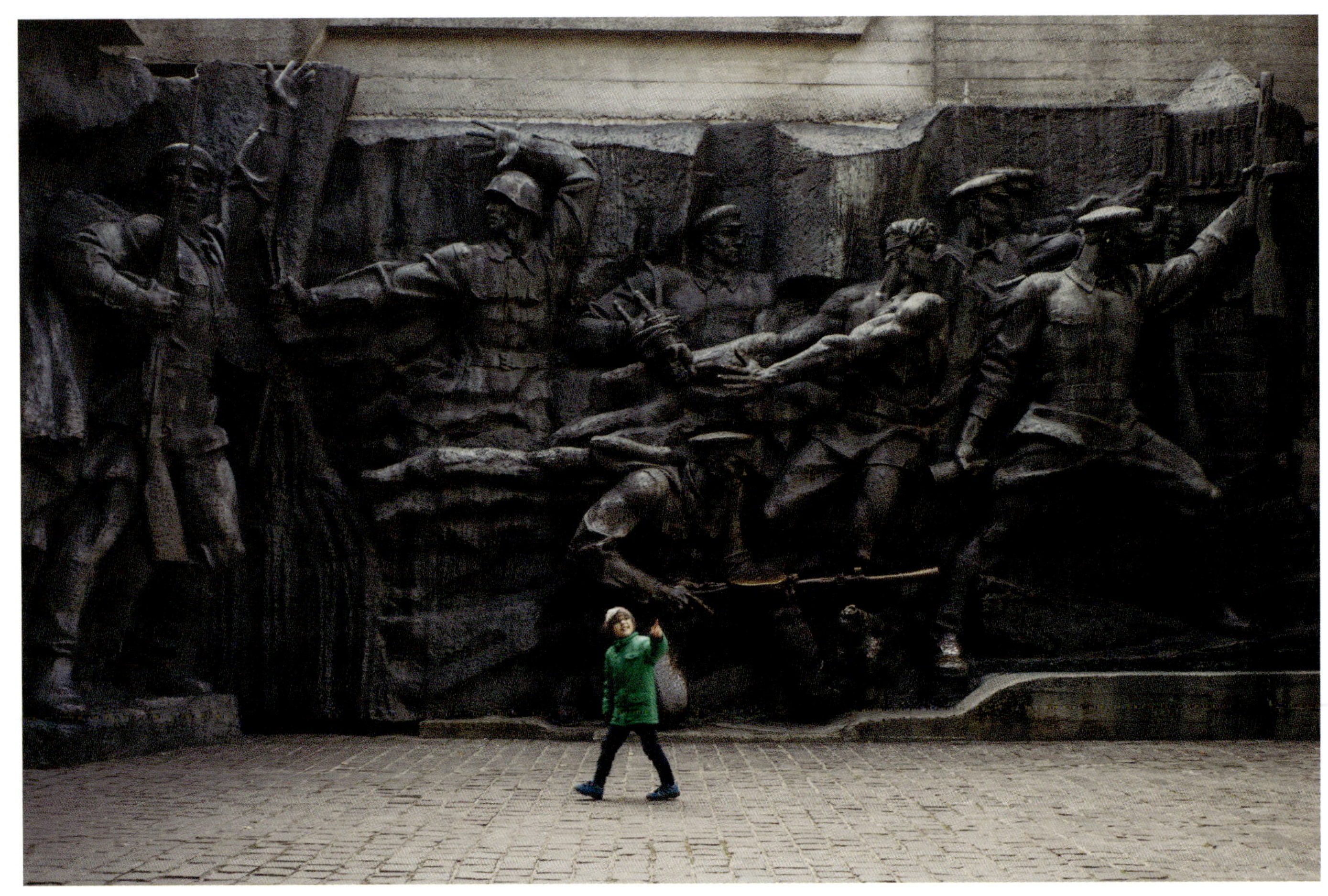

Memorial Complex of the Museum of the History of the Great Patriotic War
KIEV, UKRAINE
Built in 1974
Designers: E. Vuchetich, E. Stamo et al.

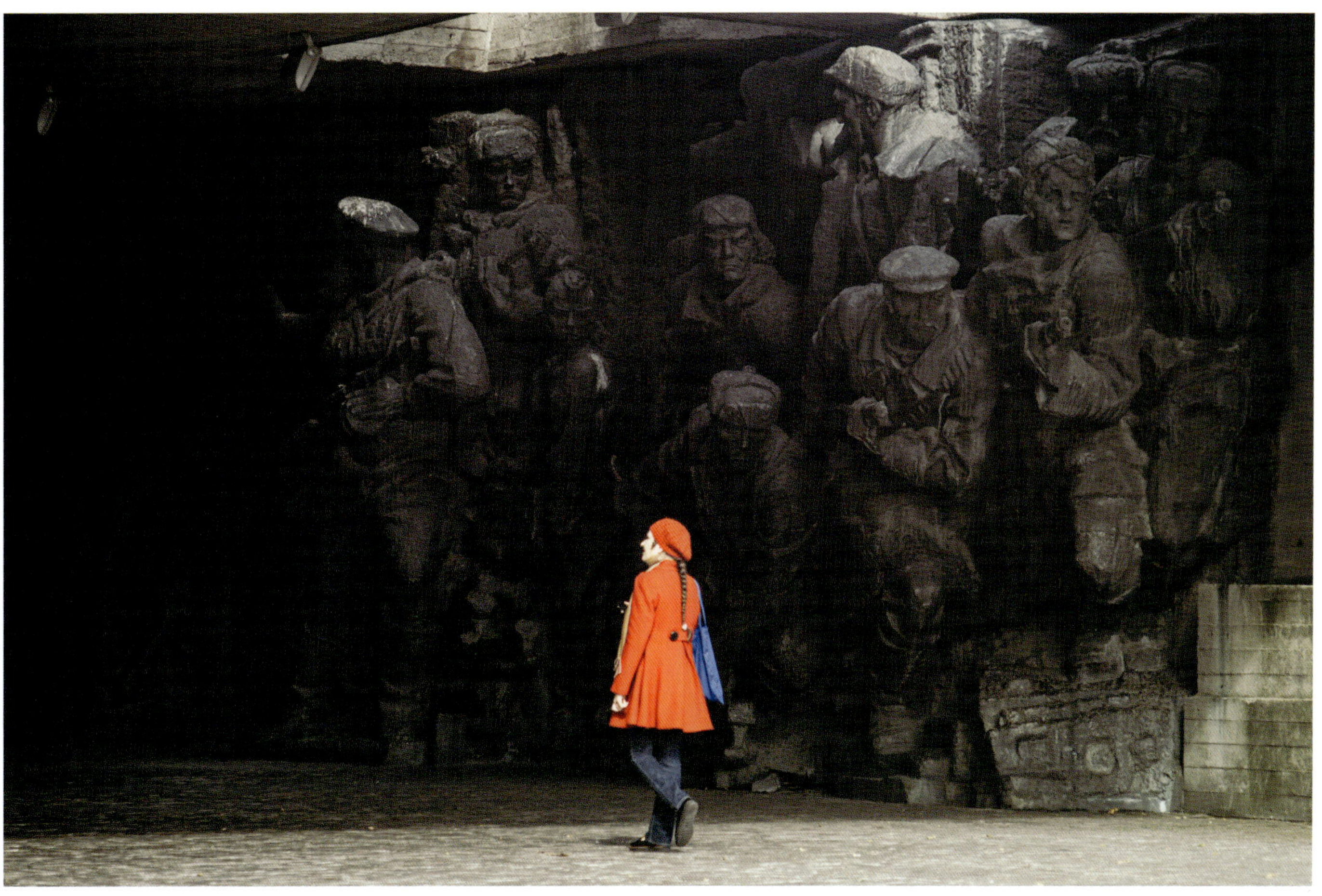

A walkway on the slopes of the right bank of the Dnieper river leads to the main entrance to the museum, built underneath the huge 'Motherland' monument. Lining the route, a 5-metre high bronze relief depicts important aspects of Ukraine's World War II campaign: 'The First Frontier Battles' (the heroic defence of the Soviet border against attack by Germany); 'Unconquered' (the horrors of German occupation); 'Heroic Underground Guerrillas' (the partisan struggle); and 'From Rear to Front' (labour on the home front).

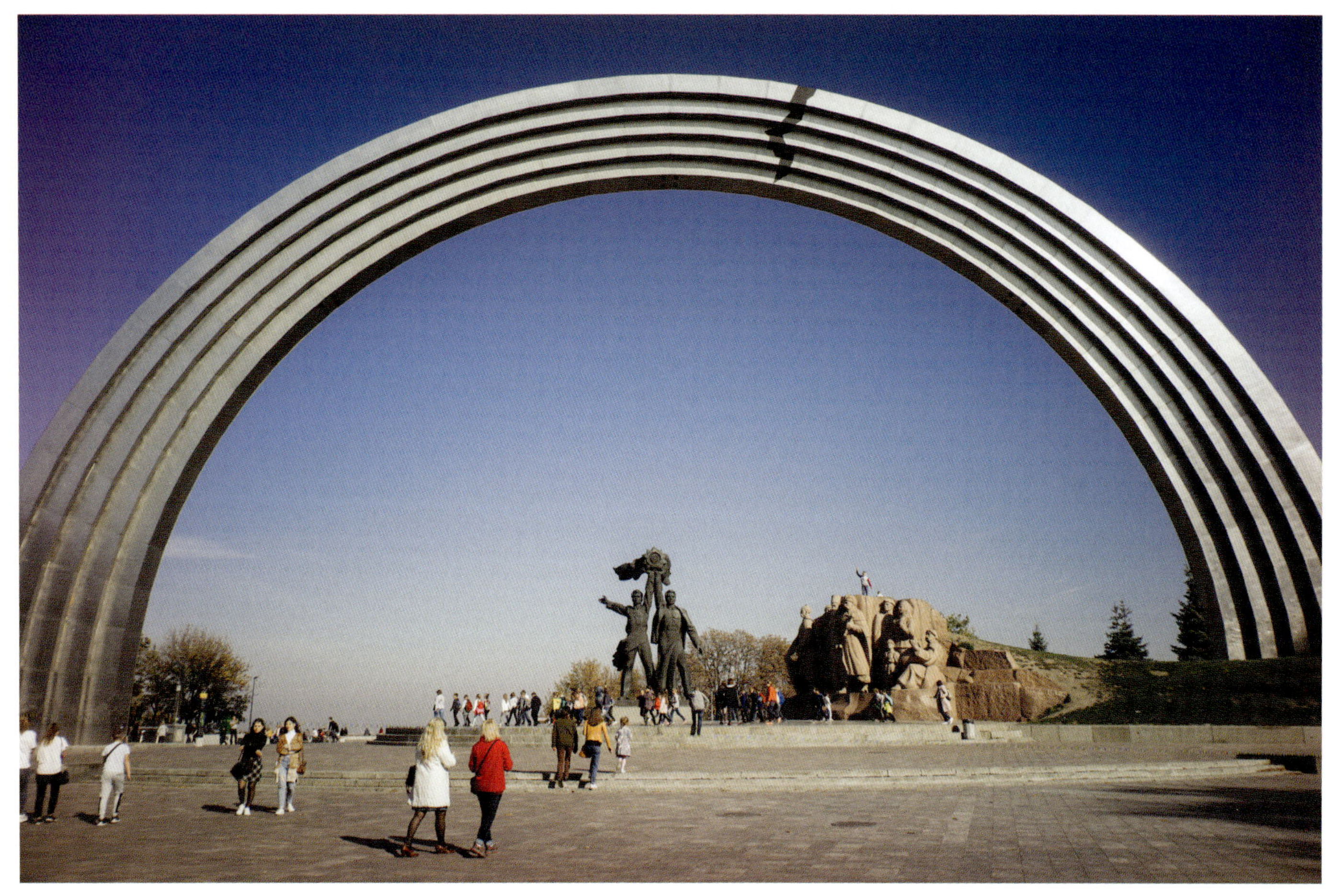

The Peoples' Friendship Arch
KIEV, UKRAINE
Erected in 1982
Designers: A. Skoblikov, I. Ivanov, et al.

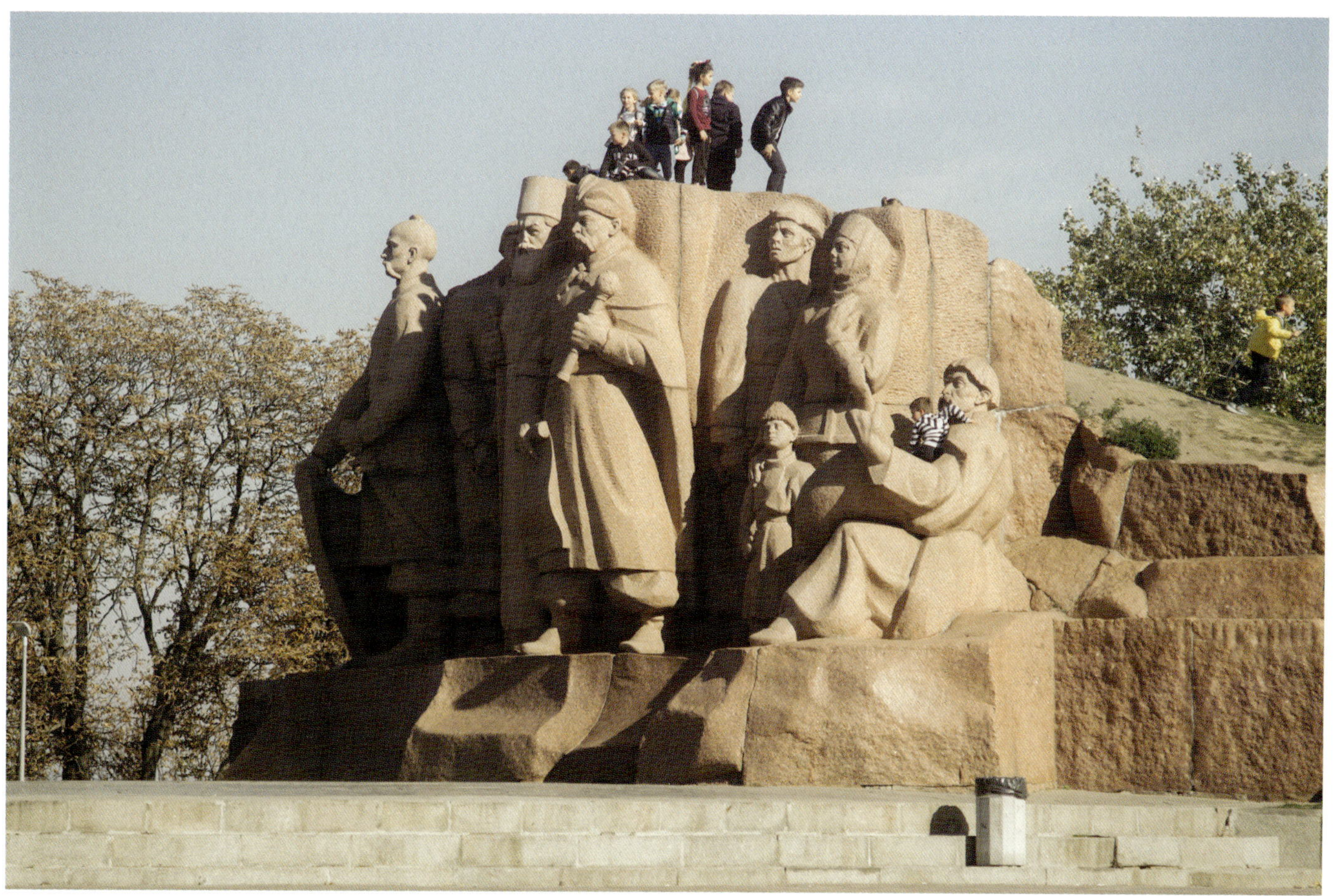

The Peoples' Friendship Arch monument comprises three elements: a bronze sculpture of two workers, a depiction of the Pereyaslavskaya Rada meeting and the arch itself, in the form of a giant rainbow. In the centre of the composition is a statue of the Russian ambassador Vasily Buturlin and the Ukrainian Hetman, Bohdan Khmelnytsky. The Pereyaslavskaya Rada scene is carved from granite and symbolises the signing in 1654 of the historically significant treaty of unification between Russia and Ukraine.

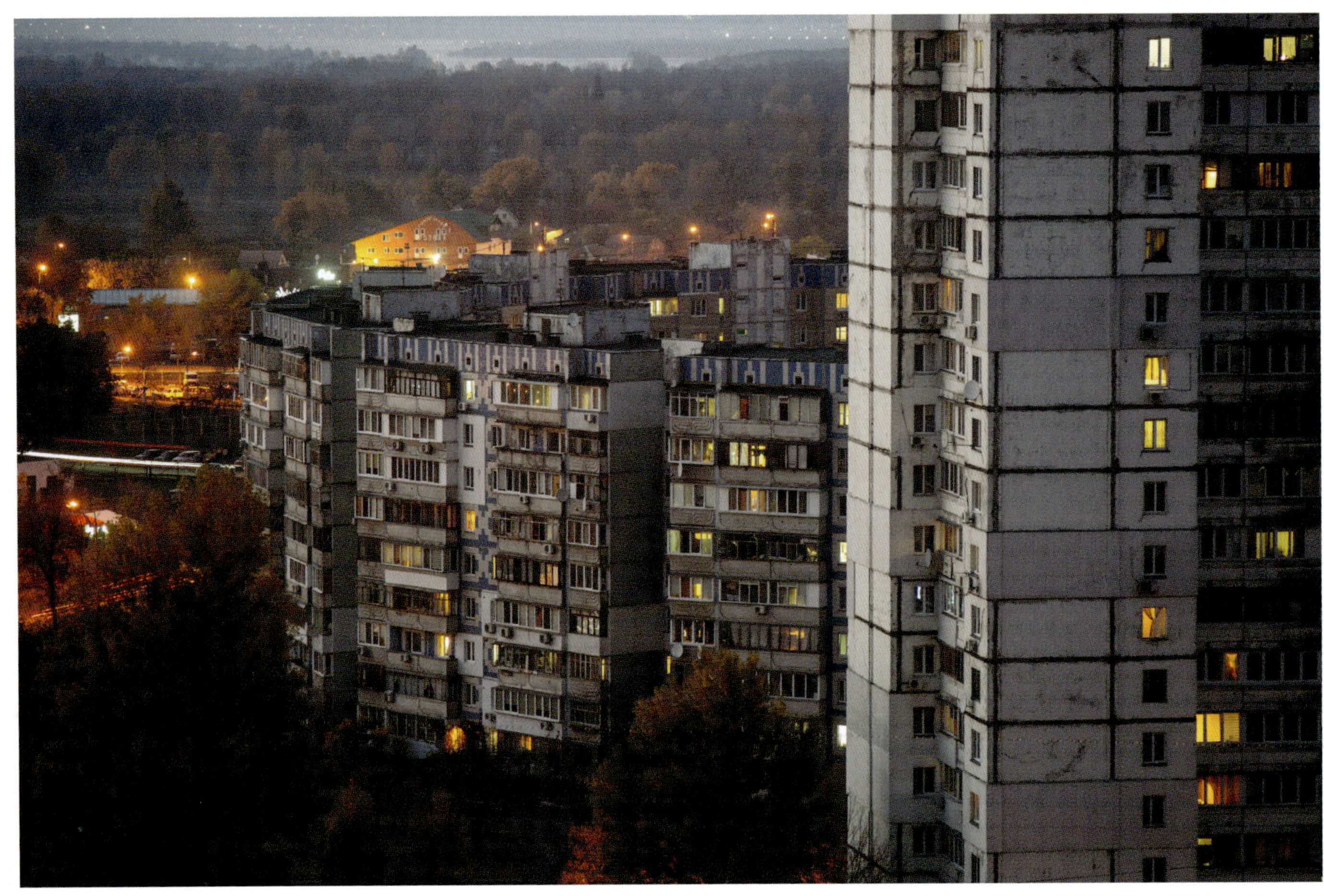

3rd Microdistrict, Troieschyna
KIEV, UKRAINE
Built in the 1980s
Architects: Yu. Paskevich, G. Slutsky et al.

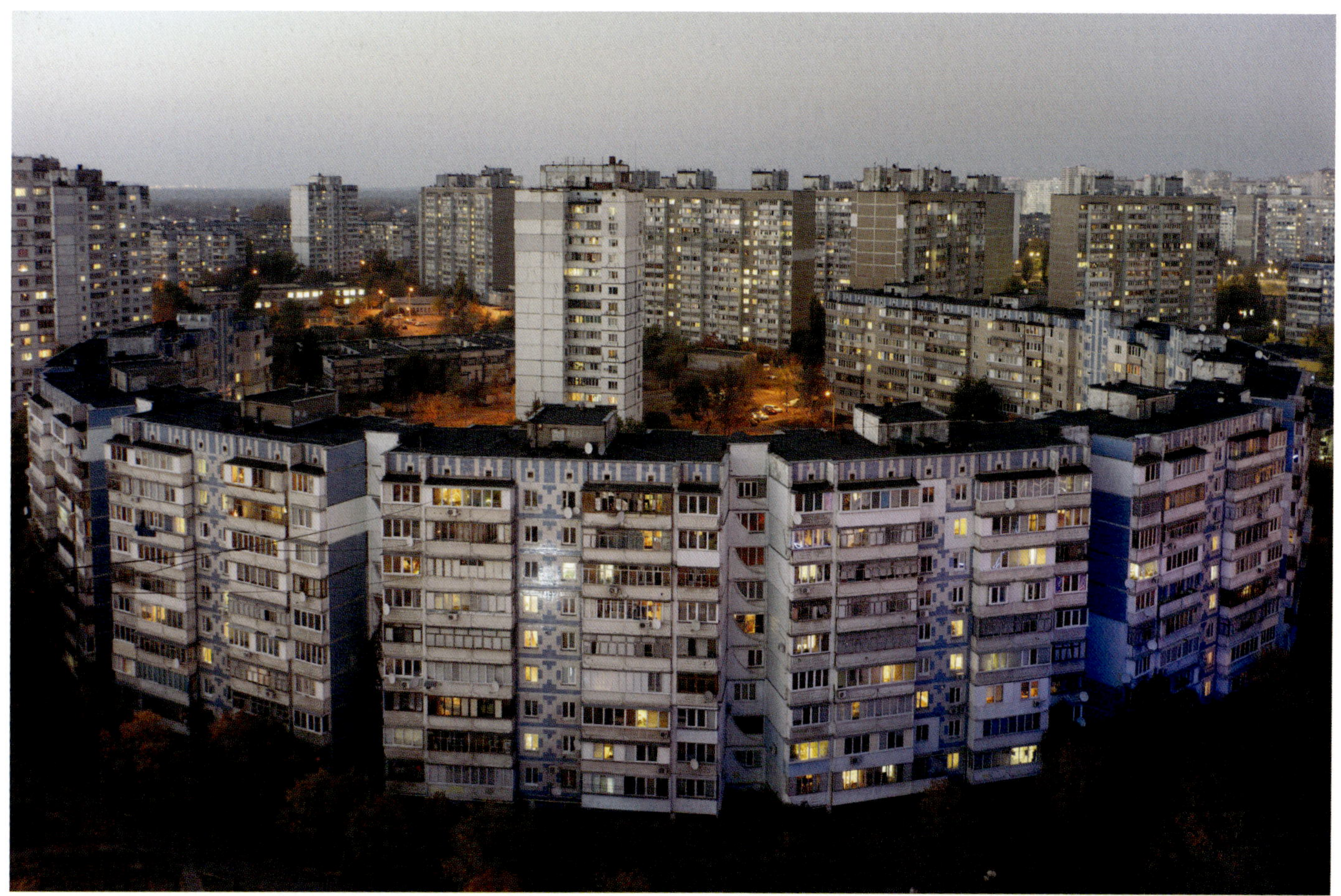

The history of the Troieschyna neighbourhood begins in the early 1980s. At that time, new residential areas on Kiev's left bank (to the east of the Dnieper), such as Bereznyaki, Lesnoy, Rusanovka and Voskresenka, had already been developed. The Troieschyna site to the north was occupied by villages whose inhabitants still lived in a traditional fashion, herding cattle, growing vegetables, drawing water from wells. Troyeschina, primarily a residential district, now has a population of more than 240,000.

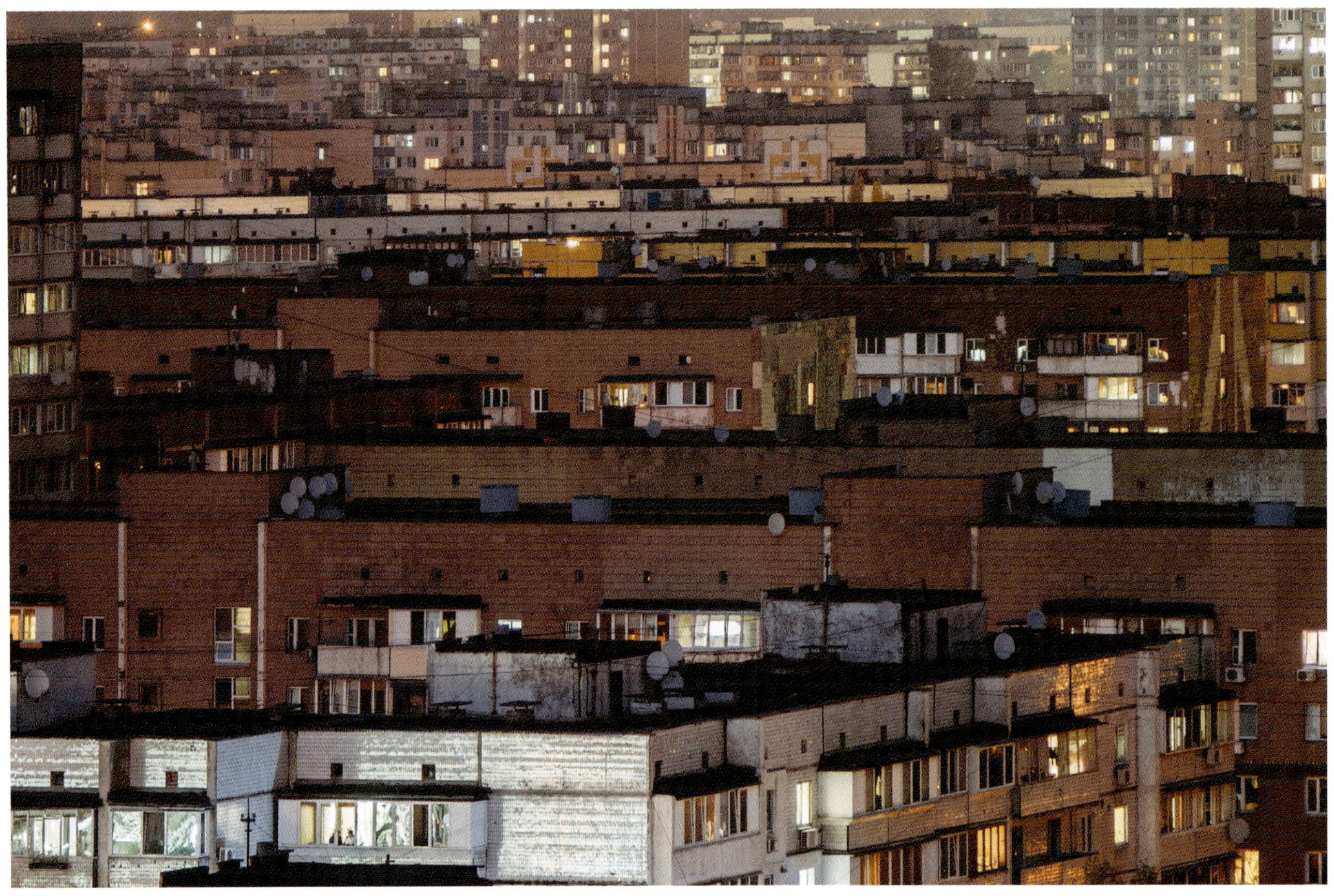

1st Microdistrict, Troieschyna
KIEV, UKRAINE
Built in the 1980s
Architect: G. Gurenkov

After the Moskovsky Bridge opened in the 1970s, redevelopment began on land on the left bank of the city. In addition to housing, many schools and kindergartens were built in the Troieschyna neighbourhood, attracting young parents to the area.

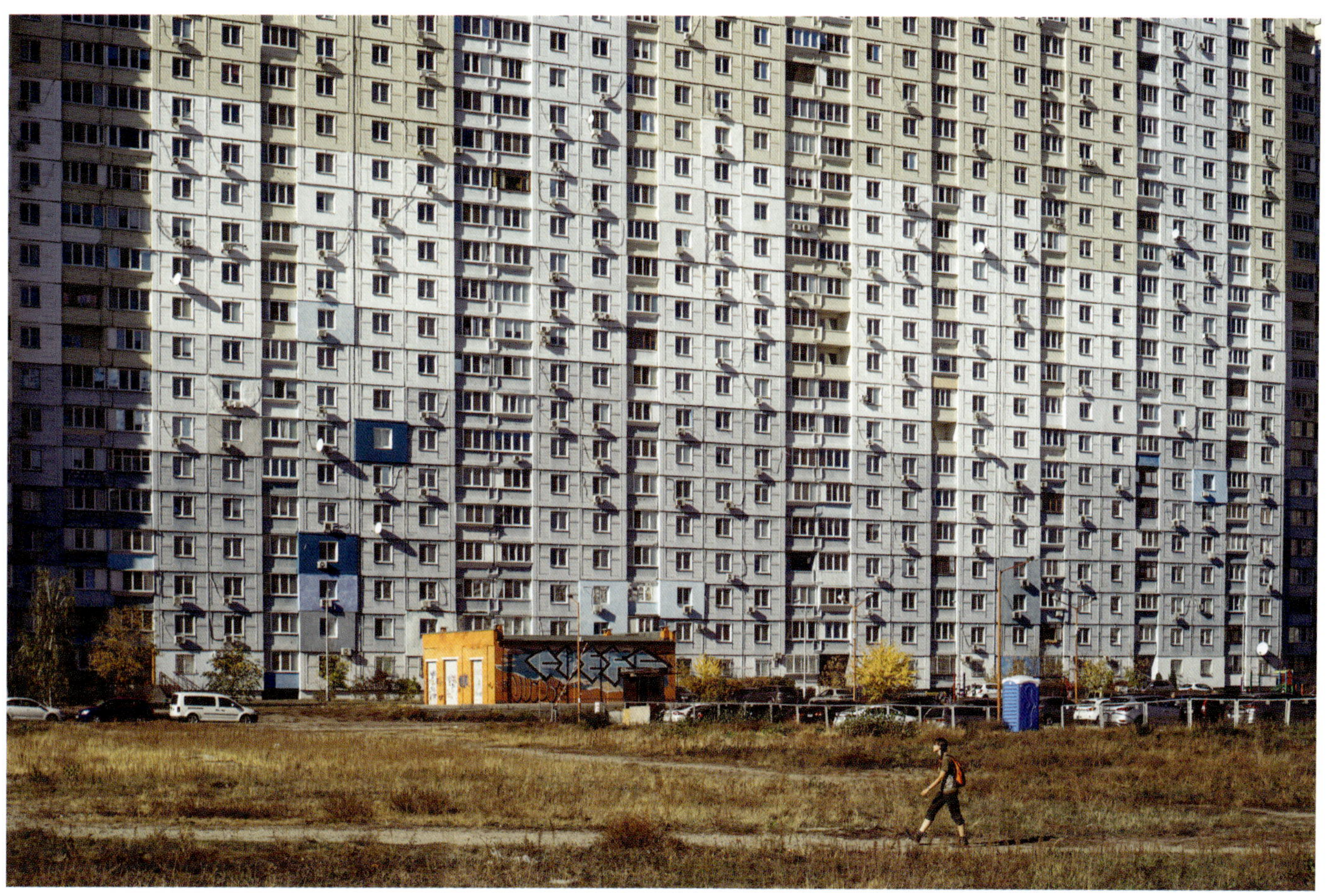

10th Microdistrict, Troieschyna
KIEV, UKRAINE
Built in the 1980s

The area suffers from inadequate transport links to the city centre. To remedy this, an extension was planned for the Kiev Metro. However, this proved too expensive and instead plans were made to expand the existing light-railway service.

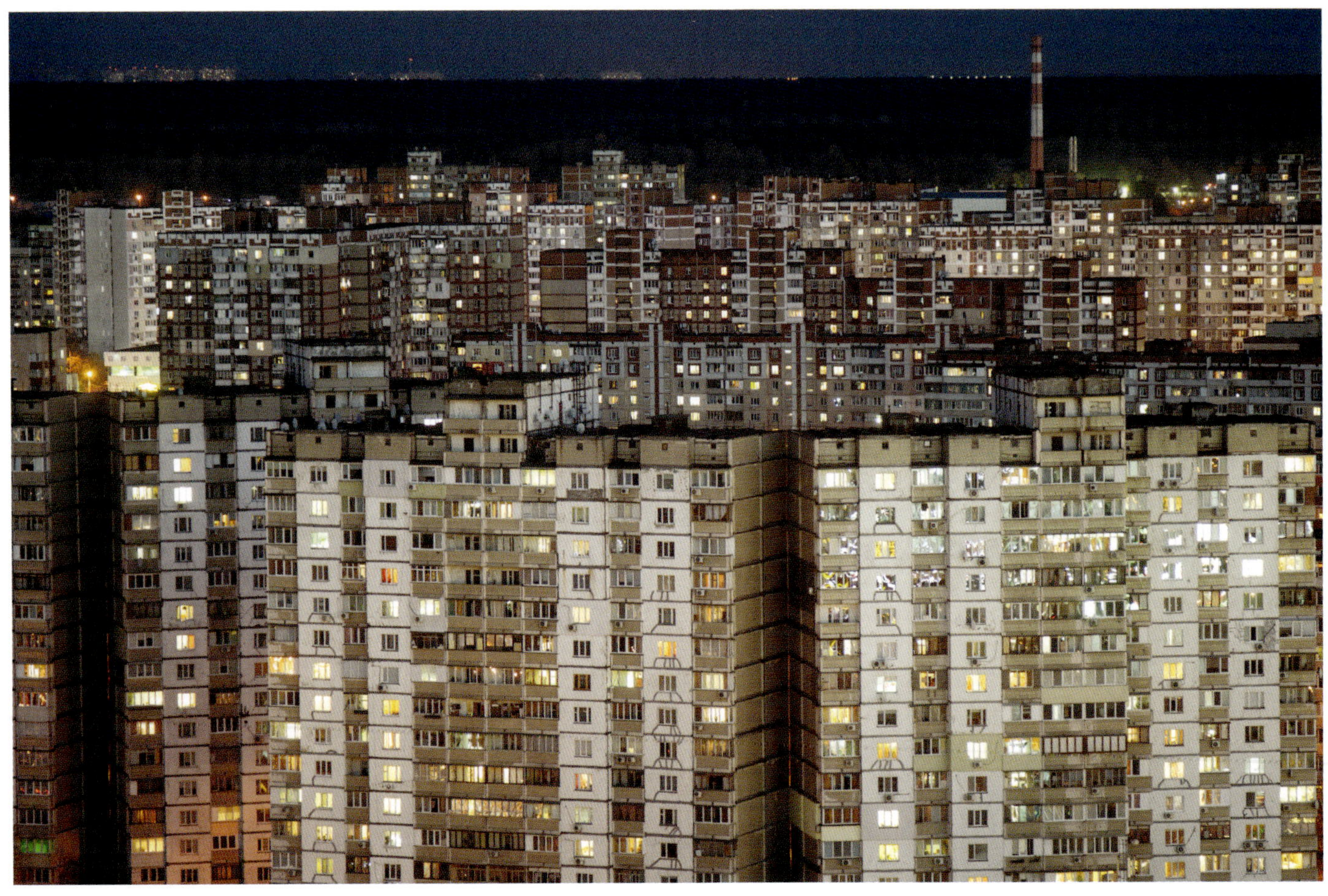

9th Microdistrict, Troieschyna
KIEV, UKRAINE
Built in the 1980s

After the Chernobyl disaster in 1986, a large number of evacuees from the 30-kilometre Exclusion Zone (the majority from Pripyat, a satellite town of the Chernobyl Nuclear Power Plant) were rehoused in Troieschyna. Almost 18,000 victims of the disaster still live here.

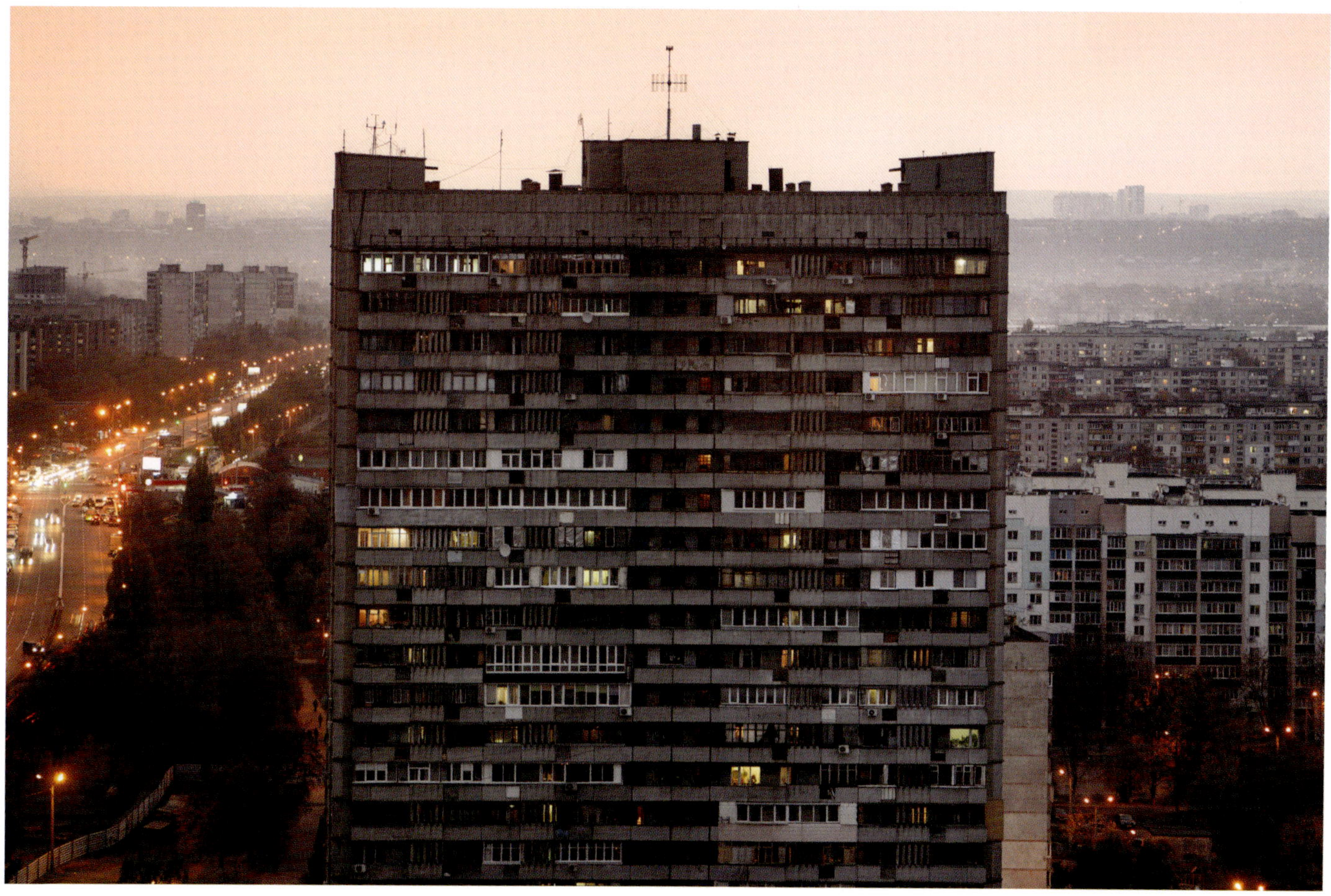

24-storey building, Saltovka
KHARKOV, UKRAINE
Built in 1979

From the time of its construction until the 2000s, this building was the tallest in the city. During the Soviet era, the top floor was disguised as ordinary residential apartments, but was used by the government as a radio monitoring and interception post.

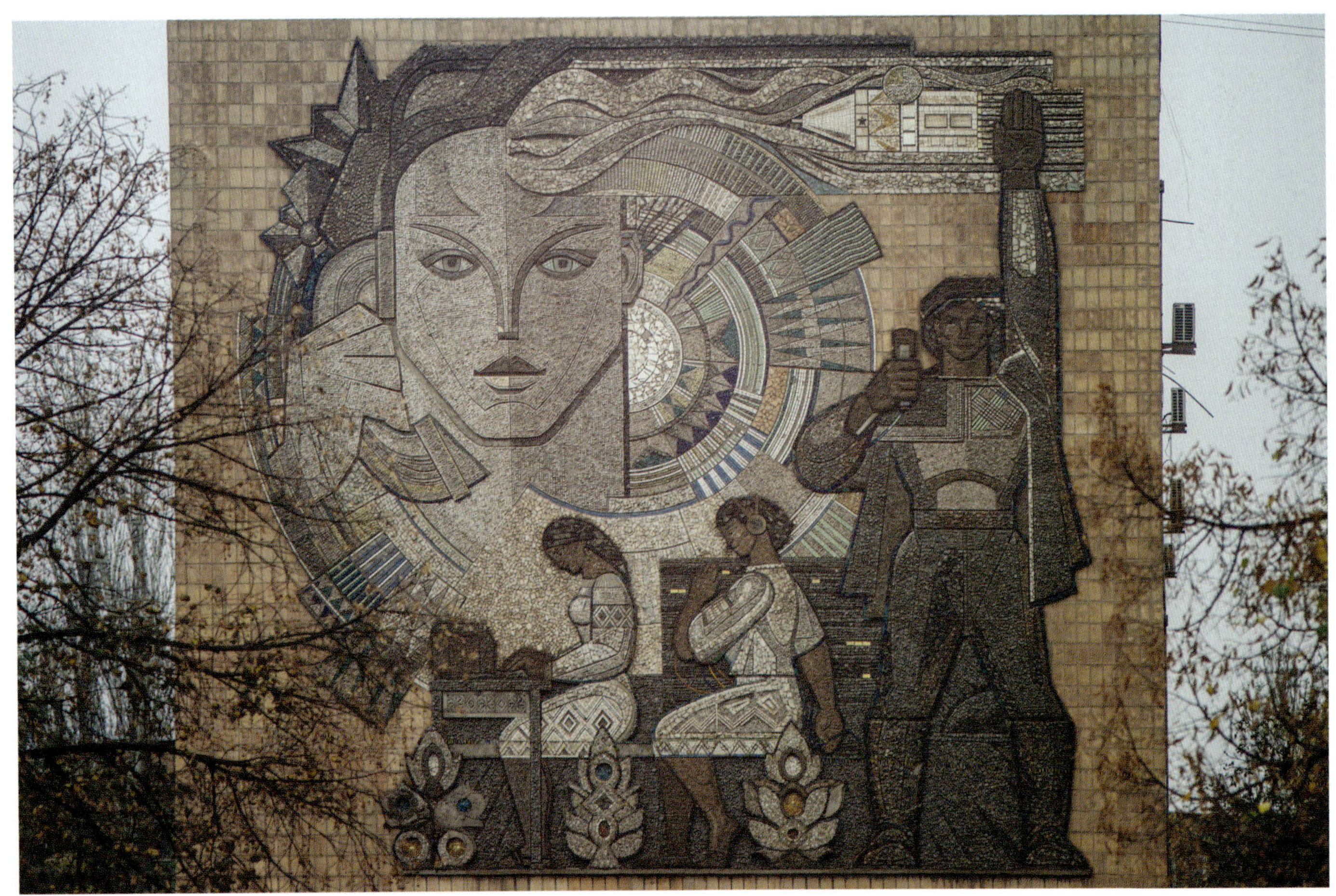

'Communication' mosaic, International Telephone Station
KRIVOY ROG, UKRAINE

This type of station assisted with telephone calls at a time when the network across the USSR was underdeveloped. From here it was possible to speak with people who did not have a phone, or who lived in settlements possessing only basic communication equipment.

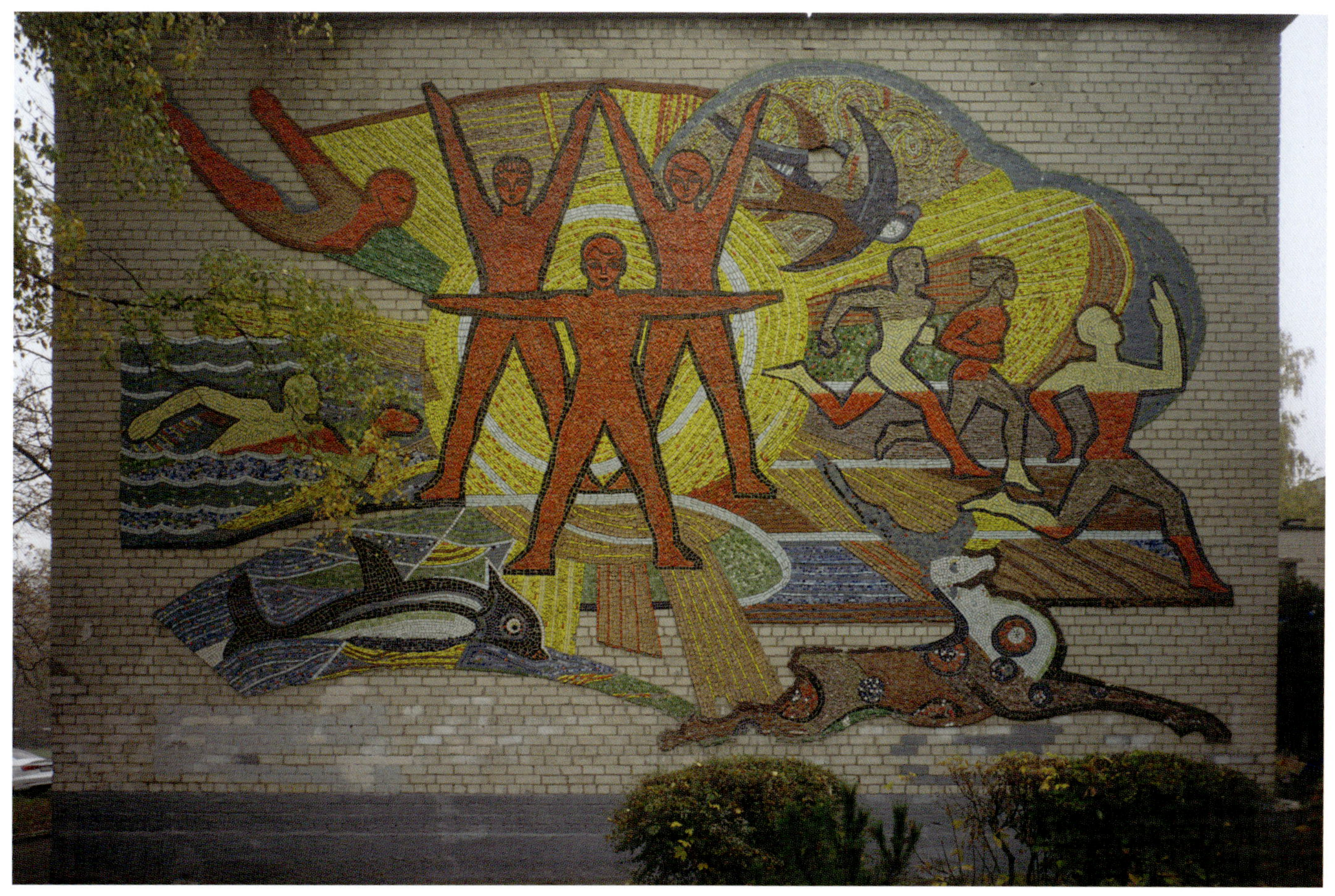

Mosaic, School No.37
DNIPROPETROVSK, UKRAINE

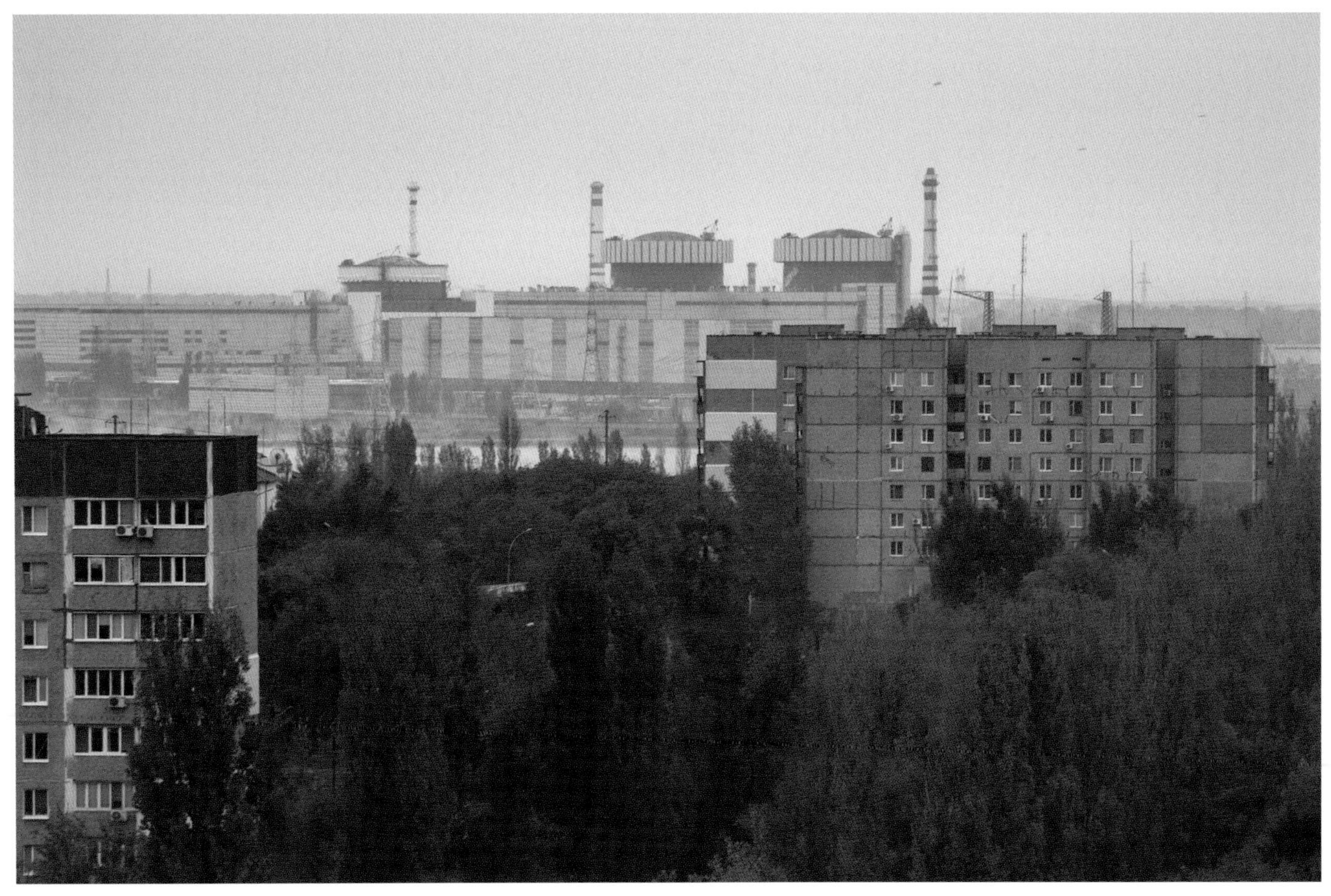

Yuzhnoukrainsk Nuclear Power Plant
YUZHNOUKRAINSK, UKRAINE
Built in 1982

Construction of this plant, alongside its satellite town, began in 1975. It has three reactors, each with a capacity of 1,000 MW. The first reactor unit was incorporated into the power network in 1982 and the remaining two in 1989.

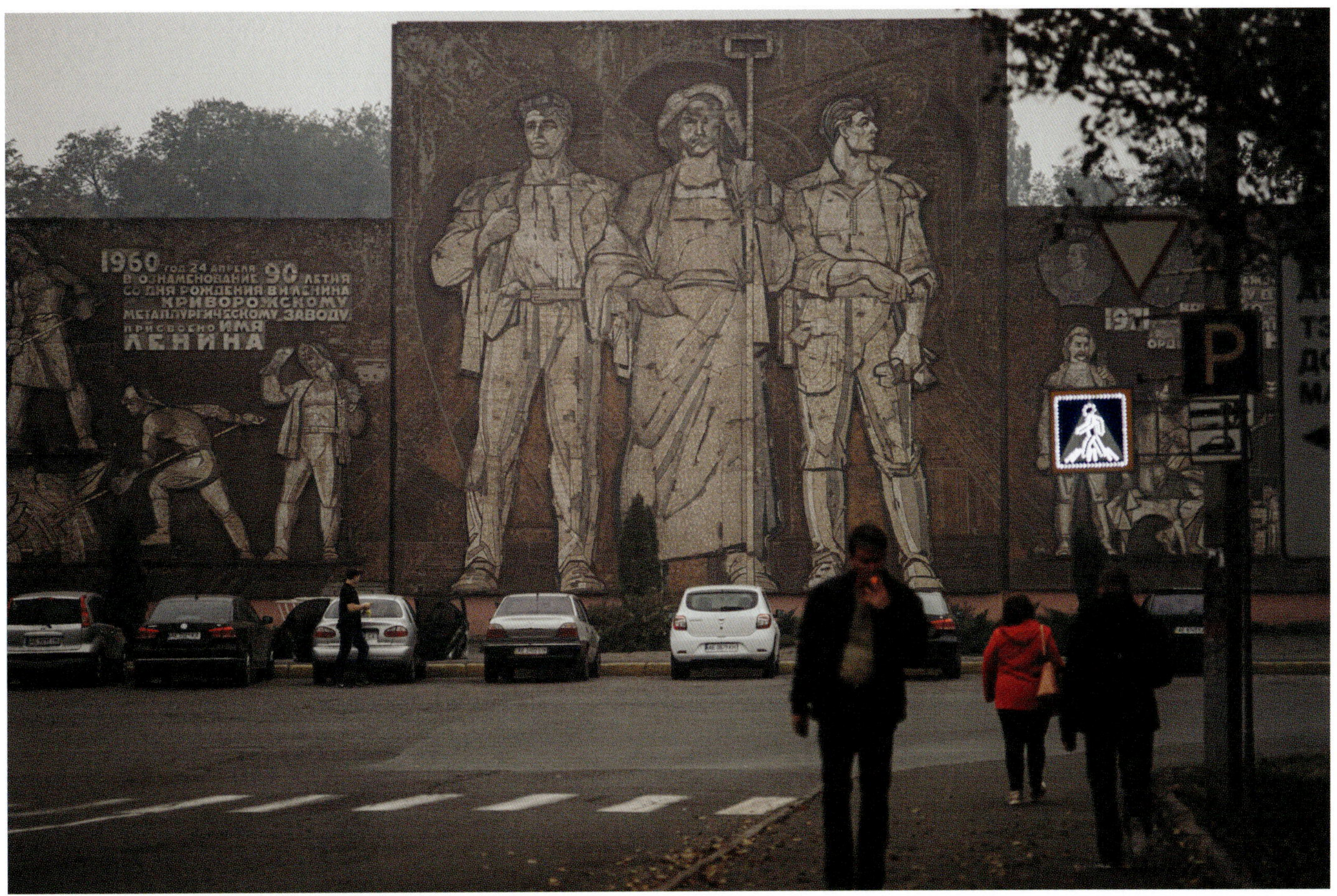

Mosaic panel dedicated to the steelworkers of
Krivorozhstal Metallurgical Plant
KRIVOY ROG, UKRAINE

The inscriptions read: 1934 – the first smelting of cast iron is issued
by our Komsomolka; 1960 – the plant was named after Lenin; 1939 –
awarded the Order of the Red Banner of Labour; 1971 – awarded the
Order of Lenin; [Our] Homeland needs more iron, steel, rolled metal!

195

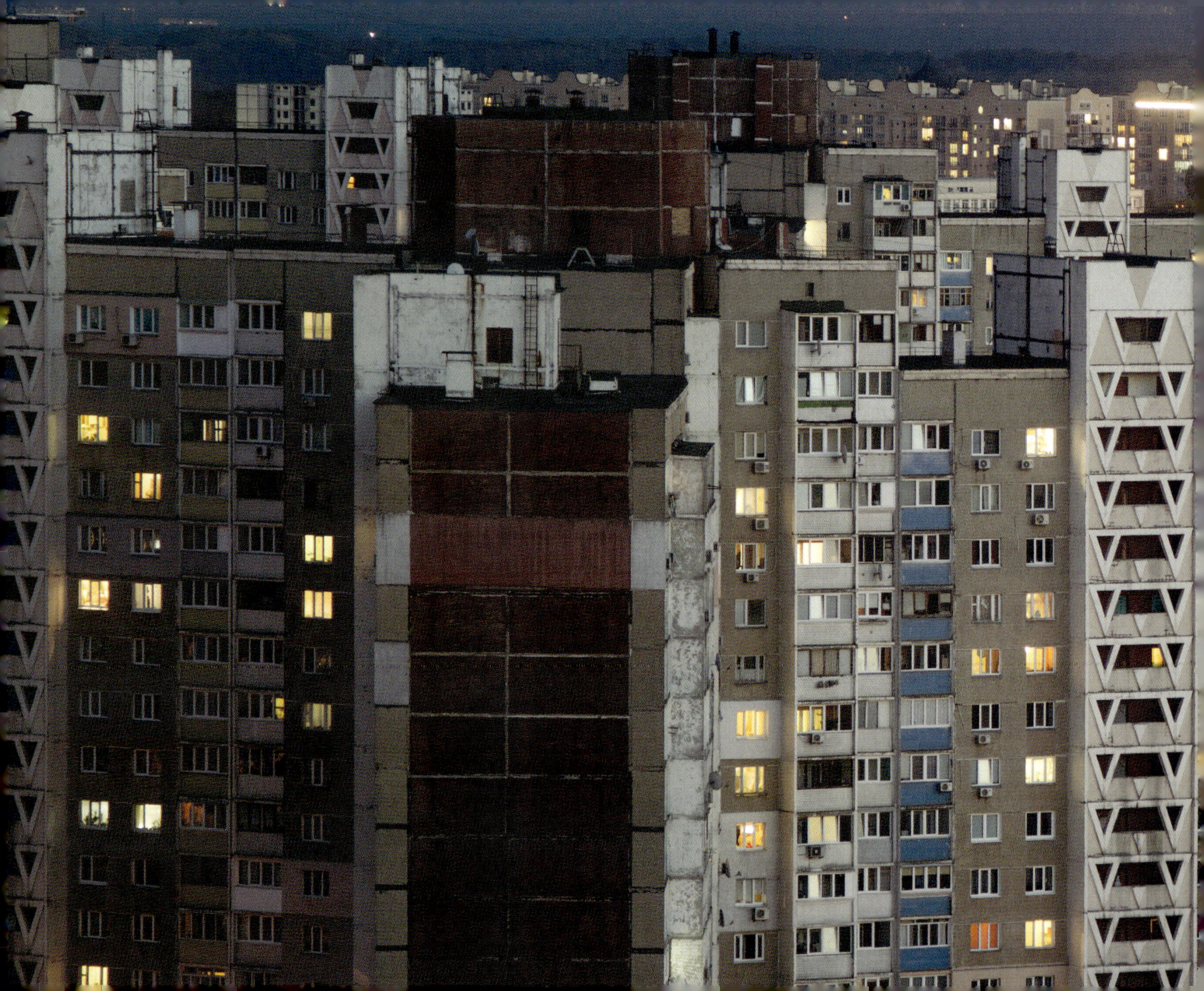

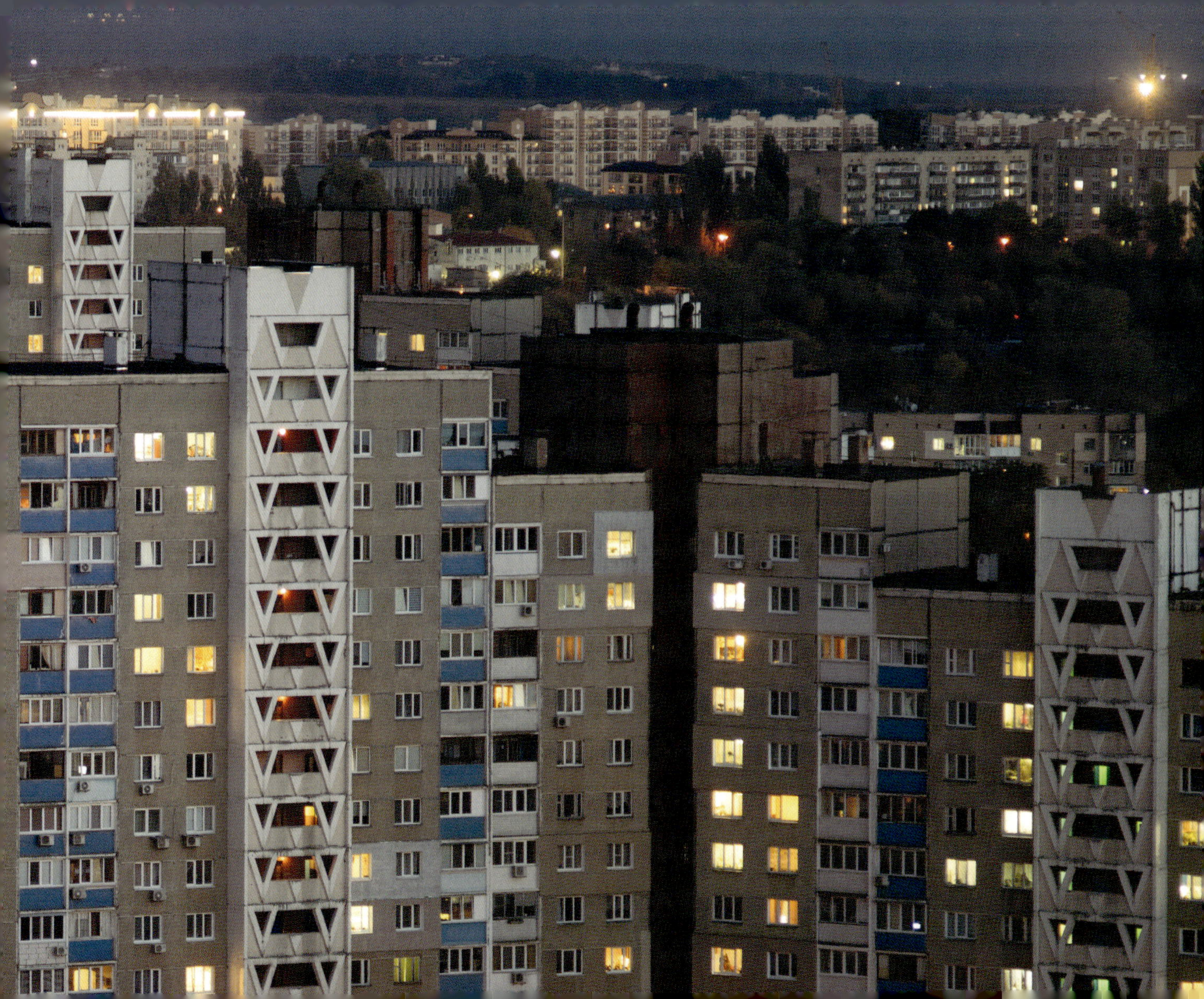

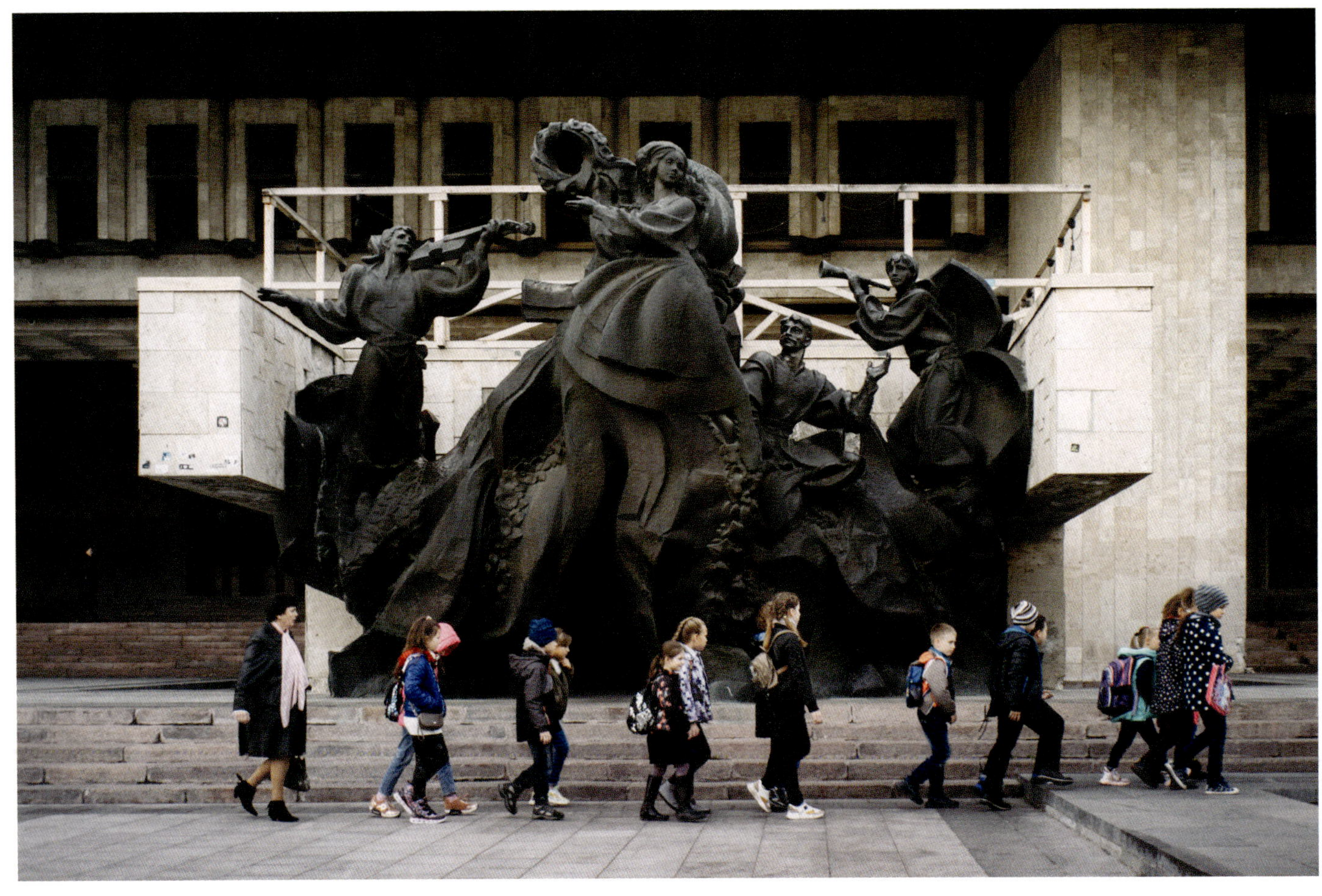

'Music of N.V. Lysenko' sculpture
KHARKOV, UKRAINE
Erected in 1991
Designer: S. Yastrebova

previous page
The longest building in Kiev, Teremki-1 Microdistrict
KIEV, UKRAINE
Built between 1987 and 1990
Architects: F. Borovik, V. Ezhov, A. Zavarov, V. Iriskin

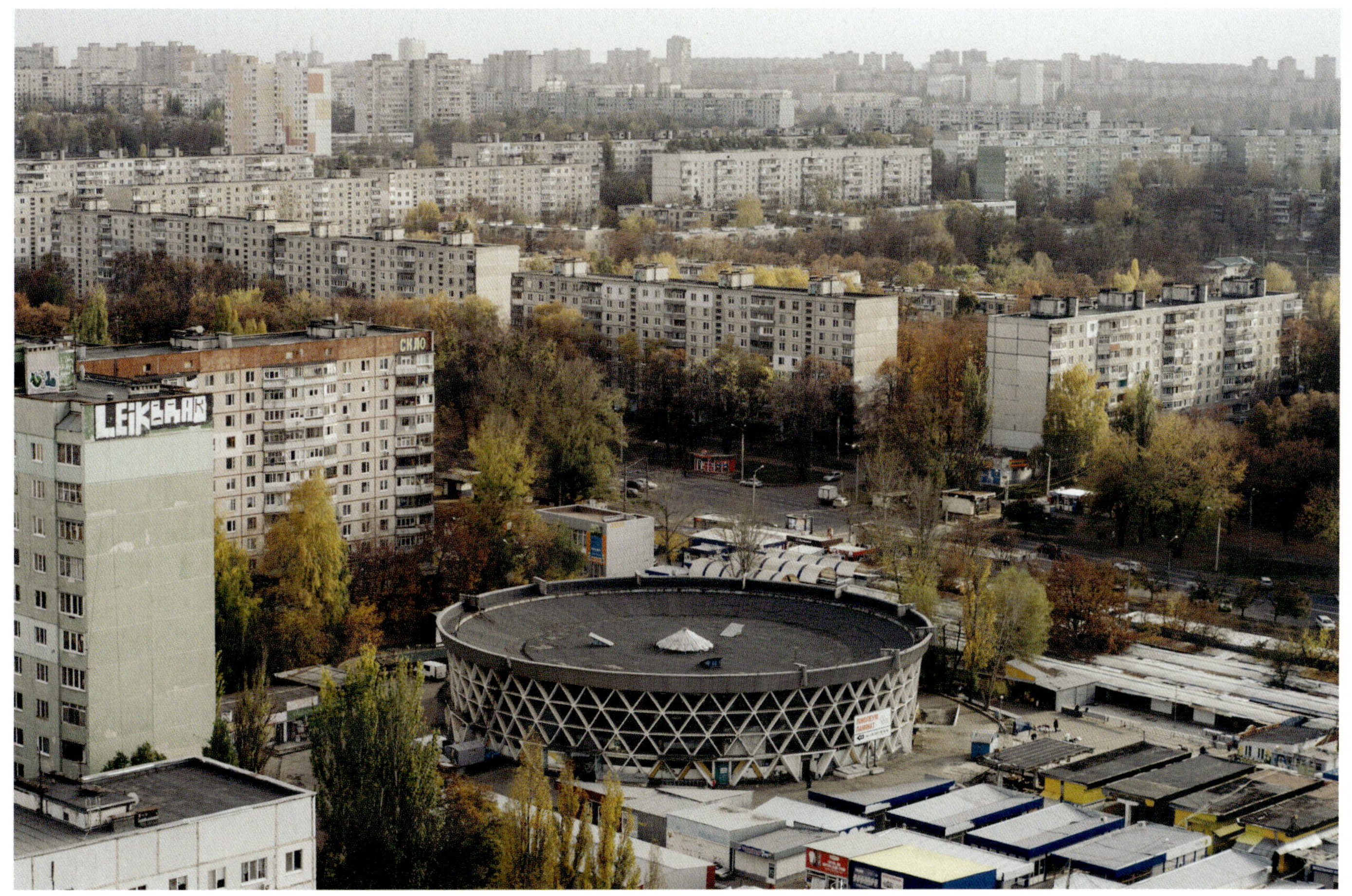

Saltovsky Covered Collective Farm Market
KHARKOV, UKRAINE
Built in 1980
Architects: V. Bakhtin, O. Dunaev

Saltovka is the largest residential area in Ukraine and the former Soviet Union. Today it is home to around 410,000 people. There are no industrial enterprises in Saltovka, but there are many shops and a large market.

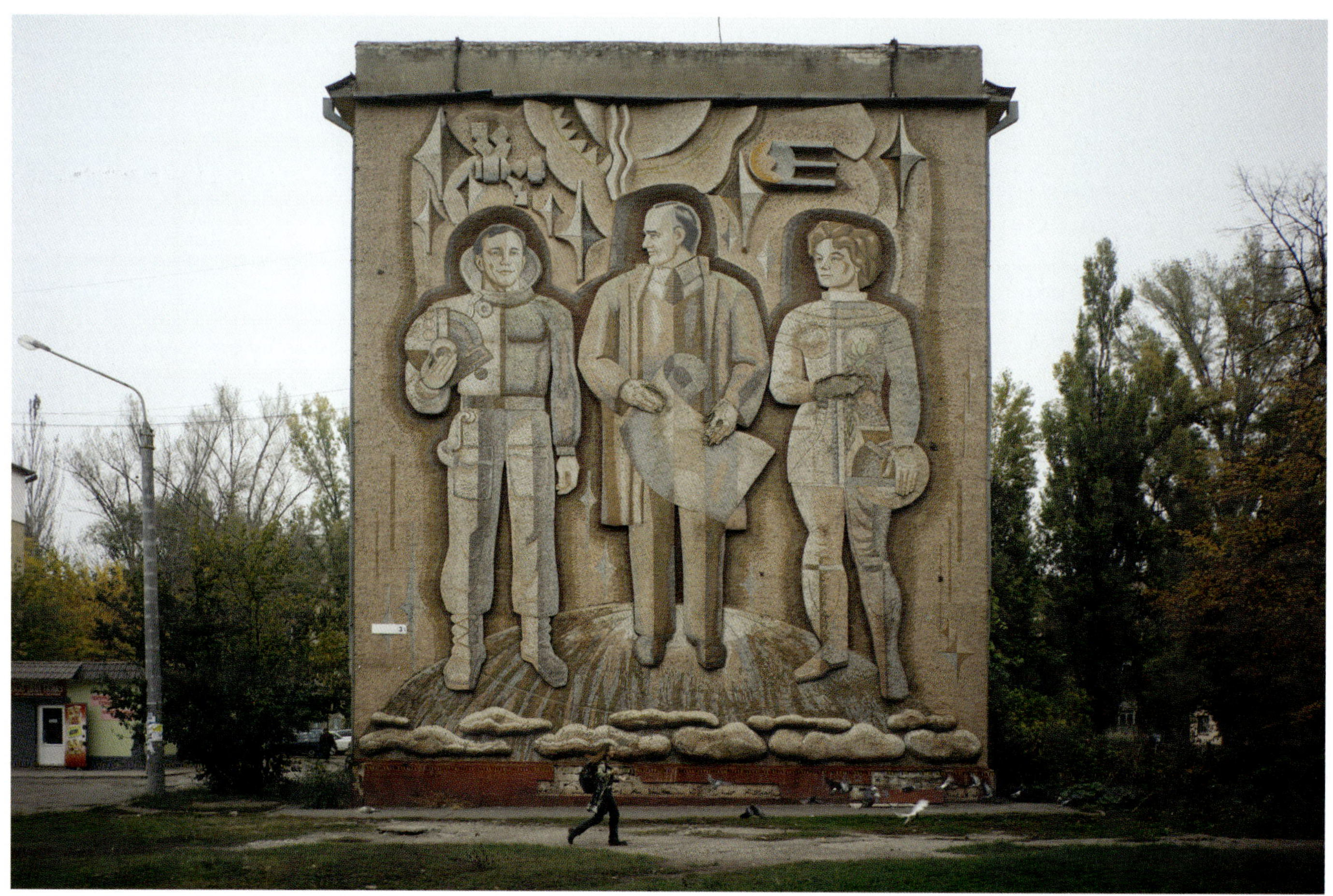

Mosaic with chief designer Korolev and cosmonauts
Tereshkova and Komarov
KRIVOY ROG, UKRAINE

Sergei Korolev (centre) was a key figure in Soviet rocket and space technology. Valentina Tereshkova was the world's first female cosmonaut. Vladimir Komarov commanded the world's first spaceship crew and was the first person to die during a space flight.

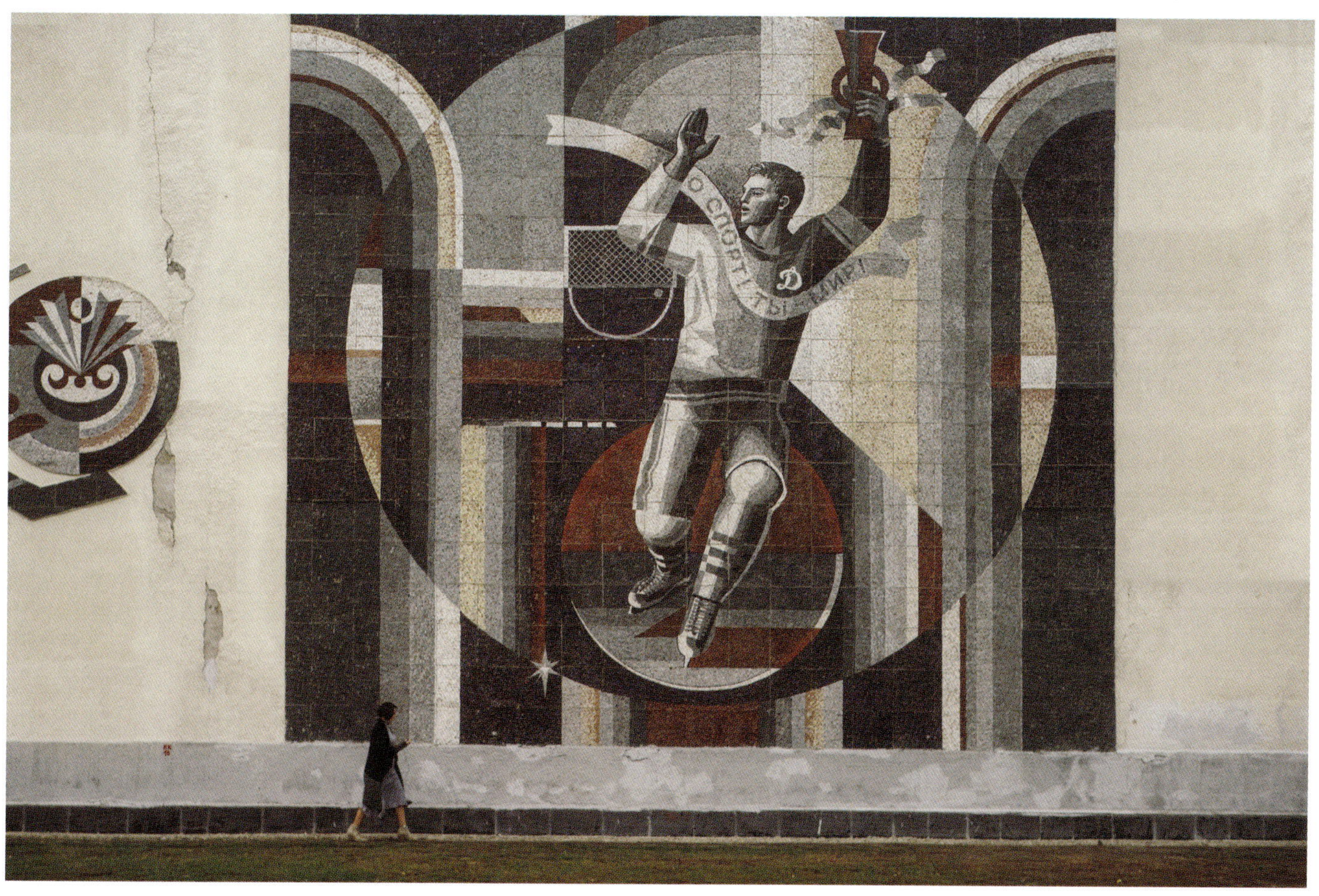

Palace of Sports mosaic
KHARKOV, UKRAINE
Created in 1977

The Palace of Sports is the largest enclosed sports facility in Kharkov.
In additon to sport, it is used for exhibitions, music performances and
other public events. The mural shows a Dynamo Kharkiv ice-hockey
player. Founded in 1979, the team was disbanded in 1992.

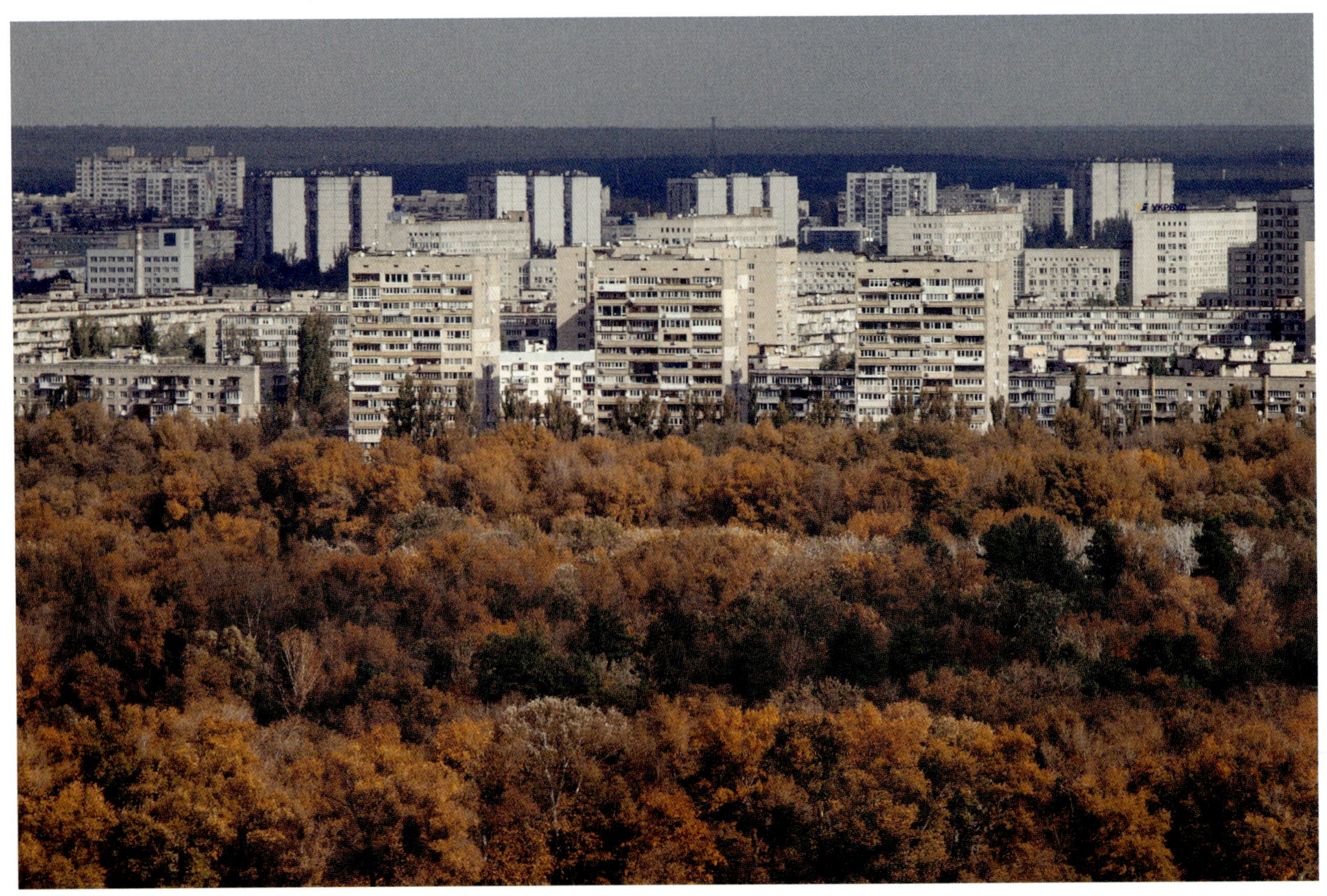

1st Microdistrict, Rusanovka
KIEV, UKRAINE

This neighbourhood consists mainly of 9-storey large-panel residential buildings. However, three 16-storey buildings were erected on the embankment, creating a high-rise silhouette when viewed from the city centre.

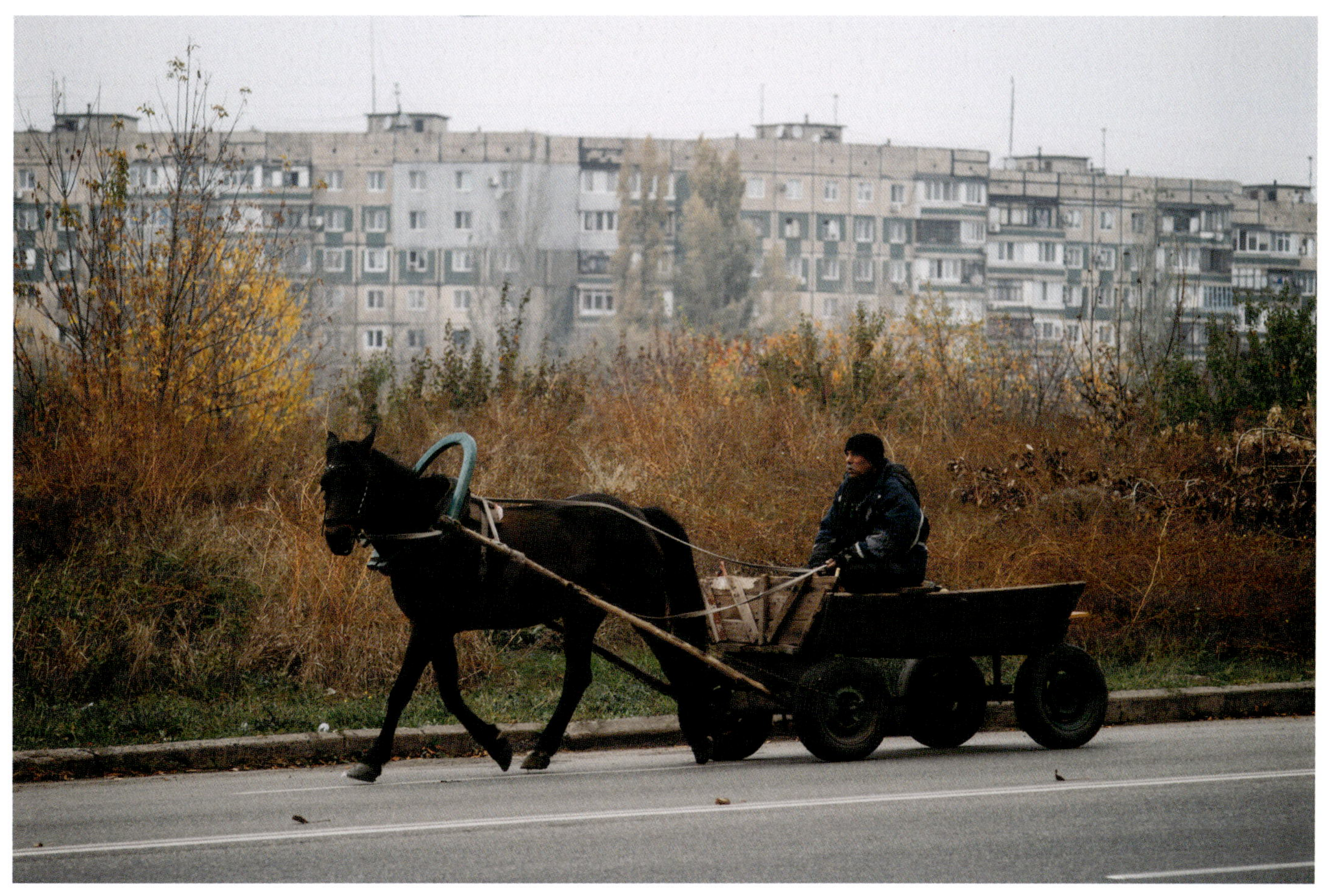

6th October Microdistrict
KRIVOY ROG, UKRAINE

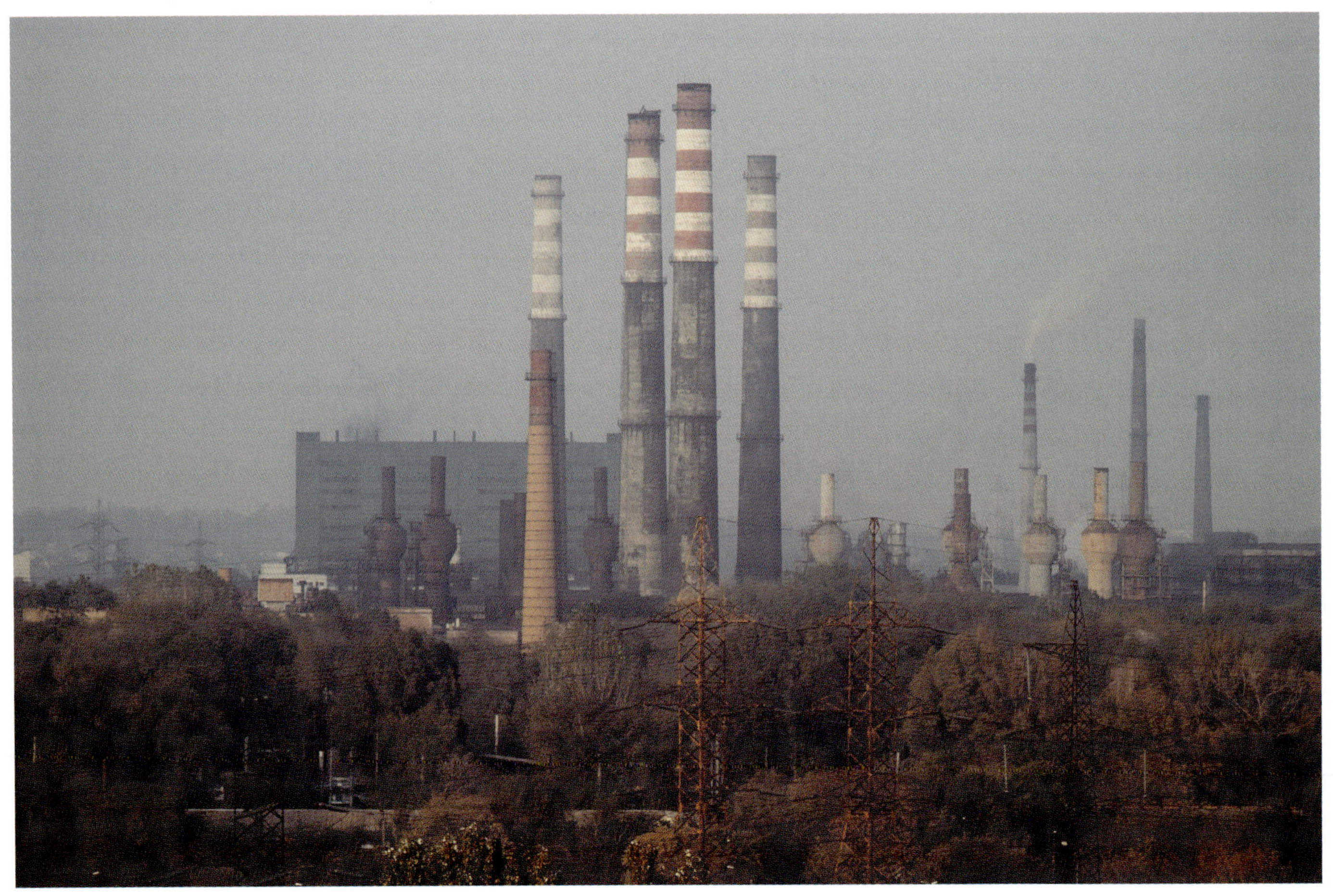

Dnieper aluminium smelter chimneys
ZAPORIZHZHIA, UKRAINE

When the construction of this aluminium smelter began in 1930, it was the first in the USSR and the biggest in Europe. Production continued until 2008, when the dire economic situation forced the complete suspension of works and the loss of a significant number of jobs.

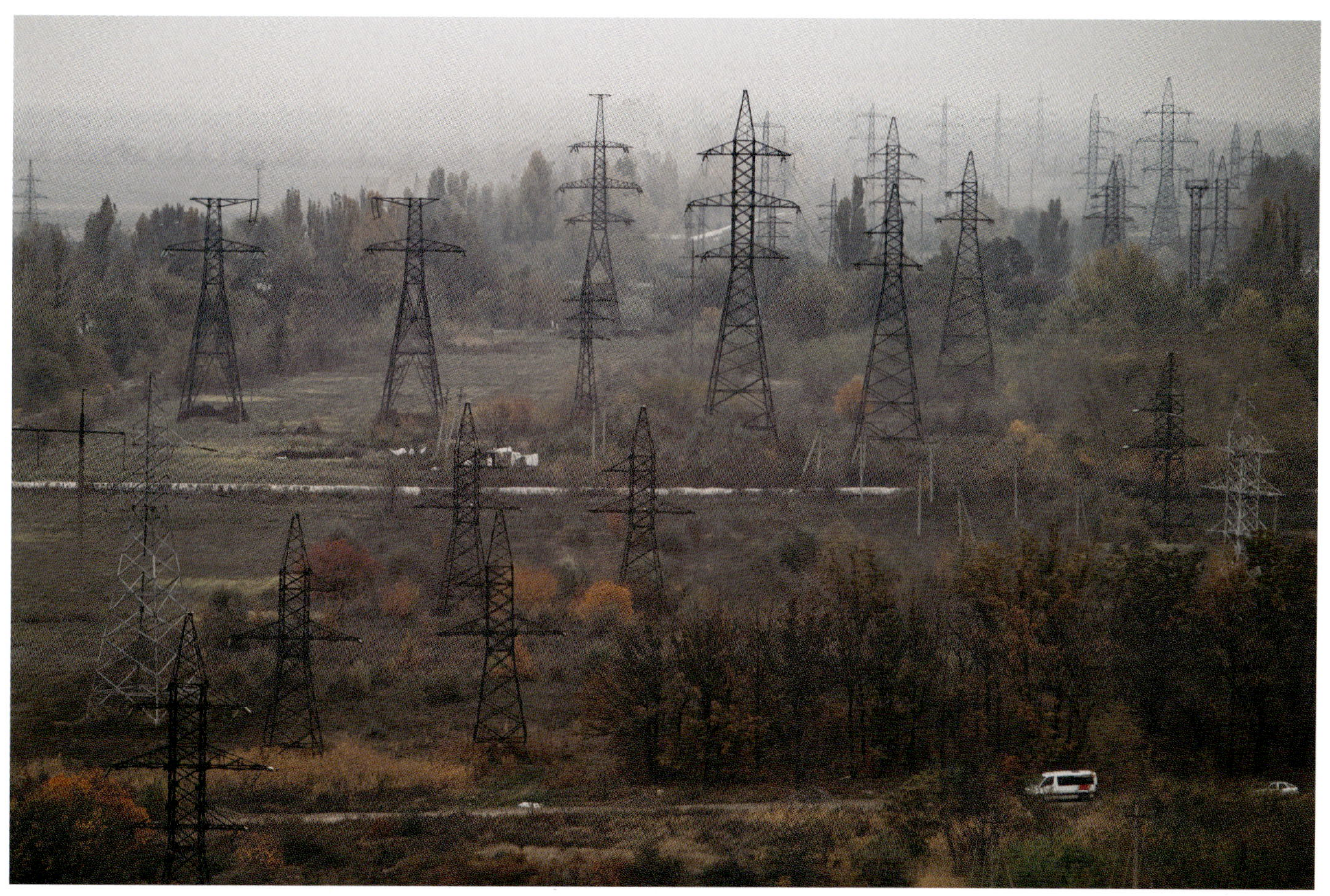

Pylons in the outskirts of the city
KRIVOY ROG, UKRAINE

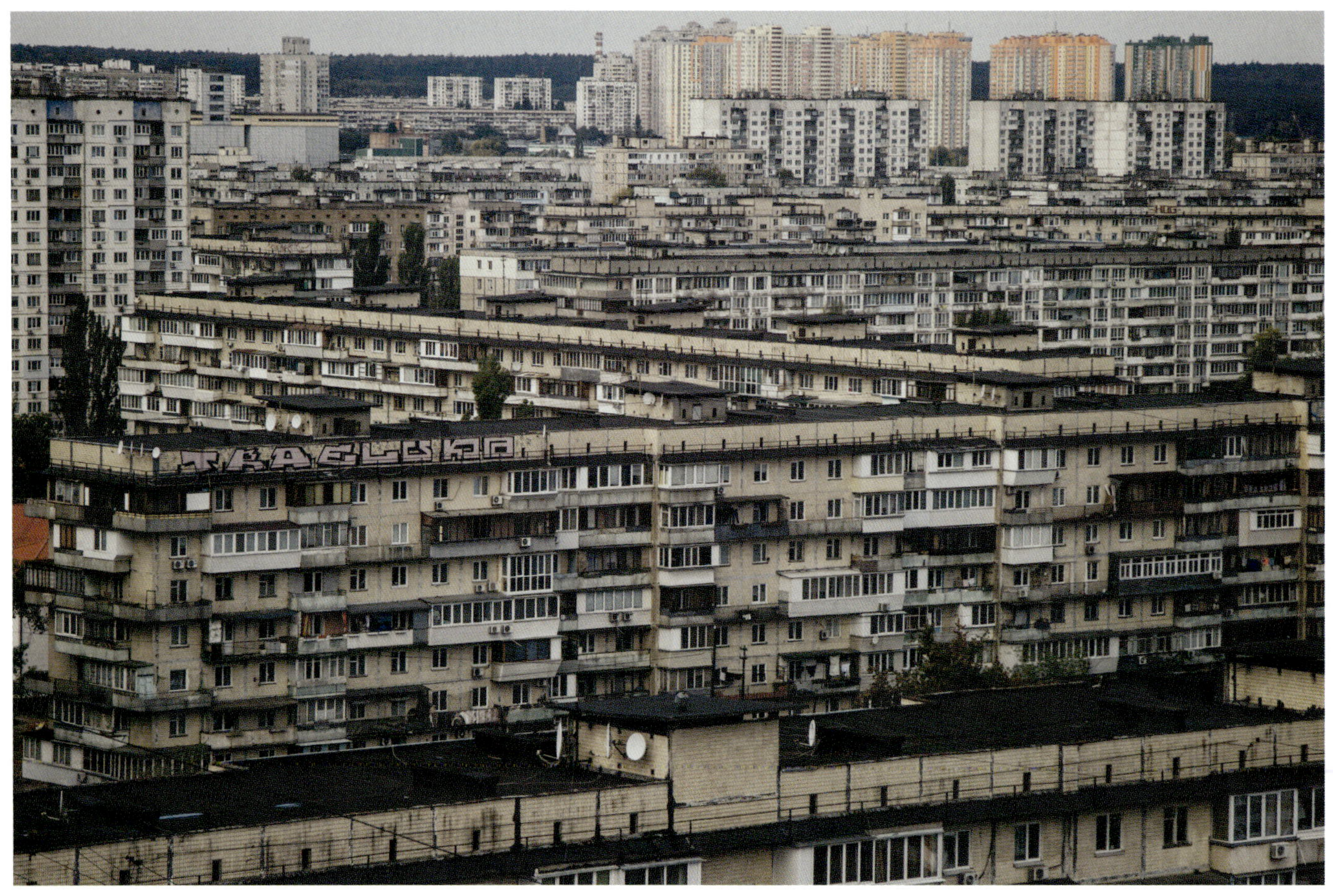

4th Microdistrict, Obolon
KIEV, UKRAINE
Built between the late 1960s and 1980s
Architects: G. Slutsky, Y. Paskevich, L. Filenko et al.

The main construction of this area took place between 1973 and 1980. It largely consists of 9- and 16-storey buildings in a honeycomb-shaped arrangement. Each section of the neighbourhood has kindergartens, schools, department stores, and cinemas.

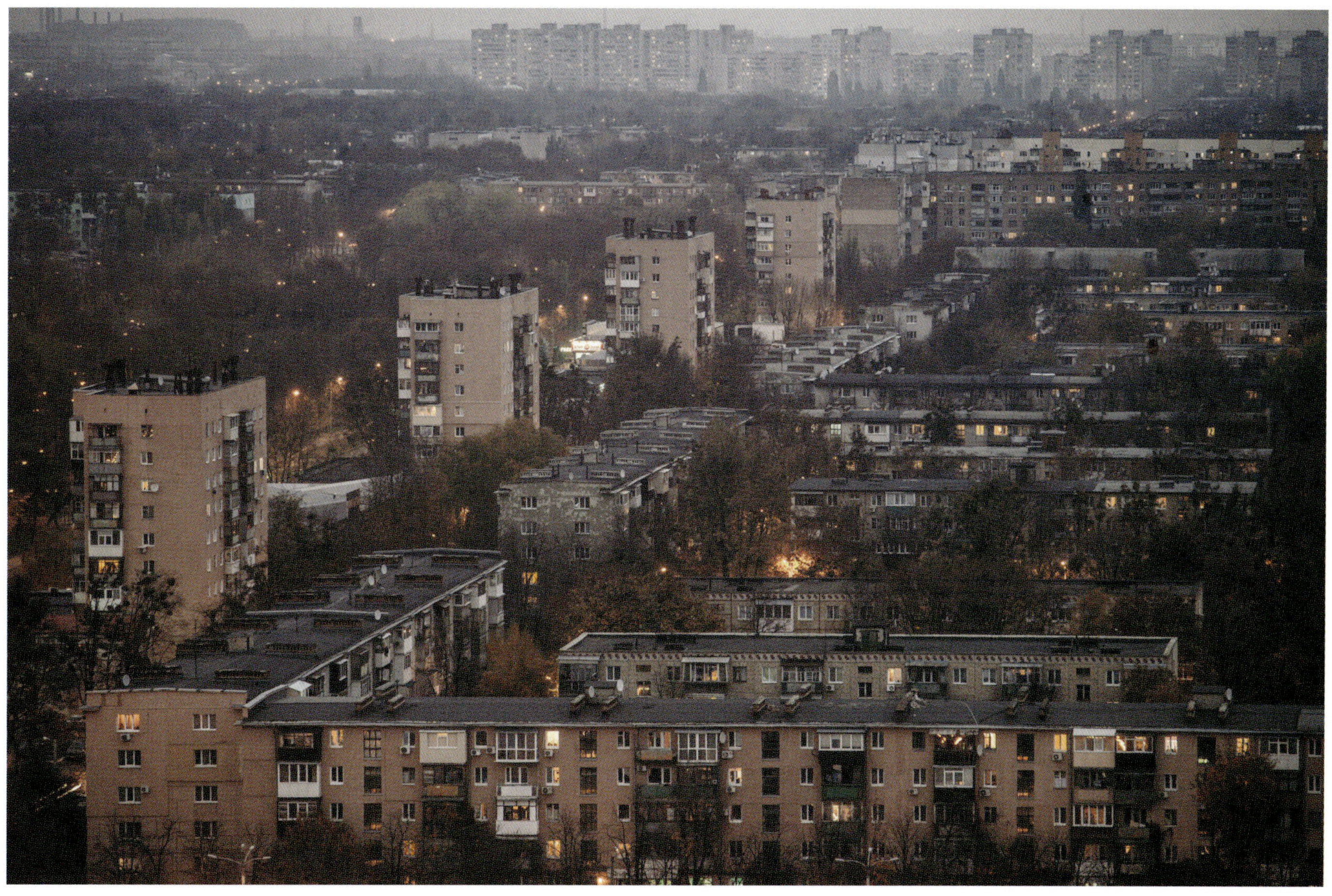

8th Microdistrict
KHARKOV, UKRAINE

Kharkov is Ukraine's second most populous city (1,443,000) and an important industrial and scientific centre. In the Soviet period, it was the largest manufacturer of tanks, tractors and turbines, and the third largest industrial, scientific and transport hub.

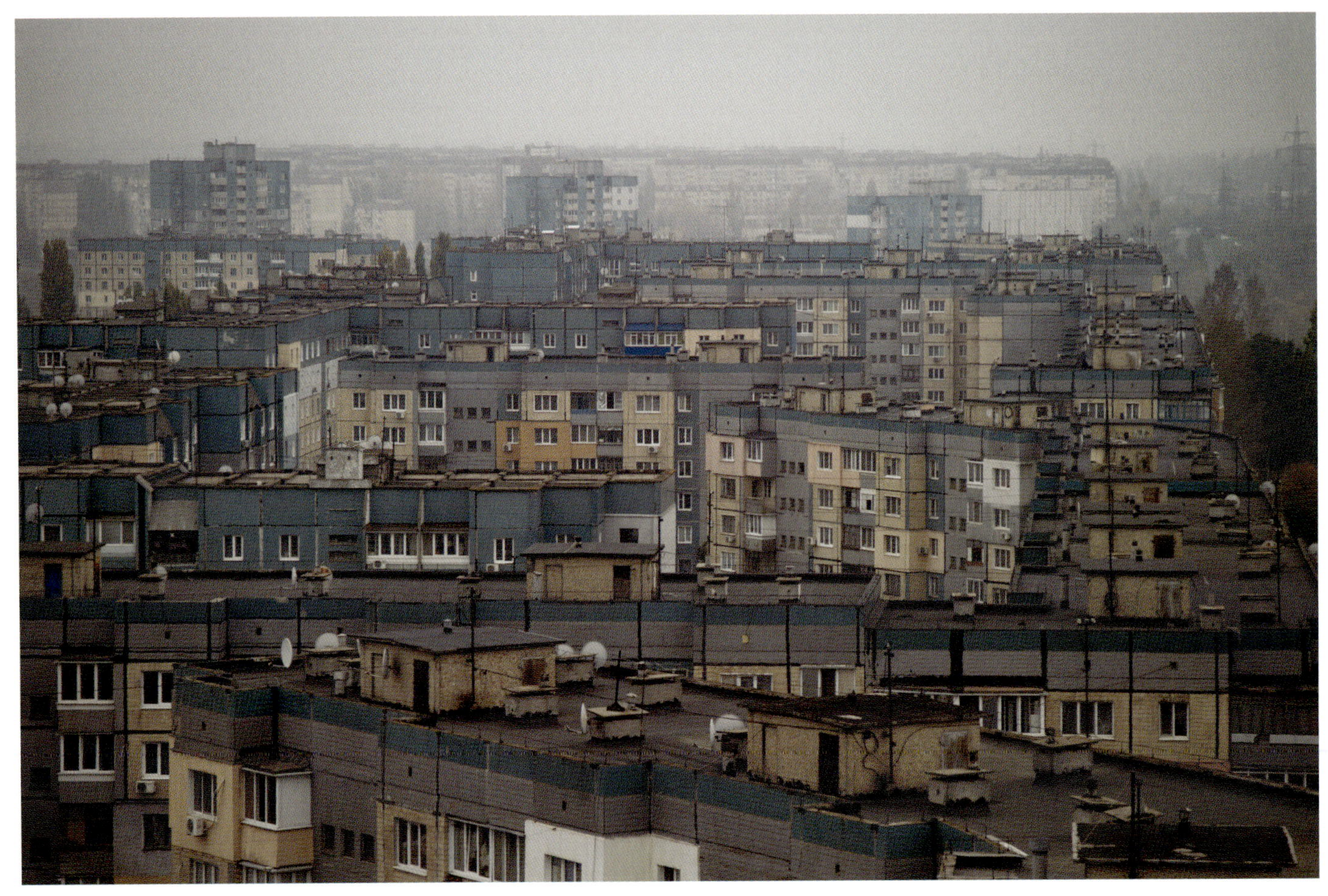

2nd and 3rd Microdistricts, Vostochny
KRIVOY ROG, UKRAINE

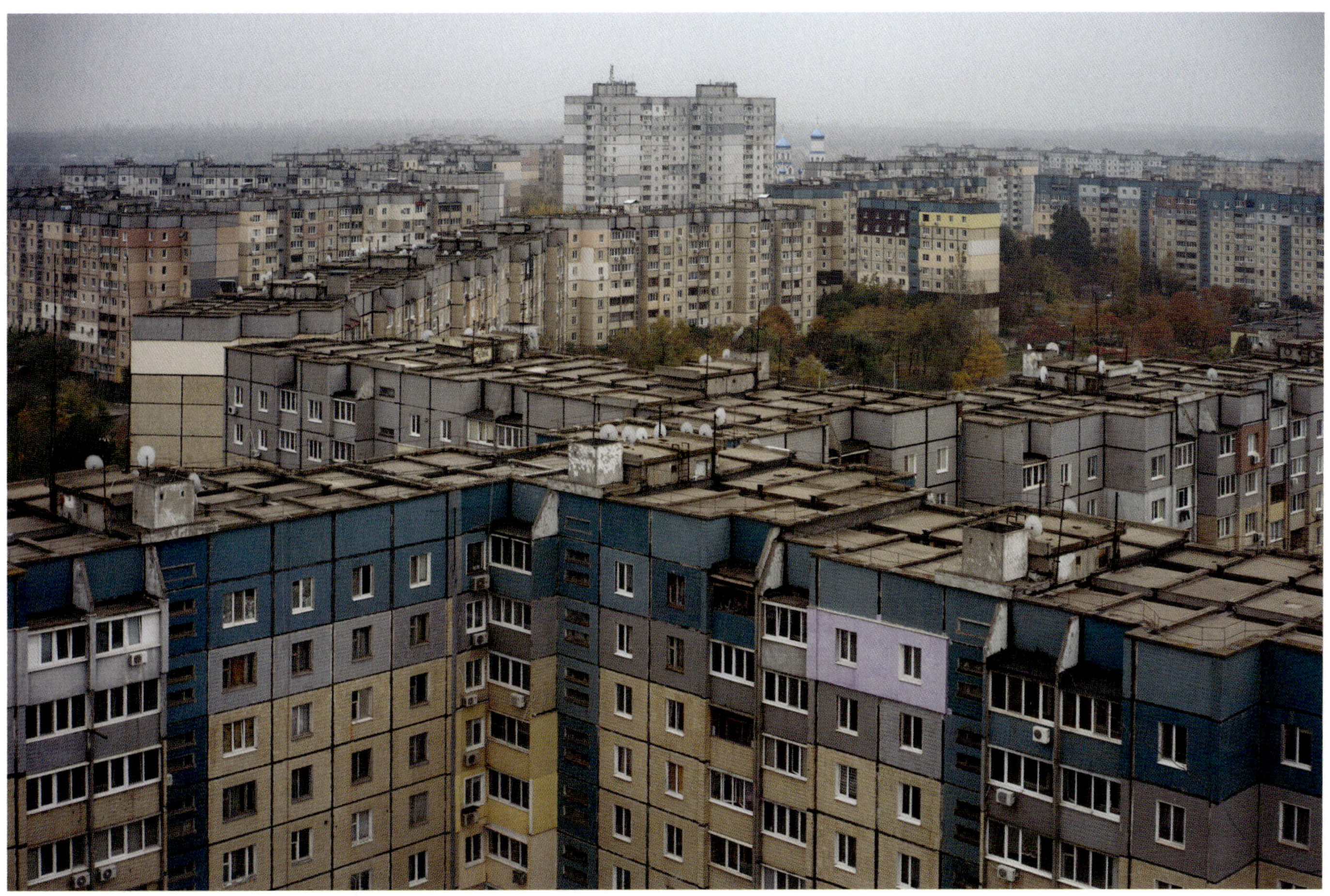

Krivoy Rog is a city in the Dnepropetrovsk region with a population of 624,000. Located at the centre of the Krivoy Rog iron-ore basin, it is considered the biggest steel-industry city in Eastern Europe. Major enterprises include productive mines, metallurgical works, ore-dressing plants, mechanical engineering, metal-working, energy and coke-chemical industries. During the Soviet period, the 27 kilometre underground Krivoy Rog Metrotram rail network was constructed in the city.

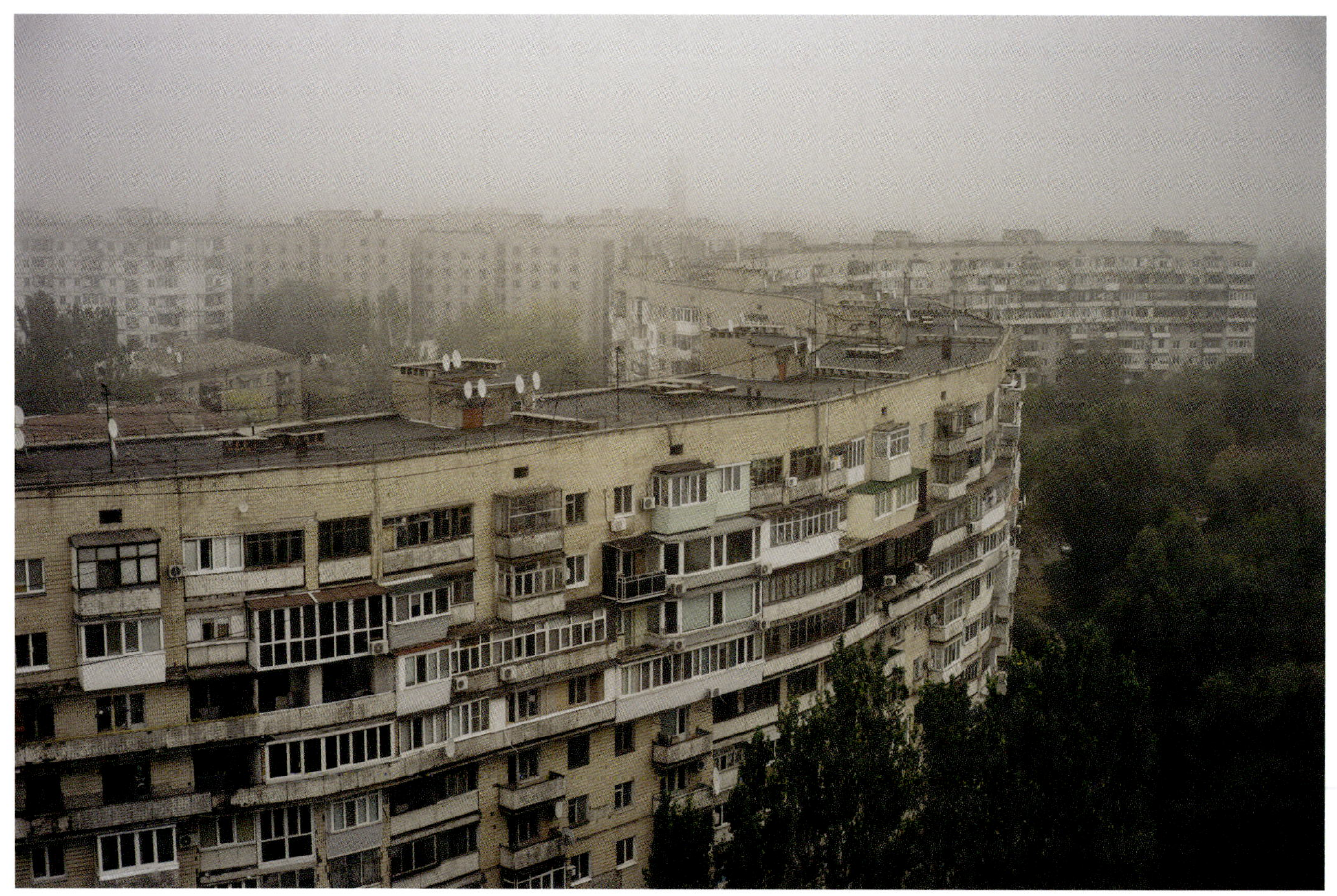

'Drunken Building'
ZAPORIZHZHIA, UKRAINE
Architect: Y. Yegorov

The city of Zaporizhzhia is one of the largest administrative, industrial and cultural centres in southern Ukraine, and the fourth largest industrial region. It is known for the production of steel, aluminium, aircraft engines, transformers and other heavy industries.

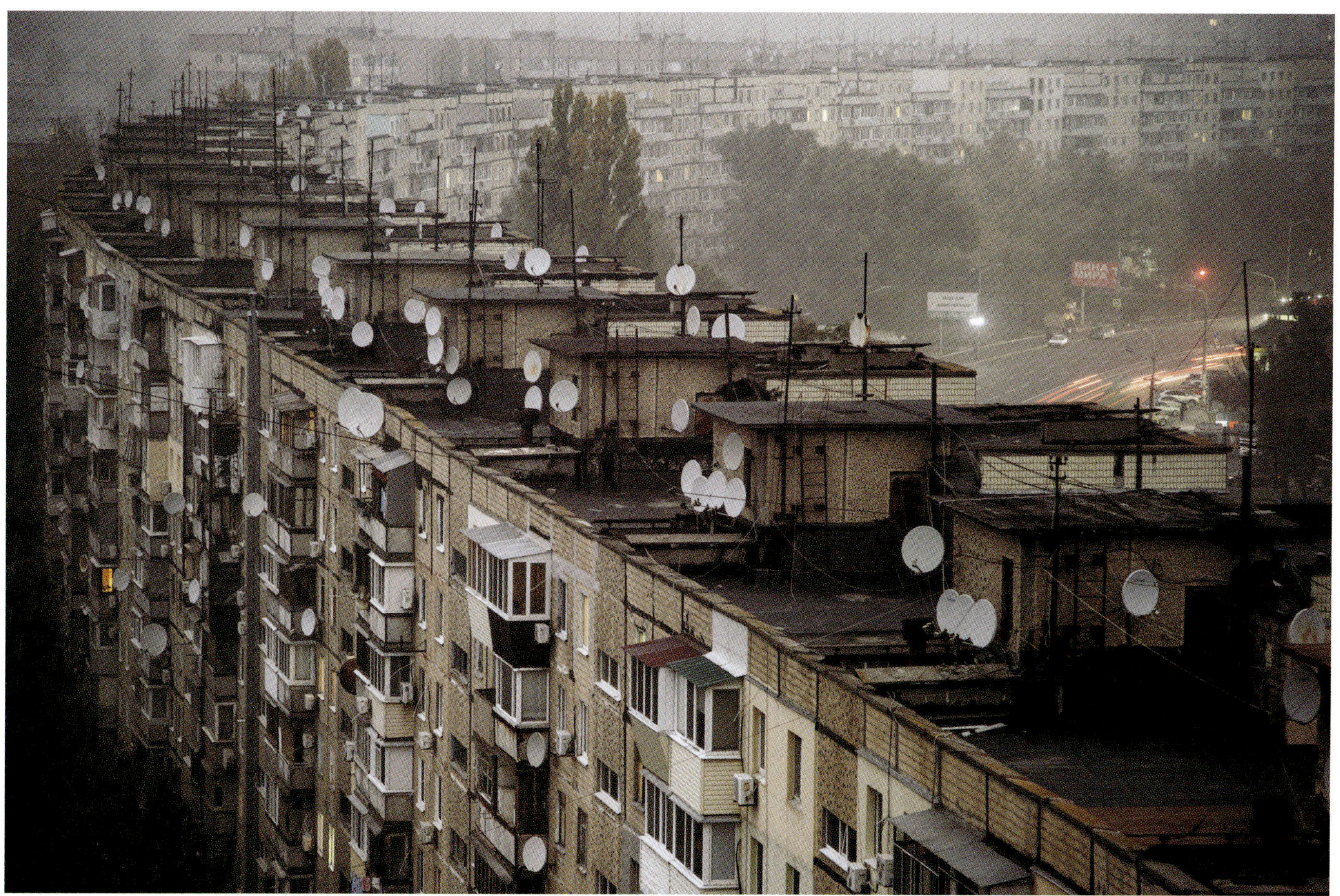

'Chinese Wall'
DNIPRO, UKRAINE
Built in 1974
Architects: O. Khavkin, P. Nirinberg and others

The curve of the road is followed for almost a kilometre by the façade of this 9-storey residential building. It acts as an architectural border between the new district and the older, low-rise buildings situated on the hillside.

In autumn 2019, I travelled to Ukraine to visit the Chernobyl Exclusion Zone. I specifically chose this time of year so I could photograph the abandoned city engulfed in fading nature. The single-day hike from the border of the Zone to Pripyat – necessary to evade security patrols – was the longest I'd ever undertaken. My girlfriend and I walked about 55 kilometres that day, seeing elk and even a herd of Przewalski's horses. At night, wolves howled shrilly nearby.

Pripyat itself leaves an indelible impression. The majority of its buildings remain more or less intact, some with collapsed roofs and others with collapsed walls, with any formerly open spaces now overgrown with trees and bushes. We managed to visit more than a dozen residential buildings, a hotel, several schools and kindergartens, cafés and shops, a swimming pool and a cinema. But most of all, I was impressed by the monumental Soviet street art. Many buildings are still decorated with mosaics, interiors retain painted murals and a fantastic stained-glass window has survived in the café.

The building of Pripyat was declared an All-Union Komosol 'shock construction' project, with volunteers from all corners of the USSR answering the call of the Party to lend a hand. According to the development plan, Pripyat was intended to house 80,000 people. It was once one of the most beautiful atomic cities ('atomograd' in Russian – meaning a satellite city, built for the workers of the nuclear power plant) in Ukraine. When it was first constructed, it was considered a model city, a city of the future. This was how the authorities had envisioned the urban centres of the Soviet Union, and Pripyat was recognised for the quality of its architecture.

The basic planning concept followed the principle of 'triangular' building, a system characterised by a mix of standard and high-rise residential blocks with expansive open spaces between them that had been developed by a group of Moscow architects led by Nikolai Ostozhenko. In contrast to old towns with their narrow streets and densely packed houses, Pripyat was designed to be open and comfortable to live in. In addition to an increase in urban space, this was achieved by the arrangement of streets and avenues in a grid to help prevent traffic congestion.

Such planning was unique at the time, though in parallel with the development of Pripyat, the same scheme was used for a dozen other cities in the Soviet Union. Some Pripyat neighbourhoods thus bear a close resemblance to residential areas in other atomic cities, in particular Kurchatov, Semipalatinsk-21, Volgodonsk and the autograd Togliatti. But Pripyat was no average city. The majority of its institutions had not been funded using conventional budgets, but instead from sources specially designated for closed cities, inhabited by a military and nuclear-industry elite. It was recognised as a model of Soviet architectural extravagance.

The composition of the neighbourhoods circling the city centre gave Pripyat a distinctive look. Administrative, cultural and recreational buildings, food and grocery stores and a hotel complex were concentrated in the centre, embellished with monumental and decorative art, neon and brightly panelled façades. Many more amenities were planned, with two shopping centres, a Palace of Pioneers, a two-screen cinema, a Palace of Arts, another hotel and two more sports complexes all scheduled to open in 1988. Because residents had an average age of only 26, special attention was paid to creating sports and pre-school facilities, including fifteen kindergartens. Every year more than 1,000 babies were born here, taking the total population to 49,000. In the evenings, young families strolled along pristine avenues, pushing prams.

But this socialist idyll came to an end on 26 April 1986, when an explosion destroyed Reactor 4 of the Chernobyl Nuclear Power Plant. At the time of the accident, the plant was the most powerful in the USSR. As the destroyed reactor spewed out deadly radiation, the city continued with ordinary life. For more than a day, the authorities concealed the news of the accident, not only from Pripyat residents and the country, but from the world. The evacuation of the city was finally initiated 36 hours after the accident. The state later attempted to justify this lack of immediate action with the explanation that it didn't want to cause panic.

Officially, 31 people died in the first three months following the disaster and 134 people suffered radiation sickness of varying severity. More than 115,000 were evacuated from a 30-kilometre zone around the plant. Considerable resources were mobilised to manage the consequences, with 530,000 workers taking part in the clean-up operation. Over the next fifteen years, the long-term effects of radiation exposure resulted in a (much disputed) death toll of around 80 people.

The cloud from the burning reactor dispersed radioactive materials, in particular iodine and cesium radionuclides, over a large part of Europe. The greatest concentration of fallout was in the areas of the Soviet Union closest to the plant, including Belarus, Russia and Ukraine. The Chernobyl accident was an event of great social and political significance for the USSR, but it was not until 14 May, almost three weeks after the explosion, that Soviet leader Mikhail Gorbachev appeared on national television to talk about the disaster. The accident had serious economic ramifications: it has been estimated that sums equivalent to between 20 and 30 per cent of Soviet gross domestic product were spent tackling the disaster and dealing with its aftermath.

In addition, the catastrophe and the suppression of its effects undermined the Soviet economy and exposed ineffective management systems, intensifying Gorbachev's desire to reform and in the process mitigate the prospect of nuclear confrontation. Chernobyl was also an important link in a chain of failures (the anti-alcohol campaign, Afghanistan, rail crashes and ethnic conflicts) that shook faith in the ability of the Soviet leadership successfully to govern the country.

References: *Pripyat – a model of Soviet urban planning*, Vladimir Dvorzhetsky, 1985; *Native Pripyat* (booklet), 1984

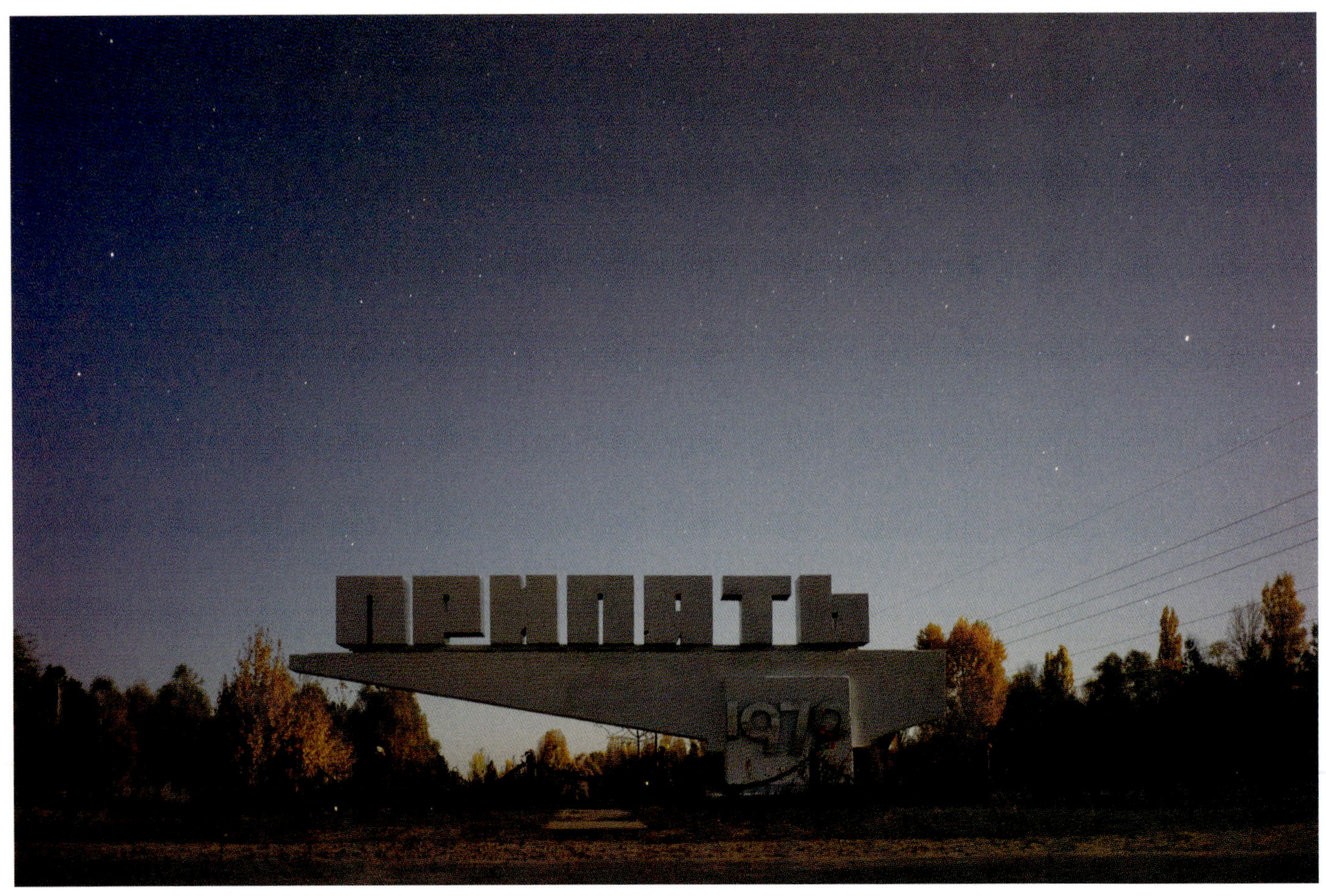

City entrance sign
PRIPYAT, UKRAINE
Erected in 1970

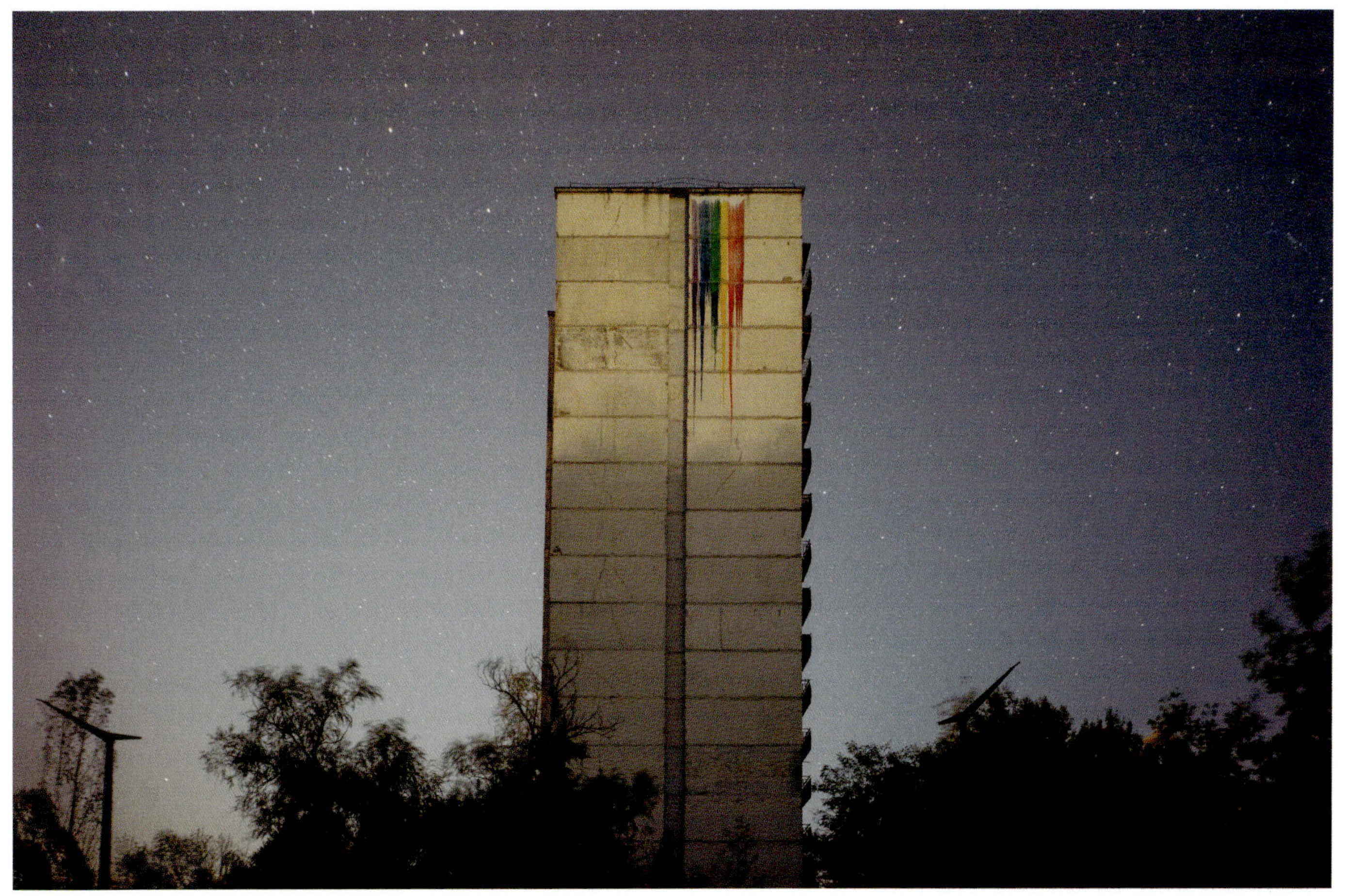

16-storey building at 52 Lesi Ukrainki Street
PRIPYAT, UKRAINE

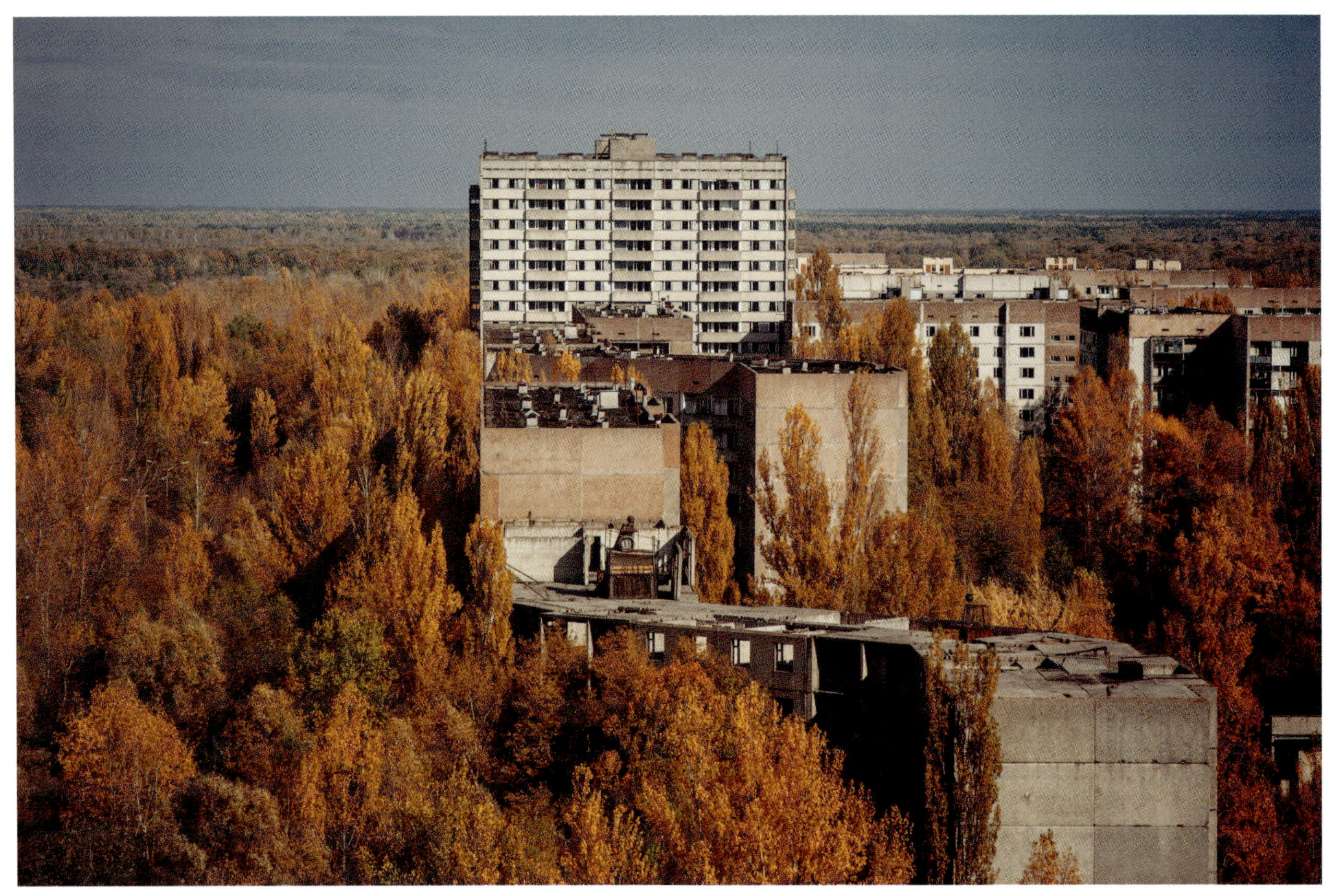

4th Microdistrict
PRIPYAT, UKRAINE

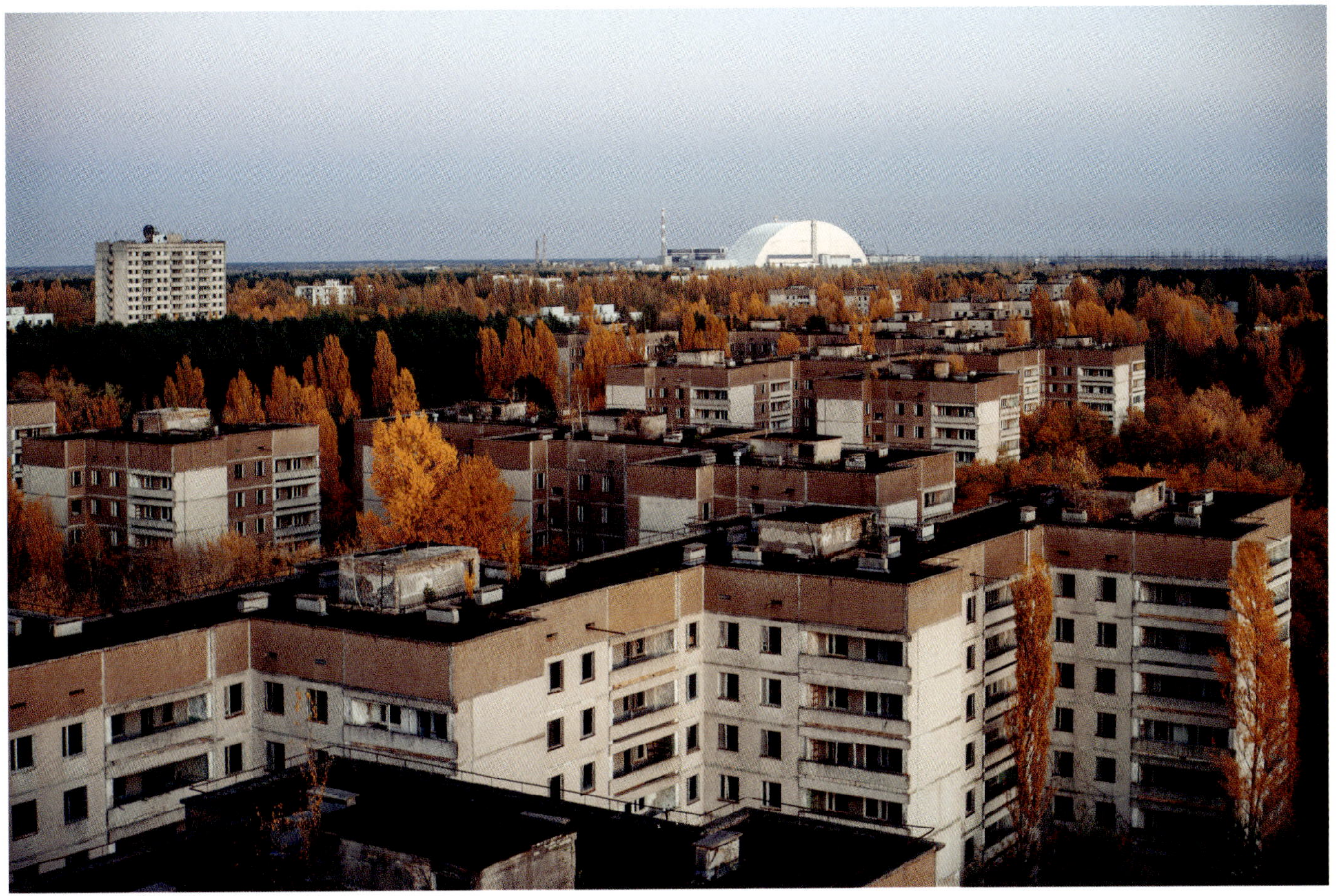

New Arch over Chernobyl Nuclear Power Plant
PRIPYAT, UKRAINE

The New Arch is a structure built to confine the remains of Reactor 4 for the next 100 years. It is designed to prevent the release of radiation, protect the reactor from external influence, allow its decommissioning and disassembly, and prevent water intrusion.

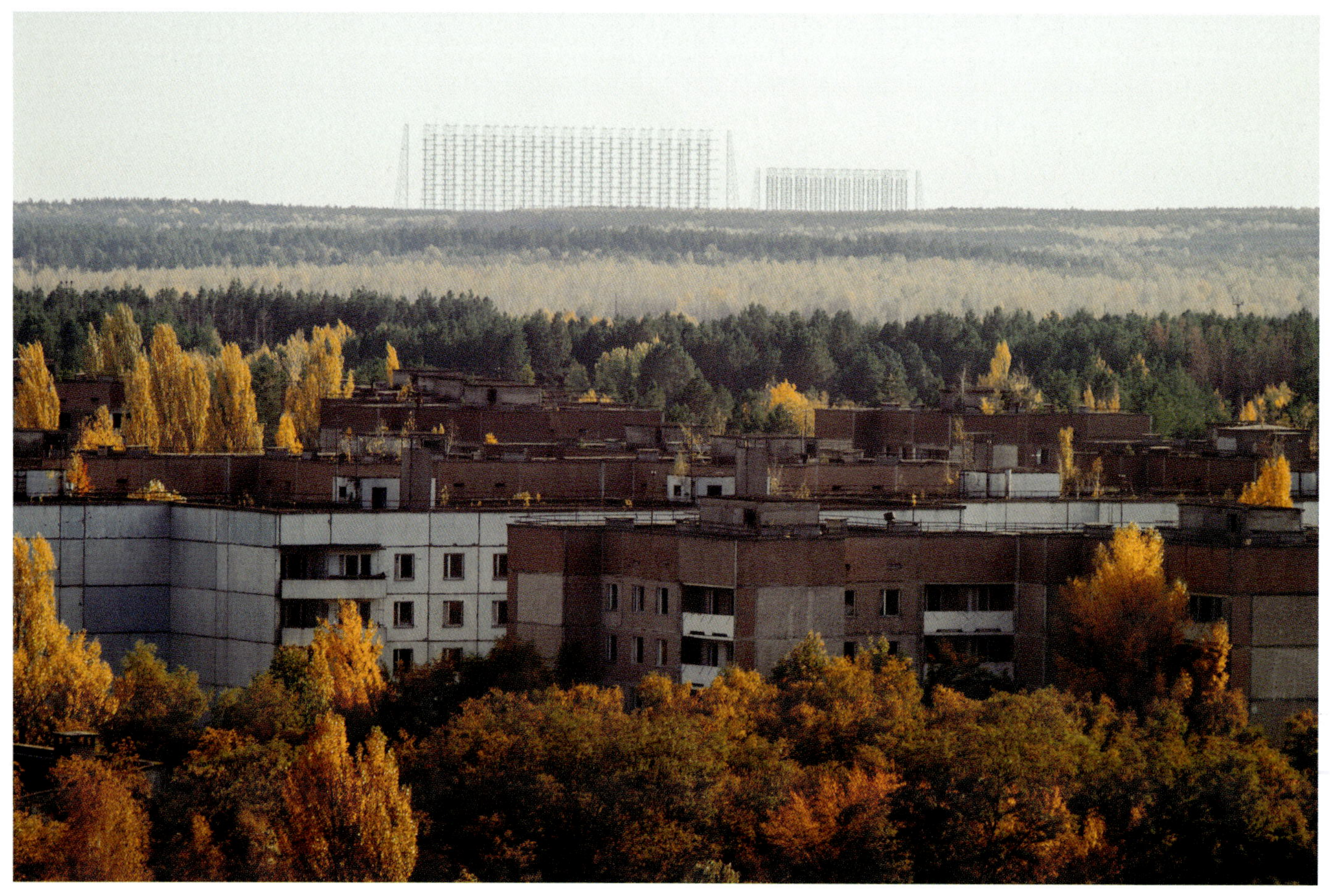

Duga-1 on the horizon
PRIPYAT, UKRAINE

Duga ('Arc' in Russian) is an over-the-horizon radar station, used for the early detection of intercontinental ballistic missiles. From 1976 to 1989, the powerful system broadcast over shortwave frequencies, its distinctive sound earning it the nickname 'Russian Woodpecker'.

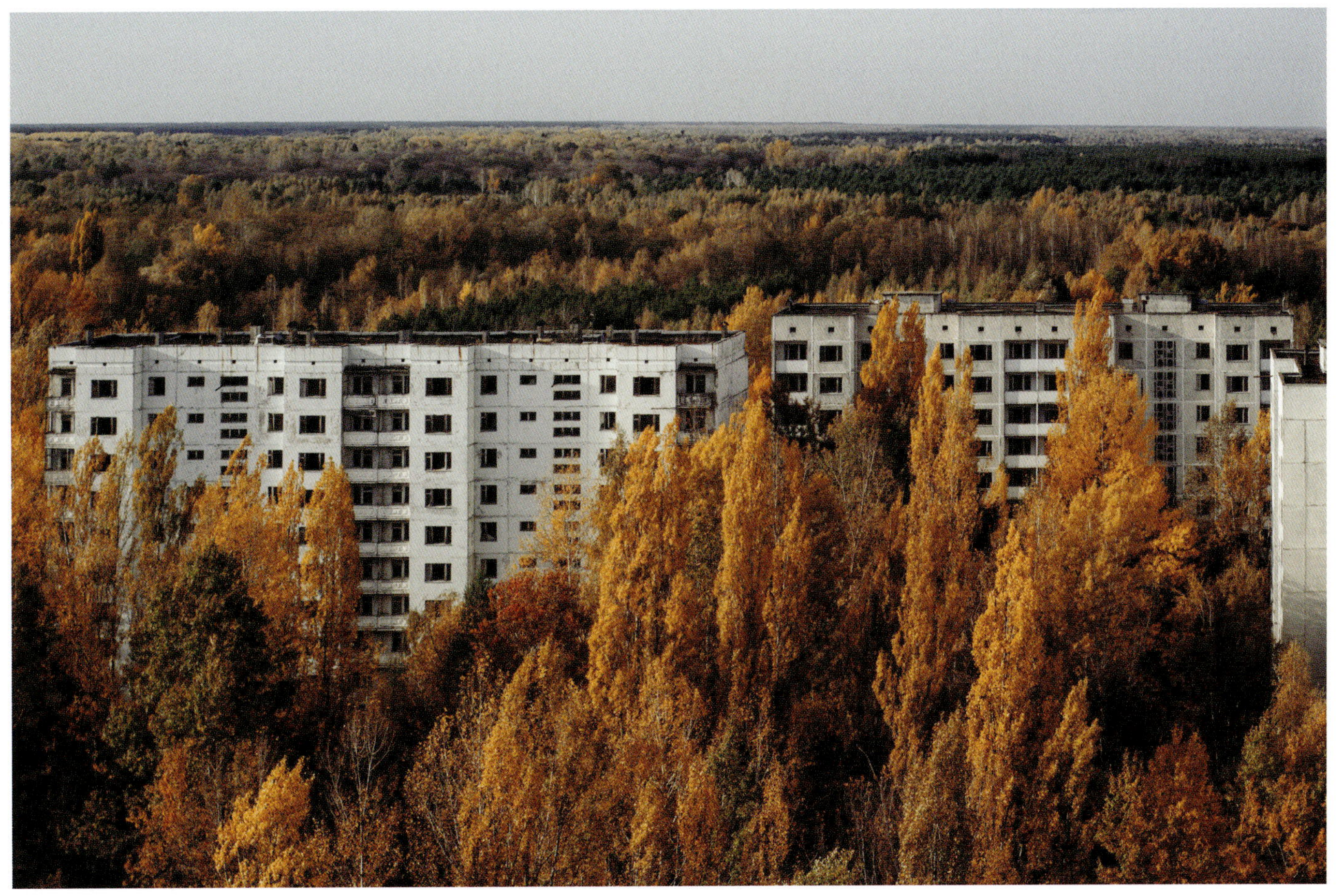

5th Microdistrict, the last to be built
PRIPYAT, UKRAINE

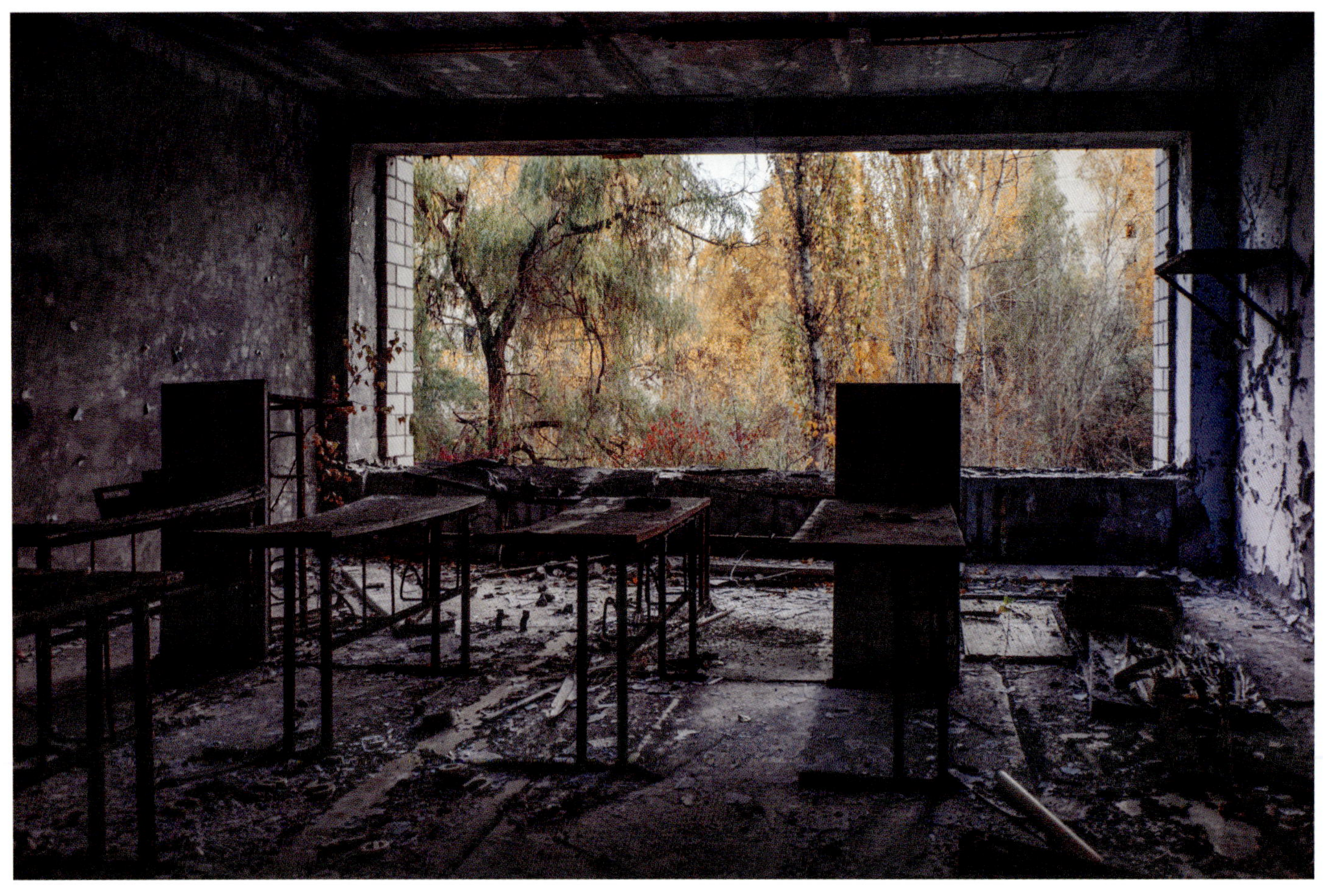

Secondary School No.4, built according to project 224-1-314
PRIPYAT, UKRAINE

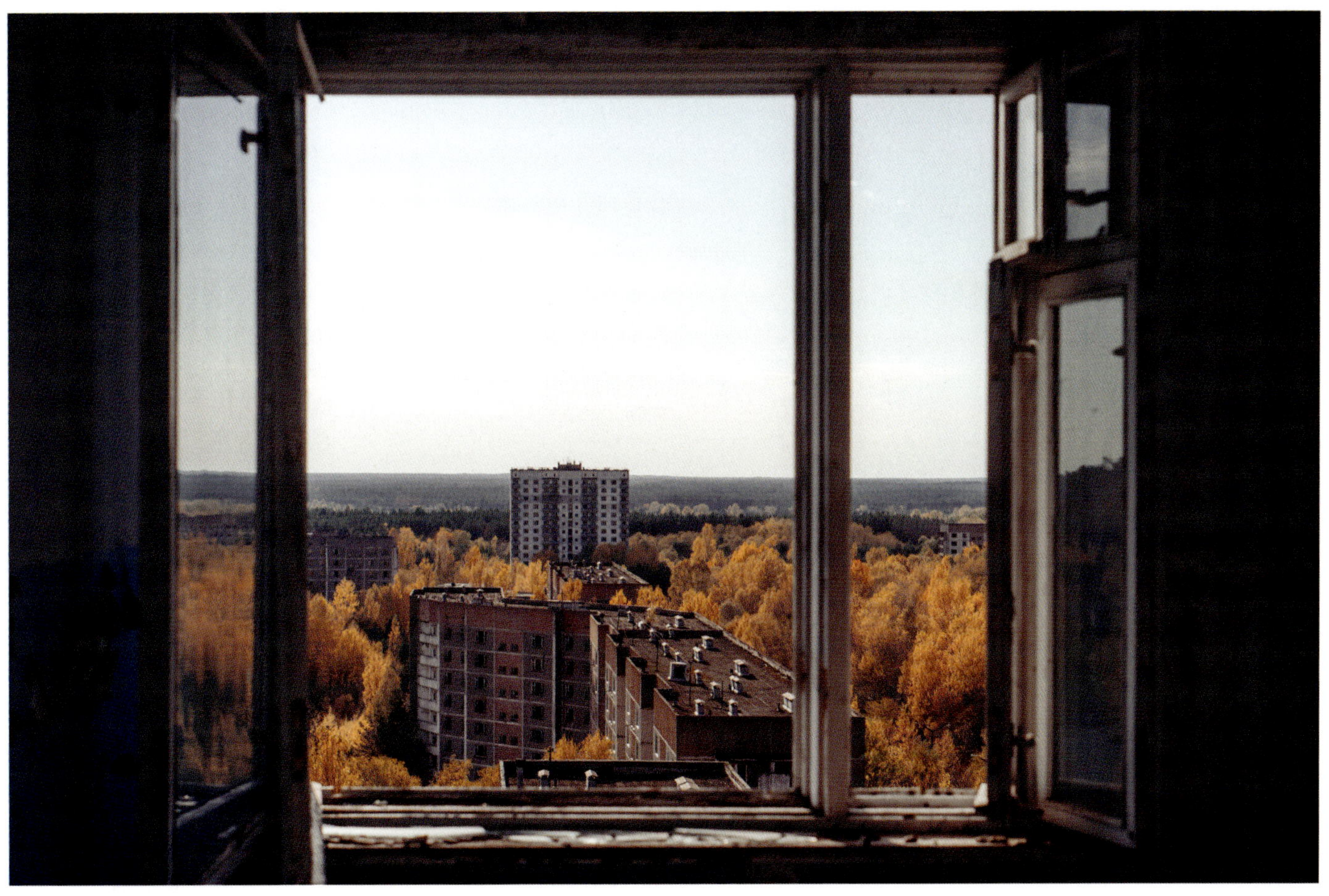

4th Microdistrict
PRIPYAT, UKRAINE

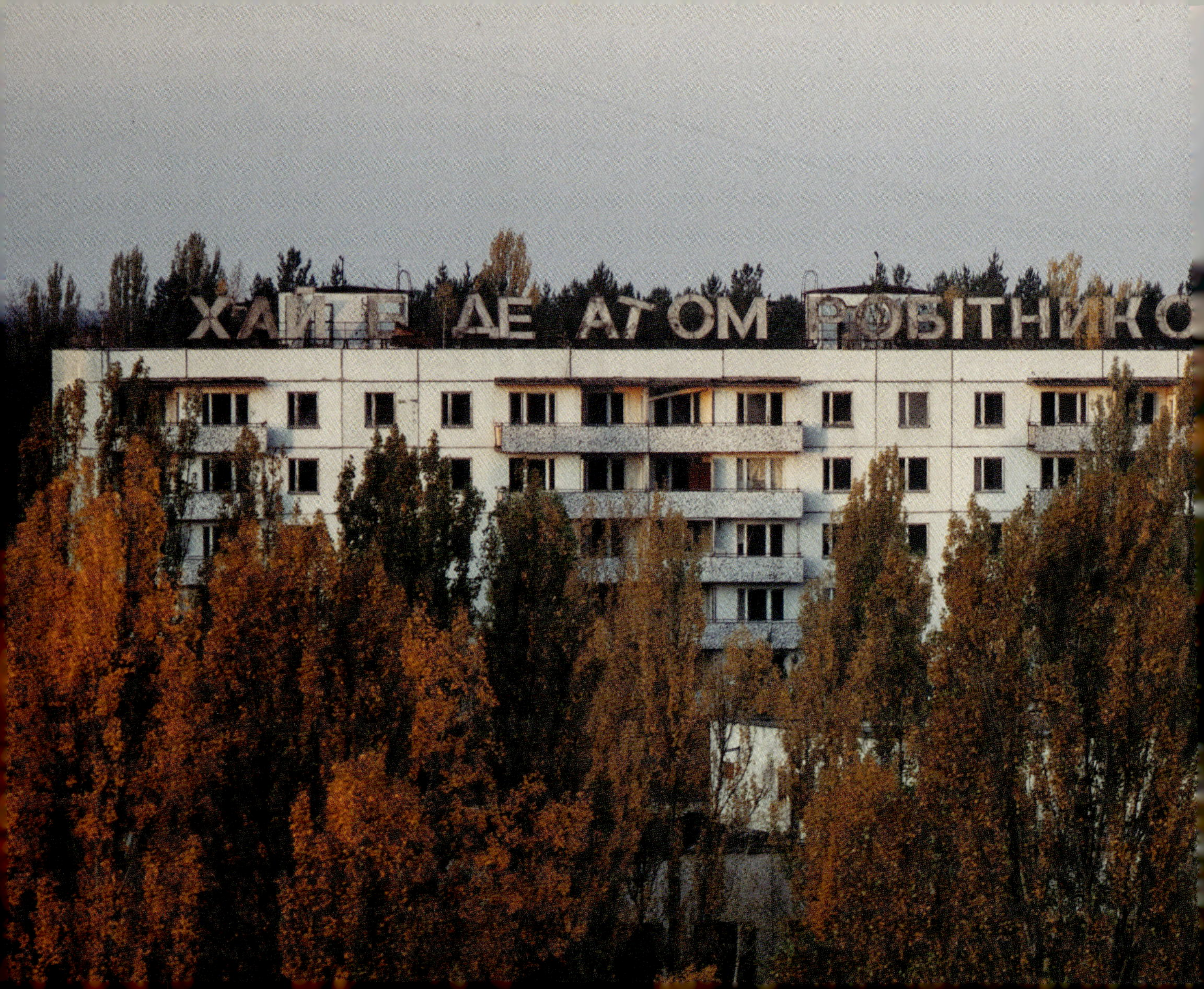
ХАЙ... ДЕ АТОМ РОБІТНИКО

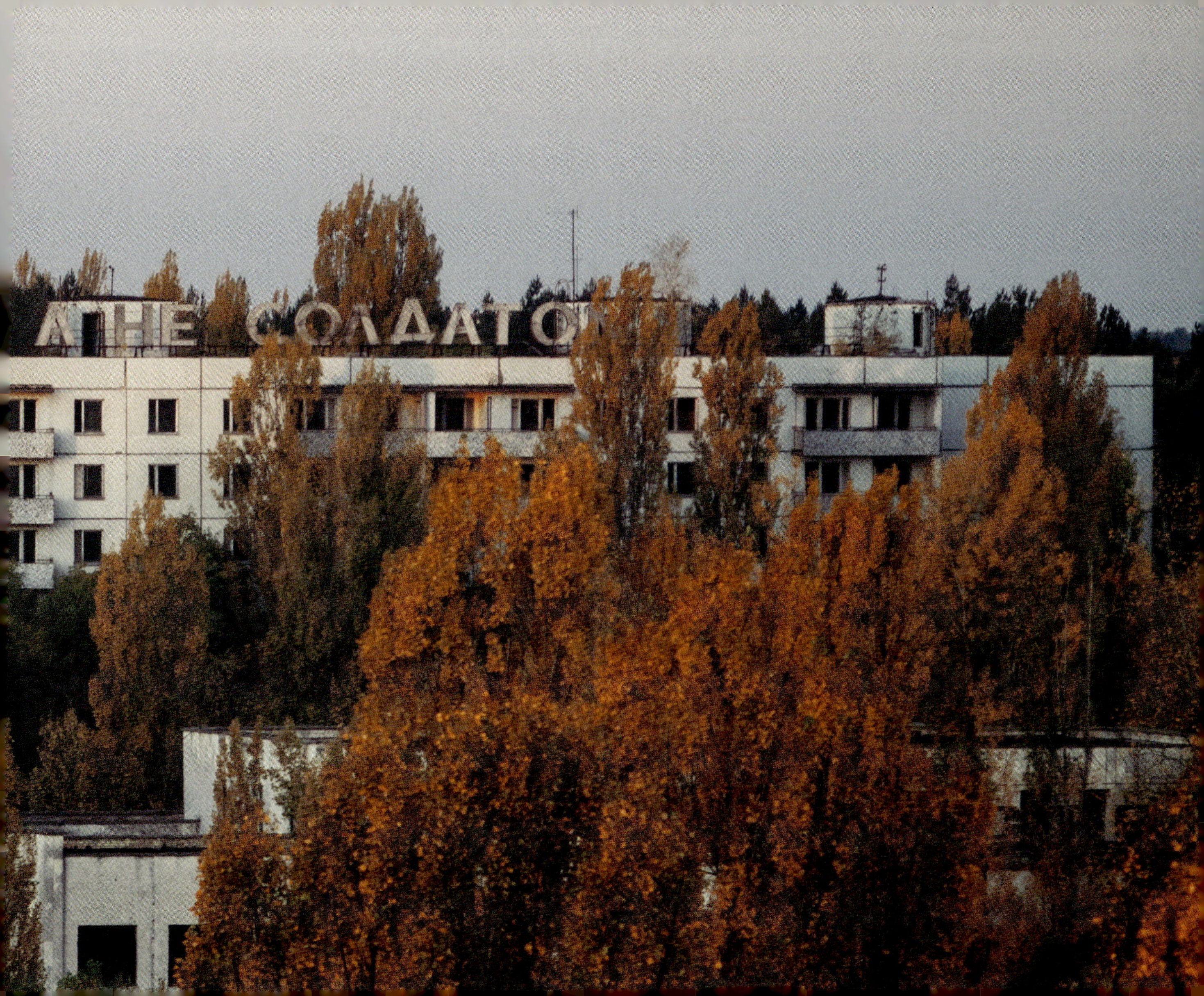
Л НЕ СОЛДАТОМ

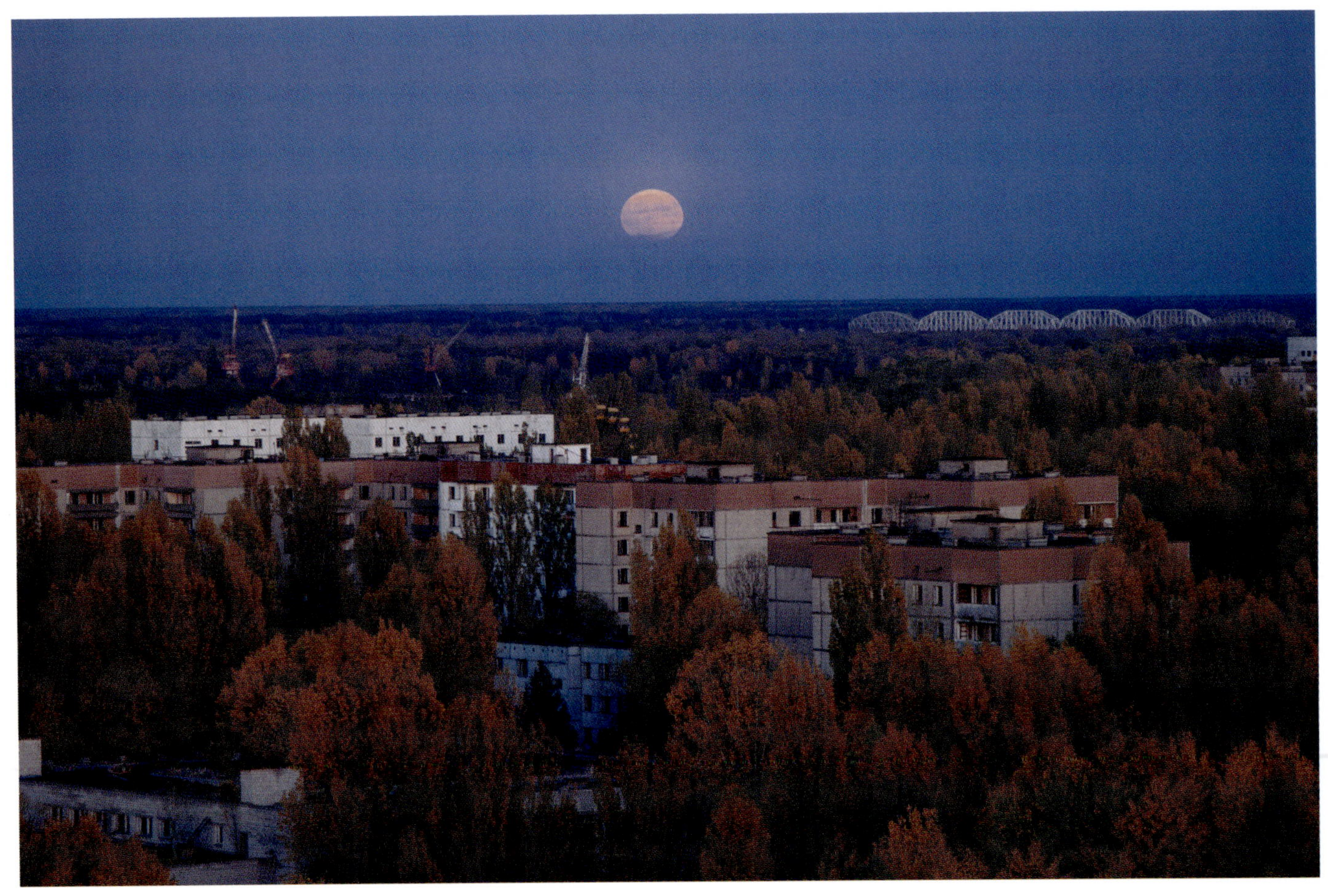

The Moon at dawn
PRIPYAT, UKRAINE

previous page
'Let atom be a worker, not a soldier' on a 9-storey panel building of
the 121T Series.

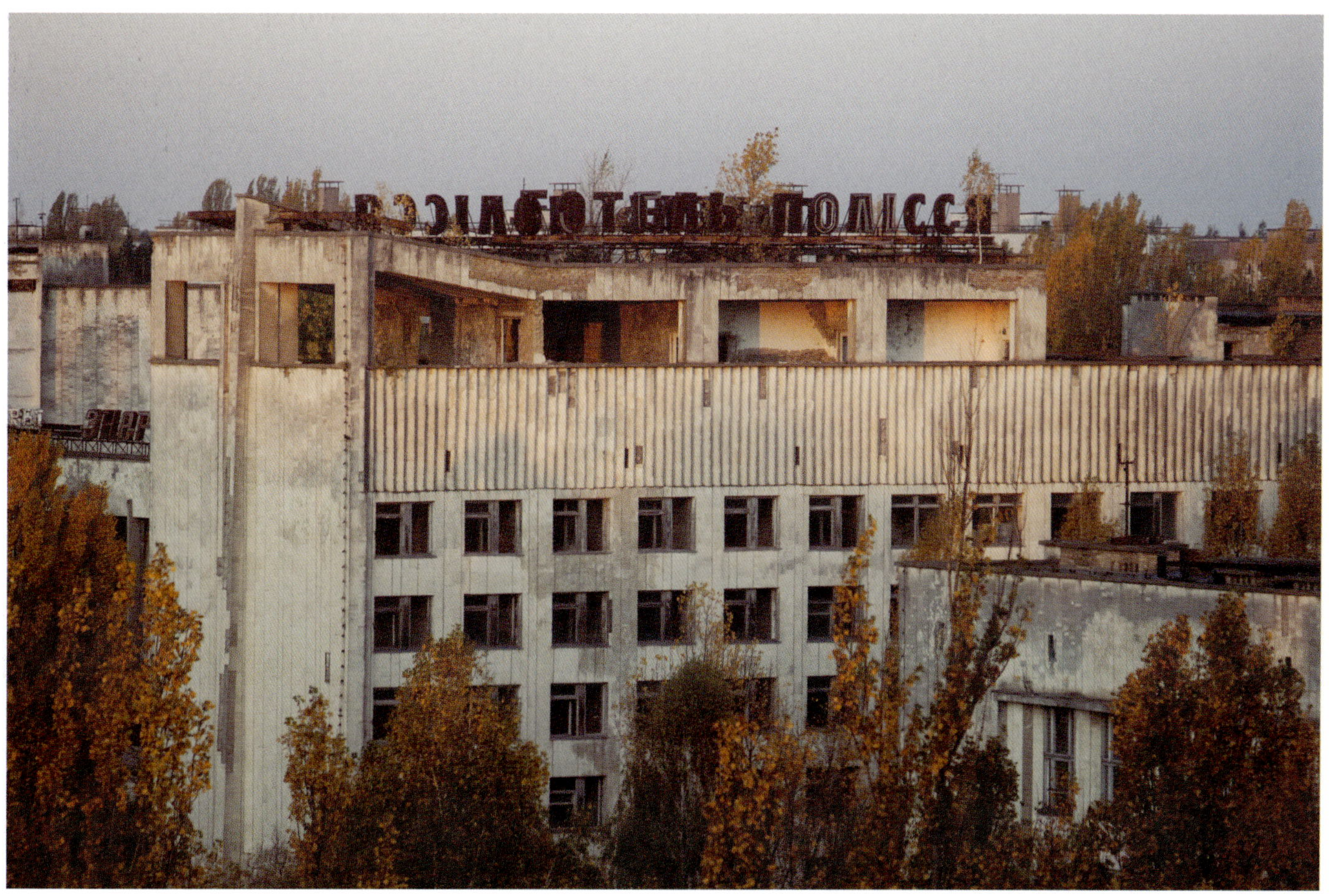

Polissya Hotel
PRIPYAT, UKRAINE
Built in the mid-1970s

This hotel has a direct line of sight to the plant. Immediately after the accident, helicopters were directed from its roof to drop boron, sand and lead onto the burning reactor. It was also used as accommodation by liquidators during the clean-up operation.

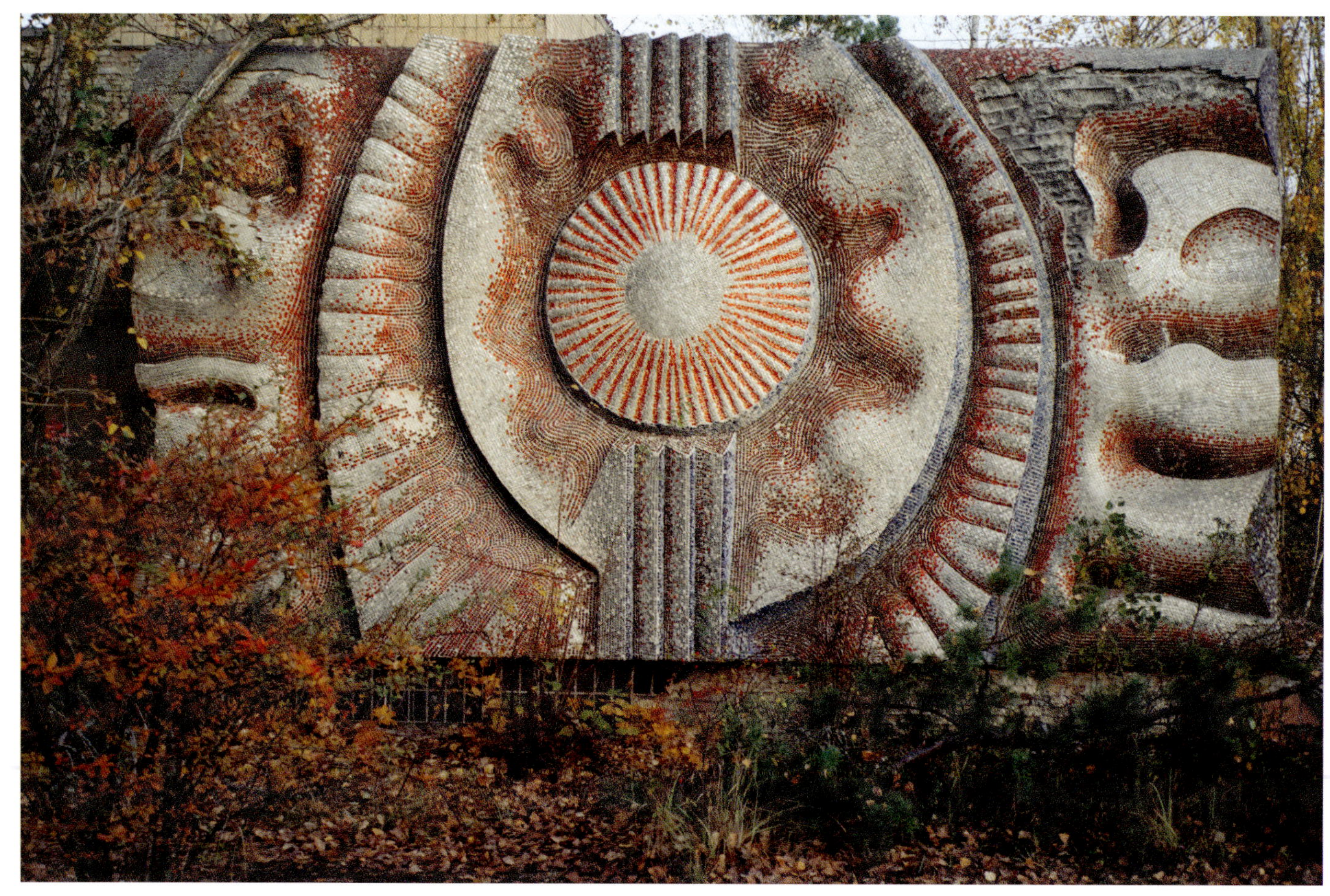

'Energy' relief mosaic, Prometheus Cinema
PRIPYAT, UKRAINE
Built in 1977
Designer: I. Litovchenko

Ivan Litovchenko was a Soviet artist who specialised in large-scale decorative and monumental work. Many of his Pripyat artworks remain in reasonable condition and can still be seen on the streets today.

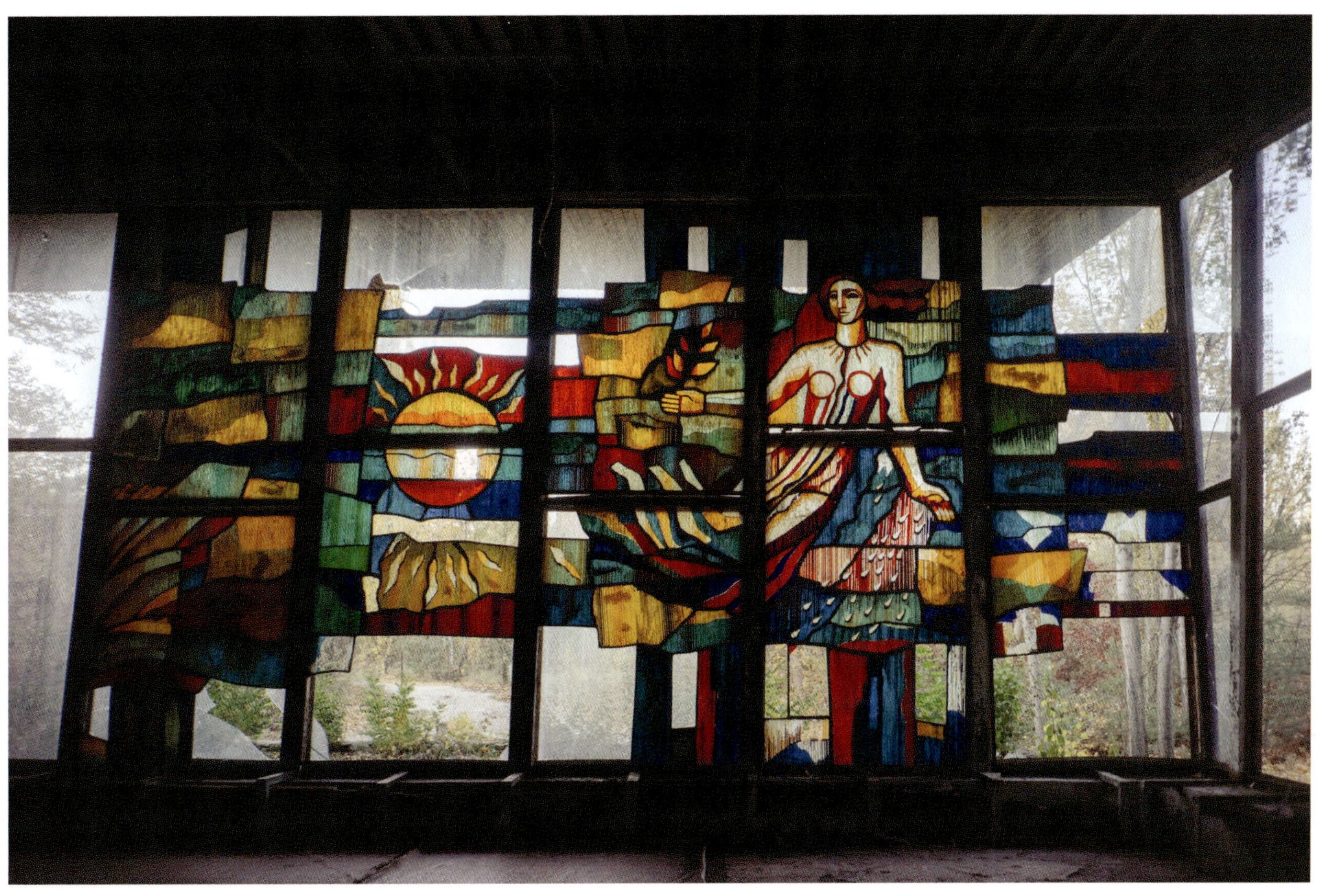

Stained-glass window in Pripyat Café
PRIPYAT, UKRAINE

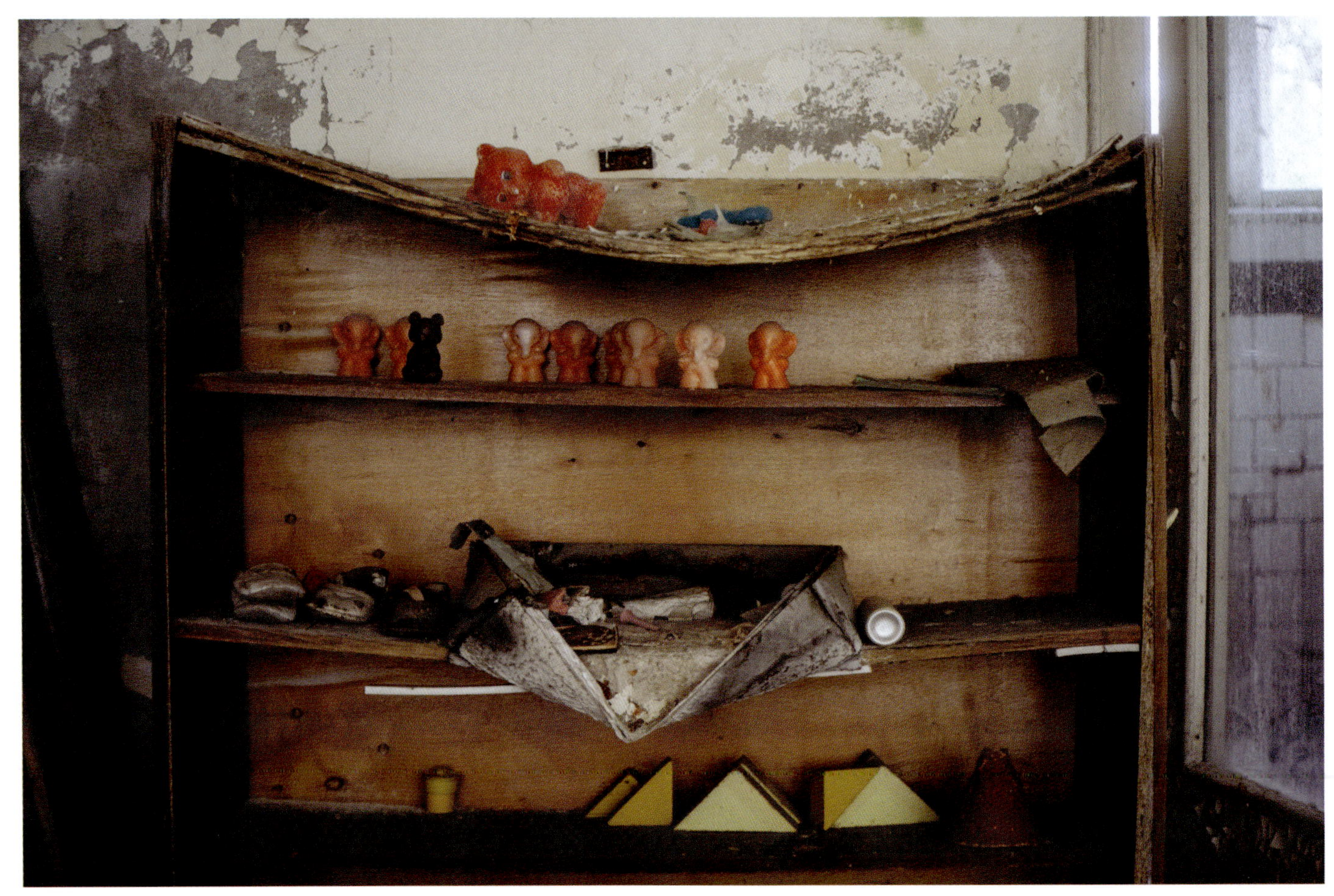

Interior, 'Children's combine' No.14 kindergarten
PRIPYAT, UKRAINE

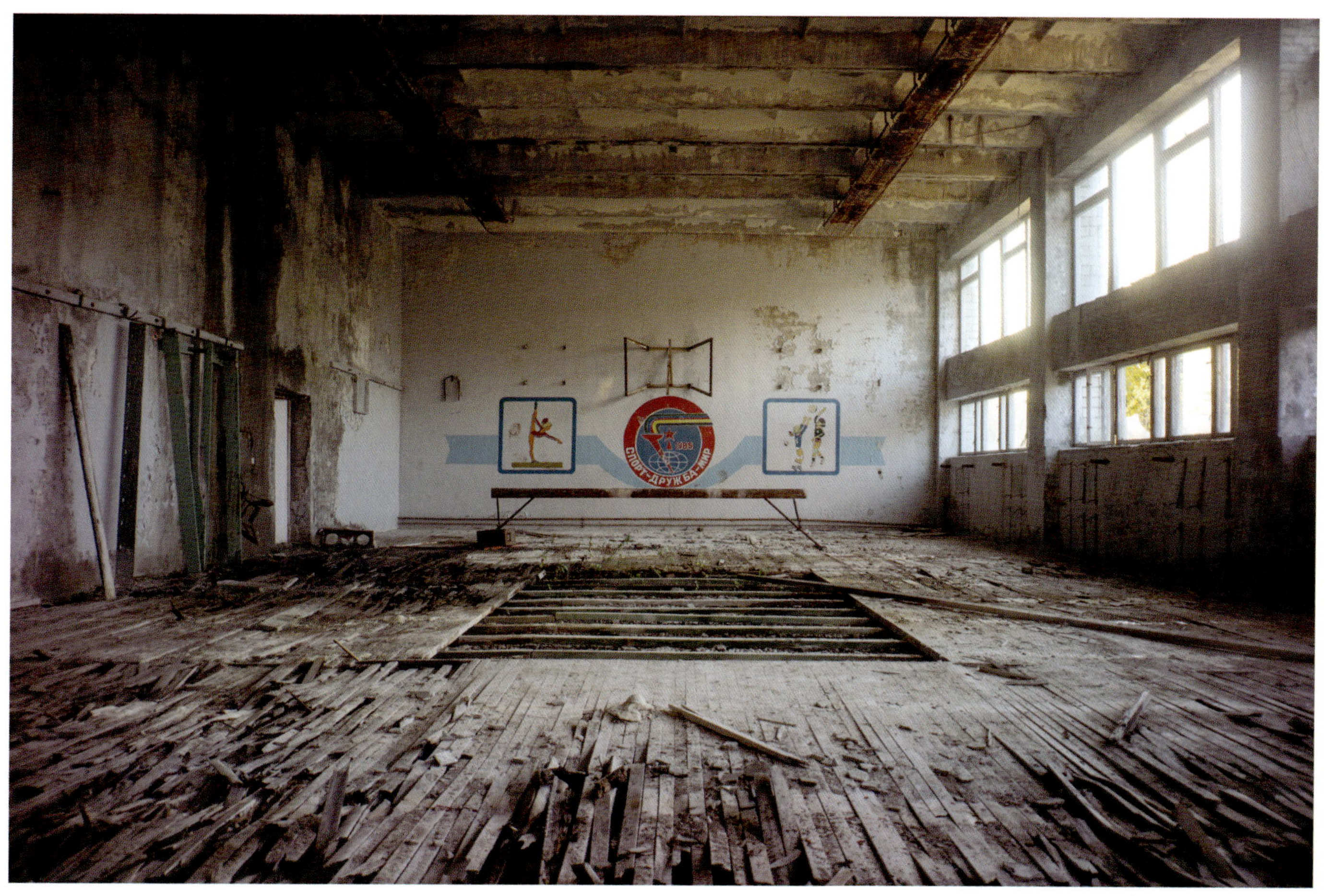

Gym, Secondary School No.4
PRIPYAT, UKRAINE

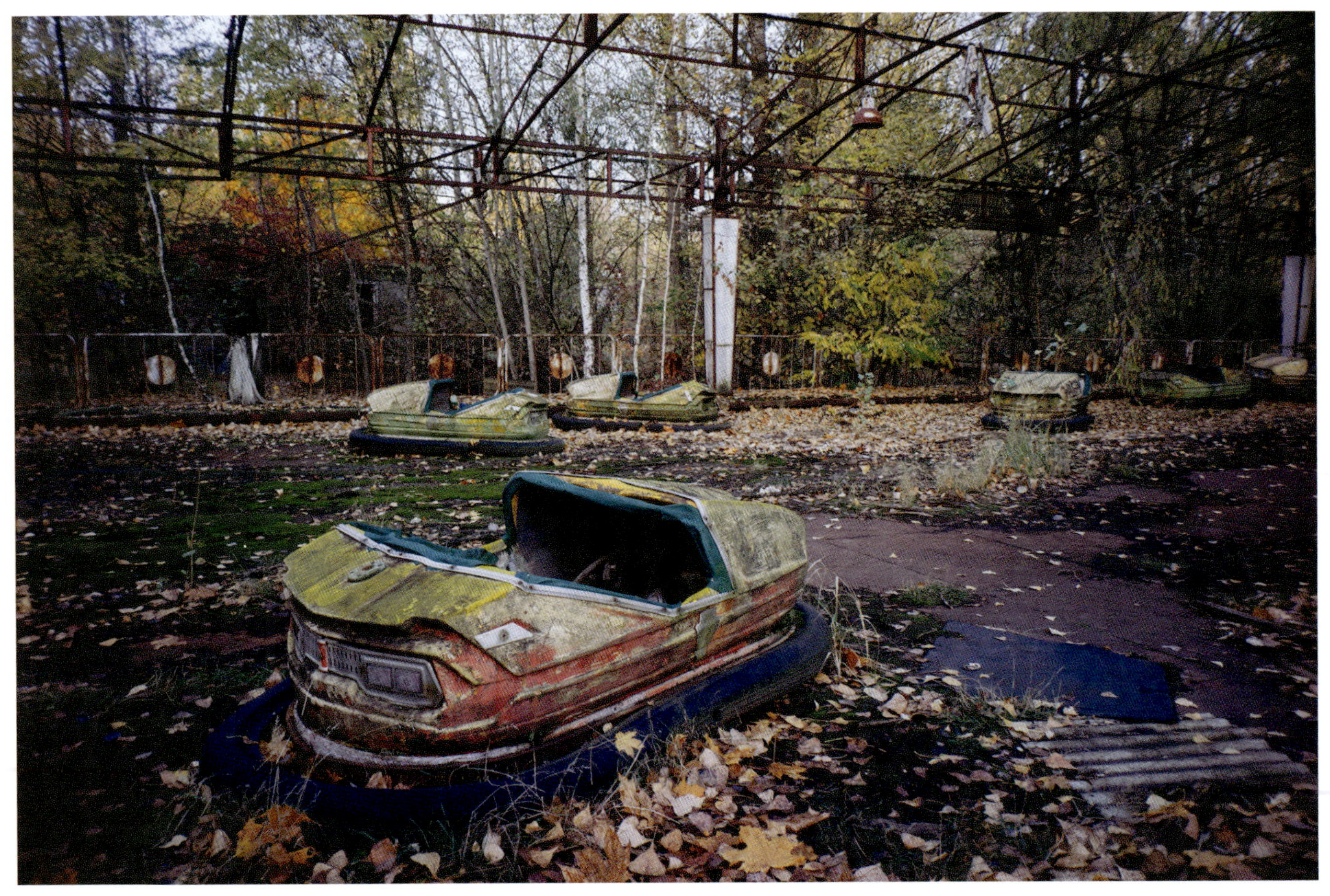

Bumper cars, Pripyat Amusement Park
PRIPYAT, UKRAINE

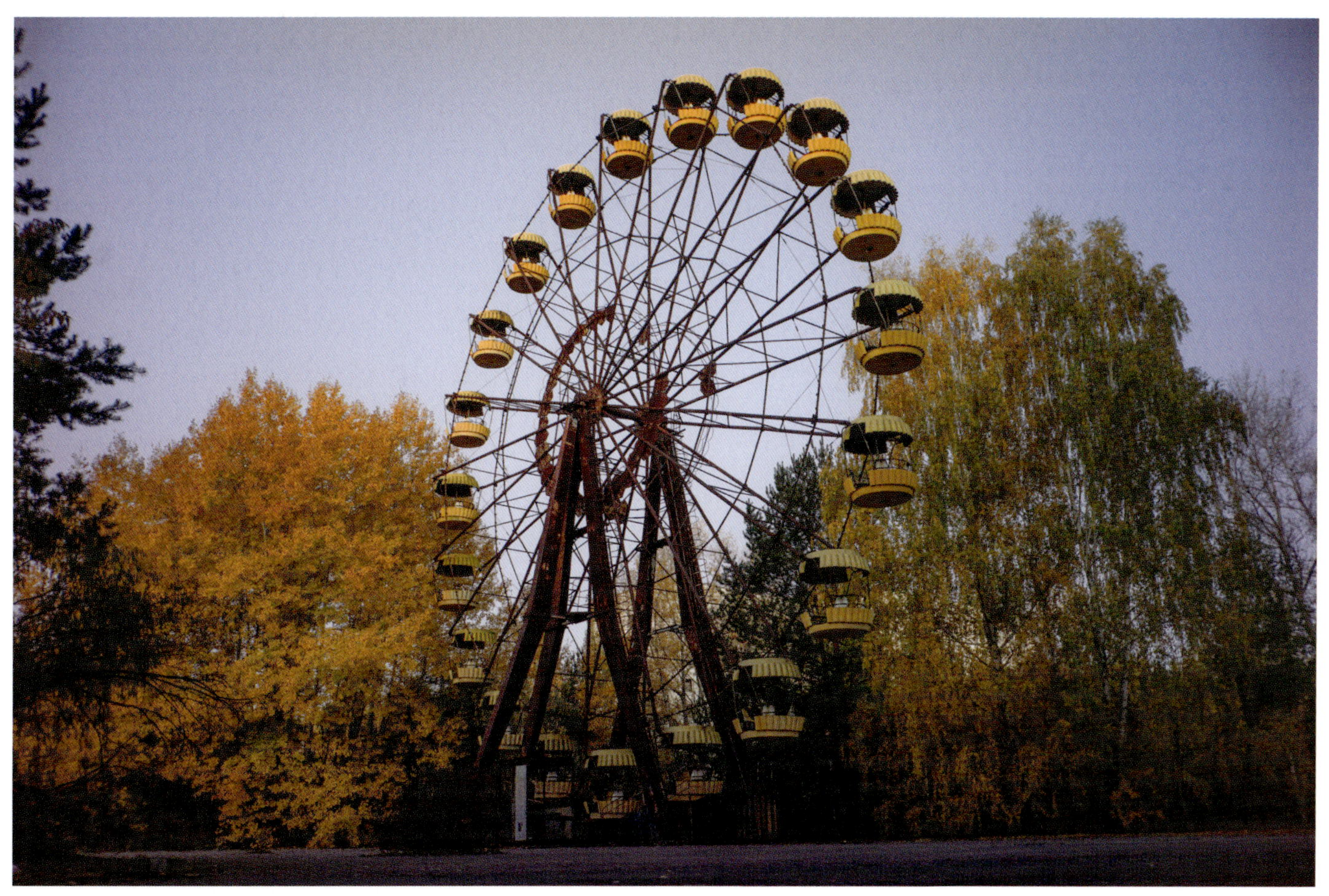

Ferris wheel, due to open 1 May 1986
PRIPYAT, UKRAINE

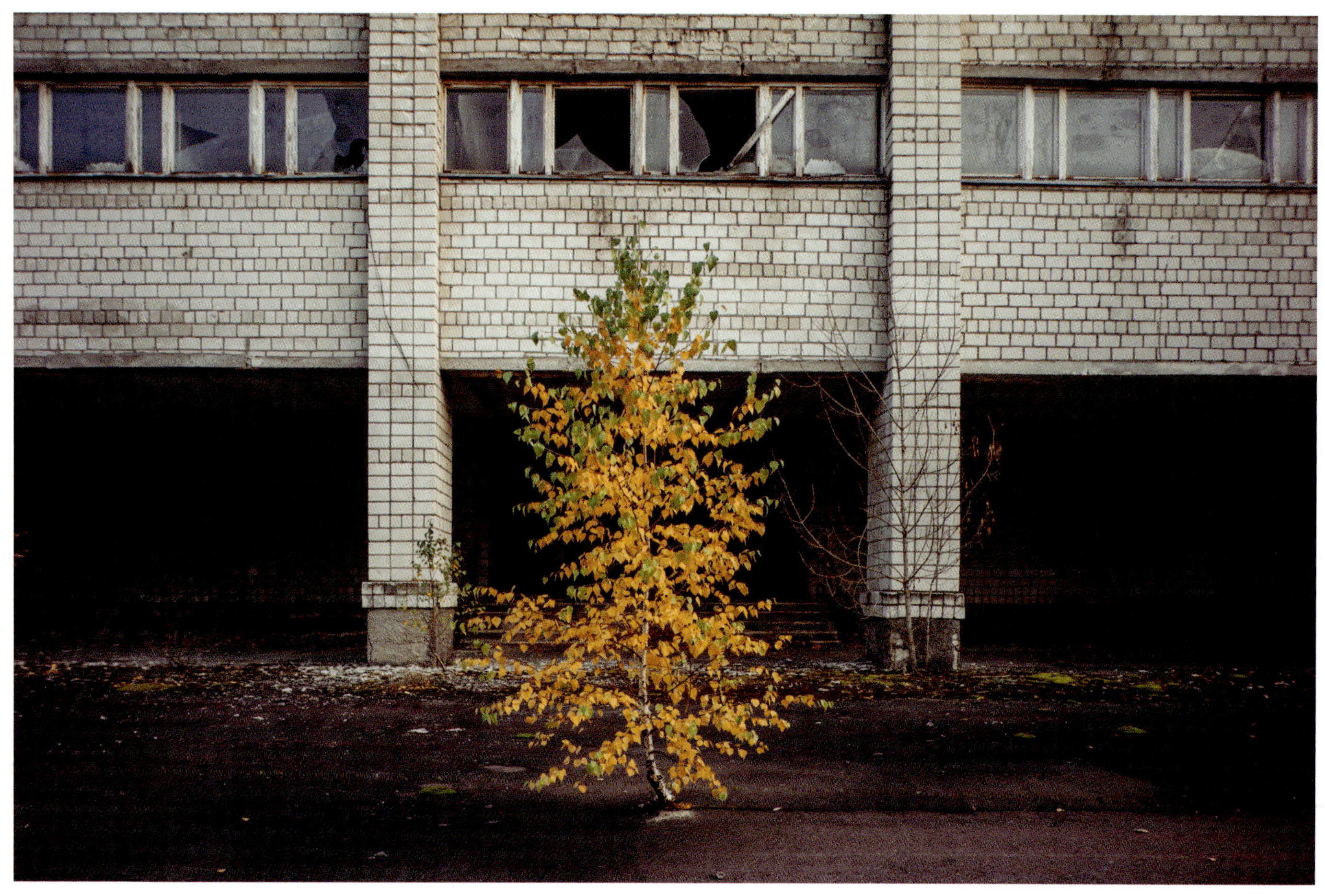

Main entrance, Secondary School No.4
PRIPYAT, UKRAINE

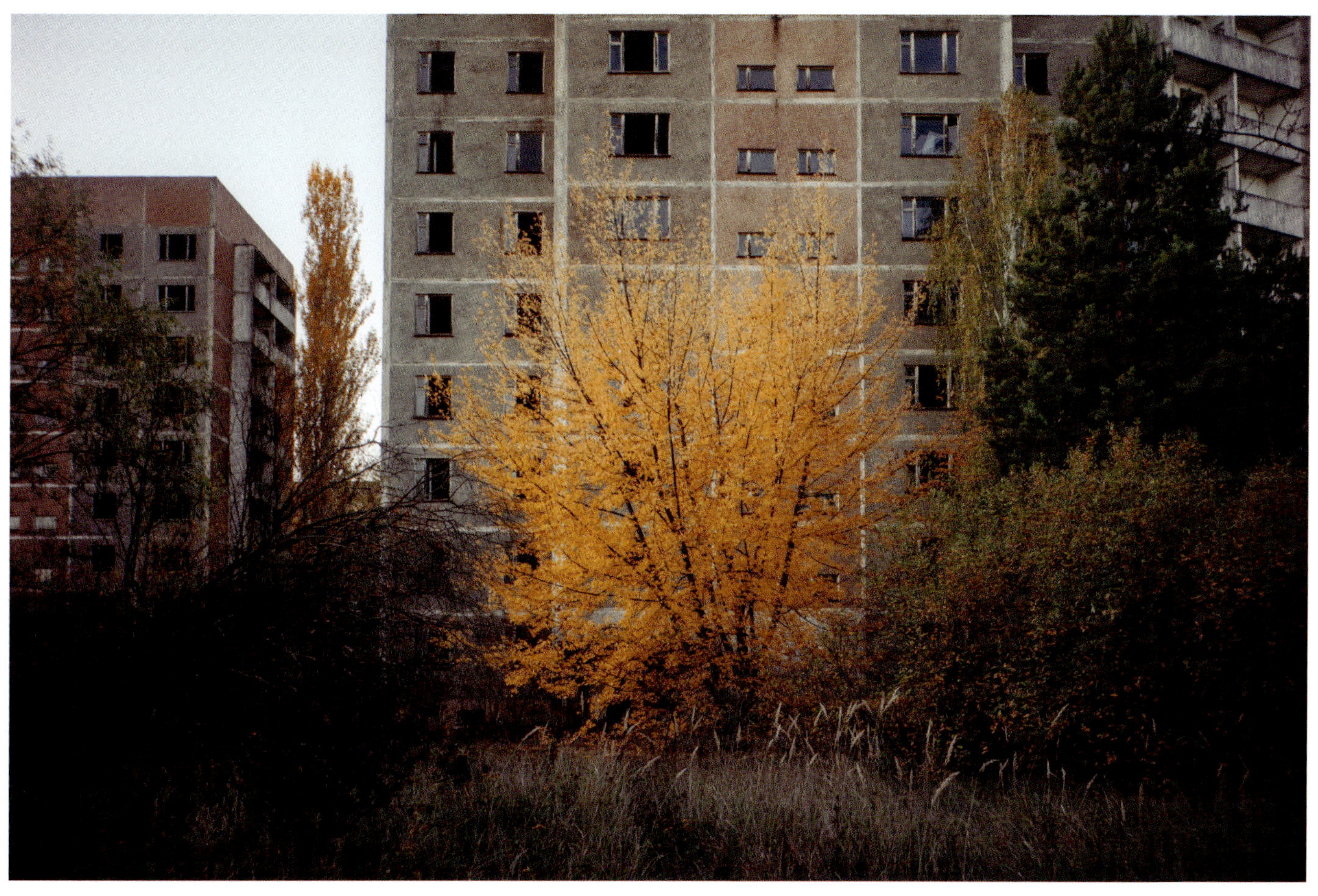

3rd Microdistrict
PRIPYAT, UKRAINE

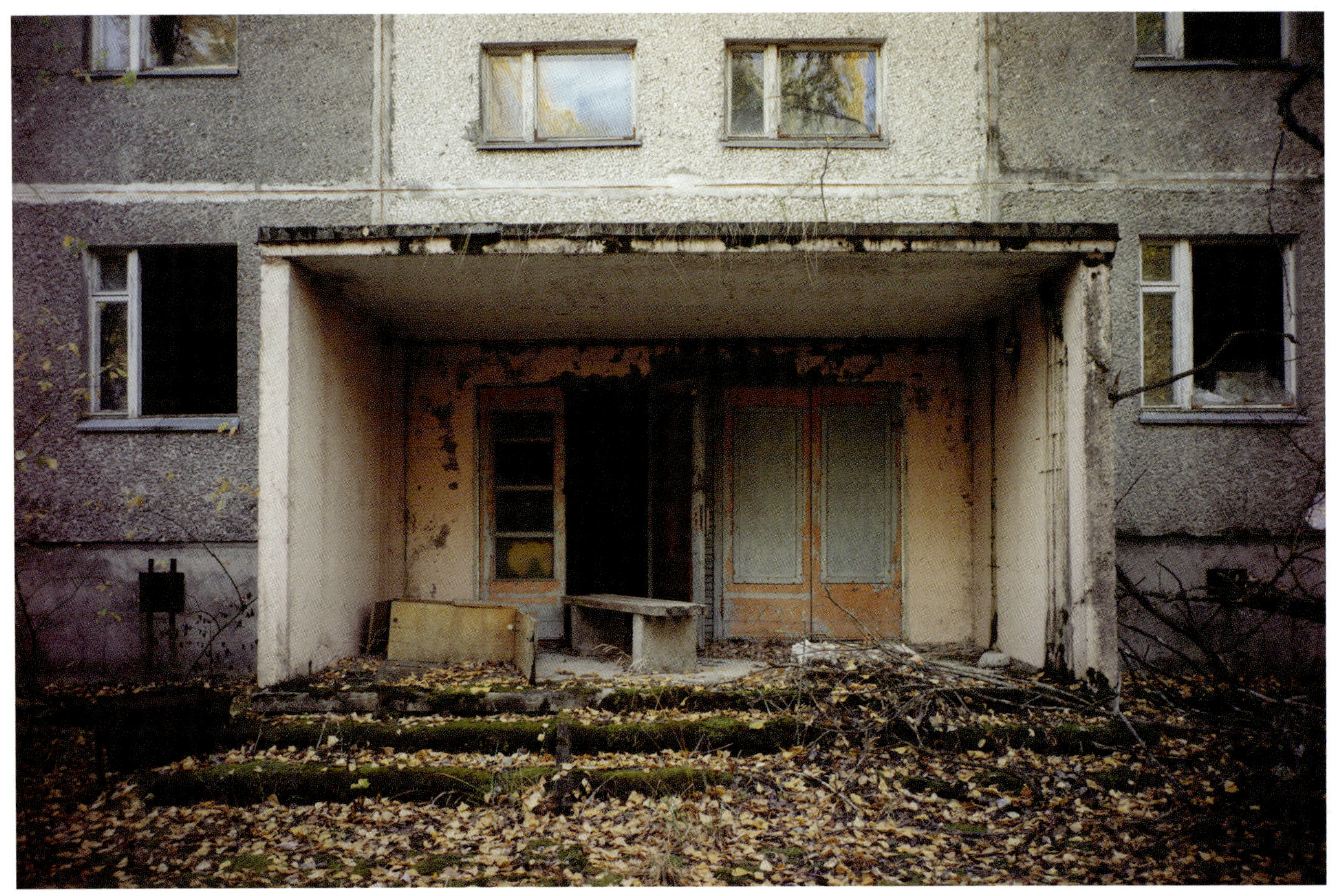

Entrance to a 9-storey panel building, 121-60-25 Series
PRIPYAT, UKRAINE

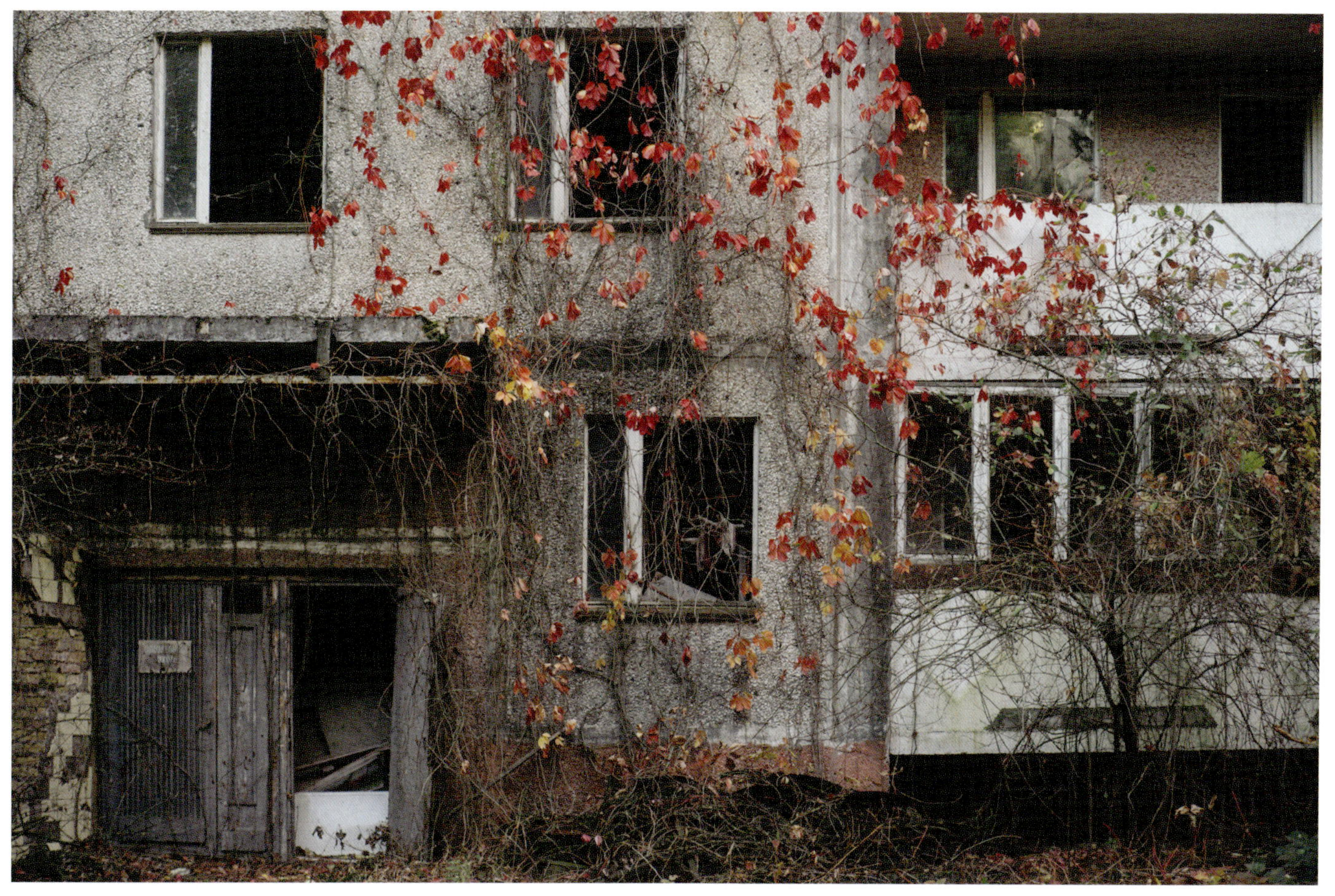

Entrance to a 9-storey panel building, 111-84 Series
PRIPYAT, UKRAINE

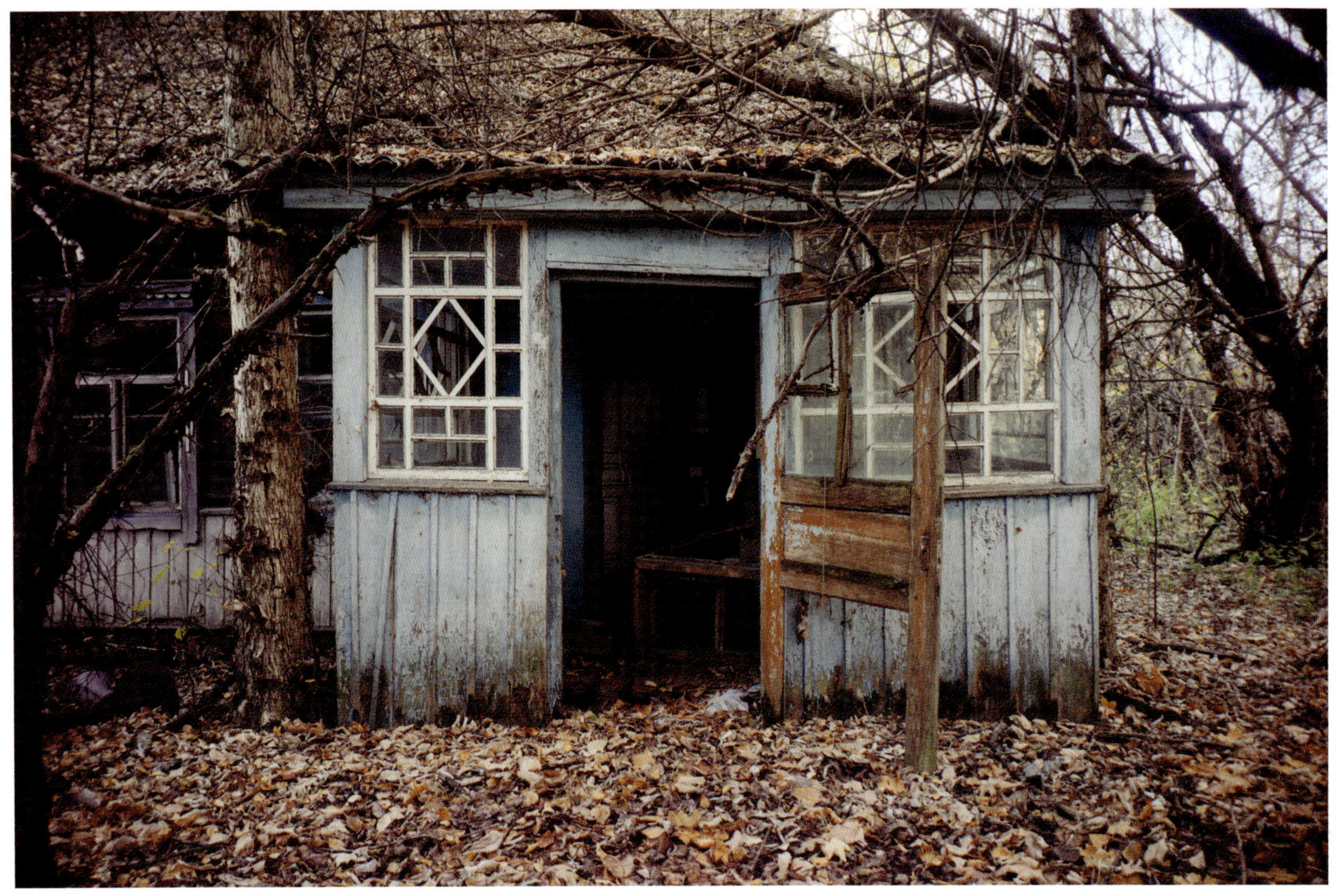

Abandoned wooden house, Korogod village
CHERNOBYL EXCLUSION ZONE, UKRAINE

Following significant radioactive contamination after the Chernobyl accident, Korogod residents were resettled to the Borodyansk District in the Kiev region. In 1999, the village was struck from administrative records.

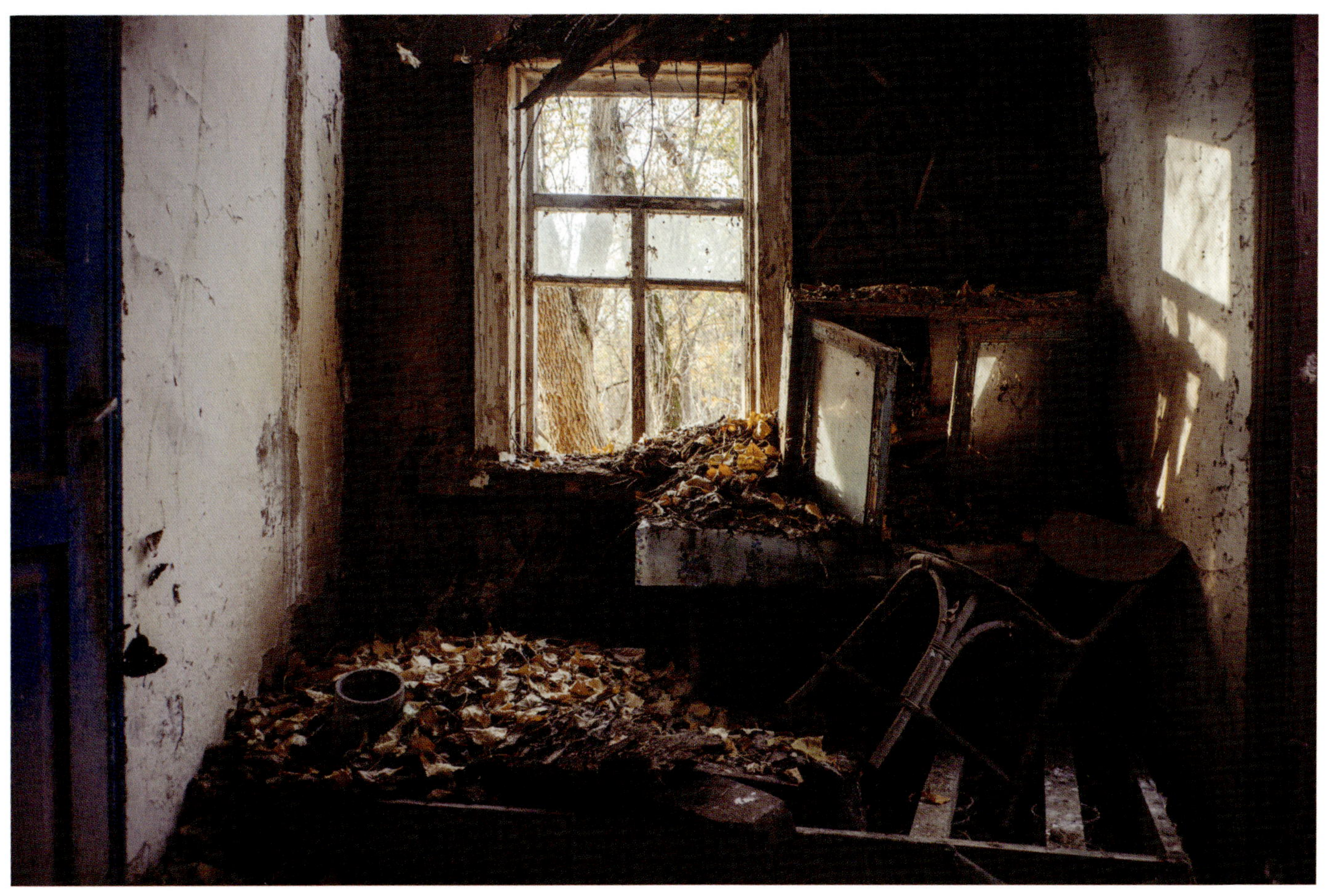

Interior, abandoned house, Korogod village
CHERNOBYL EXCLUSION ZONE, UKRAINE

Thank you to the following people who backed this book:

Adam Benway	Ben Hutchins	Darya Perekosova	Santos Lourenco	Jan Kolarik
Adam Julian	Ben McFetridge	Dave Denney	François Robert	Jan Vachek
Aderonke Babajide	Benjamin Cull	Davey Lyon	Friederike Krump	Jana Klaus
Adrian Crapciu	Benjamin Kasep	David Hasler	Galia Loupan-Richard	Janeton Sylvain
Adrian Shaughnessy	Benjamin Kraco	David Zimmermann	Galley Frédéric	Jason Gormley
Adrian Wynne	Benjamin Wisely	Dean Tantillo	Gareth Robinson	Jay Weeks
Ahmed Bougacha	Bernhard Aichner	Delcimar Almeida	Gary Shu	Jean-François Poulin
Alana de Carvalho	Berti Rosella	Denis Azaare	George Campbell	Jean-Paul Batisse
Alberto González Casanovas	Bob Leenen	Diffley Matthew	Gerald Wagner	Jef Farnsworth
Aleksandra Zuliani	Bobbie Kirby	Dimitri Henning	Gideon Leventhall-Airley	Jeroen van den Boorn
Alena Nikitina	Bruno Vandermueren	Dimitri Koeznetsov	Giuseppe Mussi	Jimmy Fritze
Alessandra Radaelli	Camille Quancard	Dmitrii Belianinov	Glagolev Vladislav Maximovich	Jiri Skopek
Alessandro M Naboni	Carl de Boulloche	Dmitrii Vorobev	Glen Bucher	Joanne Ang
Alex Antonov	Carl Moss	Dmitriy Zhukov	Götz Widiger	Joaquín Fuentes Numancia
Alex Schoelcher	Carola Hesch	Dmitry	Graham Noble	Joe Farage
Alexa Kaul	Caroline Gibson	Duncan MacGregor	Gunilla Davidsson	Joel Otterloo Kuronen
Alexander Fuller	Caroline Miklosi	Edita Krisciuniene	Gunnar Aune	Joey Luchsinger
Alexander Summerfield	Cassidy Berton	Edward Edvards	Gunter Kampitsch	Johan Holgersson
Alexander Wright	Cassie	Edward Etkin	Gustavo Korzune Gurgel	Johann Jimenez
Alexander Wuerthwein	Catharine McLaren	Edwin Bol	Guy West-McDonald	Johanna Egger
Alice (Philippa) Foreman	Charles Miller	Edwin van den Bergh	Hannah Stephens-Jones	John Fahlgren
Amie Ferris-Rotman	Charlie Lewis	Ekaterina Sivertseva	Heather Brown	John Grant
Amy Reams	Charlotte Rees	Elena Tolstykh	Helen Fuller	John Zhao
Andras Keresztes	Charlotte Schaus	Elsie Hupp	Helene Weissbecker	Jon Ashelford
Andre Kishimoto	Chartan Maeva	Emilio M. Valvini	Henrik Svensson	Jonathan Smith
Andreas Huttenlocher	Chris McMahon	Emma Gedge	Ian Baguley	Jordan Jimenez
Andreas Mattsson	Christian Weidenhiller	Emma Sturm	Ian Morton	Jordan Rodgers
Andrés Falo Morales	Christoph Dillgen	Enrique Saugar Gómez	Ibai Wangki Cruz Uzquiano	Jordan Smith
Andres Võlu	Christopher Martin Sullivan	Eric Mandonnet	Ieva Buzinskaite	Jordyn Dechant
Andrew Fisher	Clair Rogers	Eric Quek	Igor Lomachevskyi	Jorge Fortuna
Angela Pesavento	Clémence Amat	Erik Grauer	Ioan Suhov	Jose L. Equiza
Anna Benn	Cody Van Voorhis	Erik Strömbom	Iris E. Aldwell	Josh Reznick
Anthony Dyer	Conny Fanta Lundgren	Erik Vermij	Isaak Granzer	Josheil Azores
Antoine Mourier	Conor Cafferkey	Euan Innes	Isaiah Whisner	Jouvencel Guillaume
Anton Friman	Craig Wright	Eugene Masterov	Jacob Kaplan	Julian Benton
Antonio Alonso Dominguez	Dane Lloyd	Evan Stanley	Jacob Lindmeier	Justine Buisson
Arnaud Martheleur	Daniel Brooker	Evgeny Sh	Jacob Woolan	Karen Nicolaides
Arthur Valk	Daniel Delgado Coloma	Fabian Haak	James Kelleher	Karina Andreeva
Arwish Kisoensingh	Daniel Granado Deza	Fabio Paltenghi	James Robert Triggs	Karl Anderson
Aurelija Prasmuntaite	Daniel Jedfelt	Felix Wittern	James Tanner	Katarzyna Bobinska
Axier Nuñez	Daniel Martinez Calonge	Florian Diesing	James Torney	Kate Armstrong
Barrucand Tanguy	Daniele Binci	Francesc Albert Tortosa	James Welch	Katie Wheeler
Bartosz Machalski	Danny 'Deni' Jovancic	Francesco Maria Barillà	Jan Eberhart	Keith Slote
Ben Dummer	Dario Majone	Francisco Andre	Jan Hempel	Kevin Moll

Kochanov Evgenii
Konstantin Ptitsyn
Konstantinos Kandiliotis
Krzysztof Szczurek
Kseniya Silant'eva
Kylie Walker
Langlois Lisa
Laura Buhnevici
Laure Julie Perdrix
Lawrence and June Staden
Leah Namour
Lehmann William
Lennon Don Leikam
Leo Sikstel
Leon Brunzel
Leonidas Arvanitakis
Linnea ReAlgebra
Lionel Royemans
Lisa Ann Moment
Lisa Thumwood
Loïc Charlot
Lorenzo Dutto
Lorna Van Oss
Louise Kay
Ludwig Rink
Luis Laguna Estaún
M.M. Jones/Bauzeitgeist
Malcolm Goldie
Manon Cassara
Manuel Casal
Marc Sweeney
Marco Cescatti
Marcus Fowler
Maria Torres Pereira
Mariana Loperfido
Marijn Groenendijk
Marin Curić
Marion Hoe
Mark Brill
Mark Vicente
Mark Waller
Markéta Korinkova Taplin
Marta Jankowska
Martin Harris

Martin Smekal
Martina Horcickova
Mary Safro
Mathias Pozsgai
Matthew Mueller
Matthias Pflumm
Matthias Stevens
Maurizio Sorge
Mauro Moar
Max Hetzler
Maxwell Langridge
Maya Michulis
Melanie Manchot
Melanie Wipf
Michael Deevy
Michael Halls
Michael Wood
Michal Ivanic
Michele Dalponte
Michiel Martin Verkuijlen
Mihai Evoiu
Mijung Kim
Miloš Machek
Miriam Mogilevsky
Mohammed Umair Hassan
Natalia Santana
Natalya Shelest
Neik Lamoree
Neil Ingram
Neil McCallum
Nestor Hiebl
Nickie Buckner
Nickolay Pronin
Nicolas Salmon
Nigel Ball
Nikita Kharlamov
Nikita Kozlov
Nikolay Borozenets
Nikolay Chupriyanov
Normala Binte Aszeman
Oleg Ginter
Oleh Aloshkin
Olga Lewis
Oliver Steele

Ouliana Panova
Oxana Pangina
Paolo Cavallotti
Pascal Caillaud
Patrick Binksma
Patrick Dibben
Paul Douglas
Paul Riegel
Paul Rossi
Paulius Dascioras
Pavel Chernukhin
Paweł Timofiejuk
Pedro Pereira
Per Eriksson
Peter Halliday
Peter Kulak
Peter Sacotte
Peter Van Velsen
Petrov Anton
Philip Vorborg Rosing
Pier Giuseppe Ranza
Piero Cioffi
Pierre Pasquet
Pierre-Yves Morvan
Polina Chizhova
Pospelov Vladimir
Preben Randhol
Radoslaw Miszkiel
Rafael Gaya Ribas
Ralph Brydon Chilton
Ravenel Mansfield
Rebecca Warren
Renaud Besnard
René Stienen
Renza Michetti
Richard Morten
Richard Raghoo
Richard Rossi
Rick Petersen
Rob Schofield
Robert Diament
Robert Oorthuysen-Dunne
Roberto Ayala
Robin Palmer

Rodolphe Millet
Rogier Barendregt
Romany Redman
Ronald Olufunwa
Roxane Pavot
Russell Garwood
Sammy Pearson
Santiago Soto-Aguilar
Sarah Withers
Serena Kini-Cramer
Shcherbinin Kirill
   Vladimirovich
Simon Boynton
Simone Vasco
Sina Mesdaghi
Siri Bjoner
Sklias Panos
Sophie Baudens
Sophie Kilfoyle
Stanislav Filipcik
Stefan Floerkemeier
Stefan Jung
Stefano Ascani
Stefano Rivella
Stephen Leggett
Steven Harrell
Steven Monev
Sujata Ravi
Susan Skelly
Susanne Gmoser
Sussi Pettersson
Szymon Krukowski
Tatjana Yaguteva
Terje Nilsen Madsen
Terry Hecker
Theodore Martell-Turner
Thomas McGinn
Thomas Morley
Thomas Schaupp
Thomas Vercauteren
Thomas Wolkenstörfer
Tim Köhler & Emely Benfer
Tim Meier
Tim Stobo

Timothée Bourbeau
   Prud'homme
Timothy Pitts
Tobias Gantner
Tobias Mallock
Toby Nolan
Tom Stanek
Tom Walker
Tomáš Fedor
Tomas Leach
Tomasz Politański
Tonni Lolch Pedersen
Toshihiko Nogami
Trent Hutton
Uku Visnapuu
Utku Vardar
Uwe Diehl
Valentin Augsburger
Valentina Coppo
Varvara
Ville Ikonen
Vincent Valk
Vladimir Opsenica
Volker Markmiller
Walter Broek
Wayne Healy
Willem Daris
William Armstrong
William McKee
WIlliam Telford
Wing Kit Chan
Xiaoyan Wu
Yang Wong
Yannis Papadopoulos
Yu Ando
Yvonne McCombie
Zizy Kiss
Zoe Bluffstone
Zvonimir Vidovic

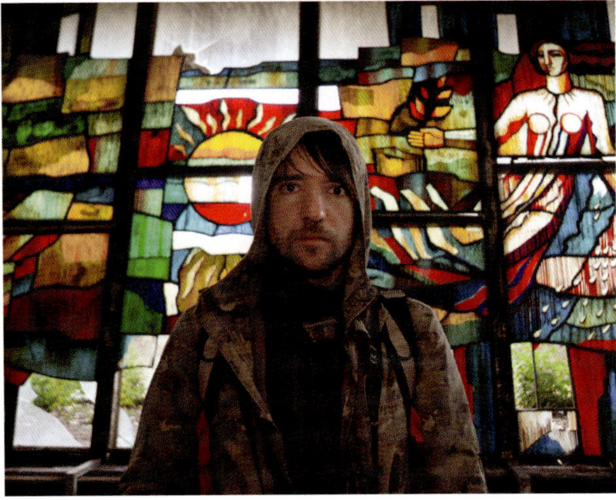

Author portrait
Pripyat Café
PRIPYAT, UKRAINE

Front cover
Spurs of the Putorana Plateau above the panel buildings of Talnakh
5th Microdistrict
NORILSK, RUSSIA

Back cover
Mount Schmidt over 16th Microdistrict
NORILSK, RUSSIA

Front endpapers
View of the city from Mount Aykuayvenchorr
KIROVSK, RUSSIA

Lenin mosaic panel in the grounds of the former sanatorium of the
Strategic Missile Forces
SUKHUM, ABKHAZIA

Back endpapers
Iron Fountain
GYUMRI (FORMERLY LENINAKAN), ARMENIA
Built in 1982
Architect: A. Tarkhanyan

Talnah District
NORILSK, RUSSIA

Published in 2021

FUEL Design & Publishing
33 Fournier Street
London E1 6QE

fuel-design.com

Design and edit by Murray & Sorrell FUEL

Distribution by Thames & Hudson / D. A. P.
ISBN: 978-1-9162184-5-1
Printed in China

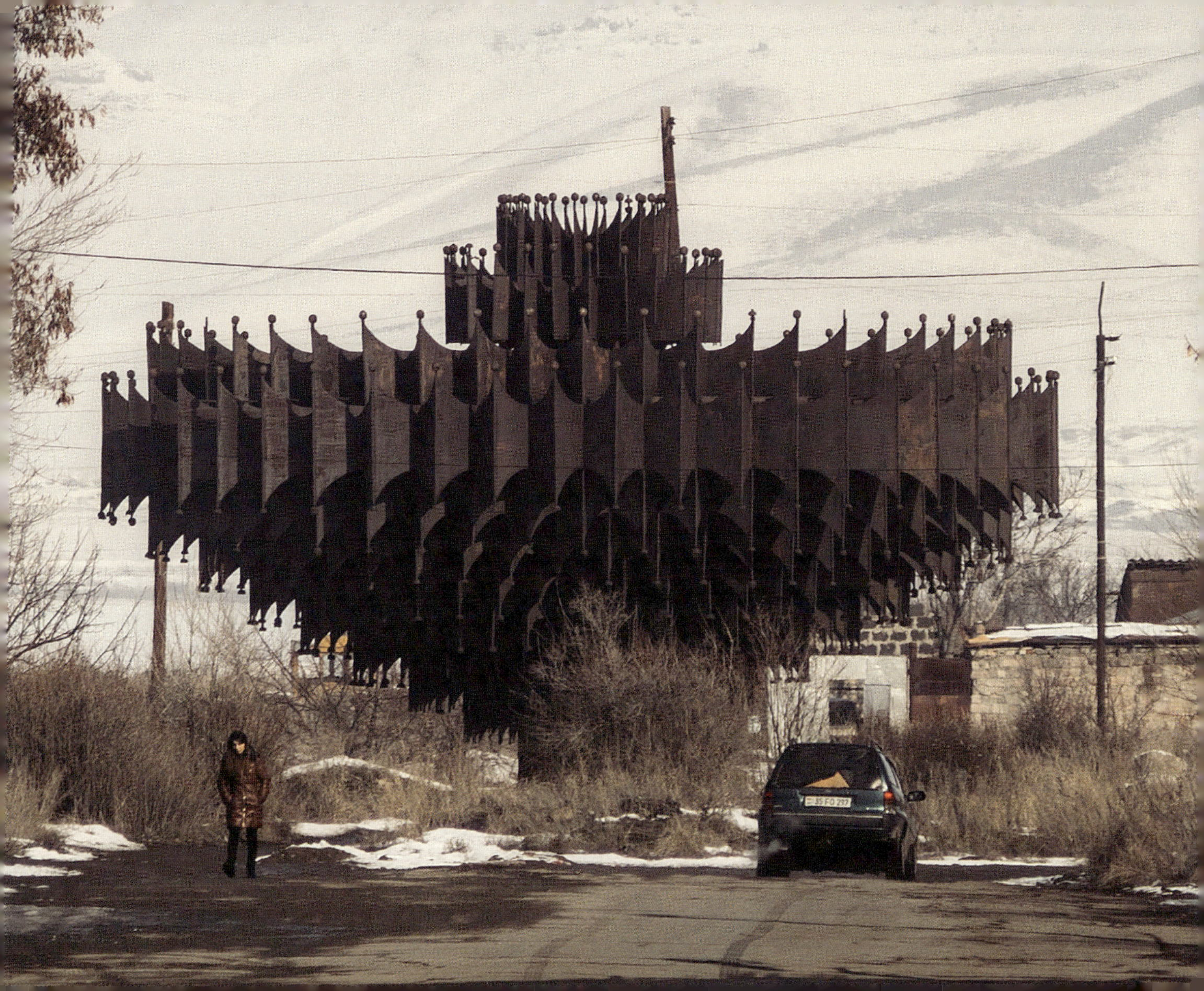

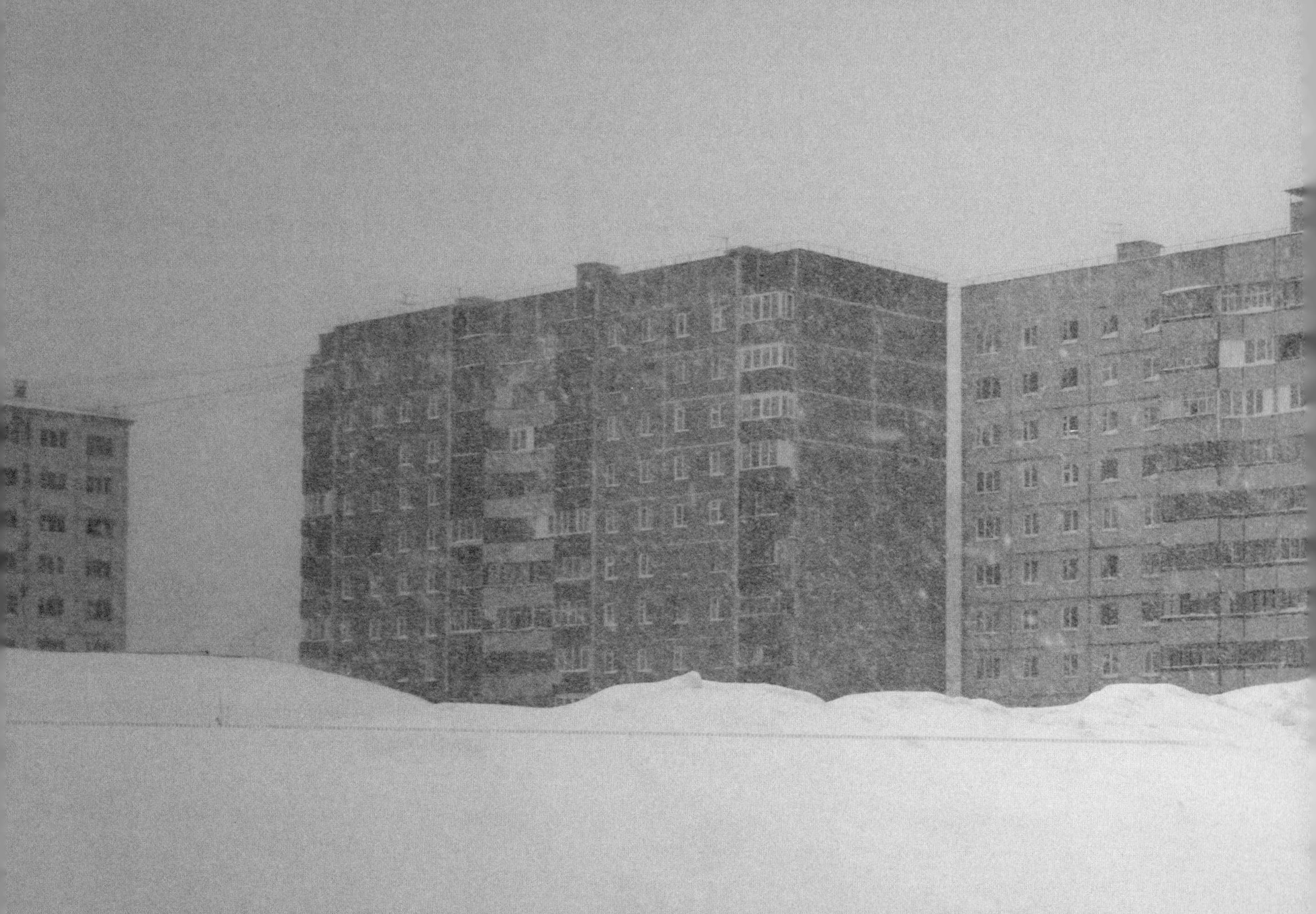